Introduction to Sport Law

SECOND EDITION

John O. Spengler, JD, PhD

Paul M. Anderson, JD

Daniel P. Connaughton, EdD

Thomas A. Baker III, JD, PhD

HUMAN KINETICS

Library of Congress Cataloging-in-Publication Data

Spengler, John O. (John Otto), 1962- author.
  Introduction to sport law / John O. Spengler, Paul M. Anderson, Daniel P. Connaughton, Thomas A. Baker III. -- Second edition.
      pages cm
  Includes bibliographical references and index.
  1. Sports--Law and legislation--United States. I. Anderson, Paul M. (Paul Martin), 1969- author. II. Connaughton, Daniel, 1963- author. III. Baker, Thomas A., author. IV. Title.
  KF3989.S637 2015
  344.73'099--dc23

                        2015018859

ISBN: 978-1-4504-5700-2 (print)

The web addresses cited in this text were current as of August 2015, unless otherwise noted.

Acquisitions Editor: Myles Schrag
Developmental Editor: Ragen E. Sanner
Managing Editor: Karla Walsh
Associate Managing Editor: Shevone Myrick
Copyeditor: Bob Replinger
Indexer: Susan Danzi Hernandez
Permissions Manager: Dalene Reeder
Senior Graphic Designer: Keri Evans
Cover Designer: Keith Blomberg
Photographs (interior): © Human Kinetics, unless otherwise noted. Chapter opening collage: Junial Enterprises/Fotolia (top left), Human Kinetics (bottom left), iStockphoto/Christopher O Driscoll (right).
Photo Asset Manager: Laura Fitch
Photo Production Manager: Jason Allen
Art Manager: Kelly Hendren
Associate Art Manager: Alan L. Wilborn
Illustrations: © Human Kinetics
Printer: Sheridan Books

Printed in the United States of America   10 9 8 7 6 5 4 3 2 1

The paper in this book is certified under a sustainable forestry program.

Human Kinetics
Website: www.HumanKinetics.com

United States: Human Kinetics
P.O. Box 5076
Champaign, IL 61825-5076
800-747-4457
e-mail: info@hkusa.com

Canada: Human Kinetics
475 Devonshire Road Unit 100
Windsor, ON N8Y 2L5
800-465-7301 (in Canada only)
e-mail: info@hkcanada.com

Europe: Human Kinetics
107 Bradford Road
Stanningley
Leeds LS28 6AT, United Kingdom
+44 (0) 113 255 5665
e-mail: hk@hkeurope.com

Australia: Human Kinetics
57A Price Avenue
Lower Mitcham, South Australia 5062
08 8372 0999
e-mail: info@hkaustralia.com

New Zealand: Human Kinetics
P.O. Box 80
Mitcham Shopping Centre, South Australia 5062
0800 222 062
e-mail: info@hknewzealand.com

E5971

Contents

Preface

Given the importance of law in our society and the increasing amount of litigation encountered in sport, the study of law in sport management programs has become a standard part of required coursework. This book is intended to serve as the text for undergraduate students in an introductory sport law class. Prior legal knowledge or experience is not required of students who use this book.

Introduction to Sport Law provides undergraduate sport management students with information in a way that is both approachable and interesting. The purpose of this text is to help undergraduate students learn the common legal concepts taught in sport management curricula. (Please note that the contents of this book are for educational purposes only and do not constitute legal advice.) This book was developed because of a common feeling among sport management students and faculty that available sport law texts were too lengthy, contained too much legalese, were more suited for law students than undergraduate students, lacked relevance for sport management professionals, or failed to cover the topics of most interest to undergraduate sport management students. *Introduction to Sport Law* was written to address these issues and provide a book well suited for undergraduate students interested in the study of sport law.

How to Use This Book

The legal topics presented in the text are covered in most sport law courses and are intended to introduce students to the legal issues that are most critical to the management of sport. The authors' approach to this text is to begin with topics that are most fundamental to faculty and students, as well as those subjects that are most practical and relevant, and to follow with subjects that are commonly taught in sport law courses but that might have greater theoretical value than practical application.

Chapter 1 presents an overview of the U.S. legal system, including different types of law and the U.S. court system. Chapter 2 looks at tort law and product liability, and chapter 3 focuses on risk management. Chapter 4 looks at agency law, and chapter 5 covers contract law. Chapter 6 looks at employment law, including types of employment discrimination. Chapter 7 introduces the reader to constitutional law, and chapter 8 covers gender equity issues. Chapter 9 looks at intellectual property law, including trademarks, patents, and copyrights. Chapter 10 focuses on antitrust laws. Finally, chapter 11 addresses labor law in the context of sport.

The chapters are organized to provide the student with unique perspectives on the topic, the importance of the topic from the perspective of both sport managers and lawyers, a clear and concise description of the law related to the topic, and legal cases and real-world examples designed to tie concepts together and provide a clear picture and understanding of how the material is applied. The organization of the chapters is designed to enhance learning. Each chapter begins with chapter objectives and a short introduction to the topic to place the topic into context for the reader. The topic is addressed from a legal perspective, written with enough technical language to state the legal concepts accurately and clearly while staying away from too much legalese. After the legal topics have been described, the legal concepts are brought to life through myriad case law examples. Unique case law examples are highlighted in the In the Courtroom sidebars. Next, important points and topics are summarized, and discussion questions provide opportunities to engage students in in-class discussions. Finally, chapters 2 through 11 include moot court cases, which are hypothetical sport law scenarios that students can use as the basis for a classroom mock trial in which hypothetical witnesses are called and students form teams to argue different sides of a case.

Accompanying Ancillaries

This book comes with a full array of ancillaries. The ancillaries are available at www.HumanKinetics.com/Introduction ToSportLaw. The Presentation Package contains 298 slides that present the content of the chapters in convenient PowerPoint form, making it easier for instructors to prepare for and present lectures. The Test Package has 173 questions, making it easy for the instructor to prepare tests and quizzes based on the content of the book. The Instructor Guide contains a sample syllabus, suggestions for group projects and topics for papers, suggested readings, and a complete explanation of how to use the moot court cases in class.

Also included is access to the e-book of the companion text *Case Studies in Sport Law, Second Edition*. That text contains case studies that will allow students to see how concepts discussed in this book have been applied in real-life cases. At the beginning of each chapter in this book, you will find a *Case Studies in Sport Law* Connection feature, which lists the cases in the companion text that relate to the chapter's topic. Using the casebook will help to add meaning and context to the concepts discussed in this book.

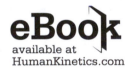

eBook
available at
HumanKinetics.com

Summary

Introduction to Sport Law will challenge the sport law undergraduate student to think about sport law concepts and apply them to the practical world of sport management. This book will serve the needs of undergraduate sport management students in terms of both learning and practice.

Introduction

All sport management students and practitioners need a basic understanding of the law, although for different reasons. Some students may wish to study law after completing undergraduate studies, so an introduction to legal issues is the first step in a long journey of learning. For most students, however, this area of study applies to their careers in sport.

Sport law affects sport at every level, from Little League teams to the highest levels of professional sports. If you plan to work in the sport industry at any level, you must understand legal principles relevant to sport. This book addresses major legal issues that you might face as a sport manager. It also introduces you to legal concepts and applications to prepare you for further study and on-the-job learning. In this introduction, you will see how various areas of law are applicable to specific levels of sport.

Tort law applies to situations in which a civil wrong has been committed. Tort law does not involve criminal conduct, but rather addresses conduct that is either careless or intentional and results in harm or injury to a person or property. Unlike criminal law cases, when a penalty or jail time might be imposed, a tort law case might result in an award of money (damages) from the person or organization (the defendant) that caused harm or injury. Types of torts include negligence and intentional torts, which are highly relevant to sport managers given the frequency with which these torts occur.

For those who work in recreational sports, tort law might be at issue when a counselor, coach, or supervisor fails to provide adequate instruction or supervision of players under his care. Another situation that gives rise to tort law claims is player and participant violence. Player-to-player incidents might involve negligence such as reckless conduct in a pickup basketball game. Players or participants might cause an intentional tort such as battery (e.g., an angry parent hits a volunteer coach). Tort law cases at the high school level often involve students injured in a physical education class or athletes injured in games or practices. In sport law cases in the high school setting, supervision is often at issue. Also, high schools commonly transport student athletes, coaches, and fans in connection with their athletic programs. Transportation is a liability exposure for any institution or school district, and it creates unique risk management issues that administrators must address.

For those who work in universities, tort law cases (negligence and intentional torts) often center on the provision of safe programs and facilities for students and a safe environment for spectators who attend collegiate athletic events. Also in the university setting, students often take sport and fitness courses for credit as part of their curriculum. When injury in a sport and fitness class results in a tort claim, supervision is often the issue. Another issue that universities must address is the provision of emergency care for athletes who are injured in practices or games and the duty owed to intercollegiate athletes by institutions for which they play.

In professional sports, tort law cases often involve alleged negligent or intentional conduct that harms another person. The parties involved on either side (plaintiff or defendant) may include managers, coaches, players, or spectators. Allegations of negligent conduct on the part of management generally result from conditions or situations at arenas or stadiums. Lawsuits have been brought, for example, when a spectator is hit by a foul ball at a baseball game while being distracted by a mascot. Another example in professional sport is an allegation that management is negligent because they fail to provide adequate security at a game (we are all familiar with recent, well-publicized incidents of players who engage in violent behavior with fans). Examples are becoming numerous, from incidents in professional basketball (e.g., the aggressive acts of players who entered the stands at an Indiana Pacers game) to professional baseball (e.g., players who throw objects into the stands). Incidents of fan violence or misconduct (e.g., storming the field after a victory) also may give rise to negligence claims against management for failing to take proper security measures.

Risk management is a process or course of action that is designed to reduce the risk (probability or likelihood) of injury and loss to sport participants, spectators, employees, management, and organizations. The key terms in this definition are *reduction of risk* and *injury and loss*. Risk management often emphasizes risk reduction, given that the prevention or elimination of all risk is often not feasible. Sport often involves some element of physical risk, from competitive sports such as football and ice hockey to recreational sports such as swimming and jogging.

Some students may wish to become risk managers for sport organizations—managing risk, improving safety, and striving to limit the liability of their organization.

Others will be motivated to reduce the organization's risk of liability through their roles as managers and leaders in organizations. Think about the many examples of risk in sport:

- A basketball player hits her head on an unpadded wall.
- A racquetball player injures his ankle on a slick floor.
- A tennis player is injured after tripping on a defect in the court surface.
- A golf spectator is struck by lightning.
- A baseball spectator is struck by a foul ball after being distracted by a mascot.
- A swimmer is paralyzed after diving into shallow water.
- A baseball player is injured after sliding into an immovable base.

A risk manager would be responsible for safety in a multitude of situations and the prevention or reduction of loss through potential litigation.

Contract law is relevant to everyone who wishes to work in sport management, and sport agents and upper-level managers of sport organizations must have in-depth knowledge of contract law. A contract is an agreement between people that is enforceable by law if certain conditions are met. Contracts are common in sport. For example, an arena or stadium might have contracts with food and beverage providers, security companies, and employees. Player contracts (agreements to play for a particular team), scholarships, and coaching contracts (employment contracts) are common types of agreements. Additionally, sport managers will be involved in drafting (for review and approval by legal counsel and management) and administering waivers (a type of contract).

Agency law often brings up images of sport agents who represent big-time athletes and enjoy all the perceived perks of the profession. The 1990s film *Jerry Maguire* continues to intrigue people and romanticize the profession. The concept of agency, however, involves more than just sport agents. Employees within a sport organization are considered agents and act on behalf of the organization in executing contracts and performing other essential tasks. Therefore, the law of agency applies to the sport manager in numerous situations and in everyday business matters, such as when employees execute contracts on behalf of a sport business. Agency law affects all areas of sport management because the agency relationship is a key part of business operations in sport.

Employment law applies to all sport managers who are involved in personnel issues, and it encompasses an extremely wide range of issues. Issues of employment are issues about people, and people are different from one another. We differ in age, race and ethnic background, gender, the way we look, our physical abilities, our minds and emotions, and our beliefs, opinions, and outlooks on life. This uniqueness, and the interaction of personnel with management, can result in an efficient, effective work environment or something quite the opposite. When employee relations fall apart, the legal issues involved are diverse, often overlap, and sometimes become complex. Common situations in which lawsuits arise in the employment context include the following:

- A person is fired from her job.
- A qualified female personal trainer is not hired for a job.
- A qualified minority assistant athletic director is not promoted.
- A coach leaves his job before his contract expires.
- A woman's work situation is so uncomfortable that she must quit.

- A maintenance worker is injured on the job.

Therefore, employment law is a critical area for sport managers because it has relevance to most management positions in sport.

Constitutional law is directly applicable to sport. Sport is an integral part of a free society in which athletes and participants can learn, grow, and compete in a manner suited to their lifestyles. The preamble of the Constitution of the United States provides the citizens with a means to establish justice, ensure domestic tranquility, promote general welfare, and secure the blessings of liberty. By understanding the words found in the preamble, we start to understand the purpose of sport in a democratic society. All citizens enjoy four broad rights relevant to sport: personal freedom, civil rights, due process, and privacy. Constitutional rights are relevant in high school, university, and professional sport settings and address such as issues as school prayer (personal freedom), discrimination (civil rights), student-athlete drug testing (privacy), and employee rights (due process).

Gender equity is a legal issue of critical importance for sport managers, particularly those who work in schools. The primary focus of case law dealing with gender discrimination in athletics is whether educational institutions have complied with Title IX. The key compliance issues are whether institutions or organizations fall within the court's recommended proportionality range of percentage of opportunities versus percentage of total enrollment for a given gender. An understanding of gender equity issues is essential to coaches and school officials in selecting which sports will be made available.

Intellectual property law encompasses copyright, trademark, the right of publicity, and patent issues. The purpose of this area of law is to protect the creative endeavors of individuals and organizations.

Copyright laws provide protection to authors of written works, musical works and performances, movies, and other audiovisual works. Television and radio broadcasts of live sporting events are also covered under copyright law. Intellectual property law is applicable to many who work in the sport industry, including such areas as university and professional sports, sports media, marketing, and sports equipment manufacturing and sales.

Antitrust law centers on the issue of competitive markets. Although this area of law is complex, the premise is easy to comprehend: Markets should be competitive and free of restraints. To this end, state and federal laws have been enacted to protect markets from unlawful restraints on trade and from activities such as price fixing and the formation of monopolies (in which a market has only one provider of a product or service). The primary federal laws that govern antitrust issues are the Sherman Act, Clayton Act, Sports Broadcasting Act, and Curt Flood Act. Antitrust issues are more common than you might suspect and have been at the forefront of several highly publicized media events involving player salaries, the movement of professional teams to new cities, draft and eligibility issues, broadcasting rights, and sponsorships. Thus, those who work in professional and collegiate sports, sports media and broadcasting, and a variety of other areas need to understand antitrust law.

Labor law governs the workplace relationship in professional sports. Employees and employers have certain rights and responsibilities. Likewise, they are prohibited from taking certain action under the law. The history and framework of federal labor law in the United States provides a useful background to the study of sport law. Employee athletes are provided specific rights under labor law, and those rights have been and continue to be used in the sport landscape. Further, employers and labor organizations are prohibited from engaging in various actions, but they can use several legal strategies, called economic weapons, in workplace-related negotiations.

The implications and importance of law to sport management are clear. If you are involved directly with a lawsuit, an understanding of legal issues and implications may help you handle the legal process and the subsequent stresses. More important, an understanding of law might help you avoid liability in the first place by knowing how to plan and prepare for potential problems.

U.S. Legal System

Chapter Objectives

After reading this chapter, you will know the following:

- The primary sources of law in the U.S. legal system

- The function and process of the federal and state court systems

- The key types of law in the United States

- Common legal resources

An understanding of the U.S. legal system is important for all sport managers. In today's litigious society, sport managers can benefit from understanding and operating within the law. Sport managers also should know how to obtain legal and risk management information—such as statutes, case law, and published standards and guidelines—that can be used to demonstrate the standard of care owed to clients, athletes, and participants. This chapter introduces the U.S. legal system by discussing sources of law, the court system, common legal resources, and types of law.

Sources of U.S. Law

A primary source of U.S. law is the common law tradition that began in medieval England. Another important source is constitutional law, which incorporates the U.S. Constitution and all of the 50 state constitutions. Statutory law includes statutes enacted by Congress and state legislatures as well as ordinances passed by city and county governments. Another source of U.S. law is administrative law, created by the many administrative agencies (such as the Federal Trade Commission, National Labor Relations Board, Internal Revenue Service, and Food and Drug Administration). These important sources of law are briefly described in the following sections.

Common Law

The English common law system forms the basis of many countries' legal systems, including the U.S. legal system. This system of laws was derived from centuries of general rules, customs, and experience. Courts developed common law rules based on decisions of actual legal disputes. In an effort to be consistent, judges based their decisions on the principles of previously decided cases. Using former cases, or precedents, to assist in deciding new cases is the basis of the American and English judicial systems. The doctrine of **stare decisis** supports the use of precedent. It is typically used to require equal and lower-level courts to follow the legal precedents (prior decisions) that have been established by higher-level courts in their jurisdiction. When deciding a case with similar facts and issues of law, lower state courts are normally bound to the decisions established by the appellate courts within the same state. Likewise, lower federal courts are bound by the decisions previously made by higher-level appellate courts within their jurisdiction. Today, this source of law is referred to as common law, judge-made law, or case law.

Constitutional Law

The U.S. federal government and every state have separate written constitutions that set forth the organization, powers, and limits of their respective governments. **Constitutional law** is the law expressed in those constitutions. State constitutions vary; some are modeled closely after the U.S. Constitution, and others provide even greater rights to their citizens. The U.S. Constitution, the supreme law of the United States, was adopted in 1787 by representatives of the 13 newly formed states. Initially, people expressed fear that the federal government might abuse its power. To alleviate such concerns, the first Congress approved 10 amendments to the U.S. Constitution, commonly known as the Bill of Rights, which were adopted in 1791. The Bill of Rights limits the powers and authority of the federal government and guarantees many civil (individual) rights and protections.

Although the Bill of Rights does not directly apply to the states, the U.S. Supreme Court has held that the Fourteenth Amendment includes many of the principal guarantees of the Bill of Rights, thereby making them applicable to the individual states. So, neither the federal government nor state governments can deprive individuals of those rights and protections. The rights provided by the Bill of Rights, however, are not absolute. Many of the rights guaranteed by the Bill of Rights are described in very broad terms. For instance, the Fourth Amendment prohibits unreasonable search and seizure but does not define what this concept entails. Ultimately, the U.S. Supreme Court interprets the Constitution, thereby defining our rights and the government's boundaries. More information about how constitutional law affects the field of sport management is provided in chapter 7.

Statutory Law

State and federal legislators enact laws termed *statutes*. Local governments, such as cities and counties, create laws termed *ordinances*. Together, these statutes and ordinances are known as statutory law. **Statutory law** covers a myriad of subjects, such as crime, civil rights, housing, and all matters that the legislative branch has constitutional power to legislate. Statutory

law is limited to matters of jurisdiction. For example, federal statutory law is limited to matters of federal jurisdiction; similar limitations hold for local and state ordinances and statutes. When jurisdictions overlap (e.g., when two levels of governments have jurisdiction), conflicts may arise. When this happens, the **doctrine of supremacy** applies; federal law prevails over state law, and state law prevails over local law (Carper & McKinsey, 2012). Statutory law also cannot violate the U.S. Constitution or the relevant state constitution.

Several federal statutes apply to sport management, including the Amateur Sports Act, Americans with Disabilities Act (ADA), Title IX, and the Volunteer Immunity Act. State statutes vary from state to state and include laws that involve concussion safety, sport agents, the use of automated external defibrillators, as well as various immunity provisions such as good Samaritan and recreational user statutes.

Administrative Law

Thousands of local, state, and federal **administrative agencies**, which are specialized bodies created by legislation at all three (local, state, and federal) governmental levels, are granted lawmaking authority to regulate certain activities. These agencies investigate problems within their own jurisdictions, create laws termed **rules and regulations**, and conduct hearings, similar to court trials, to decide whether their rules have been violated and, if so, what sanctions should be levied. Federal administrative agencies—including the National Labor Relations Board (NLRB), Internal Revenue Service (IRS), and Occupational Safety and Health Administration (OSHA), as well as a number of local and state agencies—enact and enforce numerous laws every year that affect sport management.

Types of U.S. Law

U.S. law may be classified into criminal and civil law. Both criminal and civil law attempt to persuade citizens to act in ways that are not harmful to others. Nevertheless, these types of law differ in their means of doing so.

Criminal Law

Criminal law is the body of law that identifies what behavior is criminal and stipulates penalties for violations. The majority of criminal laws are statutes, enacted by the U.S. Congress or a state legislature. The statutory law of individual states regarding criminal law is found in books typically termed *penal codes*.

In a criminal court, which hears only cases involving the alleged commission of misdemeanors and felonies, the people (general public) are represented by a governmental representative (district attorney). To convict a criminal, the district attorney must show beyond a reasonable doubt that the accused person committed the crime. A convicted criminal may be punished by fines, community service, probation, imprisonment, or any combination of these. Although the courts have the power to order restitution to a victim of a crime, the victim usually leaves the courtroom empty handed. Athletes and sport managers may face criminal charges if they violate criminal statutes on theft; stalking; illegal sports wagering or point shaving; robbery; use, sale, or possession of performance-enhancing drugs; or assault and battery.

Civil Law

Civil law is the body of state and federal law that pertains to civil, or private, rights that are enforced by civil actions. The vast major-

People who commit a crime may face a jury of their peers during sentencing in a federal court under criminal law.

ity of lawsuits involving sport management involve civil law. Civil courts hear noncriminal matters between individuals, organizations, businesses, and governmental units and agencies. The two parties involved in a civil lawsuit are the plaintiff, which is the person, group, or organization bringing the lawsuit (e.g., a participant injured in a sport event), and the defendant, which is the person, group, or organization being sued (e.g., the coaches and athletic director). Several defendants are commonly named in a civil suit. In a civil trial, a plaintiff only has to show by a preponderance (a greater amount) of evidence that the defendant is liable. The burden of proof in a criminal trial requires that a court find the criminal guilty beyond a reasonable doubt, whereas the civil standard only requires finding the defendant 51% responsible (preponderance of the evidence). Unlike in a criminal trial, the plaintiff may leave the courtroom with a verdict that will require the defendant to provide financial compensation to the plaintiff. The overwhelming majority of lawsuits that involve sport managers and programs focus on civil law and claims.

Anatomy of a Civil Lawsuit

When a person decides to seek compensation through the civil court system, her attorney typically files a **complaint**. This document, which begins a lawsuit, details the facts that the plaintiff believes justify the claim and requests damages that the plaintiff is seeking from the defendant. The complaint is often served by a **summons**, typically delivered by a court officer, that notifies the defendant that a lawsuit has been filed against her and provides a certain amount of time for her to respond to the complaint.

On receiving a complaint, a defendant typically hires an attorney to represent the defendant's interests. The defendant's attor-

ney usually files an **answer**, which normally denies some or all the allegations listed in the complaint. In lieu of an answer, the defendant's attorney may seek a dismissal of the complaint. This action, referred to as a *motion to dismiss*, is used when a complaint is legally insufficient to justify an answer. The complaint and answer combined are known as **pleadings**. After the pleading stage, either party can move to dismiss the case as a matter of law. In this motion, the court can rely only on the pleadings in determining whether any question of law needs to be answered through trial. If no questions of law are present, the case may be dismissed at this early stage of litigation. Cases may also be determined through default judgments. Default judgments occur when defendants do not answer complaints.

After these initial pleadings, the case enters what is commonly known as the **discovery** phase. The discovery phase begins with the filing of the answer and ceases at the beginning of the trial. During this pretrial time both parties obtain facts and information regarding the case, including information from the other parties, to assist in preparing for trial. Common discovery procedures include requests to produce physical evidence and the use of interrogatories and depositions. A request to produce evidence occurs when one party asks the other to produce, and provide for the inspection of, any designated physical evidence that the second party controls or possesses and that the first party believes to be relevant to the case. For example, attorneys may request to inspect equipment (e.g., football helmet, treadmill, bicycle) or facilities (e.g., swimming pool, bleachers, gymnasium, softball field) that were used by a plaintiff at the time of injury. Furthermore, documents such as preseason medical records, staff training records, parental permission forms, accident or incident report forms, facility and equipment maintenance records, membership agreements, and waivers can be requested. **Interrogatories** are written questions sent by an attorney from one party in the lawsuit to another party named in the suit. These questions must be answered within a specified time, and they can be used as evidence in a trial. A **deposition** is a pretrial questioning of a witness. Attorneys representing both parties are typically present at depositions, when a witness answers questions, under oath, that are recorded by a court stenographer. Like interrogatories, deposition transcripts can be used as evidence at a trial.

If the facts of a case are not in dispute, the case may be decided without going to trial. In a motion for **summary judgment**, the moving party (the one making the request) argues that there is no question of fact (the facts are agreed on) and that the relevant law requires that he be awarded judgment. This motion can be requested at any time, but it is typically sought after discovery, when a party believes that discovery demonstrates that the facts are not in dispute. If the motion is awarded, no trial will take place.

Either party or the court can request a pretrial conference or hearing, which usually takes place after the discovery phase is complete. The main purpose of such informal conferences is to identify the matters in dispute and to plan the course of the trial. At such hearings, a judge may encourage the parties to reach an out-of-court settlement. If a settlement cannot be achieved, the case typically proceeds to trial. Most cases result in settlements.

In a civil trial, the plaintiff usually has to decide whether she wants the case to be heard by a jury. The plaintiff gives the opening statement, which may be followed by the defendant's opening statements and is designed to inform the triers of fact (the judge or the jury) about the matter and the types of evidence that will be presented during the case. Following opening statements, the plaintiff presents her case. The plaintiff then calls and examines her witnesses. Usually, witnesses are then cross-examined by the defendant, redirected by the plaintiff, and then recrossed by the defendant. The defendant then repeats the process with his witnesses.

During trial, two types of witnesses may be called. Fact witnesses are used because they have specific facts (perhaps something they saw or heard) regarding the matter. **Expert witnesses** (also referred to as *forensic experts*) are used to help educate the judge and jury by sharing their expertise and knowledge. Expert witnesses are typically asked to provide testimony regarding the professional standards that apply to the incident and the degree to which the defendant met, or did not meet, those standards.

After both parties have completed their questioning, final closing statements are made. After these final statements, the judge in a jury trial provides the jury instructions regarding the options the jury has in reaching a decision based on the applicable laws. After deliberating, the jury renders a verdict. In a trial without a jury, a judge can either recess the court while making a decision or render a decision shortly after closing statements.

After the trial court's decision, verdicts can be appealed. The party that lost the case can make a request (an appeal) to have the court proceedings reviewed by a higher court in the hope that the lower court's decision will be reversed. The appellate court can agree with (affirm) the lower court's decision, disagree with (reverse) it, send the case back to the lower court (remand) with instructions for a new trial, or modify the lower court's judgment.

U.S. Court System

The U.S. court system is hierarchical in nature (see figure 1.1) and consists of a variety of courts at both the state and federal levels as well as some specialized administrative courts. In addition, specific courts are designed to hear only certain types of legal disputes, such as bankruptcy and small claims courts. The vast majority of legal disputes are resolved before trial. If they do proceed to trial, federal and state judges preside in these courts to settle cases brought before them. The various types and levels of courts are described in the following sections.

Trial Courts

The U.S. court system is hierarchical in nature. The lowest level, or entry-level court, typically termed a *trial court* or *district court*, is followed by an intermediate appellate court; the highest court typically is a supreme court. Trial courts carry out the initial proceedings (trials) in lawsuits. These trials have three distinct purposes (Carper, McKinsey, & West, 2008):

1. To determine the facts of the dispute (What happened between the parties?)
2. To decide what rules of law should be applied to the facts
3. To administer those rules

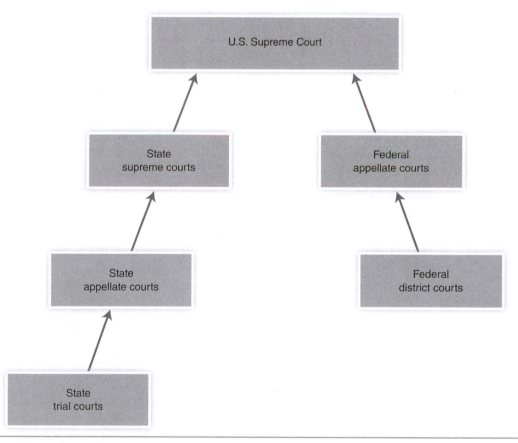

Figure 1.1   Hierarchy of the U.S. court system.

At the end of every trial, the court renders judgment in favor of one of the parties. Usually, when well-established existing law is applied, these disputes are resolved at the trial court level, and most are not appealed.

Appellate Courts

Within a certain time following a trial court's final decision, the losing party can appeal the decision. An appeal is a formal request to a higher court to review the lower court's decision. These review courts are known as *appellate courts*. Having three or more judges, these courts review lower court decisions for substantive and procedural correctness. In other words, they attempt to determine whether the proper law was correctly applied to the issue at hand.

Appellate courts must work from a court transcript of what was said and what evidence was used in the lower court, such as contracts, photographs, business records, waivers, and leases. State appellate courts do not review new evidence, listen to witnesses, make different or new determinations of fact, or use a jury. Instead, these courts review written briefs prepared by attorneys that include legal arguments about how the law was incorrectly stated or applied to the facts that were presented to the lower court. The appellate court determines whether the lower court correctly applied the law.

If an appellate court determines that a lower court incorrectly applied or interpreted the law, it will modify or reverse the lower court's decision and either provide a new revised judgment or **remand** (send back) the case to the trial court for a new trial to be conducted using the appellate court's instructions. Even if an appellate court determines that an error occurred at the trial court, it may not be sufficient to overturn the trial court's decision. A slight or insignificant error, or one that is not prejudicial to the interests of the appellant, is unlikely to affect the original ruling of a case.

If an appeals court decides a case, the judges typically write and publish a written opinion. In such an opinion, the appellate court states the rules of law applied as well as the rationale for reaching its decision. When reaching decisions, appellate courts interpret and apply relevant statutory law along with appropriate common law derived from precedent. On occasion, when no controlling statute or precedent applies to a case, an appellate court may create a new rule or extend an existing principle to the case at hand. Thus, new law is created and is termed **judge-made law** or **case law**.

Moot cases are outside the court's power because there is no case or controversy. U.S. courts will not decide moot cases. In other words, litigating a case is unnecessary unless there has been some direct negative effect on a party. A controversy must exist not only at the time the case was filed but also at the appellate stage. If the original issues in the case have substantially changed since it was filed or they no longer exist, rendering a decision would be pointless and of no practical value. A classic example of a moot case is the U.S. Supreme Court case *DeFunis v. Odegaard*, 416 U.S. 312 (1974). The plaintiff, Marco DeFunis, was a potential student who was denied admission to law school but was later admitted when the case was pending. Because DeFunis was scheduled to graduate within a few months at the time when a decision would have been rendered and the law school could take no action to prevent his graduation, the court determined that deciding the case would have no effect on DeFunis' rights. The court, therefore, dismissed the case as moot.

U.S. Federal Court System

The federal court system is a three-level model consisting of (1) trial courts known as *district courts*, (2) intermediate courts of appeal, and (3) the U.S. Supreme Court. The federal court system also includes some special courts such as maritime, military, and bankruptcy courts. The federal court system conducts trials involving federal matters, such as the enforcement of federal laws. Therefore, when a federal question arises (when a federal law is at issue in a case), the case will likely be held in federal court. Even where a federal law is at issue, however, the damages (i.e., money sought) in a case must be at least $75,000 for the case to go to federal court. Another way for a case to be brought to federal court, as opposed to state court, is when diversity jurisdiction is present. **Diversity jurisdiction** occurs when parties (individuals or organizations) to the lawsuit are from different states. For example, a fan from Tennessee might be injured at a stadium in Alabama; a subsequent lawsuit might be held in federal court, given that the person and the organization (stadium management) are from different states.

The United States is divided into 96 federal judicial districts, and at least one U.S. district court is located in each state and territory. The number of district courts per state varies depending on population changes and caseloads. The U.S. courts of appeal consist of 13 federal judicial circuits (see figure 1.2), which hear cases appealed from the U.S. district courts. The highest

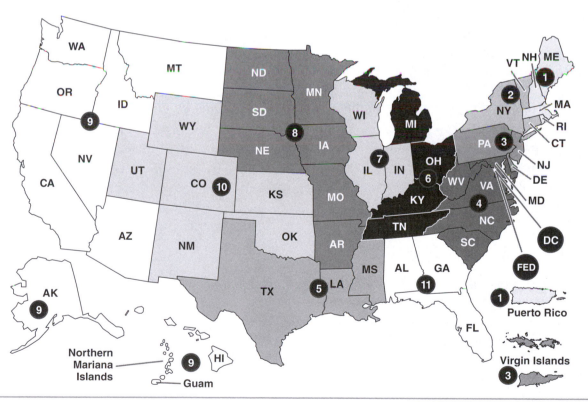

Figure 1.2   Federal judicial circuits.

level of the federal court system is the U.S. Supreme Court. Nine justices, appointed by the U.S. president for lifetime appointments, sit on the U.S. Supreme Court. The Supreme Court acts as the final appeal for the federal courts of appeals. Further information on U.S. federal courts may be found at www.uscourts.gov.

State Court System

The state court system parallels the federal system, although the states may give their courts different names than those used in the federal system. All states have entry-level (trial) courts, but they may be called a *circuit court* in one state, a *supreme court* in another, and something else in a third. Trial court decisions are made by judges or juries. These decisions, made at the local level, are not published. Therefore, the full case decisions that are publicly available for you to read come only from the upper-level state courts (courts of appeal and supreme courts), not the trial courts. Every state also has some form of an appellate system and specialized courts for specific legal matters. The typical hierarchy of the state court system is the trial court, the court of appeals, and the state supreme court. Further information about state court systems can be found at the National Center for State Courts website at www.ncsc.org.

Legal Resources

Sport managers and practitioners should study aspects of the law that relate to the field, although at times they may have to obtain specific legal information. Legal resources can be grouped into primary and secondary sources. **Primary sources** consist of court decisions (case law), U.S. and state constitutions, statutes, and administrative agency regulations. Primary sources are the actual law and therefore are the primary legal sources relied on in determining what the law requires. In contrast, **secondary sources** examine, inform, or review various legal topics and issues. Examples of secondary sources include law review articles and legal encyclopedias, textbooks, dictionaries, and journals (e.g., *The Sport & Recreation Law Reporter*, *Journal of Legal Aspects of Sport, Marquette Sports Law Review*). Although secondary sources should never be relied on as legal authority, they can be useful to the sport manager by providing information about a specific legal issue.

Case law (also referred to as *court opinions*) is published in a series of books known as reporters. At the federal level, all reported U.S. district court cases are published in the reporter known as the *Federal Supplement*. U.S. circuit court cases (courts of appeal) are reported in the *Federal Reporter*. U.S. Supreme Court cases are typically reported in three major sets of reporters: the *Supreme Court Reporter*, the *United States Reports*, and the *United States Supreme Court Reports Lawyers' Edition*.

Most state court opinions are published by the West Publishing Company in a set of reporters referred to as *regional reporters*. Every regional reporter prints opinions from courts in a specific geographical region. Each of seven regional reporters prints decisions for a number of states (Southern [So.], Southeastern [S.E.], Southwestern [S.W.], Northeastern [N.E.], Northwestern [N.W.], Pacific [P.], and Atlantic [A.] reporters), and California and New York each has its own official reporter for publishing decisions from its courts. Additionally, reporters are grouped according to series, starting with a first series and moving to additional series designated as "2d," "3d," and so on.

Although reports and the cases they contain are typically found in law libraries, case decisions can also be obtained from the Internet. Although some legal search engines and databases, such as *Lexis* and *Westlaw*, may only be accessed for a fee and therefore are primarily used only by members of the legal profession, the *Lexis/Nexis Academic Universe* database is available through many academic institutions. This database permits students and researchers to obtain primary and secondary sources and offers keyword search engines for law reviews, legal news, statutes (i.e., codes), and case law. Contact your local or institutional library to see whether you have access to *Lexis/Nexis Academic Universe*.

LEARNING AIDS

Summary

A challenge for sport managers is to recognize and understand legal issues, effectively manage such issues, and reduce the possibility that legal problems will occur. A sport manager can best manage such issues by understanding the sources of law, the U.S. court system, types of legal resources, and the steps in a lawsuit. By being familiar with these legal topics, as well as the relevant laws and legal issues that affect the sport industry, a sport manager can reduce or eliminate many legal problems.

Knowledge and understanding of key aspects of the law have become increasingly important for sport managers in today's litigious environment. Sport managers should know how to obtain legal information, such as statutes, case law, and published standards and guidelines. Likewise, understanding when it is best to obtain legal assistance is important. Because the law is constantly changing, a wise professional will stay abreast by attending relevant conferences, reading the professional literature, and seeking advice from legal professionals.

Discussion Questions

1. Identify and describe the major sources of U.S. law. Provide a sport-related example of each.
2. Explain the primary differences between criminal and civil law.
3. Describe the names and structure of your state's court system. Where is your state's supreme court located? How many justices serve on the state supreme court?
4. What is the location of the U.S. district court closest to you? What federal regional circuit court of appeals does your state belong to?
5. Identify and explain the steps in a civil trial.
6. Identify which reporter publishes your state's court opinions.
7. Locate and read a sport management–related case opinion from a reporter or from the Internet. Outline the key facts and legal issues. What was the court's decision, and why did they decide that way? Do you agree with the decision? Why or why not?
8. Obtain, read, and summarize a sport law–related article from a sport-related secondary source (journal, law review, blog, etc.).
9. Identify two specific, sport-related primary legal sources as well as two secondary legal sources. What is the major difference between primary and secondary sources?
10. Using the Internet, identify three expert witnesses who focus on sport and physical activity cases.

Tort Law and Product Liability

2

Chapter Objectives

After reading this chapter, you will know the following:

- The elements of negligence liability and how it applies to sport

- The defenses to the tort of negligence and the application to sport management

- Intentional torts and their application to sport settings

- Product liability and its application to sport management

Case Studies in Sport Law Connection

Check out the following case studies related to this chapter in the accompanying e-book, *Case Studies in Sport Law, Second Edition* (Pittman, Spengler, & Young, 2016):

Averill, Jr. v. Luttrell

Baugh v. Redmond

Benjamin v. State

Byrns v. Riddell, Inc.

Crawn v. Campo

DeMauro v. Tusculum College, Inc.

Dilger v. Moyles

Dotzler v. Tuttle

Dudley Sports Co. v. Schmitt

Eddy v. Syracuse University

Everett v. Bucky Warren, Inc.

Filler v. Rayex Corp.

Foster v. Board of Trustees of Butler County Community College

Friedman v. Houston Sports Association

Gehling v. St. George's University School of Medicine, Ltd.

Gillespie v. Southern Utah State College

Hanson v. Kynast

Hauter v. Zogarts

Hayden v. University of Notre Dame

Hemphill v. Sayers

Jaworski v. Kiernan

Knight v. Jewett

Lofy v. Joint Union School Dist. No. 2, City of Cumberland

Lowe v. California League of Professional Baseball

Miller v. United States

Nabozny v. Barnhill

Pell v. Victor J. Andrew High School

Rawlings Sporting Goods Company, Inc. v. Daniels

Rispone v. Louisiana State University and Agricultural and Mechanical College

Sallis v. City of Bossier City

Schiffman v. Spring

Vargo v. Svitchan

This chapter addresses a topic with important practical implications for sport managers: tort law. A **tort** is a category of law that encompasses situations in which a civil wrong has been committed. A tort does not involve criminal conduct but rather conduct that is either careless or intentional that results in harm or injury to a person or property. Unlike criminal law, in which a penalty or jail time might be imposed, a tort might result in an award of money (**damages**) from the person or organization (the defendant) that caused injury or harm. Types of torts include negligence and intentional torts, which are discussed in this chapter and are of critical importance to sport managers, given the frequency in which they occur. This chapter discusses negligence, intentional torts, and product liability as they apply to sport management.

Negligence

Negligence occurs when someone sustains personal injury but there is no intent to cause injury. The injured person (the plaintiff) may initiate a negligence lawsuit in which she seeks money for the injury. Examples of negligence include lawsuits against fast-food chains for claims that fast food made a person overweight or obese and the famous case of the woman who sued McDonald's after she spilled hot coffee in her lap. Most negligence cases never go to trial, because the cases are settled by the attorneys and their clients.

Many examples of negligence can be found in the sport world. Within the broad category of torts, negligence is the most likely type of lawsuit a sport manager will face. We know about many of these negligence cases from either the media or published legal decisions. Thousands of published cases involve negligence in sport. An example of a negligence case in the sport setting is *Green v. Konawa Independent School District* (2005). After participating in an elementary school track and field competition at the Konawa track and field facilities, Green, a fourth-grade student, was instructed by a teacher to sit on one of the stands outside the facility to wait until the event ended. Four students, including Green, climbed to the top level of the stands. One of the students, who weighed more than 200 pounds (91 kg), leaned over the top rail, causing the stands to collapse. Green was hurt in the fall, and his father sued the school district, alleging that the school was negligent for failing to secure the stands and adequately supervise the students.

In this section we look at the elements of negligence, gross negligence, and defenses to negligence.

Elements of Negligence

The plaintiff (injured person) has the burden of proving her case when negligence is alleged. When lawsuits are brought, the plaintiff goes on the offensive and attempts to provide reasons why she should prevail in a lawsuit, but the plaintiff must follow rules set forth by the legal system. The rules, or parts of the case, that must be proved are often called *elements*. With negligence, four key elements must be proved:

- Standard of care
- Breach of duty
- Causation
- Injury (damages)

Each element must be found to exist before a plaintiff may recover (be awarded money) in a negligence case. Figure 2.1 illustrates the elements of negligence.

Standard of Care

Negligent conduct occurs when a defendant fails to meet his duty or responsibility (standard of care) for the protection of others and, as a result, causes another to be injured or harmed. Establishing the standard of care is critical to whether a case is won or lost. The **standard of care** is the duty or responsibility owed by a defendant (this could be a person or an organization)

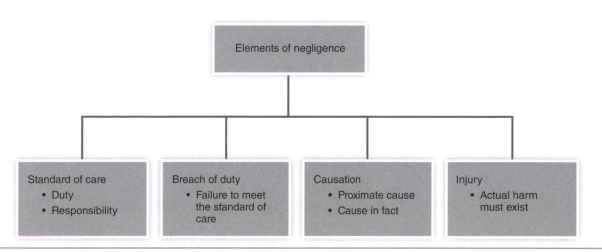

Figure 2.1 Elements of negligence.

to another. The responsibility of the sport practitioner is often viewed in the context of providing a reasonably safe sport environment for those under her care. The following list provides factors that a court might consider when determining the standard of care. Often, a combination of these factors influences the final determination of the standard of care, or responsibility, owed by a sport manager.

- *Case precedent.* Courts refer to the outcomes and facts of prior cases to determine the standard of care (the duty or responsibility of the plaintiff). The practice of using prior legal decisions with similar facts to determine the outcome of later cases is referred to as stare decisis. This doctrine, which provides stability and predictability in the law, is also flexible because some courts may overrule prior decisions in cases in which public policy or other relevant legal matters dictate the need for change.

- *Rules and regulations.* The standard of care might be written in a rule put forth by a regulatory agency. For example, rules govern sliding in high school baseball games, the number of lifeguards required for a pool of a certain size, slide tackling in soccer, and contact in college football. Certain sport-specific rules might help determine the standard of care in a sport negligence lawsuit.

- *State and federal laws.* Legislation may mandate a certain act. For example, in some states, fitness centers and high school athletic departments are required to have automated external defibrillators (AEDs) on the premises. State law dictates the standard of care for these facilities, mandating a duty to have these devices on the premises and specifying the circumstances in which they should be used.

- *Community practice or industry standard.* The standard of care might be influenced by what others in the industry (i.e., **industry standard**) or community are doing. For example, do other softball complexes in the city or state adhere to certain safety practices or have similar safety features at their facilities? If, for example, most facility supervisors in the region have lightning safety plans in place to protect players from injury, a lightning safety plan for softball complexes in that region might be considered the standard of care. Therefore, the sport manager should know what others in the community and industry are doing with regard to safety.

- *Federal regulatory agencies.* Certain federal agencies may have guidelines and recommendations relevant to sport safety with bearing on the standard of care in sport negligence cases. For example, the **Consumer Product Safety Commission (CPSC)** has guidelines regarding the safety of moveable soccer goals; these guidelines may be used by courts in determining whether the standard of care was met. The CPSC recommends that moveable soccer goals provide warnings, be anchored on level ground, and be constructed according to certain guidelines. These recommendations might be used by a court in determining the standard of care if a person is injured when a soccer goal tips over on him.

- *Professional associations.* **Position statements** are often published by organizations such as the National Collegiate Athletic Association (NCAA), the American College of Sports Medicine (ACSM), and the National Athletic Trainer's Association (NATA) that provide guidelines on subjects as diverse as lightning safety and equipment safety. Guidelines contained in association position statements might be used by the courts in determining the standard of care.

• *Agency and organization manuals.* An agency's own policies and procedures manual might be used in determining whether it met its own standards. Lawyers in negligence cases often seek out the agency policy as evidence in determining the standard of care. For example, if language in an agency policy manual states that staff members must call 911 in the event of a head injury, this guidance might be construed as the standard of care as it pertains to the emergency action plan.

• *Expert opinion.* The opinions of **forensic experts** from various fields might be used to help a court determine the standard of care. In sport, experts come from a variety of disciplines: sport management, engineering, medicine, psychology, economics, and others. Engineers might be called to consult on a sport negligence case in which structural or equipment design defects are at issue. Economists might provide testimony about lost future earnings when a young victim loses the ability to work for the remainder of his life as he had anticipated. Sport safety experts might provide testimony about supervision, instruction, emergency planning, or other issues specific to the sport setting.

A person or organization's duty (standard of care) is triggered by the relationship with the injured person (the plaintiff). Certain relationships automatically give rise to a duty to protect another person from an unreasonable risk of harm. For example, although a swimming pool patron is under no legal obligation to rescue a fellow swimmer in distress, lifeguards are responsible because of the nature of their relationship to the patron (e.g., the lifeguard's job is to render assistance). The same idea holds true for coaches (an obligation to players), sport instructors (an obligation to students), and others who provide a service with an associated obligation. Consider the case in the Duty of Care sidebar, in which the court recognized a duty owed by the school and coach to an injured student-athlete.

The duty might arise in another context, even where the types of relationships described previously don't exist. For example, although a person has no general duty to come to someone's aid, after someone voluntarily begins to render assistance, she must proceed with reasonable care. For example, a coach attending a game as a spectator sees a player collapse on the field and decides to render aid. If the player has a neck injury and the off-duty coach (spectator) moves the player and aggravates the injury, the coach may be liable for negligence even though he did not have a duty to render aid based on a player–coach relationship. Thus, the off-duty coach assumed a duty that normally he would not possess.

The final way in which a duty may be found is if it is set forth by statute. For example, state law prohibits the sale of alcohol to minors. Suppose that a 17-year-old high school student becomes intoxicated after drinking beer that was sold to him illegally by arena concessions staff. While driving home from the game, this intoxicated person runs into a pedestrian; the arena and concessionaire have likely breached a duty owed to the pedestrian. As such, the arena and concessionaire may be deemed negligent per se for selling alcohol to a minor, resulting in injury to the pedestrian. If a defendant violates a statutory duty and is deemed **negligent per se**, then the defendant is negligent as a matter of law (*Restatement [Third] of Torts* § 324, 2005). In such a case, the plaintiff need only prove the elements of causation and actual harm to prevail in court. Thus, the statute sets up both the legal duty and the standard of care for the plaintiff. Determining whether

IN THE COURTROOM

Duty of Care

Avila v. Citrus Community College District (2003)

Jose Luis Avila was a 19-year-old student at Rio Hondo Community College and played on the school's baseball team. During a game against Citrus College, Avila was hit in the head with a pitch that was thrown with such force that it cracked his helmet. He alleged that the pitch was deliberately thrown to retaliate for a Rio Honda pitch that hit a Citrus College batter.

After being hit by the pitch, Avila staggered, felt dizzy, and was in pain. The Citrus College coaching staff did not check him, provide any aid, or summon medical care. His coach told him to go to first base. After going to first base, Avila complained to the first-base coach, but the coach told him to stay in the game. After Avila reached second base, he still felt dizzy and in pain. An opposing player yelled to Rio Honda's dugout that they needed a different runner. Avila walked to his bench, but his injuries were not tended to.

Avila alleged, among other things, that Citrus College was negligent for not providing or calling for medical aid when it was obvious that he needed medical attention. He also claimed that Citrus College was negligent for failing to supervise and control the pitcher and the game,

provide umpires or other supervisors to control the game and prevent retaliatory or reckless pitching, and provide an adequate helmet to protect him from serious head injury. Finally, Avila alleged that Citrus College was negligent for failing to train and supervise coaches, managers, trainers, and employees in providing medical care to injured players and for holding an illegal pre-season practice game in violation of community college baseball rules. Citrus College contended that it was immune under government code (section 831.7) on recreational immunity and that it had no duty to supervise Avila. The trial court dismissed the case in favor of the defendants.

On appeal, the court ruled that extending immunity to this case based on section 831.7 was not appropriate. The court stated that "coaches and instructors owe a duty of due care to persons in their charge" and section 831.7 "was not intended to affect the relationship between schools and their students" (p. 818). Regarding the duty allegation, the court stated, "It is surely foreseeable that a student might be injured if supervision is lax (or non-existent) at a school-sponsored sports event, and if medical care is not summoned when an injury occurs" (p. 819). The trial court's decision was reversed (*Avila v. Citrus Community College District*, 2003).

---

a duty is owed and what standard of care is applicable is a key element of a negligence case. After the duty, or standard of care, is established, the next step for the plaintiff is to prove that the defendant failed to meet the standard of care.

Breach of Duty

The second element of negligence, **breach of duty**, requires the plaintiff to prove

that the defendant breached the duty of care. The plaintiff must establish that the defendant failed to conform to the duty of care owed to the plaintiff (*Restatement [Second] of Torts* § 282, 1965). To show that the duty of care was breached, the plaintiff must prove that the defendant's conduct, viewed as of the time it occurred, imposed an unreasonable risk of harm (Keeton, 1984).

By establishing the existence of an unreasonable risk of harm, the plaintiff shows that the defendant breached the standard of care that was owed under the circumstances. A good way to conceptualize breach of duty is first to think about the standard of care and where it comes from and then think about situations when the standard of care is not met. The following example should help you understand the concept of breach.

• *Case precedent as basis for breach.* During a baseball game, a batted ball passes through a hole in the netting that was designed to protect spectators behind home plate and strikes an elderly spectator in the face, fracturing her jaw. Suppose that case precedent has determined that fans assume the risk of being struck by foul balls only when they sit outside protected areas but that stadiums have a duty to provide a safe environment behind netted areas. Based on the duty identified through case precedent, a breach of the standard of care has occurred.

• *Violation of rules and regulations as basis for breach.* A county municipal health code regulation states that pools in the county must have a minimum of six lifeguards on duty at all times for a pool of a certain size. Four lifeguards are on duty when a child drowns in the pool. If the municipal rules regulating the number of lifeguards are determined to be the standard of care, then the pool management has breached its duty (not met the standard of care) in guarding the pool.

• *Violation of state or federal law as basis for breach.* You operate a fitness facility in a state that requires all health and fitness centers in the state to have at least two AEDs on the premises. Suppose that the statute also requires staff to be trained in the use of the AED. If someone suffers sudden cardiac arrest and dies, and you had neither an AED nor anyone trained in its use, you would have violated your duty as required by state law, also possibly invoking the doctrine of negligence per se.

• *Violation of federal regulatory agency guidelines as basis for breach.* A court determines that the CPSC guidelines for moveable soccer goals are the standard of care in a negligence case. The guidelines state that goals must be constructed properly, placed on level ground, and anchored. If an injury and subsequent negligence lawsuit arose after a goal tipped over on a child, and the goal in question was top heavy and not anchored, the standard of care would have been breached.

• *Professional association position statements.* Safety guidelines relevant to lightning safety contained in a position statement from a well-recognized professional association require that sport participants wait at least 30 minutes after a lightning storm has passed to return to the field of play, and these guidelines are determined to represent the standard of care. If a coach or sport supervisor returns the team to the field 15 minutes after the storm has passed and a player is struck and killed, the supervisor has breached the duty of care.

• *Violation of agency policy as breach.* An organization has a policy that requires all staff to call 911 immediately in the event of a suspected head injury. If a staff member fails to call 911 at all, or fails to call in a timely manner, and further injury results, the staff member has breached the standard of care as contained in the organization's policy.

In all these hypothetical cases, the issue will turn on whether the defendant's actions posed an unreasonable risk of harm to the plaintiff. Consider the Causation as an Element of Negligence sidebar and evaluate whether the defendant's actions created an unreasonable risk of harm to the student-athlete.

IN THE COURTROOM

Causation as an Element of Negligence

Day v. Ouachita Parish School Board et al. (2002)

As a member of the freshman football team at West Monroe High School (WMHS), Morgan Day was required to participate in a weight-training class held during school hours. The class was supervised by WMHS' strength coach and three other coaches. Sixty football players were divided into five groups and were supervised by one of the coaches. Several senior students on the team helped the coaches supervise and instruct the class participants.

During one of the classes, Morgan injured his back while lifting weights. The next day, he played in a freshman football game even though his back was bothering him. Shortly thereafter, Morgan sought medical treatment. After an examination, the treating orthopedic surgeon provided Morgan with a written medical excuse that stated, "(1) No football for 1 week (2) No weightlifting, squats or power cleans. Diagnosis—lumbar strain and injured L-5 disc" (p. 1040).

Morgan presented the note to the freshman coach, and the note was posted in the office. The coaches testified that they believed the physician's note meant that Morgan could not participate in football or weightlifting for 1 week. Morgan and his mother claimed that they interpreted the note to mean that Morgan could not play football for 1 week and could not lift weights for an indefinite amount of time.

One day after the medical excuse was posted, Morgan was observing the class but not lifting weights when an assistant coach instructed him to perform a dumbbell power clean push press. Morgan reminded the coach that he was medically excused, but the coach insisted that the exercise would not affect his low back. After performing a few repetitions of the exercise, Morgan experienced severe pain and needed to lie down.

Morgan again saw the orthopedic surgeon and complained of back pain. Magnetic resonance imaging revealed a disc protrusion between the fourth and fifth vertebrae. The physician wrote another medical excuse that prohibited Morgan from all weightlifting and football activities until further notice. Morgan was referred to another specialist. He also went to other orthopedic surgeons and a neurosurgeon.

After the disc injury, Morgan was unable to play high school football or baseball. He lost interest in school and failed his classes because of excessive absences. He withdrew from WMHS and enrolled in an alternative school. Morgan's mother sued the school board and the coach who instructed Morgan to perform the lift after the medical excuse had been delivered. The trial court found the defendants liable for Morgan's back injury (*Day v. Ouachita Parish School Board et al.*, 2002).

Causation

Causation is the third element that must be proved in a negligence case. *Causation* refers to the claim in a negligence case that the acts or inaction of the defendant brought about injury to the plaintiff. Proof of causation is often a key part of a negligence case; the outcome hinges on its resolution. A court might consider two types of causation, depending on the jurisdiction (state where the case is brought), when rendering decisions in negligence cases: cause in fact and proximate cause.

Consider this case in the context of causation. John Lowe (plaintiff) was seriously injured when struck on the left side of his face by a foul ball at a professional baseball game. The Quakes, at their home games, feature a mascot who goes by the name of Tremor. He is a caricature of a dinosaur, standing 7 feet (2.1 m) tall and having a tail that protrudes from the costume. Tremor was performing his antics in the stands just along the left-field foul line. Tremor's tail touched the plaintiff, who was standing in front of Tremor. The plaintiff was distracted and turned toward Tremor. In the next moment, just as the plaintiff returned his attention to the playing field, he was struck by a foul ball before he could react to it. Serious injuries resulted from the impact. As a result, the underlying action was commenced against the California League of Professional Baseball and Valley Baseball Club, Inc., which does business as the Quakes (defendants) (*Lowe v. California League of Professional Baseball*, 1997).

Did the baseball club cause the injury to the spectator? Should it be liable? Consider this case in light of the types of causation described next.

Cause in Fact

Even if a breach of the duty of care owed to another occurs, it remains to be proved that the defendant's breach was the factual cause (**cause in fact**) of the plaintiff's harm. In other words, the plaintiff's **cause of action** for negligence must have some reasonable, direct connection to the defendant's action or omission (Keeton, 1984). An act or omission is not a cause of an event if the event would have occurred without it. This maxim has been used by courts to establish a "but for" or "sin qua non" rule. Simply put, causation in fact requires a finding that but for the defendant's conduct, the plaintiff would not have been hurt. In the Lowe case mentioned earlier, "but for" the distractive actions of Tremor, would the plaintiff spectator been hit by the foul ball, or would he have had greater awareness to the extent that he could have seen the ball coming and avoided it?

In some jurisdictions, causation may be found not to have occurred if it can be shown that something else caused the plaintiff's harm. But the law recognizes that there can be more than one cause for a plaintiff's harm. Accordingly, if a plaintiff can prove that any of two or more causes would have brought about the harm, then the plaintiff may recover against any or all of the actors. The substantial factor test is used to determine whether multiple causes each resulted in the plaintiff's harm (Keeton, 1984). If the defendant's conduct played a substantial factor in causing the plaintiff's harm, then the defendant's conduct factually caused the plaintiff's harm. Thus, if the actions or omissions of multiple defendants each played a substantial factor in bringing about the plaintiff's harm, then all the defendants would be deemed liable and the plaintiff may recover against any single defendant or all the defendants for compensation (*Restatement [Second] of Torts* § 432, 1965).

Proximate Causation

Proximate cause is another type of causation used in courts in various jurisdictions. Under this type of causation, the plaintiff must establish that the defendant's negligence was the proximate cause of the injuries (Wong, 2002). The concept of **proximate cause** stems from policy considerations that place manageable limits on liability caused by negligent conduct (57A American Jurisprudence 2nd § 427, 2003). The proximate cause requirement is based on the premise that defendants should not be liable for all the consequences of their actions, especially far-reaching consequences. There are two conflicting applications of the policy. The first is termed the *direct causation* view. It holds that defendants are liable for all consequences of their negligent acts if no superseding intervening causes occur. The second application, which is more popular and is widely used, is termed the *foreseeability* or *scope of risk* view (Keeton, 1984). Jurisdictions that incorporate **foreseeability** into their proximate cause determination require plaintiffs to prove that the injury was foreseen by the defendant, or reasonably should have been foreseen, and was the natural and probable result of the negligence (57A American Jurisprudence 2nd § 429, 2005). Accordingly, the foreseeability component of proximate cause is satisfied if a person of ordinary caution and prudence could have foreseen the likelihood of injury (*Regions Bank & Trust v. Stone County Skilled Nursing Facility, Inc.*, 2001).

Injury

For any cause of action based on negligence, some **actual harm** or injury must exist (*Restatement [Second] of Torts* § 907, Comment a, 1965; Wong, 2002). Proof of damage is an essential part of the plaintiff's case in negligence because negligent conduct in and of itself does not rise to the type of interference with the interests of society as a whole to warrant a complaint (Keeton, 1984). For example, many of us experience negligent acts committed by others every day. We have all likely experienced a near miss by a car running a red light. An event like this upsets us because the other driver breached the standard of care (broke the traffic law) and caused us distress. The act of the driver was careless, if not negligent, but we have no cause of action for negligence because we suffered no physical harm and the emotional distress was minimal and of a degree that is common to most throughout a normal day. For negligence to be found, in addition to the previously mentioned elements, some real (actual) physical or emotional harm must exist.

After actual harm or injury is established, many types of damages may be recovered to compensate the plaintiff. The types of damages available depend on the circumstances but may include compensation (**compensatory damages**) for physical pain and suffering, mental distress, direct economic loss, **loss of consortium**, and wrongful death (van der Smissen, 2003). In some jurisdictions, a plaintiff may possibly recover **punitive damages** against the defendant. Punitive damages differ from compensatory damages because punitive damages are awarded to punish the defendant rather than compensate the victim (Keeton, 1984). Punitive damages, however, are awarded only to punish outrageous, reckless, willful, or wanton conduct (Wong, 2002). For example, punitive damages may be sought against a stadium concessionaire who sells alcohol to a visibly intoxicated patron who injures another in a car wreck or against a hockey player who uses his stick to hit another player, resulting in serious injury.

Gross Negligence

Thus far, this chapter has focused on what is required for ordinary negligence. But the common law recognizes that tortuous conduct may be so great that it amounts to more than just negligence, even though it falls short of being intentional (Keeton, 1984). For these situations, courts have distinguished between ordinary negligence and situations in which the defendant acts with a heightened degree of carelessness, or gross negligence (*Fidelity Leasing Corp. v. Dun & Bradstreet, Inc.*, 1980). In **gross negligence**, the defendant's responsibility is magnified so that it is at a higher degree than that found in ordinary negligence (57A American Jurisprudence § 227, 2005). Some courts have stated that gross negligence amounts to a failure to exercise even the care that a careless person would use (*Whitley v. Com.*, 2000). Other courts, however, have interpreted gross negligence to require a showing of willful, wanton, or reckless misconduct (Keeton, 1984). The majority of jurisdictions distinguish between acts that are willful, wanton, or reckless and those that involve gross negligence (Keeton, 1984). Regardless of type, the determination is subjective.

A good case example to consider when thinking about the concept of gross negligence is one involving a professional football player who died of heat stroke, resulting in a wrongful death claim for improper medical care. After reading the Negligence Cause of Action and Heat Illness in Football sidebar, think about whether the acts of the coaching staff were grossly negligent.

IN THE COURTROOM

Negligence Cause of Action and Heat Illness in Football

Stringer v. Minnesota Vikings Football Club, LLC (2005)

In the case of *Stringer v. Minnesota Vikings Football Club, LLC* (2005), a professional football player, Korey Stringer, died from heat stroke after the second day of practice at the 2001 Minnesota Vikings training camp. In the 2 days of training camp and before his death, Stringer vomited several times and fell to his knees or the ground several times, although he stood up by himself. Because of these events, Stringer was treated by the Vikings' medical service coordinator and by an assistant trainer. Both of these practice days were hot and humid, and 11 players were treated for heat-related illness on the second day of practice.

During the morning practice of the second day, Stringer became sick and vomited again but continued to practice. Shortly after that practice ended, Stringer dropped to his knees, fell on his right side, and then lay down on his back. The assistant trainer, who thought that Stringer was doing fine, took him to an air-conditioned trailer as a preventive measure. While in the trailer, Stringer relaxed for several minutes. He was given water to drink and an iced-down towel for his forehead. After the trainer removed the player's socks and shoes, Stringer lay on the table and began humming and moving his head back and forth for 10 minutes or more. The assistant trainer eventually called the training room to request a golf cart to transport Stringer, but when the cart arrived, Stringer was unresponsive. This was the first time anyone checked any of Stringer's vital signs, including his pulse, which was steady and slow. At this point no one had called for an ambulance. A few minutes later, the medical coordinator arrived and, believing that Stringer was hyperventilating, treated him for such. Soon thereafter, those present attempted to reach a physician who provided medical services for the Vikings. A few minutes later, the physician telephoned, and a decision was made to call an ambulance. An ambulance arrived 8 minutes after it was dispatched, and the ambulance transported Stringer to a hospital. Hospital staff reported that Stringer's body temperature was 108.8 °F (42.7 °C). Despite attempts to cool and treat Stringer, his condition worsened. He died from heat stroke less than 2 hours after arriving at the hospital.

Stringer's wife filed suit, alleging that the coordinator of medical services and the assistant trainer had a personal duty to protect and care for Stringer's health and that they were grossly negligent in performing such duty. By alleging that the medical coordinator and assistant trainer were grossly negligent, the plaintiffs were saying that the actions, and inaction, taken by these people amounted to extremely careless conduct. Whether actions amount to gross negligence is a subjective determination based on the facts of a case. A key issue here was whether the time delay in getting emergency medical services on site amounted to gross negligence. The Supreme Court of Minnesota upheld the lower court's ruling in favor of summary judgment for the respondents.

As previously stated, some jurisdictions distinguish between gross negligence and willful, wanton, and reckless conduct. These jurisdictions recognize situations in which a defendant may act with intentional indifference to the point that her actions exceed the culpability required for gross negligence (Keeton, 1984). Even though a defendant acts with intentional indifference, the defendant's actions remain negligent rather than intentional because the defendant did not intend to bring about the harm. In these situations, the risk of harm is so great that the defendant probably knows that the harm will follow (*Restatement [Second] of Torts* § 500, 1965). Some courts have tried to differentiate willful, wanton, and reckless conduct (*Neary v. Northern Pacific Railway*, 1910). For most jurisdictions, however, these terms can be used collectively or interchangeably (*Mania v. Kaminski*, 1980). A defendant who is found liable for willful, wanton, and reckless conduct may incur civil sanction through punitive damages (*Hackbart v. Cincinnati Bengals, Inc.*, 1979).

In *Hackbart v. Cincinnati Bengals*, a professional football player was struck in the head by an opposing player after a play had ended. The plaintiff (Hackbart) was seriously injured as a result. The reckless nature of the act was considered in light of the fact that it was committed after a play had ended and in light of the manner in which the incident occurred. Also, consider the case of *Nabozny v. Barnhill* (1975), in which a soccer player was seriously injured after being kicked in the head by an opposing player. The plaintiff (Nabozny) was kicked during a game after he had dropped to one knee, caught the soccer ball, and held it to his chest while in the penalty area. The defendant (Barnhill) continued to run in the plaintiff's direction and kicked the side of his head in the penalty area. The court held that a player is liable for an injury in tort if the conduct of the defendant was either deliberate, willful, or with reckless disregard for the safety of another. The case was remanded to the trial court for a factual determination of the issue.

Legal Protections

Sport managers can use several defenses when defending against negligence claims. Most of these defenses focus on the plaintiff's conduct. Plaintiffs must show all the elements of negligence to prevail in court. Sport managers who are defendants in negligence actions can prevail against a plaintiff's negligence suit if they show that not all the required elements have been met. If a plaintiff has established each of the required negligence elements, then the defendant's case will rest on whether one of the following defenses to negligence exists.

Assumption of Risk

Assumption of risk is a legal defense by which plaintiffs may not recover for injuries in negligence when they have voluntarily exposed themselves to known and appreciated dangers (Keeton, 1984). Three elements to assumption of risk must be established (*Leakas v. Columbia Country Club*, 1993):

- The risk must be inherent to the sport.
- The participant must voluntarily consent to be exposed to the risk.
- The participant must know, understand, and appreciate the inherent risks of the activity.

Inherent Risks

Inherent risks are those that cannot be removed from an activity without fundamentally altering the nature of the activity. For example, risks are associated with tackling in football. Football would be a much safer activity if players simply pulled flags off other players to stop their progress rather than hit them with their bodies in a manner that causes them to fall to the ground. But removing the skill of tackling, and all the risks associated with tackling, would fundamentally alter the game of football. Thus, risks associated with tackling are inherent to the sport.

Voluntary Consent

Certain aspects of a sport, such as physical contact, are accepted (consented to) as part of the sport. Obvious examples of situations in which there is **voluntary consent** to contact and potential injury are legal tackles in football and legal checking in hockey. Even some sports that are technically considered noncontact, such as basketball, involve physical contact that is a known and accepted part of the game (e.g., setting picks). When physical contact resulting in injury goes outside the rules of the game (e.g., helmet-to-helmet contact in football) or when unnecessary physical contact resulting in injury occurs between plays or outside game time, consent fails to be a valid defense. The participant must voluntarily consent to be exposed to the risk for a successful defense to be raised.

Knowledge, Understanding, and Appreciation

After the defendant establishes that the risk leading to injury was inherent and voluntary, it must be shown that the plaintiff knew, understood, and appreciated the risk. The knowledge aspect of assumption of risk requires the defendant to show that the plaintiff knew the nature of the activity and the risks associated with that activity. Continuing with the football example, let's say that a child wishes to play football in a youth sport league but has no knowledge of the game or the way in which it is played. If the child is thrown into a scrimmage game on the first day of practice and is injured when tackled for the first time, the league

Young athletes may not be able to understand all the inherent risks associated with a sport.

would likely be unable to establish that the child had knowledge of the risks associated with tackling in football.

Similarly, defendants must show that plaintiffs understood the activity in terms of their own condition and skill. To show that a plaintiff legally volunteered to risk exposure, the defendant must show that the plaintiff understood his own abilities and physical condition in relation to the risks associated with the activity. If someone knows that he has a specific health condition that should prevent him from playing tackle football but that person does so anyway, it could be shown that he had the requisite understanding of the risks associated with the activity.

Finally, it must be shown that the plaintiff appreciated the type of injuries that are associated with the activity. Sport activity leaders have a legal duty to warn participants of the dangers inherent in the activities and the types of injuries that participants could sustain. Someone might know of risks associated with an activity and have a general understanding of her own condition and skill in relation to those risks, but if she does not appreciate the injuries associated with that activity, then there is no assumption of risk. How can it be shown that a person has made an informed decision to expose herself voluntarily to risks associated with an activity when she doesn't even appreciate the injuries that could possibly occur through participation? The common theme running through the knowledge, understanding, and appreciation requirements of assumption of risk is information. To assume a risk, a person must make an informed decision to expose herself to that risk.

Express and Implied Assumption of Risk

The two types of assumption of risk are express and implied. Express assumption of risk occurs when the participant uses language to evidence that he has assumed the risks of an activity (Keeton, 1984). The language used by the participant can be either oral or written. For example, after a sport activity leader informs a participant of risks associated with an activity, the participant may verbally inform the sport activity leader that he knows, understands, and appreciates the risks of the activity but would like to participate anyway. An example of a written expression of assumption of risk is a participation agreement, a document that sport managers often require sport participants to sign before participation. If the participant is a minor, parental signatures are also required. These participation agreements contain language expressing the dangers associated with

an activity and state that the participant assumes the risks associated with the activity.

Implied assumption of risk exists when the participant's conduct or actions show that he voluntarily assumed the risks by taking part in the activity (Keeton, 1984). For example, Paul played organized football throughout childhood and high school, and now he decides to play in a recreational adult football league. Simply by playing in the league, Paul assumes risks that he has known, understood, and appreciated for many years.

Typically, the courts have found that spectators assume the risk of injuries that might be caused by implements flying into the spectators' seats (e.g., foul balls being hit into the stands along the first- or third-base line) when the person is sitting outside a protected area, as the Assumption of Risk sidebar illustrates.

Contributory Negligence and Comparative Fault

Contributory negligence is a defense to negligence that focuses on the negligent conduct of the plaintiff. Contributory negligence is also an absolute defense in that it precludes recovery for the plaintiff if contributory negligence is established. The **theory** provides that plaintiffs may not recover if they are negligent and their negligence contributes proximately to their injuries. Thus, the defense is a complete one. It shifts the loss totally from the defendant to the plaintiff, even if the plaintiff's failure to exercise reasonable care is much less marked than that of the defendant. Because of the harsh results for plaintiffs, only a few states have retained contributory negligence as a defense.

Most jurisdictions have adopted **comparative negligence**, a system that apportions damages according to the degree to which

IN THE COURTROOM

Assumption of Risk

Costa v. Boston Red Sox Baseball (2004)

In *Costa v. Boston Red Sox Baseball* (2004), the plaintiff was struck in the face by a batted ball while attending a baseball game at the defendant's stadium. She filed suit and claimed that the defendant owed her a duty to warn her of the danger of being hit by the batted ball.

After arriving late to the game, the plaintiff and three companions took their seats in an unscreened area in Fenway Park. Their seats were on the first baseline behind the Red Sox dugout. A player hit a line drive foul ball that struck the plaintiff's face, causing severe and permanent injuries. She had been at the game no more than 10 minutes before being injured.

The plaintiff claimed marked ignorance of the sport of baseball. She had been to a baseball game only once, when she was 8 years old. She had not seen baseball on television except when she had changed channels. Before the injury, she had no subjective understanding of the risks posed by a foul ball.

The plaintiff claimed that she was entitled to a reasonable warning of the dangers of sitting in an unprotected area so that she could have made an informed decision whether to remain sitting there. She acknowledged that a disclaimer existed on her admission ticket but claimed that she did not look at the ticket. Furthermore, she claimed that the disclaimer was inadequate to relieve the defendant's duty to warn, especially because the print was very small. After her injury, signage was installed that stated, "Be Alert. Foul Balls and Bats Hurt" (p. 301). The plaintiff claimed that the signage was necessary before the accident, and that if she had been adequately informed of the danger, she would not have accepted the risk posed by her seat.

The trial court granted the defendant's motion for summary judgment, and the appellate court affirmed, stating,

> Even someone of limited personal experience with the sport of baseball reasonably may be assumed to know that a central feature of the game is that batters will forcefully hit balls that may go astray from their intended direction. We therefore hold that the defendant had no duty to warn the plaintiff of the obvious danger of a foul ball hit into the stands. The result we reach is consistent with the vast majority of reported decisions involving injuries to spectators at baseball games. (p. 303)

each party (plaintiff and defendant) is at fault. In comparing fault, jurisdictions either go with a pure comparative fault system or modify the concept. A pure comparative fault system is one in which plaintiffs recover no matter how negligent they are. For example, if a plaintiff is 90% at fault, the plaintiff still recovers 10% of the financial award for damages incurred. Some jurisdictions require the defendant to be more at fault than the plaintiff before financial recovery is available to the plaintiff. These states are called modified rule jurisdictions because they have modified the concept of comparative fault to prevent plaintiffs from recovering if they are more at fault than the defendant is. For example, if it is determined that the plaintiff is 51% responsible for the harm, the plaintiff is barred from recovering for damages incurred.

Unforeseeable Consequences

Unforeseeable consequences are the results of actions or situations that could not have been predicted or foreseen by a reasonable person. Sometimes events occur that cause an accident but are not foreseeable by a normal, rational person. When this circumstance can be proved, it is possible that negligence liability will not be found. For example, consider the following hypothetical. A man is standing behind an L-screen in a batting cage pitching to a high school baseball player who is warming up for a game. The batting cage is supported by thin metal poles on the sides and corners of the batting cage. Imagine that a pitched ball is batted back toward the pitcher but veers toward the side, striking a pole and ricocheting off at just the right angle to fly behind the protective L-screen and strike the pitcher in the face. If considered an unforeseeable circumstance, or "freak accident," then the concept of foreseeability might act as a protection from liability for the organization responsible for either the design or use of the batting cage.

Waivers

Another type of legal protection from negligence liability in sport is a waiver. A waiver is a contract that sport organizations often use to protect themselves and their business from lawsuits that might occur when people are injured at an event or facility. Waivers should be considered in sport activities because of both the litigious nature of our society and the element of risk contained in most, if not all, sports. Contact sports, adventure sports, distance running, and others have the potential for substantial injury risk. If created and implemented properly, waivers can be used to inform the participant of the risks and potentially free the organization from liability. Waivers and releases have often been found to protect organizations from liability, though only when certain legal requirements to find a valid contract are met. The chapter on contracts in this book explains the elements of a contract that are necessary to create a valid contract. Because a waiver is a contract, those elements apply to waivers as well.

Intentional Torts

Unlike the tort of negligence, in which a careless act is committed, an **intentional tort** is what its name implies—a tort (civil wrong resulting in harm to person or property) that is committed with intent. Committing an intentional tort does not mean that a person meant harm or had an evil motivation. Instead, intent means that a person (the defendant) intended the consequences of the act or knew with substantial certainty that a particular consequence (specific outcome) would result from the act.

In sport, intentional acts are sometimes committed that result in harm to officials, athletes, and sport spectators. The business of sport places unique stressors on people working in the profession. Arena, stadium, and event managers, for example, often work extremely long hours. Sport participants (and parents of youth sport participants) can be especially abusive and hostile toward coaches and referees. Physical and emotional fatigue can take a toll on even the most well-intentioned people. Therefore, some types of intentional torts may affect the sport profession. The types of situations that might result in or be construed as intentional torts include making verbal threats, touching someone without his permission, spreading rumors, dealing with abusive patrons inappropriately, holding someone against his will, and entering the land or taking the property of another without his permission. Intentional torts are broken into two main categories: harm to persons and harm to property. Figure 2.2 shows the categories of intentional torts that these acts encompass.

Harm to Persons

In the realm of sport, certain intentional acts result in personal harm to others. The harm can be in the form of physical injury, emotional injury, or damage to a person's reputation. The following text describes certain types of intentional torts that address this type of harm. The lawsuits dealing with personal harm are battery, assault, defamation, false imprisonment, intentional infliction of emotional distress, and invasion of the right to privacy.

Battery and Assault

Civil law often makes a technical distinction between assault and battery that differs from the common perceptions of these acts. The distinction is that battery involves touching someone, whereas assault is the threat to touch someone.

Battery is generally defined as the intentional, harmful, or offensive touching of another that is unprivileged and unpermitted. Intent comes into play in terms of the person's intent to make contact with another, either directly or indirectly (e.g., throwing a baseball at a group of spectators). You don't have to bruise or physically

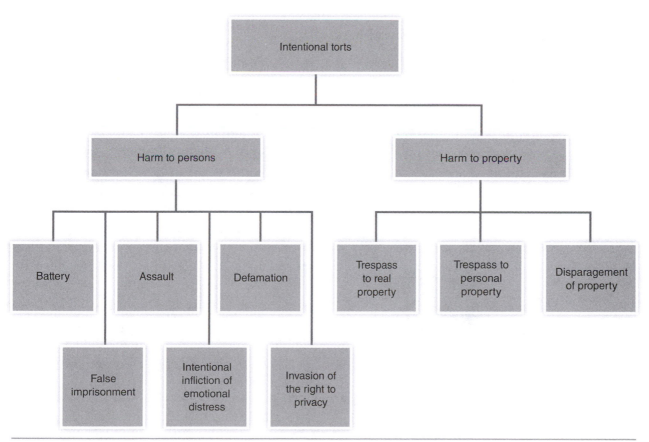

Figure 2.2   Categories of intentional torts.

hurt someone to commit battery, as battery includes both touch that is *harmful* and that which is merely *offensive*. Offensive touching may arise in conjunction with a sexual harassment claim. Harmful touching is common in sport, but often there is no liability because it is permitted (or consented to) as a part of the game. Situations that might involve battery include those in which aggressive spectators hit referees, a sport instructor or coach touches a student or player inappropriately, or a professional athlete rushes into the stands and strikes a heckler. Organizations often put rules in place to avoid situations that might lead to battery and subsequent lawsuits against the organization; such rules might apply to touching, discipline, hazing, and ways that referees should handle conflicts.

Battery can occur in sport settings if harm occurs outside the accepted rules and conduct of the game.

Assault is closely associated with battery but differs in that assault is the threat of a battery (the threat of harmful or offensive touching). The importance of assault is that an organization might be held liable for the acts of an employee who threatens to touch another in a harmful or offensive way. Employees should be instructed not to take matters into their own hands, not only by not hitting or touching another but also by not threatening another. Waiting for the proper authority to handle a heated situation is usually the best measure.

Defamation

Most people have heard about the intentional tort of **defamation**. Gossip in the workplace, untrue and harmful media reports that are made to increase sales, untrue negative remarks that are made without knowing that they were overheard, and negative untrue evaluations of work performance can all lead to defamation under the right circumstances. The two specific types of defamation are libel and slander. **Slander** is the oral form of defamation, whereas **libel** is the written form. A defamation lawsuit proposes that someone has been injured because of something written or spoken about her that was untrue or false, harmful, and made known to another person.

The law uses certain terms to describe that which is harmful and made public. The term used for harm is *defamatory*; therefore, one element of defamation is making a statement that is defamatory. The term used to describe a statement that is made public is *published to a third party*. This means that a third person, someone other than the person making the statement and the person affected by the statement, hears what is said. The rules for defamation differ by whether the affected person is a public figure or an ordinary citizen. Public figures generally have less protection for untrue and negative statements made about them. For public figures, actual malice or a reckless disregard for the truth must be shown. Also, some categories of defamatory statements are potentially more libelous than others, such as statements about someone's moral character (e.g., falsely calling someone a child molester), statements about a person's chastity (e.g., accusations of sexual promiscuity), statements that a person has a "loathsome disease," and statements that affect a person's occupation and profession. Sport managers should discourage gossip in the workplace, back up performance evaluations with facts, and instruct staff and employees to avoid saying harmful things about others and to say nothing at all about a matter if they are unsure of the truth regarding that matter.

False Imprisonment

Another type of intentional tort is the tort of **false imprisonment**. Although the word *imprisonment* brings to mind being locked in a prison or elsewhere, in the eyes of the law confinement does not necessarily have to occur to prove false imprisonment. It may be interpreted, depending on the court and jurisdiction, that a person is "imprisoned" merely if he believes that he cannot leave a certain location (e.g., a child is told by an adult to stay in one place for an unreasonable length of time, or someone believes that she cannot leave an area without being harmed). False imprisonment may arise from seemingly innocent situations. A child might be held against her will as punishment, without the coach or supervisor realizing his error in keeping that child from leaving a certain area for an unreasonable length of time. An innocent person might be held against her will because a store manager falsely but innocently believed that the person had stolen an item from the store. Because of the potential for false imprisonment claims, the sport manager should

be extremely careful in holding someone against his will. Some issues for sport managers to consider involve the reasonableness of their actions. For example, did the sport manager have reasonable suspicion to detain the person? Was the person detained for a reasonable length of time? Were the use and amount of force reasonable? Was the person brought back from a reasonable distance outside the business after leaving the premises? The sport manager should consider and discuss such issues with legal counsel before acting.

Intentional Infliction of Emotional Distress

Intentional infliction of emotional distress is a type of tort that arises when someone intentionally commits an act that represents extreme and outrageous conduct and results in severe emotional distress to another person. The person (the defendant in a lawsuit) intended to commit the outrageous act, and the injury is severe and emotional, not physical. A type of act considered extreme and outrageous enough to result in severe emotional harm to another person is sexual harassment, which sometimes includes claims for intentional infliction of emotional distress. A woman, for example, might be called, text-messaged, or e-mailed repeatedly with language that is sexual in nature and highly offensive, enough so to be considered extreme and outrageous. Additionally, the messages or the manner in which the messages are sent might be so offensive as to result in severe emotional distress or trauma to the victim.

Intentional infliction of emotional distress might also arise when someone intends to play a practical joke on another that goes well beyond the bounds of decency. Suppose that someone calls another and tells him (falsely) that a member of his family has been involved in a life-threatening accident. Upon hearing this, the person receiving the call would likely become severely emotionally distressed. Such a message would likely be considered extreme and outrageous. In this situation, battery (touching) or assault (threat) has not occurred. The tort of intentional infliction of emotional distress therefore covers situations in which injury arises from acts that are not covered under other types of tort causes of action.

In the sport context, a coach might be sued for intentional infliction of emotional distress under certain circumstances. Suppose that a football coach tells his player, a 225-pound (102 kg) senior linebacker, to go out and intentionally injure by spearing (using the helmet as a weapon) a 140-pound (64 kg) freshman quarterback who is playing for the first time on an opposing team. The mother of the freshman player sees her son become seriously injured because of an illegal spearing by the senior player. A suit for intentional infliction of emotional distress

might be brought by the mother because of the extreme and outrageous acts of the opposing coach and the resulting severe emotional injury that those acts caused her. Consider the Liability in Coaching Behavior sidebar and ask yourself whether the actions of the coach were extreme and outrageous and, more important, what a coach would need to do before his actions would rise to that level.

Invasion of the Right to Privacy

The **invasion of the right to privacy** concept encompasses several types of intentional torts, all of which are relevant to sport. The United States Supreme Court has interpreted various amendments of the U.S. Constitution to find that U.S. citizens have a fundamental right to privacy. Some states have taken this a step further by enacting legislation that specifically provides for rights to privacy. The intentional tort of the

IN THE COURTROOM

Liability in Coaching Behavior

Kavanagh v. Trustees of Boston University (2003)

In *Kavanagh v. Trustees of Boston University* (2003), Kevin Kavanagh, a member of the Manhattan College basketball team, was punched in the nose by an opposing Boston University (BU) player during an intercollegiate basketball game. The punch resulted in a broken nose, but Kavanagh later returned to play in the game. The player who threw the punch was immediately ejected from the game. Kavanagh brought suit against the trustees of BU and BU's basketball coach, alleging that the university was vicariously liable for the actions of its scholarship athlete and that the university and coach were negligent because

they took no steps to prevent the act. Additionally, Kavanagh alleged that the BU coach intentionally inflicted emotional distress on him because of the actions of the player whom he coached. Kavanagh claimed that the coach incited the team's aggressiveness by shouting encouragement from the sideline, not removing from the game players who were allegedly elbowing opposing players, and praising his players, including those who were committing fouls. The court concluded that neither BU nor its coach had any reason to foresee that its student-athlete would engage in violent behavior, and Kavanagh failed to show that BU's coach engaged in reckless or intentional conduct rather than aggressive coaching. The appellate court affirmed the decision.

invasion of the right to privacy provides further recourse for those who have been harmed in any of the following four ways:

• *Appropriation*. The first category of intentional tort involving privacy is **appropriation**. Appropriation occurs when someone uses, without permission and for her own benefit, the name, likeness, or other identifying characteristic of another person. Many examples could be placed in the sport context. For example, suppose that someone puts the image of a professional football player on T-shirts and sells them to the public. This is an example of appropriation if the player did not give his permission and the sale was for the benefit of the seller. Suppose that you run a youth sport league and take photos of children playing softball. You post the photos on the Internet and distribute brochures containing the photos to promote your league. This activity is an example of appropriation if the identities of the children were made known in the pictures and the pictures were taken and made public for the benefit of the league sponsors without the permission of the children, parents, or legal guardians. Therefore, when the likeness of someone is recorded (even if for innocent purposes), permission should be obtained before making the image public.

• *Intrusion*. A second type of intentional tort with privacy implications is **intrusion** (also called *intrusion on seclusion*). This tort may arise where someone invades a person's home or searches personal belongings without permission. An example might be a coach who searches the backpack of a player on an opposing team with the hope of finding performance-enhancing drugs or something else that might embarrass or incriminate the opposing player or team. Where an action of this type is done without permission, the tort of intrusion might apply. Intrusion might also be relevant when

offices, lockers, bags, or other personal belongings of players, coaches, or staff are searched without permission. Even in situations in which wrongdoing on the part of another might be suspected, a person must never invade the privacy of another by searching personal belongings without permission. In the scenario addressed here, the best approach would be to alert the proper authorities to handle a matter of suspected wrongdoing rather than take matters into one's own hands and be sued for invasion of privacy (intrusion).

• *False light*. The third type of intentional tort relevant to privacy is called **false light**. False light is similar to defamation and may be brought in tandem with a defamation lawsuit. This involves putting a person in the public spotlight over information that is untrue. Suppose that a newspaper article wrongly claims that a particular college soccer player is a strong supporter of a racist organization. This story would place the player in a false light by making the public think that the player held racist views when he did not. The story would also require the player to face the public to rebut the claims made in the story, thus interfering with his right to privacy.

• *Public disclosure of private facts*. The fourth type of intentional tort with privacy implications is **public disclosure of private facts**. This tort would arise when facts about a person's private life, which an ordinary person would find objectionable, are made public. The public is often fascinated with the personal lives of athletes. Therefore, media outlets sometimes push the limits by providing information about athletes that goes beyond their performance on the field and court. If a newspaper, for example, published a story about a star high school athlete that dealt with the athlete's sex life or finances, this action might give rise to the tort of public disclosure of private facts.

Public disclosure of private facts and the other privacy torts provide legal recourse for private citizens when someone violates their right to privacy.

Harm to Property

The intentional torts discussed to this point have all dealt with harm to people, either emotional or physical. Intentional torts, however, also involve harm committed on (or interference with) a person's property, either real or personal. **Personal property** consists of things that can be moved, such as sports equipment like soccer goals or smaller items like bats, helmets, and gloves. **Real property** is both land and objects that are permanently attached to the land, such as fields, courts, and swimming pools.

Trespass to Real Property

Trespass occurs when a person intentionally enters the land of another, or causes another person or object to enter the land of another, without permission or **necessity**. Several key points are important to your understanding of trespass. First, for the intentional tort of trespass to be found, actual physical harm to the property does not have to occur. Suppose that "No trespassing" signs are posted around a college football stadium and field to protect the turf between games during the season. Some people decide to disregard the signs and play a game of ultimate Frisbee on the field. Even if they don't harm the field in any way, they could still be found liable for the intentional tort of trespass.

The intent of this tort is not just to prevent harm to property but also to prevent people from interfering with the exclusive possession of a person's or organization's property, in this case the university. A sport organization needs to post "No trespassing" signs on their property to give notice that entry to the land is not allowed. If the trespasser has entered the property with criminal intent, however, the intruder is understood to be a trespasser even without posted signs. Conversely, trespass to land is acceptable at times. For example, entering the land of another may be necessary to protect oneself or another person from harm. Suppose that a severe thunderstorm with lightning has arisen and, to protect themselves from the weather, people enter a stadium with posted "No trespassing" signs. This action might be considered a necessity in which liability for trespass would not occur.

Trespass to Personal Property

Trespass to personal property occurs when someone takes the personal (movable) property of another without the permission of that person. For example, a person drags a movable soccer goal off the property of a sport complex and places it in her backyard. She has committed the intentional tort of trespass to personal property. The initial taking of the property constitutes trespass to personal property. If she keeps the property in her possession, then she has committed the intentional tort of **conversion**. She has deprived the owner of the possession of their personal property without a valid reason. Damages or harm might occur to the sport organization if, by virtue of not having possession of their property, they lose business. A sport organization running youth soccer leagues might lose money if they cannot effectively run their programs without necessary equipment that has been wrongfully taken from them. A catering company, for example, might lose business and profits if someone takes their delivery van and they are not able to deliver their food and provide services. Trespass to personal property and conversion mirror concepts in criminal law such as larceny and theft. Remember, however, that the discussion here centers on civil law whereby the harmed person can seek to recover monetary damages from the wrongdoer when an intentional tort of trespass or conversion has occurred.

Disparagement of Property

The final type of intentional tort discussed in this chapter is **disparagement of property**. This tort arises when someone makes a comment about the property of another that is untrue and results in harm to the person in possession of the property. The two types of disparagement of property are slander of title and slander of quality.

Slander of title occurs when someone makes false statements about the ownership or title of someone's property. This wrongdoing amounts to a statement that someone is in possession of stolen property and does not have a valid title to the property. Suppose that someone makes public a false accusation that a certain business is selling stolen baseball trading cards. People would be unlikely to buy trading cards from this business if they believe that the cards have been stolen. A loss of business and potential profits to the store would obviously occur, potentially causing subsequent financial hardship for the store owner.

A second type of disparagement of property is **slander of quality**. This type of tort arises when someone makes false statements about the quality of someone's product or merchandise. Suppose that a business sells championship rings studded with diamonds. If a person falsely accuses the business of selling rings with fake diamonds and people believe the claim, then schools or sport franchises would be unlikely to purchase rings from this business. Subsequent financial loss and hardship would be placed on the business. Slander of quality and slander of title are similar to defamation but should not be confused with latter. The distinction is that defamation deals with untrue statements about a person, whereas disparagement of property deals with untrue statements about personal property.

Product Liability

Product liability is liability for harm caused by a consumer product. At one time, consumers who were harmed by products could recover only against those who sold them the product. Thus, manufacturers would be shielded from liability if the consumer purchased the harmful product from a distributor rather than directly from the manufacturer. Laws now extend liability down the chain of manufacture. The chain of manufacture includes any person or entity who made or distributed the good before it reached the end user. Thus, coaches and sport organizations who sell or provide equipment to athletes may be susceptible to product liability claims.

For example, Phil's parents agree to let him play youth football and purchase his helmet and pads directly from the youth sport organization. Unfortunately, the helmet sold to Phil is unreasonably designed and Phil is severely injured as a result. Phil's parents can bring a claim on his behalf against any or all of the following parties: (a) the company that made the helmet, (b) the company that distributed the helmet to the youth sport organization, and (c) the youth sport organization that sold the helmet to Phil.

Plaintiffs can use three theories when suing manufacturers under product liability: negligence, strict liability, and breach of warranty (Kiely & Ottily, 2006). The first two theories (negligence and strict liability) are found in tort law, whereas the third (breach of warranty) is a contractual remedy. Also, defenses are available to manufacturers who are sued for harm caused by their product. Most of these defenses focus on the plaintiff's actions. Defenses include (a) improper equipment installation, (b) improper modification, (c) use of the product for unforeseeable purposes, and (d) failure to use the product in accordance with instructions (Owen, Madden, & Davis, 2000).

Negligence

The first theory that plaintiffs can use to recover is negligence. Plaintiffs using negligence as a theory in their product liability claim must establish each of the four elements of negligence (duty, breach, causation, and injury [damages]) to prevail in court. Negligence is a theory of liability that can be used in all product liability cases no matter what the type of defect. But negligence is not always easily established, because plaintiffs cannot readily show that manufacturers, distributors, or other parties in the chain of manufacture acted unreasonably in the creation or sale of the product.

The case of *Sanchez v. Hillerich & Bradsby Co.* (1992) provides a sport-related example of a product liability claim. On April 2, 1999, Andrew Sanchez, a baseball player for California State University, Northridge, was pitching against the University of Southern California (USC). During the game, he was struck on the head by a ball that was hit by Dominic Correa, a player for USC. The ball was traveling extremely fast. The bat used by Correa when the injury occurred was an aluminum bat called the Air Attack 2, which was designed and manufactured by Hillerich & Bradsby Co. (H&B). Before the 1999 season, the National Collegiate Athletic Association (NCAA) notified all athletic conferences under its umbrella, including the Pac-10, of which USC is a member, that certain new aluminum bats like the Air Attack 2 were dangerous. The hazardous nature of the bats stemmed from the fact that the bats increased the speed of batted balls,

thus reducing the time that players in the field had to react to batted balls. In its notice to the conferences, the NCAA stated that it had implemented new rules to decrease the speed of batted balls and that these rules would be effective August 1, 1999.

In 2000 Sanchez filed a lawsuit against H&B and the NCAA asserting causes of action for product liability and negligence. The trial court granted summary judgment motions for H&B, USC, and Pac-10, finding that Sanchez would be unable to establish causation. Sanchez argued that the design of the bat increased his risk of injury. But the trial court held that Sanchez had to prove that the bat's design actually caused his injuries. On appeal, the case was remanded back to the trial court to determine whether the type of bat was the cause of the injury.

Strict Liability

The second theory used in product liability is called **strict liability**, a concept of liability regardless of fault. Thus, plaintiffs using this theory are not burdened with the task of showing that a party in the chain of manufacture acted unreasonably. Instead, plaintiffs using strict liability need show only that the product was defective when it left the defendant's hands and that the defect caused the plaintiff's injuries.

The policy allowing strict liability to be used in product liability cases is that between the product manufacturer and the consumer or user, the manufacturer is in the better position to anticipate hazards associated with the product and take measures to guard against said hazards. The problem with strict liability is that unlike negligence, it cannot be used in all cases. The Third **Restatement of Torts** (*Restatement [Third] of Torts,* 2005) provides that there is no strict liability for used goods, based on the idea that buyers expect a somewhat greater risk of defect when the product they are buying is not new. Special circumstances, however, may require the use of strict liability even though the goods are used. This rule is not applicable when the goods are considered "nearly new."

For example, cars are often provided to representatives of sport organizations for use during major sporting events like the Super Bowl and the World Series. These cars are lent to league representatives and other sport dignitaries a short time before the event so that the representatives and dignitaries can travel about the community that hosts the event. When the event ends, the cars are often sold at discounted prices by the car distributors who lent the cars for league use. These cars are not new but have not experienced a lot of use. Thus, these cars may be labeled "nearly new," and some jurisdictions may be willing to allow strict liability to apply to harm caused by these cars.

Breach of Warranty

The third theory that can be used by plaintiffs is **breach of warranty**. This theory is not a tort theory of liability but instead a contractual remedy. Breach of warranty is a remedy most commonly used by those who are simply dissatisfied with their product and wish to have it repaired or replaced. This theory is used every time a product breaks or fails to work properly and the consumer returns it to the store or distributor. The theory is a contractual theory because of the contractual relationship that exists between manufacturers or distributors and those who purchase their products. These contracts are found in the purchase agreements and are called warranties.

Contractual remedies typically are not used to compensate for personal injuries. But tort theories usually must be brought within a short time after the injury is known or should have been known; otherwise,

the plaintiffs are precluded from bringing a lawsuit. Conversely, plaintiffs with contract claims have a much longer time to bring their claims before they are barred. Most jurisdictions give plaintiffs 10 years to assert a breach of contract claim. Thus, plaintiffs who are harmed by a product may be barred from bringing tort actions but may still have cause to sue under breach of warranty.

The two types of warranties are express and implied. An **express warranty** arises through advertising, sales literature, product labeling, and oral statements in which the seller asserts a fact or makes a promise that relates to the quality of goods and induces the buyer to purchase the goods. Accordingly, consumers can claim a breach of an express warranty if an affirmation or promise is not satisfied. For example, if the manufacturer of a basketball shoe advertises that the shoe will improve the vertical leap of consumer athletes by 1 inch (2.5 cm) and a consumer establishes that this is not the case, the consumer might have a claim against the manufacturer for breach of an express warranty.

Implied warranties exist as a matter of law whenever consumer goods are sold. These warranties can be found in article 2 of the **Uniform Commercial Code (UCC)**. The UCC is a set of laws governing the sale of consumer goods that has been adopted by every U.S. state but Louisiana. Two types of implied warranties flow with every sale of a consumer good: the implied warranty of fitness for a particular purpose and the implied warranty of merchantability.

The **implied warranty of fitness** exists when the retailer, distributor, or manufacturer knows of a certain purpose for which the goods are required and, further, that the buyer is relying on the skill and judgment of the seller to select and furnish suitable goods. When this situation occurs, then there is an implied warranty that the goods are fit for the purpose. For example, suppose that a consumer walks into a store looking for a golf club that improves distance and is allowed on all courses. If the golf pro who sells the club to the consumer knows of the consumer's desires and sells the consumer a club that is not legal on Professional Golf Association–regulated courses, then the consumer may have a claim for breach of the implied warranty of fitness for a particular purpose.

The **implied warranty of merchantability** is satisfied when the consumer goods (a) pass without objection in the trade under the contract description; (b) are fit for the ordinary purposes for which such goods are used; (c) are adequately contained, packaged, and labeled; and (d) conform to the promises or affirmations of fact made on the container or label (Uniform Commercial Code § 2-313). In other words, the implied warranty of merchantability states that the goods will do what they are generally supposed to do. This implied warranty of merchantability is the more commonly used implied warranty because it is relied on when products do not work.

Note that the warranty is called the warranty of merchantability rather than consumerability. It is called the warranty of merchantability because it is a derivative warranty, meaning that it derives from the warranty that manufacturers have with distributors. Accordingly, the warranty is that the product will be merchantable, meaning that it can be sold. Merchants typically buy in bulk from manufacturers, so they cannot expect perfection from all the products sold to them. Similarly, consumers claiming breach of the warranty of merchantability cannot expect perfection from their products; consumers can expect only that the products are good enough to be sold.

Because warranties are based in contract, they can be modified or disclaimed like any other contract provision if the parties agree to the modification or disclaimer warranty (Kiely & Ottily, 2006). Therefore, manufacturers can limit the application of warranties or do away with them altogether. For example, a manufacturer could limit the warranty of merchantability to only 1 year. Most manufacturers do limit the warranty of merchantability to 1 year, and this limitation can be found in the warranty given to the consumer. By law, the warranty of merchantability cannot be done away with completely, but all other warranties can be disclaimed.

Types of Defects

Three types of defects can result in legal liability. The first, called a **manufacturing defect**, exists when a product is manufactured incorrectly. Manufacturing defects do not affect the entire product line. In fact, manufacturing defects are established by comparing the harmful product with other products off the same line.

The second type of defect is called a **design defect**. These defects exist when a product is unreasonably designed. Design defects exist before the product is manufactured, and thus the entire product line is defective. The Third Restatement of Torts (*Restatement [Third] of Torts*, 2005) does not impose strict liability at all for design defects but instead requires a risk–utility approach, under which a product is defective in design when the foreseeable risks of harm posed by the product could have been reduced or avoided by the adoption of a reasonable alternative design (Kiely & Ottily, 2006). The omission of this alternative design is what makes the product not reasonably safe.

For example, a company designs a new football helmet that is lighter than all other helmets while affording the same level of protection. The lightweight design, however, causes the helmet to fly off users' heads when hit from a certain angle. Using the risk–utility approach, a court will have to determine whether the risk is greater than the utility (meaning benefits or usefulness). In doing so, a court will ask whether the new lightweight design is so useful that it justifies the increased danger of having the helmet fly off. Furthermore, the court will examine whether an alternative design could have been used that would manage the risk while maintaining the utility. Ultimately, the court will find that the helmet line is defective if the risk associated with the new design outweighs the utility of the new design.

Last, manufacturers have a duty to warn their consumers of the dangers that are inherent in the reasonable use of a product. But the duty does not stop there; manufacturers must also warn customers of dangers resulting from foreseeable misuses of the product. The policy behind this rule is that manufacturers have superior knowledge of the limitations of the product because they made the product. Thus, manufacturers know more about the product than the consumer does. Manufacturers also have a responsibility to warn of defects discovered after a product has been marketed. So the duty to warn continues throughout the sales life of the product.

Warnings must be reasonable. For this reason, strict liability is generally not available in failure to warn defect cases. After all, strict liability occurs regardless of fault, meaning that plaintiffs do not have to establish that the manufacturer acted unreasonably. If no warning exists, however, then strict liability may be used. In determining whether a warning is reasonable, courts will examine whether the warning is conspicuous (i.e., easy to locate on the product). Furthermore, to be considered reasonable, a warning must be easy to read and comprehend. A warning may be unreasonable if it uses complicated language that confuses the consumer.

LEARNING AIDS

Summary

Tort law has practical implications for the day-to-day management of sport facilities and programs. A sport manager will likely encounter a tort lawsuit at some time during her career; she may be involved directly in the lawsuit, or her organization may be involved in a tort lawsuit in which she is not personally involved. Although negligence is the most likely type of lawsuit a sport manager will encounter, intentional torts and product liability lawsuits also occur in the sport setting. Knowledge about these areas of law will help the sport manager handle the emotional strain that accompanies a lawsuit as well as help her prepare for the litigation process. This important area of law is also an interesting one. You should keep this text as a resource in addition to reading tort law articles and cases to keep abreast of current issues in tort law.

Discussion Questions

1. Create a hypothetical scenario about an injury and subsequent negligence lawsuit that occurs in a sport setting. Make an argument for the plaintiff in your scenario based on the four elements of negligence.

2. Create a hypothetical scenario about an injury and subsequent negligence lawsuit that occurs in a sport setting. Make an argument for the defense in your scenario based on applicable defenses to negligence.

3. Research, find, and summarize the key components of a local rule or regulation that is applicable to a sport or recreational activity.

4. Describe the tort of battery, explain how it differs from the tort of assault, and list and describe several situations or contexts in which the tort of battery might arise.

5. Explain the doctrine of assumption of risk with examples of how express and implied assumption of risk might arise in the sport context.

6. Explain how product liability might arise in the context of a lawsuit against (a) the manufacturers of sports equipment and (b) those who buy and distribute equipment to players under their care.

MOOT COURT CASE

Sport Spectator Scenario

During the summer, Sammy Slugger attended a Triple A baseball game with his wife and four children. They had driven 30 miles (50 km) from their home and paid for the tickets at the gate before entering the game. Their seats were 20 rows up along the third-base line. The seats behind home plate were protected by a screen, but Sammy's seat was far enough up the third-base line that it was unprotected.

Sammy loved baseball, and he was enjoying the game with his family. Sammy also enjoyed watching the antics of the team mascot and eating and drinking the food and beverages offered at the game. The peanut vendor, a stadium employee, was a true favorite of the fans. Instead of walking along each row and distributing bags of peanuts by hand, this vendor had a unique method of selling peanuts. He would walk along the row beneath the spectators and throw bags of peanuts to whoever called for them. He would also throw a tennis ball with a carved hole in it to the hungry spectator, who would place money inside the ball and return it to the vendor. In the sixth inning of the game, the peanut vendor passed in front of Sammy and spotted a fan who wanted a bag. The fan was sitting several rows up and behind Sammy and his family. The vendor heaved the bag of peanuts as he always did, but on this occasion he slipped on a piece of ice and lost control of the throw. The bag flew through the air but fell short of its intended mark, hitting Sammy squarely in the chest. Sammy reached down to retrieve the bag and at that instant felt as if he had been struck by a sledgehammer. Unknown to Sammy, a player had fouled a ball directly in Sammy's direction. Distracted, Sammy had not seen it coming. He was rushed to the emergency room of the local hospital for treatment of his serious injury. Sammy, though still a fan of baseball, brings suit against the stadium management for his misfortune.

Risk Management

3

Chapter Objectives

After reading this chapter, you will know the following:

- ☐ The foundations of risk management and key elements of the decision-making process

- ☐ The essential components of an emergency action plan and a crisis management plan

- ☐ The key elements of a lightning safety plan

- ☐ Management issues for sport facilities and those with disabilities

Case Studies in Sport Law Connection

Check out the following case studies related to this chapter in the accompanying e-book, *Case Studies in Sport Law, Second Edition* (Pittman, Spengler, & Young, 2016):

Bearman v. University of Notre Dame

Kleinknecht v. Gettysburg College

Maussner v. Atlantic City Country Club, Inc.

Mogabgab v. Orleans Parish School Board

Sport law is about managing **risk** in sport. When you apply legal principles to the facts in sport law cases, practical implications for management (e.g., facility and program safety for sport participants, staff, employees, and spectators; employee relations; gender equity in sport) become evident. **Risk management** is a course of action designed to reduce the risk (probability or likelihood) of injury and loss to sport participants, spectators, employees, management, and organizations.

Risk management often centers on reducing the risk of harm given that the elimination of all risk is often not feasible. The very nature of sport involves some degree of risk: The only practical way to eliminate all risk is to close a facility, remove a risky piece of equipment, or eliminate the provision of a sport or service. To remove the risk completely from sport would have a potentially negative consequence to sport providers in that the sport activity likely would lose its appeal to most participants. For example, completely removing the risk of injury from hockey by eliminating contact through checking would not be reasonable. This change would destroy the very nature of the sport. A more reasonable approach would be to provide rules regarding contact and use of protective equipment, require coaches to teach those rules, and require referees to enforce the rules.

The types of risk that managers should consider include personnel issues, such as the risk of sexual harassment and discrimination, and issues concerning harm, such as the risk of physical injury to spectators, players, coaches, supervisors, and other employees. The potential physical risks in sport that might affect management through litigation are numerous. The possibilities are extensive and well covered in various texts (Appenzeller & Seidler, 1998; Dougherty, Goldberger, & Carpenter, 2002; Spengler, Connaughton, & Pittman, 2006).

Broad categories of risk, particularly in college and professional sports, include fan and player violence, terrorism (foreign and domestic), fan celebrations and storming the field, natural weather events such as lightning, food and beverage concessions, and health emergencies among players, coaches, and fans. For managers, additional general risk categories include blood-borne pathogens (e.g., the risk of disease transmitted through contact with blood or bodily fluid, as occurs in boxing, basketball, and fitness), sudden cardiac arrest (which gives rise to the need to purchase and install automated external defibrillators), child protection issues (protecting children from sexual predators through background checks and on-site safety procedures), fire, heat-related illness (including hydration issues and emergency action plans), lightning and other severe weather, security (protection from violence), sport-related trauma (commonly head and neck injuries), and vehicular accidents and injuries (harm resulting from incidents, usually involving vehicles transporting players and participants).

This chapter addresses perspectives on approaching risk management and the risk management process and illustrates risk management applications.

Perspectives on Approaching Risk Management

As a person who is ultimately responsible for the safety and welfare of your employees, participants, and spectators, you can approach risk management from several perspectives. Put yourself in the shoes of the following people or organizations when you think about safety in sport venues.

Manager

The manager often has a great deal of latitude in decision making. Each of us has unique personal experiences that affect our decisions, such as sport injuries or near misses; education and training through sport law and risk management courses, such as the one you are currently taking; exposure to media influence, such as hearing of sport-related lawsuits in the news; on-the-job experiences with sport-related injuries and possibly lawsuits; and other factors, such as hearing stories relayed by friends and colleagues. When making decisions, a manager must sort through this information to determine what is relevant and reliable. This process requires self-evaluation. Suppose, for example, that your nephew was seriously injured in youth football because his volunteer coach did not provide him with a properly fitting helmet. This incident may have caused you to recognize the importance of providing proper safety equipment for young athletes in your program.

Besides thinking about factors that might influence individual perceptions, the manager has practical matters to consider. For example, how much will it cost to implement safety procedures and buy safety devices and equipment (e.g., lightning monitors, automated external defibrillators, wall padding for gyms)? Other practical considerations include the availability of information necessary to develop a comprehensive safety plan, support from upper management in implementing a new safety measure, and the cost of insurance. These issues are discussed later in this chapter.

Risk Manager or Director of Loss Prevention

A risk manager or loss prevention director has primary responsibility for the safety of a sport facility. This person might be responsible for alcohol service training, safety inspections, fire prevention, blood-borne pathogen protection, weather-related risk management, food service and equipment, and emergency services, including medical services planning, emergency action plans, and crisis management. If you have a risk manager on staff, that person would handle the details and day-to-day operations of managing risk, but you as a manager—the person with ultimate responsibility—would still need to understand the important safety issues at your facility and the policy and procedures for managing specific risks. If a loss prevention expert is not on your staff, you will need an even greater understanding of safety policy and procedures and risk management.

Outside Auditor

When we live in the same environment for some time, we often filter out many of the details of our surroundings. An outside auditor would conduct a comprehensive examination of your facility or some component of your facility, taking a fresh look at the surroundings. This person is often better able to identify **hazards** because she is looking for them and seeing the facility from a different perspective. When you manage day-to-day operations of a facility, take a step back occasionally to view your surroundings as if for the first time. Make it a habit to look for actual and potential hazards. In other words, think like an outside auditor.

Insurance Company

The insurance company is interested in limiting financial loss. This type of loss often flows from damage to property or personal injury to employees, guests, or participants. The cost is often measured in terms of repair or expenses associated with litigation (either settlements or trial expenses). An insurance company considers the probability and severity of harm that might result from the program or service offered and the conditions surrounding the provision of the program or service. For example, the likelihood (probability) and severity of injury associated with having a diving board in an unguarded pool might raise the risk of financial loss to a level so high that the insurance company is not willing to insure the risk. Sometimes the potential severity of risk is great but the likelihood is relatively low (e.g., a severe weather event). The precautions that you might take in this instance are more difficult to justify. If the risk is great enough that it might result in the death of a single person, however, you must make an ethical decision (with potential legal consequences) about whether implementing a safety plan is simply the right thing to do.

Lawyer

Good lawyers think about winning cases. Personal injury cases are often won on the facts and a determination of the standard of care. The standard of care in a negligence (personal injury) case, as you learned in the previous chapter, may be determined by a number of factors. These might include (1) community or industry standard (what sort of safety measures similar organizations are putting into practice and whether these measures have themselves become accepted community or industry standards), (2) rules and regulations (whether the law requires that certain actions be taken), (3) organizational policy and procedures (your own rules), (4) prior case law, and (5) expert opinion. Therefore, you should think about your reasons for having safety plans, policies, and procedures. For example, are you keeping up with the standards that other sport organizations are meeting? Are you meeting the requirements of city codes and regulations? Are you making the same mistakes that others have made regarding safety that resulted in lawsuits and published case decisions that you have read? Thinking like a lawyer can help you avoid loss to your organization through litigation.

Jury of Your Peers

A key determination in the outcome of many legal decisions is whether a certain action was reasonable. Juries and judges in a court of law determine what is reasonable. When you are deciding whether your actions, the conditions of the facility, or other matters that might have legal consequences are legal, ask yourself what is reasonable. Ask someone you trust who has good common sense whether something that holds potential risk is unreasonably dangerous.

If you ask a lawyer, you will probably get a conservative answer. If you ask an extreme sport enthusiast, you will get an answer at the other end of the spectrum. Ask a jury of your peers, however, and you will get a good idea of what is reasonable.

A diligent and thorough assessment that incorporates some combination of the preceding ways of thinking will be a good start when you consider managing your risk and that of your sport organization.

Loss Prevention and Risk Management

Ultimately, risk management is about loss prevention. It is about providing for the safety of those to whom you owe a duty or responsibility and protecting your organization from liability through the implementation of reasonable safety measures. Losses to a sport organization because of litigation can be substantial. The following are categories of loss, some easily measured and others not.

- *Money.* Easily measured in terms of loss, money is a key concern for insurance companies. Organizations are affected if insurance rates increase or a policy is dropped after a successful lawsuit or large settlement against the sport organization. Organizations that are self-insured will also suffer financial loss.

- *Time and effort.* Lawsuits take time, some more than 10 years, to make it through the appeal process. Even with lawsuits that are settled relatively quickly, the affected parties must provide answers in the discovery process through written interrogatories and oral depositions. Preparing for depositions, traveling, and fulfilling other requirements of the discovery process can cost personnel a great deal of time and effort.

- *Stress.* The pretrial, trial, and appeals process can be stressful to both management and the affected parties. Depositions, in which a defendant can be questioned under oath and on the record for many hours, can create a great deal of stress. Picture yourself sitting across the table from an accomplished trial attorney who is questioning you about the facts surrounding an incident that holds implications for liability on the part of your organization or you personally. The goal of the questioning is to gather information from you that can potentially be used against you in court. Imagine that this attorney is aggressive in her approach toward obtaining information that supports her side of the case. This situation would likely be extremely stressful.

- *Image and good will.* An organization stands to lose its good image nationally and in the community if misdeeds and negligent acts are brought to light through media attention to the lawsuit. This incident might influence everything from ticket sales to the monetary value of an organization.

Risk Management Process

Managing risk in sport is a process. This process has three primary components that have multiple influences to each. Figure 3.1 will help you conceptualize the process and familiarize you with the components of a risk management process: recognition, analysis, and action.

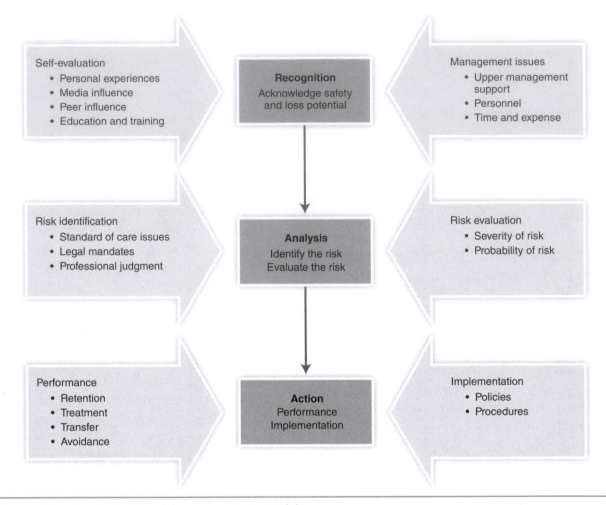

Self-evaluation
- Personal experiences
- Media influence
- Peer influence
- Education and training

Recognition
Acknowledge safety
and loss potential

Management issues
- Upper management support
- Personnel
- Time and expense

Risk identification
- Standard of care issues
- Legal mandates
- Professional judgment

Analysis
Identify the risk
Evaluate the risk

Risk evaluation
- Severity of risk
- Probability of risk

Performance
- Retention
- Treatment
- Transfer
- Avoidance

Action
Performance
Implementation

Implementation
- Policies
- Procedures

Figure 3.1 Sport decision risk management model.

Each component has unique influences, designated by the arrows in the model. The first step in the risk management process is the recognition by management of the importance of reducing or eliminating certain risks. This recognition results in a decision by management to act on either a specific risk or an identified risk category. Once recognized, risks are then analyzed through identification and evaluation, and appropriate action (performance tasks and implementation of policies and procedures) is taken. Each part of the process is discussed next.

Recognition

Recognition of risk involves thinking about both the general categories of hazards to address and the specific hazards within those categories. Managers may not always recognize the importance of addressing certain risks and the subsequent liability that might result from a failure to do so. Influences on the recognition of risks and the decision whether to address potential risks include certain practical management issues and a manager's attitudes and perceptions (self-evaluation). One important management concern is cost.

Many decisions are based on the amount of money available to an organization. Implementing new risk management plans and procedures may be expensive because of personnel or equipment costs. For example, whether the organization is able to provide automated external defibrillators (AEDs—portable lifesaving devices that a bystander can use to revive a victim of sudden cardiac arrest, including administering an electric shock to the chest when appropriate) depends, in part, on whether it can afford to purchase AEDs. When negligence lawsuits are brought against sport providers for failure to provide a safe environment, cost and financial burden to the provider are often factors in the case. Before a sport organization decides not to provide safety equipment based on cost, however, it needs to exhaust all potential funding options. Depending on the nature of the sport organization, grant or subsidy programs might be available that reduce or eliminate the cost of implementing safety standards. Some examples of alternative funding sources include local civic organizations or local businesses, government and private grants, public charities, and traditional fund-raising events. Additionally, as technologies such as AEDs evolve, their cost often falls.

Other management issues shape decisions about whether a potential specific hazard or general hazard category warrants recognition and action, such as time, effort, and human resources; information and support; and necessity. When an organization has limited personnel, decisions must be made about the best use of employees' time, skills, and energy. In some cases, management may decide that certain safety procedures are not practical given limited human resources. One factor may be the perception that too much time, effort, or expense would be needed to develop a comprehensive safety policy or procedure. This perception, however, might be inaccurate given the wealth of information regarding safety procedures available online from professional associations (often in the form of published position statements written by experts and standard-setting organizations, such as the American Society for Testing and Materials). Much of this information is easy to access and available in a format that can be transferred to fit specific organizational needs with minimal time and effort. Additionally, guidance is available from sport safety consultants and published texts.

Another management concern might be that the implementation of a sport-specific safety plan is too problematic. The perceived problems might lie with training time and costs. When an organization has limited staff, management may decide that it is not feasible to pull employees away from their daily functions and responsibilities to attend training sessions and then later to practice safety procedures on a regular basis. Despite these concerns, however, both the importance of saving lives and reducing injuries and the ever-present potential for liability in sport activities warrant attention to safety.

In an organization that has layers of authority, action on identified risks often cannot be taken at the ground level without upper-management support. Those working with day-to-day operations might need to convince managers about the liability and harm that an identified hazard might pose. Although limits on liability insurance coverage might be important factors for upper management, the importance of safety from an ethical standpoint should also be a prime consideration.

> You likewise have an ethical responsibility to provide for the safety and well-being of participants and spectators. When determining whether to implement safety measures,

emphasis is often placed on the bottom line—the impact that safety measures would have on financial resources. Yet, the cost of potential injury or death to participants in the absence of safety plans is obviously of great concern as well. Even in situations in which a plan would cost an organization more to implement than it would save in terms of protection from lawsuits, there remains an ethical responsibility to provide for the safety and well-being of patrons. (Spengler et al., 2006, p. 5)

Consider also the following aspect involved in identifying risks that need to be addressed:

It is also wise for those responsible for safety to examine their personal motivations and consider the source of these motivations. For example, your decision regarding whether to implement a risk management plan for a particular risk category (e.g., lightning safety) might be influenced by your perception of risk. Be aware of factors that might influence this perception. (Spengler et al., 2006, p. 5)

For example, a coach who must decide whether to implement lightning safety procedures might be influenced by experiences. Perhaps he or a friend or relative was struck or nearly struck by lightning, or maybe a young player on his team was struck by lightning and the coach administered CPR to save the player's life. Another influence might be the media; perhaps the coach has read news stories describing the dangers of lightning in outdoor sport programs. The coach might be influenced by professional training experiences, such as a course or panel discussion on lightning safety in sport conducted by a professional association. Friends and colleagues may have told the coach stories about near misses with lightning and the importance of having lightning safety plans and procedures. In such a case, the individual should try to set aside personal perceptions and look objectively at whether there is significant risk.

Analysis

After the manager recognizes the need to address risk, she should analyze specific risks or general categories of risk. The analysis should consist of two parts, which often overlap and work together: risk identification and risk evaluation.

Risk Identification

Risk identification involves finding hazards and determining the potential liability that might result if a hazard is not properly addressed. For example, a common area for hazards is indoor and outdoor play areas and facilities. Some hazards include uneven turf on playing fields, glass doors or windows in gyms, slippery surfaces, baseball and softball fixed bases, low fences, and inadequate protective equipment. As a risk manager, how will you identify risks? One method is to review the facility's incident and accident report forms. Is a pattern or common cause associated with past incidents? If you have access to injury statistics or evidence of prior incidents for a particular sport or activity, you should investigate this area further. A record of prior incidents, however, will be available only if management has developed an emergency plan that includes maintaining proper records.

Identification, therefore, ties directly to the development of good risk management plans. A complete discussion of emergency action plans and other risk management issues relevant to sport can be found in *Risk Management in Sport and Recreation* (Spengler et al., 2006). In risk identification, an applicable rules and regulations. Statutory mandates (e.g., state laws that require a certain organization to take certain actions) often apply to sport. For example,

> in some states, it is required by law that sport and recreation organizations implement safety measures or comply with certain safety standards. For example, it may be that the case that high schools, park districts, and even health clubs must have automated external defibrillators (AEDs) at their facilities. If required by state law, and compliance is mandatory, the decision regarding whether to implement a particular safety measure has been made for you. It is therefore important to be familiar with—or seek counsel from someone familiar with—laws relevant to your organization and program. (Spengler et al., 2006, p. 3)

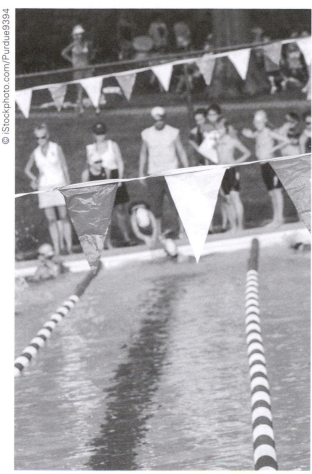

What potential risk factors can you identify in this photo of a facility? Identifying potential risk is part of developing a sound risk management plan.

The manager's background, education, and training, in combination with the previously addressed issues, are key factors in her ability to identify hazards and risks to the sport organization. University classes, continuing education, and on-the-job training are vital in helping the manager understand legal and safety issues in sport.

Risk Evaluation

The second component of analysis is the evaluation of risks. A risk may appear to be hazardous, but more analysis is necessary to determine the extent of risk that the hazard poses. This part of the analysis involves an evaluation by the sport manager of both the frequency and the severity of the identified risk. This procedure enables sport managers to prioritize their risks and attend to them in a timely manner. Not all hazards or risks are worthy of attention. The possibility of injury from

element of common sense or professional judgment often is involved. Common sense, in this context, refers to the natural ability of a person—absent study, investigation, or research—to recognize a hazard. The hazards identified through common sense likely are obvious and should be addressed first.

Other hazards, however, might not be so obvious. For these, we would look to the origins of the standard of care. These might include industry or community standards, published guidelines, standards and recommendations from professional associations, case precedent, statutory mandates, and a potential hazard might be so remote that it would happen only through a freak accident. Thus, managers should focus on hazards that are serious enough and likely enough to result in appreciable injury to someone. How do we evaluate the likelihood of injury? This evaluation is tied to risk identification: When you identify risks, you should also evaluate them. When we consider the likelihood that an event (e.g., injury from slipping on a wet floor) will occur, we are applying the legal concept of foreseeability. When it is reasonably foreseeable that a hazard (the wet floor) might injure a participant, the potential for liability on the part of the sport organization increases. A risk might be considered foreseeable if it occurs in places or situations where injuries have occurred in the past (e.g., a high likelihood of risk is present), places of high inherent risk or danger, and situations in which participants do not understand or appreciate a particular risk because of a lack of education, training, skill, or maturity (this circumstance often refers to children). Less foreseeable risks are those in which no incident has occurred over a reasonably long period, common sense dictates that the risk is low, or experts or other authority would determine the risk to be low. Skilled athletes in a well-supervised and controlled environment would likely incur less risk of personal injury than children who, for example, are learning a higher-risk activity such as gymnastics or swimming.

Besides evaluating the likelihood of injury, a manager must assess how serious a potential injury might be. You can probably guess the types of sport activities, facilities, and programs that hold the greatest prospect for serious injury. Swimming and diving, gymnastics, cheer stunts, certain contact sports, exercise in extreme weather (e.g., hot and humid conditions), and competitive cycling all carry a high degree of risk for personal injury. Risk can be eval-

uated either subjectively or objectively, and both the severity and probability of risk should be viewed in combination. If an objective approach is taken, the severity and probability of risk can be ranked. Action to reduce the risk becomes more necessary as the severity and likelihood of the risk increase (figure 3.2).

Where the severity of a potential injury is high and the likelihood of injury is high, the organization clearly must reduce or, if possible, eliminate the risk of injury or death. A more difficult situation arises, however, when the likelihood is moderate to high and the severity is low (e.g., the potential injury is quite minor—a scrape or bruise), or the combination of severity and frequency lies in some middle-ground range. Management must make a judgment call about whether to take action and, if so, what action to take. This takes us to the third step of the process: action.

Action

After a risk has been recognized and analyzed, the manager must decide whether to act on the perceived risk and, if so, the type of action to take. Four options (potential actions to take) are provided by this model:

- **Retention**—keeping the situation as is
- **Treatment**—taking action to reduce the risk, such as covering an exposed sprinkler head on a playing field
- **Transfer**—placing the risk of liability on another, often through leases and contracts
- **Avoidance**—eliminating the risk by eliminating the program, facility, or service that gives rise to the potential risk

To understand the actions that each option calls for, consider the security operations of a university or professional sport stadium before and after the terrorist

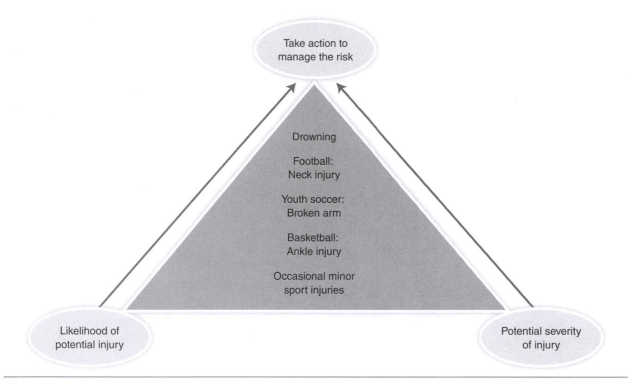

Drowning

Football:
Neck injury

Youth soccer:
Broken arm

Basketball:
Ankle injury

Occasional minor
sport injuries

Take action to
manage the risk

Likelihood of
potential injury

Potential severity
of injury

Figure 3.2 Sport risk evaluation model.

attacks of September 11, 2001. The potential severity of harm from such an attack is obviously quite high at any time. The perceived likelihood or probability of harm, however, changed after September 11. Before the terrorist events, the perceived risk of a terrorist attack at a sport stadium was moderate to low. Therefore, standard security operations in place at that time were often deemed adequate and were *retained*. The threat to the security of public places was elevated after September 11. Therefore, security measures were developed in an effort to *treat* (reduce) the risk of a terrorist attack on sport stadium facilities. Treatment options at some stadiums included the prohibition of certain items from entering the stadium premises, physical barriers at entrance points to keep vehicles a safe distance from the facility, heightened security and searches of event patrons, and no-fly zones around the stadium.

Besides treating the risk through tangible risk reduction measures, stadium managers also sought ways to *transfer* the risk of financial loss to others. The primary method was through insurance. Increased premiums thus became a substantial additional cost for stadiums. In other contexts, some organizations attempt to transfer their liability through leases and contracts. The manner in which a contract is written is critical to whether an organization will be protected from liability. Another option for organizations with large financial assets is self-insurance. This approach involves setting aside a large sum of money to deal with financial losses that result from risk (e.g., litigation costs). The final option, and the most dramatic one, is to *avoid* the risk. Some sport events were cancelled immediately after September 11, both to show support for the victims, their families, and the United States and to plan and implement additional security measures.

To formalize the specific actions that are chosen, the manager will produce and implement policies and procedures. A policy is a written rule governing the conduct of the agency's activities and programs, whereas a procedure is a written statement regarding employee actions in given circumstances. Information relevant to forming risk management policies and procedures is often available from professional associations and regulatory agencies as well as online. Thus, the Internet has had a great influence on the availability of risk management procedures. Table 3.1 provides examples of information relevant to risk implementation given various categories of risk (Spengler et al., 2006). A good example of how the Internet has influenced the availability and accessibility of sport safety information is in procedures for lightning safety. Easily accessible sources from a variety of organizations (e.g., National Oceanographic and Atmospheric Association [NOAA], professional sport organizations) provide lightning safety procedures that are applicable to sport organizations and venues. Sport managers can access this information with relative ease and develop their own procedures from these sources.

Traditionally, policies and procedures were printed and bound into books or pamphlets, whereas now this information is usually available in electronic form. The challenge for organizations with bound copies of policies and procedures was to see that they were read by employees and did not just sit on a bookshelf and gather dust. In our electronic age, managers face the same dilemma without the dust. In whatever form, safety policies and procedures must be available to employees and others (e.g., volunteers) in sport programs and facilities, and these people must read and follow the policies and procedures. If a policy or procedure exists but has not been properly communicated or followed, and an injury and lawsuit subsequently arise, the potential for liability is great. The plaintiff's lawyers can build their case using the sport organization's own policies and procedures, which will be reproduced and enlarged for

Table 3.1   Safety Issue and Risk Implementation Sources

Safety issue	Organization	Abbreviation	Home page
Sports equipment	American Academy of Orthopaedic Surgeons	AAOS	www.aaos.org
Child-protective equipment	American Academy of Pediatrics	AAP	www.aap.org
Aquatics	American Red Cross	ARC	www.redcross.org
Emergency policy for health and fitness	American College of Sports Medicine	ACSM	www.acsm.org
Sports equipment and facilities	American Society for Testing and Materials	ASTM	www.astm.org
Soccer goals	Consumer Product Safety Commission	CPSC	www.cpsc.gov
Lightning	National Athletic Trainers' Association	NATA	www.nata.org
College athletics	National Collegiate Athletic Association	NCAA	www.ncaa.org
Crisis planning for schools	U.S. Department of Education	USDOE	www.ed.gov
Concussion in youth sports	Centers for Disease Control: Heads Up to Youth Sports	CDC	www.cdc.gov

Adapted, by permission, from J.O. Spengler, D.P. Connaughton, & A.T. Pittman, 2006, *Risk management in sport and recreation* (Champaign, IL: Human Kinetics), 2.

use in court. An expert witness may even base her opinion regarding the standard of care on these policies and procedures. Therefore, the sport manager must ensure that safety policies and procedures are communicated, implemented, and documented.

One common procedure for sport organizations is routine maintenance and inspection of facilities. Inspections may occur frequently, often on a set schedule. For example, bleachers may be inspected weekly for structural defects or weakness. If the schedule is provided as part of a formal safety inspection procedure, the sport manager responsible for oversight of maintenance and inspection must ensure that the schedule is adhered to. We can easily imagine what an expert witness and lawyer for a plaintiff would say if the bleachers failed and someone was injured because the schedule was not followed and a problem was missed. Besides conducting regular maintenance and inspection, sport facility managers sometimes bring in outside experts to conduct facility audits. These audits are detailed examinations of facilities or certain facility components. Audits are conducted less frequently (maybe only once or twice a year) than inspections and are much more detailed, including detailed checklists for many items. As with inspections, however, after a problem has been found, the sport manager must determine whether that item represents a safety hazard that warrants attention. If the manager decides that the problem poses a threat to safety (through an evaluation of the risk), measures must be taken to either reduce or eliminate the risk of harm.

The case in the Issues of Liability With Alcohol at Sport Venues sidebar is from the published decision (later settled for an undisclosed amount) in the appellate court case of *Verni v. Aramark et al.* (2006). The case raises the issue of managing the risk of alcohol service in sport stadiums and arenas.

Maintaining and Providing Proper Equipment and Premises

Common sources of injuries in sport and recreation include dangerous or improper equipment, hazardous premises, improper instruction, and improper supervision. Each of these issues is obviously comprehensive in scope. Much has been written on these issues and is available in books and articles. This section addresses key aspects of the broad issues and then, importantly, provides direction in terms of finding information on recommendations, standards, and guidelines relevant to these issues.

Equipment

Equipment must be in good working order to ensure the safety and well-being of your organization's participants. Understanding how to care for equipment is vital. Equipment issues are clearly at the forefront of importance for sport and recreation supervisors. Supervisors must not only provide protective or safety equipment but also instruct participants about how to use and care for the equipment properly, as well as perform basic safety inspections. These inspections would act as a supplement to inspections provided by the coach or sport supervisor. Manufacturer recommendations regarding inspection and maintenance of equipment should be followed. Also, all instructions and documentation relevant to safety and warnings should be retained. All equipment should be properly fitted, and participants should be shown how to wear it properly. Likewise, the equipment must be

Issues of Liability With Alcohol at Sport Venues

Verni v. Aramark et al. (2006)

At approximately 11 a.m. on October 24, 1999, (defendant) Lanzaro and Michael Holder arrived at Giants Stadium and attended a football game. Lanzaro admitted that he did not clearly remember all the events of the day but recalled that while tailgating before the game, he had consumed two or three of the eight 12-ounce (360 ml) beers he had in his truck. He described himself as a binge drinker. The men entered the stadium at approximately 12:30 p.m. for the 1 p.m. kickoff. Lanzaro, who had purchased his ticket from a scalper, did not sit with Holder but rather sat in the third or upper tier in section 310. Lanzaro admitted that during the first half of the game he purchased two or more 16-ounce (480 ml) light beers from an unidentified person operating a concession stand in the upper tier. Lanzaro "guzzl[ed]" the beer, drinking approximately one beer every 10 minutes, and "never had an . . . empty hand," claiming he was drunk by the end of the first quarter. Just before half-time, at approximately 2:30 p.m., Lanzaro left his seat and walked down the "spirals," the ramps leading to the various stadium levels, to meet Holder. En route, Lanzaro, purchased "four or more" 16-ounce light beers from an unidentified person operating a portable beer cart in the lower-level spiral. Lanzaro claimed he told the server how many beers he wanted and then "duked," or tipped, the server an extra $10 to bypass the stadium's two-beer limit.

Lanzaro walked approximately 50 to 75 feet (15–23 m) to meet George Lanzaro (his brother), Lisa Lanzaro (his sister-in-law), and Holder in the spiral by Gate D. George and Lisa, who had been sitting with Holder, confirmed that Lanzaro walked toward them carrying six 16-ounce beers. George claimed that Lanzaro appeared to be intoxicated because he had "a blank look," was animated and loud, and had "a very slight sway." Lisa said she gave Lanzaro a sandwich because she "thought he was drunk." Neither Lisa nor George Lanzaro observed Lanzaro buy the beer. Holder testified at trial that he could not recall whether Lanzaro had appeared intox-

icated but admitted that at depositions he had testified that Lanzaro had not seemed drunk. In any event, Lanzaro maintained that he drank only one or two of the beers he bought in the spiral and offered the rest to his family. Lanzaro then left and purchased marijuana in the spirals from an unidentified person but claimed he had only a "couple of hits" because he "was too drunk."

Lanzaro and Holder left the stadium sometime around the beginning of the third quarter. Lanzaro drank a beer in the parking lot before driving to Shakers, a go-go bar. While there, Lanzaro ordered a light beer but claimed he had only "a couple sips." Lanzaro then drove to a liquor store, where Holder bought a six-pack of beer and a bottle of champagne, which they took to The Gallery, another go-go bar. The Gallery did not have a liquor license but allowed its patrons to bring alcohol. It provided cups, ice, and service. Lanzaro and Holder remained at The Gallery for approximately 40 minutes, during which time Lanzaro admitted he might have consumed a beer but said that he and Holder did not drink the champagne because it was for the dancers. Gunther Bilali, the owner of The Gallery, set forth in deposition testimony read to the jury that he was not present at the time but that the hosts at his establishment would not allow a visibly intoxicated patron to enter. After leaving The Gallery, Lanzaro drove to a fast-food restaurant, where he and Holder ate.

At approximately 5:47 p.m., shortly after leaving the restaurant, Lanzaro swerved across the lane of traffic and struck a 1999 Toyota Corolla driven by Ronald Verni. The parties stipulated that "Lanzaro's driving was the cause of the accident." On arrival at the scene, Officer Lange and Patrolman Thomas Barnett of the East Rutherford Police Department observed that Fazila Verni was in the back seat "wedged behind the driver" and that Antonia Verni, age 2, who was also in the back seat, was unconscious. A test taken at 6:25 p.m. confirmed that Lanzaro had a blood-alcohol concentration of .266%. Lanzaro was arrested, subsequently convicted of vehicular assault, and sentenced to a 5-year term. The Verni family sued Lanzaro and multiple other parties, including Aramark, the concessionaire responsible for the beer vendors at the game. The New Jersey Court of Appeals overturned a trial court verdict for $100 million against Aramark for negligence. The case was appealed from the appellate court and subsequently settled for $25 million to compensate the family for loss due to injury.

appropriate for the activity and the physical size and skill level of participants.

A case example that illustrates the importance of providing proper equipment involves an injury to a high school football player. Richard Locilento, a senior at John A. Coleman Catholic High School, was participating in an annual, informal intramural tackle football game. The game was officiated by two instructors from the school, and no protective equipment was provided. Locilento sustained a dislocated shoulder while attempting to tackle another player. He filed suit, alleging that the school failed to supervise the game properly and provide necessary equipment and training. At trial, the jury held for Locilento, and the school appealed. The higher court reasoned that the likelihood of injury was greater because of the school's failure to provide the necessary protective equipment (*Locilento v. John A. Coleman Catholic High School*, 1987).

Playing tackle football without protective equipment might seem like an extreme example. Consider, however, whether a similar result might occur if a young girl is hit in the face by a softball when a catcher's mask was neither required nor made available, or when shin guards were not made available for young soccer players.

With the importance of providing, maintaining, and often requiring proper and safe equipment of obvious importance, understanding how and where to find information regarding important equipment issues is necessary. Organizations such as American Academy of Pediatrics (AAP), the American College of Sports Medicine, the American Camping Association (ACA), the American Academy of Orthopaedic Surgeons (AAOS),

the American Academy of Pediatric Dentistry (AAPD), Sanford Health, and other medical and health groups have information relevant to the safety of sport participants and those who supervise them.

For collegiate sports, information on recommended safety equipment is provided in the *2013–2014 NCAA Sports Medicine Handbook*. The *Handbook* provides information on mandatory equipment and prohibited items for sports such as baseball, basketball, fencing, field hockey, football, gymnastics, ice hockey, lacrosse, shooting, soccer, snow skiing, softball, swimming and diving, track and field, volleyball, water polo, and wrestling. The *2013–2014 NCAA Sports Medicine Handbook* is available online at www.ncaapublications.com/p-4328-2013-14-ncaa-sports-medicine-handbook.aspx. Other safety equipment issues addressed separately in the *Handbook* include guidelines for fitting and removing helmets, eye safety, and mouth protection.

For high school sports, information on protective equipment is available from the National Federation of State High School Associations through their website: www.nfhs.org. Equipment issues are covered in the section Activities and Sports. This source of information is valuable for high school coaches and administrators.

For sport activities, particularly those involving contact, equipment that protects the face and head is of critical importance.

Premises

The premises for sport play and events must also be in good working order and maintained to ensure the safety and well-being of your organization's participants. When planning to develop, renovate, or perform extensive maintenance on facilities, an expert in facilities should be consulted in the early stages. Various agencies, associations, and organizations publish standards and guidelines that may affect your facility. Laws and regulations may also apply. These may include but are not limited to laws and regulations of the Occupational Safety and Health Administration, Americans with Disabilities Act, American Society for Testing and Materials, the American National Standards Institute, ACSM's Health/Fitness Facility Standards and Guidelines, as well as various local and state health and fire codes.

To reduce the risk of injury, administrators, teachers, and coaches of sport and recreational activities should take reasonable precautions to provide a safe environment. Part of doing so includes inspecting facilities for risks. Administrators, teachers, and coaches can be held liable for an injury caused by hazards they should have discovered. Additionally, if they are aware of a hazard they may be held liable if they failed to take reasonable steps to remedy the hazard or to offer adequate warning to participants.

Facility and equipment inspections may be classified according to type and frequency. An inspection may be generalized for an entire facility or tailored to focus on a designated location. Inspections should be conducted regularly and may occur daily, weekly, monthly, seasonally, or annually (Peterson & Hronek, 2001). The frequency of the inspections depends on several factors including but not limited to manufacturer recommendations, facility and equipment standards, condition of the facility and equipment, and the amount of usage. Generally, the higher the risk, the more frequent the inspections should be. Daily inspections can be developed to address such risks as checking for water or debris on activity

courts, holes in fields, or doors that should be locked. Less frequent inspections can provide a more specialized inspection for equipment, facilities, and premises including items such as frayed cables on an exercise machine, loose boards on bleachers, or loose anchors for soccer goals. Also, periodic inspections should be conducted to determine whether facilities are compliant with all code requirements for equipment such as emergency lighting and fire extinguishers.

If a hazard is detected, it should be corrected immediately. If it cannot be immediately repaired or replaced, cordon off the area, warn participants, remove the damaged equipment, cancel or modify the activity, or do whatever else is necessary to provide a reasonably safe environment. Participants also can be taught how to perform basic safety inspections of the facility and equipment that they will be using. These inspections should supplement the inspection being performed by the coach, teacher, or supervisor. Participants should be instructed to report immediately any obvious or questionable defects to the supervisor.

Using an inspection report or checklist, administrators, teachers, and coaches can document their inspections. If faced with litigation, the sponsoring organization's proof that they sufficiently inspected for risks may prevent or limit liability. Inspection checklists should be created and then approved by an organization's administration and legal counsel. This type of documentation should be retained for the length of the state's statute of limitations.

Regularly scheduled maintenance of facilities and equipment is another component of providing a reasonably safe environment. Regular maintenance helps reduce risks that might be overlooked during inspection. Maintenance should be performed according to manufacturer's recommendations, and formal documentation of these preventive maintenance measures should be retained.

In *Byrd v. State* (1995), the court ruled that the state fulfilled its duty to maintain a park in a safe condition by conducting daily inspections and correcting defects as soon as possible. Although not all potential risks can ever be fully eliminated, the court ruling in *Byrd* shows that an effective, formalized facility and equipment inspection program, coupled with a preventive maintenance plan, may help protect administrators, teachers, coaches, and the sponsoring organization from liability.

Facilities and equipment should meet or exceed the relevant recommended space and safety specifications (e.g., unobstructed space around playing area, size and thickness of matting, number and size of signage). Finally, facilities should be secure when they are not open and intended for use.

Instruction and Supervision

When managing risk in sport settings, planning for and providing reasonable instruction and supervision is important. Supervision and instruction addresses issues such as properly matching participants when choosing sides for practices or games, teaching sport progression to ensure safety, and using arms-length or close and specific supervision when circumstances dictate. The concepts of supervision and instruction are closely related and are often listed together in a negligence claim.

Instruction

Coaches, physical educators, and other physical activity providers are expected to select activities that are appropriate for the ability levels and ages of their participants. Instruction is expected to be proper, accurate, and delivered in a manner that maxi-

mizes the potential for participant success. Instruction should be supplemented with warnings regarding the inherent dangers of the activity; the provision of proper safety equipment and protective measures; and appropriate feedback, which allows the participant to evaluate and modify her performance (Dougherty et al., 2002). Dougherty recommends the following instructional guidelines (Dougherty et al., 2002):

- Activities selected should be within the reasonable abilities of participants.

- Participants should be warned of the inherent risks in an activity. Safety rules should be explained and regularly enforced.

- All instruction should be consistent with the latest, professionally accepted standards, guidelines, and information. Before instructing, the physical activity provider should be familiar with curriculum materials, specific activity and sport standards and guidelines, and relevant safety information. Physical activity providers should thoroughly understand the activities they teach or coach.

- Participant readiness should be individualized. Evaluation and screening, documentation, and individualized progressions are keys to safety and success.

- The use of comprehensive lesson plans that document sound instructional strategies and reasonable progressions are important to instructional success.

- Participants should not be required or coerced to perform when they are, by their own admission, afraid or unprepared for the task.

- Regular feedback and corrective instruction should be provided.

- Injured or ill participants should not be allowed to participate without appropriate medical clearance.

- In activities in which physical contact is possible, steps should be taken to minimize the risk associated with mismatches.

A mismatch may be defined as an inequity in the size, strength, or ability of the competitors that, if not properly controlled, can unreasonably increase the risk to the overmatched athlete. Size, physical maturity, skill, experience, and fatigue are important factors that should be considered when matching participants. Be especially alert to mismatches among participants who have substantially different levels of conditioning, those recovering from injury, those with physical or mental challenges, and those unduly fatigued. Always determine whether it is necessary or beneficial to allow any adult to participate in an activity or if it would create a potentially dangerous mismatch. If it is reasonably foreseeable that the situation may lead to a mismatch and a possible injury, teachers and coaches should proceed cautiously. If adults are allowed to participate, consider creating guidelines for their behaviors. Discussing potential dangers and establishing rules for their participation (e.g., regarding their intensity levels) may be appropriate.

Supervision

Supervisors of sport and recreational programs have a great deal of responsibility. They hold a unique relationship with those under their care. Examples of this type of relationship include teacher–student, coach–athlete, recreation supervisor–participant, and supervisor–facility user. The responsibility of the supervisor is to exercise reasonable care for the protection of participants under his supervision. To meet this responsibility, having a supervisory plan is important. A plan is outlined here to address key issues in supervision. It is intended as a tool to provide guidance in planning.

• Consider the circumstances. When developing a supervisory plan, it is important to consider the circumstances (e.g.,

Physical educators must provide sufficient instruction and supervision to keep students safe.

type of activity, skill and maturity of participants, level of risk). The type of supervision depends on the circumstances and can be simply categorized as one of two types: general or specific. **General supervision** involves staying within sight and hearing of participants. The supervisor can hear and see what is happening on the court or field but is not necessarily in close contact with the participants. An example would be a person who is supervising a basketball game or tennis match. Participants are usually older and more mature, or more skilled, and the activity is lower risk. By contrast, **specific supervision** involves staying within close contact and proximity of participants. The supervisor is providing hands-on assistance or is immediately ready to do so. Examples would include supervision of young, beginning swimmers, gymnasts, or cheerleaders. Participants are usually younger and less mature, or less skilled, and the activity is higher risk. The type of supervision should be planned by considering both the activity and the participants.

• Have the proper qualifications. Supervisors should have the requisite qualifications (e.g., education, experience, or certification). Besides having the appropriate qualifications, supervisors should be present in sufficient numbers to oversee the activity properly, and they should be located in the proper positions to supervise the activity.

• Provide safety information first. Every supervisory plan should begin with safety. It should be documented that instructions involved safety first. Although true for all activities, safety instruction is particularly important when children are involved. Warnings should also be given regarding inherent dangers in the activity.

• Have a plan for replacements. Circumstances often arise that might pull a supervisor away from her assigned area of responsibility. When this happens, the participants still might need supervision, especially when specific supervision is preferred. A supervi-

sory plan should include the identification of a person who has the requisite knowledge, training, and qualifications to supervise the activity properly until the primary supervisor returns.

• Plan for progression. Participants often learn in stages and are able to advance to higher-risk activities or levels only after progressing in skill to that point. The plan should ensure that participants are not placed in situations above their skill level that would pose an unreasonable risk of harm to them. A plan should teach safety first and move participants to higher-risk situations only when their skill and ability levels will allow.

• Consider an emergency action plan. Communication, training, certification, and emergency equipment are all important aspects of preparing for emergencies.

Risk Management Applications

The applications of risk management to sport are numerous. Several issues important to sport managers are discussed here: emergency action planning, crisis management, and lightning safety. Given that risk management issues often arise in the context of managing facilities, a discussion would not be complete without addressing the issue of disabled participants and application of the Americans with Disabilities Act.

Emergency Action Planning

An important issue at all levels of sport is the provision of emergency care for athletes who are injured in practices or games. The outcome of a lawsuit may hinge on the degree of care that was provided to an injured person after an initial injury. If improper care is provided, or too much time is taken in rendering aid, an injury can substantially worsen. For example, improperly moving an athlete with a suspected neck or head injury can result in permanent, devastating injury. Additionally, waiting too long to perform CPR can result in brain damage or death. Therefore, an essential risk management function is to prepare, communicate, and practice an **emergency action plan (EAP)** specific to the sport program or facility.

A properly planned and rehearsed EAP can help an organization reduce the time required to respond to a medical emergency and respond in a manner that results in the best possible provision of care to an injured person. Some factors in emergency planning might include knowing the distance of local EMS from your facility and an estimated response time to your facility, purchasing and locating emergency medical equipment (e.g., automated external defibrillators

[AEDs]), having staff properly trained and certified in CPR and first aid, having athletic trainers on staff when feasible, and having proper communication devices and phone numbers available to call for emergency assistance. After emergency medical plans have been developed, they must be communicated to staff and rehearsed on a regular basis. The rehearsal of EAPs helps reduce apprehension and potential panic should an actual medical emergency occur. The case of *Kleinknecht v. Gettysburg College* (1993) (see the Medical Emergency Action Planning in College Athletics sidebar) addressed the duty of emergency care owed to university athletes by institutions for which they play.

Crisis Management

Besides the potential for medical emergencies to occur in the sport setting, greater harm can come to a sport organization.

IN THE COURTROOM

Medical Emergency Action Planning in College Athletics

Kleinknecht v. Gettysburg College (1993)

Kleinknecht, a 20-year-old college student, was playing lacrosse with his team at a practice field at Gettysburg College. While playing, he fell to the ground and was unresponsive. Team members and coaches rushed to help him, but no one had the proper training (e.g., CPR training) to render the needed assistance. The school did not have a plan in place for an emergency. The nearest phone was 250 yards (230 m) away in a training room. An 8-foot (2.4 m) fence barrier separated the training room from the field. The team captain searched and found a student trainer, head trainer, and band member who

were trained in CPR. They performed CPR on Kleinknecht until an ambulance arrived. Despite attempts to save him, Kleinknecht later died at the hospital. The Kleinknecht family sued the college, claiming that the college breached its duty when it failed to provide prompt and adequate medical services. The court held that the college owed a duty to its students to provide prompt and adequate emergency medical care. Because lacrosse is a contact sport and life-threating injuries can happen, the court reasoned that a college owes student-athletes a duty to take reasonable precautions against the risk of death (e.g., having coaches trained in CPR or certified trainers on site) during sport practices and games.

This broad category of harm is termed a **crisis**. Crises are large in scope, negative, and disruptive, and they can threaten an organization's mission and reputation. During a crisis, the mission of the organization is usually placed on hold until the crisis is resolved. Examples of crises are catastrophic weather events, fires, and terrorist events. When crises occur, the goal of the organization should be to react quickly and effectively to stabilize the situation and then to act in a positive manner to return the situation to normal. Because most crises catch people and organizations by surprise, placing them in a reactive mode, the sport manager needs to develop a sound plan before the onset of a crisis. This plan is called a **crisis management plan (CMP)**. A CMP is similar to an emergency action plan (EAP) but is specific to emergencies that are greater in scope and generally more damaging to more people. A comprehensive CMP should cover a wide range of potential crises.

The primary goal of crisis management planning is to develop comprehensive written contingency plans based on existing resources and operational capabilities that will enable sport managers to deal effectively with crises. CMPs must be specifically developed for every sport program. Every program has unique factors that must be considered, including the nature and location of the program, the participants, the staff, the response time of local emergency medical services (EMS), and the facility and equipment involved. Despite the uniqueness of each program, several components should form the foundation of all CMPs.

Create a Planning Team

The first component is the planning stage in developing the CMP. This step requires the formation of a planning team who will begin the process. The team's primary task is to identify the possible risks and crises that may arise in the organization. Several methods of identifying potential risks and crises exist,

including consultation with outside experts, reviewing industry trends, and studying accident and injury report forms. Locations where past incidents occurred, the nature of the incidents, and the way in which they were handled will be valuable to the sport manager in developing a CMP.

Develop an Action Plan

The second component is the development of an action plan for crisis response for each major category of hazard that may confront the organization. The action plan should include several key considerations for the sport manager. The first planning issue for the sport manager to consider is personnel—those who will be critical to crisis response. The action plan should identify, by job title, the employees who will handle the crisis. Specific duties and responsibilities of each responder must be carefully outlined in a simple and clear format. It is recommended and often required that certain employees be certified in CPR and first aid. The second planning issue to consider is the sport facility. The location of emergency exits and shelters; gas, power, and water shutoff valves; alarm systems; backup power systems; main electrical panels; and fire hoses and extinguishers should be clearly identified. Locations for meeting EMS should also be identified, and evacuation procedures should be developed. A third planning issue, in addition to those related to the facility, is an evaluation of emergency equipment. The plan should identify and catalog the type of equipment available (e.g., public address and communication equipment, firefighting equipment, first aid kits, automated external defibrillators, and backboards), where it is stored, and who will have access to it.

Establish Emergency Communication Rules

A third issue of importance in developing the CMP is communication. Before a crisis occurs, the sport organization should identify outside experts who will work side by side with the organization in a crisis. Internally, the sport organization should designate who will be responsible for emergency communications. All staff should be trained regarding where and how to make emergency communications. For example, all staff should know the exact location of telephones or other communication devices and know the procedures for making emergency phone calls. Specifically, staff should be trained on dialing the correct emergency number. This training may be as simple as informing staff that they must dial a 9 or other number to reach an outside line before dialing 911 or other emergency number. Staff should be trained to stay calm and provide accurate information to emergency responders. In the event of a crisis, staff should know not to hang up the phone until the operator or dispatcher states that he has all the necessary information.

Establish Postcrisis Communication Rules

The fourth component of importance to the CMP is postcrisis communication. The organization should determine who will meet with staff for debriefing and who will meet with the media. Preparations for a timely, accurate, and appropriate response must begin soon after a crisis has occurred. News media will expect and demand an immediate response. A decision on whether a news conference or release would be an appropriate means of conveying information to the news media and public must be made. The means of internal communication to be used if the crisis affects employees and participants must also be determined. The main switchboard or operator must be informed about where to refer phone calls pertaining to the crisis. At the earliest possible stage, staff members must be advised of the crisis. Clear instructions on handling the media and telephone calls concerning the situation should be communicated, and staff should be told that that they may be called on to perform special duties related to the incident. The organization should address alternative or additional means of conveying information, which might include such items as letters to parents or fans, letters to newspaper editors, and consultation with boards or other entities.

Create Postcrisis Reports

The fifth component of importance to the CMP is postcrisis reports. In response to a crisis, the sport organization should determine who completes reports and when. All crises should be carefully documented with the use of an appropriate incident or injury report form approved by the organization's legal counsel. Staff members should be familiar with these forms and the policies and procedures regarding their use. For example, it is typically required that these forms be brought to the administration's attention within 24 hours of the incident. They must be retained for at least the length of the respective states' statutes of limitations. Assigned personnel should know how to complete them and to whom they should be sent. Policies should be established for filing and retaining reports. Additionally, postcrisis responses should adhere to certain follow-up procedures. For example, it should be determined who (e.g., injured participants, parents, EMS, law enforcement, risk management, insurance companies) is contacted and when. The organization should also determine how contacts are to be made (e.g., phone calls, visits to those injured) and by whom. Finally, a preassigned spokesperson who will speak to the media should be selected. All personnel should be informed that only the media contact person speaks to the media.

Test the Plan

The final component of importance to the CMP is testing the plan. After a CMP has been developed, it must be tested. A crisis manager or committee designated by the sport organization should discuss the plan, event by event, situation by situation, and develop schematics of how the plan works. The CMP should then be tested in conditions as close to real life as possible and adjusted accordingly. A final CMP draft should then be developed and circulated to all affected parties (Connaughton, Spengler, & Bennett, 2001).

After all components of the CMP have been addressed, all employees should be provided with a written copy, or access to a copy, of the organization's CMP. Additionally, all employees should be trained in the CMP at the beginning of their employment and periodically thereafter. Students and certain program participants can also be trained to assist in the event of a crisis.

Depending on the program, its location, and the participants' age, they may be able to do things such as ensure that EMS or certain administrators have been notified, retrieve first aid supplies, or, at the very least, behave in a manner that does not impede the CMP. CMPs must be regularly practiced, evaluated, and updated. Practicing CMPs will assist in working out any flaws. Announced and unannounced practice of the CMPs should be conducted on at least a yearly basis (Appenzeller & Seidler, 1998). Consideration should be given, however, to parents and children in advance of the practice to ease tensions and fear. Sport and recreation managers, physical educators, coaches, fitness instructors, and others involved in providing physical activities should establish a plan if a crisis occurs. Developing a CMP with the advice of appropriate counsel is an important proactive measure that might lessen the negative consequences of a crisis.

Careful planning for how to manage a crisis is important, but putting the plan to practice in realistic scenarios will help all members of the crisis management team fully understand their roles if a crisis hits.

Lightning Safety

Another risk for sport managers involves injuries and fatalities to players or participants from lightning strikes. For outdoor sports, particularly when supervision of youth is at issue, lightning safety and potential liability are major concerns. Fortunately, guidance on managing the risk of lightning in sport programs and facilities is accessible. This guidance comes in the form of position statements from professional associations. Sport managers should be aware of professional associations that have lightning safety recommendations or guidelines that are relevant to their programs. If they wish to follow the recommendations, they would ultimately need to develop a risk management plan that addresses lightning safety and identifies policies and procedures that reduce the risk of injury and death from lightning.

Professional associations in the field of sport and recreation management that have published and adopted lightning safety recommendations include the National Athletic Trainer's Association (NATA) and the National Collegiate Athletic Association (NCAA). The NATA has published a position statement on lightning safety for athletics and recreation (Walsh et al., 2013), which other associations have adopted in some form. The recommendations are similar to those set forth by the American Meteorological Society (Holle & Lopez, 1999).

The National Athletic Trainer's Association has been instrumental in formulating lightning safety recommendations that are focused on both sports and recreation. The NATA recommends the formulation and implementation of a "comprehensive, proactive lightning safety policy or emergency action plan specific to lightning safety" (Walsh et al., 2013, p. 259). The NATA identified five essential components of a lightning-specific emergency action plan for each venue:

1. Promote lightning-safety slogans supported by the National Weather Service. "NO Place Outside Is Safe When Thunderstorms Are in the Area!" "When Thunder Roars, Go Indoors!" "Half an Hour Since Thunder Roars, Now It's Safe to Go Outdoors!"

2. Establish a chain of command that identifies a specific person (or role) who is to make the decision to remove individuals from the field or activity. This person must have recognized and unchallengeable authority to suspend activity.

3. Use a reliable means of monitoring the local weather. Before the event, identify a specific person (a weather watcher) who is responsible for actively looking for threatening weather and is charged with notifying the chain of command.

4. Identify safe locations from the lightning hazard in advance of the event for each venue.

5. Identify specific criteria for suspending and resuming activity in the EAP. (p. 259)

The National Collegiate Athletic Association has also developed lightning safety guidelines for collegiate athletic programs (National Collegiate Athletic Association, 2001):

1. The NCAA suggests that a chain of command be designated to determine who will monitor threatening weather and who will make the decision to remove athletes from a site or event. An emergency plan should be developed that indicates instructions for participants as well as spectators.

2. A weather report should be reviewed each day to determine the potential risk of threatening weather.

3. During events, the National Weather Service should be monitored for severe weather or thunderstorm watches or warnings.

4. Coaches and athletes should know the closest safe structure or location to the field or playing area and the time required to get there.

5. Athletic officials and coaches should be aware of how close lightning is to the field or playing area. Proximity may be determined by several measures, including the flash-to-bang count and lightning predictors or detectors.

Sport managers need to understand the scope and nature of lightning safety policies and procedures in sport programs. The NATA, NCAA, NOAA, and other organizations provide excellent reference and guidance on lightning safety policies and procedures. By following these recommendations, facilities and programs can be designed and managed to minimize the risk from lightning strikes. If the risks associated with lightning are understood and if measures are implemented to reduce the risk of lightning-related injury, sport managers can provide better protection to participants.

Facilities and the Americans with Disabilities Act

When managing risk for sport facilities, safety measures should be implemented with concern for everyone, including both able-bodied people and those with disabilities. The Americans with Disabilities Act of 1990 (ADA) was passed to provide a national mandate furthering the elimination of discrimination against people with disabilities (Americans with Disabilities Act of 1990, 42 U.S.C. §12101(b)(1), 2008). The ADA enhances the protections provided by the Rehabilitation Act of 1973, which prohibits discrimination against people with disabilities by government agencies that receive federal funds (Rehabilitation Act of 1973, Pub. L. No. 93-112, 1973).

To understand whether the ADA applies to a particular person, that person must first be classified as disabled as defined in the statute. This inquiry is important because a person may be disabled in some way as understood in normal parlance but not be disabled under the definition found in the statute. According to the ADA, a person is disabled if she has a physical or mental impairment that substantially limits one or more of the major life activities, has a record of such impairment, or is regarded as having such an impairment (42 U.S.C. § 12102(2)). For purposes of the statute, a physical or mental impairment involves any of the following:

- Any physiological disorder or condition, cosmetic disfigurement, or anatomical loss affecting one or more of the following body systems: neurological, musculoskeletal, special sense organs, respiratory including speech organs, cardiovascular, reproductive, digestive, genitourinary, hemic and lymphatic, skin, and endocrine

- Any mental or psychological disorder such as mental retardation, organic brain syndrome, emotional or mental illness, and specific learning disabilities

- Contagious and noncontagious diseases and conditions such as orthopedic, visual, speech, and hearing impairments; cerebral palsy; epilepsy; muscular dystrophy; multiple sclerosis; cancer; heart disease; diabetes; mental retardation; emotional illness; specific learning disabilities; HIV disease (whether symptomatic or asymptomatic); tuberculosis; drug addiction; and alcoholism (Definitions, 28 C.F.R. § 36.104(1), 2008)

Perhaps most important for many situations that develop in the high school and college setting is that learning disabilities are specifically mentioned as impairments that qualify someone as disabled under the statute. In addition, a major life activity is defined as "functions such as caring for oneself, performing manual tasks, walking, seeing, hearing, speaking, breathing, learning, and working" (Definitions, 28 C.F.R. § 36.104(2), 2008). As a result, the ADA can have an effect on a person's participation in sport because it may involve the major life activities of seeing, hearing, walking, or other aspects of this definition.

After a determination that a person is disabled under these definitions, the analysis then shifts to the part of the ADA that may apply to the particular situation. Title III applies to the sport context, perhaps most important in regard to accessing sport facilities. Title III (42 U.S.C. §12182(a), 2008) bars discrimination against disabled people "in the full and equal enjoyment of the goods, services, facilities, privileges, advantages, or accommodations of any place of public accommodation by any person who owns, leases (or leases to), or operates a place of public accommodation." The statute specifically includes gymnasiums, golf courses, and other places of exercise and recreation as places of accommodation covered under this part.

Many forms of discrimination are banned under Title III. Perhaps most important in connection to sport and recreational activities is barring people with disabilities from enjoying the goods and services of the place of public accommodation, failure to make reasonable modifications unless such modifications would fundamentally alter the nature of the goods and services of the place of public accommodation, and failure to remove structural and other facility barriers to disabled people. Many lawsuits have been brought within the sport context with regard to access to sport and recreational facilities themselves. Cases have been brought against the architects, designers, and owners of these facilities to force them to comply with the regulations of the ADA. Facilities constructed before

January 26, 1993, are considered existing facilities that must remove architectural barriers only where such removal is readily achievable in relation to the effectiveness, practicality, and cost of such removal.

Facilities designed and constructed for first occupancy after January 26, 1993, are viewed as new construction and must comply with the ADA's more strict accessibility standards (Nondiscrimination on the Basis of Disability by Public Accommodations and in Commercial Facilities, 28 C.F.R. subpart A, 2006). These regulations, the Americans with Disabilities Act Accessibility Guidelines (ADAAG), put forth minimum technical requirements for new construction and alterations of existing facilities so that both accommodate people with disabilities. These guidelines are especially important in the sport and recreation industry because they can affect every stage of the design and building process. At every stage of this process, the builder, owner, tenants, and all others involved must make sure that the facility being built will accommodate disabled patrons in specific technical ways. For instance, facilities must remove architectural barriers by installing ramps; making curb cuts in sidewalks and entrances; rearranging tables, chairs, vending machines, display racks, and other furniture; repositioning telephones; widening doors; and eliminating turnstiles or providing alternative accessible paths (28 C.F.R. §36.304(b)).

Edward Resnick, a quadriplegic man who uses a wheelchair, sued the owners of Pro Player Stadium, home of the Miami Dolphins and Florida Marlins, when he was unable to purchase accessible seating for football and baseball games (*Access Now et al. v. South Florida Stadium Corp. et al.*, 2001). Pro Player Stadium was constructed in 1987, before the enactment of the ADA. Therefore, the stadium had to comply with the ADA's "readily achievable" standard applicable to existing facilities; barriers have to be removed only when such measures are effective, practical, and fiscally manageable. Although Resnick demonstrated several ways in which access to the stadium could be improved for people with disabilities, he was unable to show that the facility was not in accord with the ADA and its architectural guidelines. Therefore, the court found that Pro Player Stadium was not in violation of the ADA, and the stadium owner had no legal obligation to make the facility modifications that he suggested.

LEARNING AIDS

Summary

Decisions pertaining to safety are the most important decisions that sport managers make. These decisions often result in the formation of risk management policies and procedures. Risk management is a process that begins with the recognition by management of the importance of reducing or eliminating certain risks. This recognition results in a decision by management to act on either a specific risk or an identified risk category. Once recognized, risks are analyzed. Appropriate action is taken, and safety measures are implemented as deemed necessary. An effective risk management plan that is communicated to employees and staff and that is properly carried out can help an organization reduce the probability of injury to its patrons and the subsequent liability that often results.

A key question in many injury-related lawsuits is whether the injured participant was physically capable of successful participation and whether he was properly prepared and instructed. Although certain risks may be allowed, they should be well thought out and justified, and the potential for participant injury must be minimized (Dougherty et al., 2002). In an effort to reduce injuries and maximize participant success, proper and accurate instruction must be appropriately provided. Coaches and other physical activity providers should continue to update and refine their instructional skills by attending conferences, workshops, and in-service trainings.

Supervisors should not only provide protective or safety equipment but also instruct participants about how to use, care for, and inspect the equipment. Additionally, some safety equipment is mandatory, so supervisors and coaches must require that it be worn or used. Fortunately, guidance from professional organizations is available regarding the use of sport and recreational equipment. This chapter has provided links to some of these valuable resources.

Supervisors of sport and recreational programs have a great deal of responsibility. To help meet this responsibility, a supervisory plan is a valuable tool. This chapter provided some key elements of a supervisory plan. The plan that you develop, with these or additional elements, will be of value to you in helping to provide a reasonably safe sport or recreation program.

Discussion Questions

1. Discuss issues relevant to the standard of care that would help you identify risks in a sport facility. For example, one might be case precedent.

2. Provide a brief explanation with examples of the four elements of performance (retention, treatment, transfer, and avoidance).

3. Locate a position statement related to the issue of injury prevention in sport from a national association (sport or medicine) and provide a synopsis of the recommendations.

4. Describe what is meant by the term *progression* in sport instruction and why this concept is important to safety.

5. Outline the components of an emergency plan for a crisis of your choosing.

6. Create a lesson plan for a sport activity of your choosing with an emphasis on safety as discussed in this chapter.

MOOT COURT CASE

Supervised Recreational Sport Scenario

Doug was the supervisor of an after-school sport program (run by ASP, Inc.). Doug was also an avid fan of dodgeball, having played the sport since childhood, and he enjoyed the adrenaline rush and competitive nature of the game. Dodgeball was just one sport in a series of activities provided by the after-school sport program that included kickball, basketball, soccer, volleyball, and various other games.

On a particularly hot day in early August, Doug was supervising a group of eight 6th graders in an outdoor basketball game. The children were complaining about the heat, and the heat appeared to be taking a toll on several of them. Doug, mindful of the dangers of heat illness, believed that it was best to take his group inside. It was getting late in the day anyway, and only an hour was left until activities ended for the day. Doug took the children inside into a multipurpose play area that was set up for volleyball. Christie, a counselor with the program, was with her group of 8th graders, who were playing volleyball. She also had eight in her group. Doug suggested that they play dodgeball because Christie's group was tired of playing volleyball, and putting both groups together on one volleyball court didn't seem like a good idea. Doug suggested that they take down the net. They would leave the posts up and just warn the players to stay away from them because taking them down was too much work. Doug and Christie split the groups so that each team had four 6th graders and four 8th graders. They also warned the children about the volleyball posts. The children began play and seemed to enjoy it. To make the game more interesting, players who were hit with the ball would sit out for only a few minutes and could then return to the game. They were instructed to sit behind the volleyball posts near the centerline when hit by a ball.

Suzie was one of the 6th graders in Doug's group. Despite her age, she was one of the best players on the court. While throwing a ball, she was struck in the waist by a ball thrown by a member of the opposing team. Suzie was disappointed but ran to the sidelines to sit out. As she was running, a ball thrown by an 8th grader on the other team struck her ankle and she lost her balance. Suzie fell forward and struck one of the volleyball posts with the side of her head. Both counselors immediately came to her aid and asked her how she felt. She said that her head hurt somewhat but that she was OK and wanted to keep playing. Doug and Suzie looked for swelling but saw none. Although they knew she had struck the post with a lot of force, they decided that she could keep playing. Thirty minutes later, the game ended. Suzie told Doug that her head was hurting worse. The class was ending in 10 minutes, and parents were already arriving to pick up their children. Doug wasn't sure of the policy or standards relevant to head injuries, but he asked Christie to call 911. She went to make the call. She returned 10 minutes later and said that she was delayed because she didn't know that she needed to dial 9 first to call out. She finally figured this out on her own. By this time, Suzie was nauseous and incoherent and could not stand up. Her mother had just arrived and was holding her. The ambulance arrived 10 minutes later and took Suzie to the hospital. It was determined later that she had suffered a serious head injury. Suzie's mother sued Doug and ASP, Inc., for negligence.

Agency Law

Chapter Objectives

After reading this chapter, you will know the following:

- How agency relationships work and what authority agents have

- The function of a sport agent

- The duties of agents and principals within the agency relationship

- The many ways in which athlete agents are regulated

Sport managers work with many types of agents in the sport industry. The focus in sport is often on athlete or player agents, but many other types of agents are involved in the industry, from marketing, sponsor, and endorser agents to representatives of coaches and team and facility owners. When one person represents a second person or entity in negotiations with a third person or entity, that initial person is acting as an agent of the second party.

This chapter focuses on the law related to agents. We begin with a discussion of the history of sport agents and the role they serve. Next we focus on principals of **agency law**, including establishment of the agency relationship, authority of agents, and the duties agents must uphold. We then move to an analysis of agency contracts, followed by an in-depth look at the regulation of player agents. The focus then shifts to an analysis of contract law, criminal law, and tort law disputes involving agents. The chapter ends with a discussion of the future of sport agency.

Although agents are involved at virtually every level of the sport industry, player agents are the focus of regulations, disputes, litigation, and most of the analysis within the industry. Therefore, although this chapter discusses principles of agency that apply to all agents, the examples provided frequently involve player agents. This focus does not change the analysis; it merely reflects the fact that player agents are the most regulated professionals within the U.S. sport industry, to the point that specific state and federal laws apply only to player agents.

Sport Agents

Determining when the first person in the sport industry entered into an **agency relationship** is impossible. A clearer historical record can be established related to player agents. The first well-known player to hire an agent to represent him in contract negotiations was early football star Red Grange. In 1925 Grange hired an agent to negotiate his contract with the NFL's Chicago Bears. Still, the profession did not truly expand until the 1960s, when attorney Mark McCormack began to work with legendary golfer Arnold Palmer. As Palmer began to make more money from sponsorship and endorsement deals, athletes from other sports began to seek the representation of player agents.

At the time, not all teams were excited about working with player agents. In the early 1960s NFL Hall of Fame center Jim Ringo of the Green Bay Packers hired an agent to renegotiate his contract with legendary Packers coach Vince Lombardi. When Lombardi saw the agent, he left the room for a short time and returned to tell Ringo that the negotiations were over because he had been traded to the Washington Redskins.

The player agent profession did not see explosive growth until the 1970s. Until then, most athletes in professional team sports were bound by reserve clauses (discussed further in chapter 10) in their contracts stipulating that if the player did not automatically sign a new contract with the team for the next season, all the provisions of his present contract would be automatically renewed. Therefore, players had no freedom to move from team to team seeking higher salaries. In the 1970s the professional sports leagues adopted free agency, and players were free to offer their services to other teams and often relied on agents to help them in their negotiations.

Continuous growth has occurred in the field of sport agency. Each of the four major professional sports leagues in the United States currently has hundreds of registered player agents, although many individual agents represent multiple players (see table 4.1). For instance, notorious baseball player agent Scott Boras represents more than 100 baseball players at the major and minor league level (Wikipedia, n.d.), and football player agent Drew Rosenhaus represents over 100 football players ("Drew Rosenhaus Net Worth," n.d.).

Sport agents assume many roles for the player, team, coach, or owner for whom they work. These roles include the following:

- Negotiating employment contracts
- Negotiating concession agreements with concessionaires
- Representing an organization in negotiations with sponsors, advertisers, and media outlets
- Representing an organization, athlete, or coach in negotiations with endorsers
- Entering the team or organization into events
- Entering into contracts with security, ushers, merchandisers, and others associated with games and other events
- Managing the relationship with outside entities including community organizations, facility boards, and charitable foundations
- Conducting estate, tax, and financial planning for athlete, coach, and organization clients
- Securing investment and appearance opportunities for the athlete or coach
- Working as the conduit between an athlete, coach, or organization in developing an Internet presence or marketing campaign

To understand the nature of this relationship, we next look at the principles of agency law.

Concepts in Agency Law

The law of agency is often understood by reference to the Restatements of the Law.

Table 4.1 Number of Player Agents in Professional Team Sports

League	No. of agents	No. of players
Major League Baseball	>300	750 (active roster)–1,200 (40-man roster)
National Basketball Association	>350	448
National Football League	877	2,407 (active rosters)
National Hockey League	1	2,067

The information for the number of agents in each league was collected from the league union websites in April 2015.

Written by legal scholars who are members of the American Law Institute, the Restatements explain what the law is in a certain area and how it is changing. Courts often rely on the Restatements to provide consistent explanations of certain areas of law. One of the most widely used Restatements is the *Restatement of Agency*.

The Restatement defines an agency as "the fiduciary relationship that arises when one person (a 'principal') manifests assent to another person (an 'agent') that the agent shall act on the principal's behalf and subject to the principal's control, and the agent manifests assent or otherwise consents so to act" (*Restatement [Third] of Agency*, § 1.01, 2006). In simpler terms, *agency* refers to the relationship between two parties in which one party, known as the *agent*, agrees to act as the representative of the other party, known as the *principal*. Of particular note, the agent should act for the benefit of the principal and subject to the control of the principal. In sport, these relationships are everywhere:

- Students who sell their university's merchandise at a game are acting as agents of their school (the principal).
- Ticket sellers who sell tickets for games or other events are acting as agents of the team (the principal) they work for.
- Sport managers who promote a facility as a possible location for playoff or other games and events are acting as agents of the facility (the principal).
- Health club workers who try to draw in clients for the club are acting as agents of that club (the principal).

Agency law refers to the law that applies to and explains these situations and specifically defines the rights and responsibilities of both principals and agents, the authority of the agent as she works for the principal,

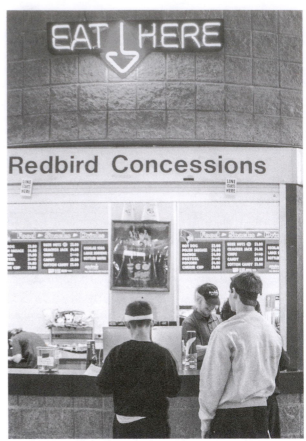

There are many types of agency relationships in sport, particularly informal agency relationships, such as this one between the fans and the concession staff.

and the creation of the agency relationship itself. This relationship between the agent and the principal is governed by law and bears further examination.

Agency Relationship

An agency relationship is the relationship between the principal and the agent. Such relationships are consensual, meaning that both parties agree to become part of the relationship. In addition, although agency relationships often are described by contracts between the principal and agent (such as a student employment agreement stipulating that the student will work in a merchandise store for the school), agency relationships also can be created simply by oral agreement. But for any agency relationship to be established by an agreement, both parties must have the legal capacity to enter into the agreement (as discussed in chapter 5).

Generally, no formality is required to create an agency relationship. All that is necessary is that the parties agree to enter into an agency relationship. This lack of formality can lead to problems when one party disputes the existence of the agency relationship. In evaluating whether an agency relationship has been created, courts typically focus on whether the principal did or said something that the agent could have reasonably interpreted as the principal's intent to allow the agent to act on the principal's behalf. Consider the following hypothetical example.

Al is an agent for the Greater Milwaukee Open (GMO), a professional golf tournament. As part of his job, Al attends charity functions and industry mixers to meet golfers, sponsors, and others in the industry. At one event, he happens to stand next to Tiger Woods and so introduces himself. Al tells Tiger about the GMO and describes how wonderful the tournament is. Tiger says, "That sounds great. I would love it if you could help me play at that event this year." Tiger is then quickly pulled aside by the media before Al can respond. Al is excited and tells his employers at the GMO that Tiger Woods has agreed to let Al help Tiger play in the GMO. The GMO then leaks a story that Tiger will play in the tournament next year. Ticket and sponsorship sales climb because of the announcement. In reality, Tiger never intended to play in the GMO because it conflicts with another tournament. Three weeks after the story is leaked, Tiger's player agent contacts Al to tell him that Tiger has not committed to play in the GMO. Al disputes that, claiming that he and Tiger had an oral agreement that Al would act as an agent on his behalf and help him play in the GMO. Eventually, the GMO sues Tiger Woods for lost revenue associated with the loss of sponsorships and returned tickets when the media learn that he will not play in the GMO. Although Al has a good argument that he relied on Tiger's statement that he wanted Al's help to allow him to play, the court also looks closely at what Tiger said and finds that no agency relationship was created.

Beyond simple misunderstandings, to understand what an agent can do, you need to understand the different levels of authority that an agent may possess. These different levels of authority are discussed next.

Authority

The scope of the agent's authority to act on behalf of the principal is vitally important. If the agent does not have the authority to act on behalf of the principal or exceeds the authority he was given by the principal, the agent's actions cannot bind the principal and the principal cannot be held liable for the acts of the agent.

A typical example could involve a university coach. The coach is a highly sought-after men's basketball coach and enters into a written agreement with an agent who will help him negotiate with schools to attain the best salary. The agreement, however, does not include any reference to the agent's seeking marketing and endorsement opportunities for the coach, because the coach typically talks to marketers himself. If the agent starts to negotiate with Nike, Adidas, or other apparel companies without the coach's knowledge or approval, the agent may have acted without the authority of the coach, so any apparel contract entered into would not be binding on the coach. This issue could be especially problematic because many schools enter into their own apparel contracts with apparel companies. Therefore, the coach would merely be an agent of the school concerning these apparel contracts and so not able to negotiate his own deal.

The level of an agent's authority can best be understood by analyzing the legal concepts of actual authority (including express and implied authority), apparent authority, and ratification (see figure 4.1). Each of these concepts creates and defines the particular agency relationship.

Actual Authority

An agent acts with **actual authority** when the agent reasonably believes that her actions are within the scope of authority given to her by the principal. *Scope of authority* refers to the limits on the agent's authority and typically includes the amount of authority needed to accomplish the goals of the agency relationship. The two types of actual authority are express and implied.

Express Authority

An express agency relationship is created when the agent and principal enter into a written or oral agreement. Any written or oral communication that grants the agent authority to perform an act is considered **express authority**. Any standard agency contract can establish an express agency that provides the agent with express authority. Many professional team sports unions mandate that player agents enter into **standard representation agreements** with union members (the players in the particular sport) before representing any players within the sport. These standard agreements create an express agency relationship between the player and agent that clearly defines the exact amount of authority that the agent will have in acting on behalf of the player. Such an agreement might contain language similar to that found in figure 4.2. Under this agreement, the agent's express job is to "represent, advise, counsel, and assist Player in the negotiation, execution, and enforcement of his playing contract" (NFL Players Association, 2012, appendix D).

Implied Authority

Implied authority refers to the agent's authority and ability to perform incidental acts that are reasonably necessary to

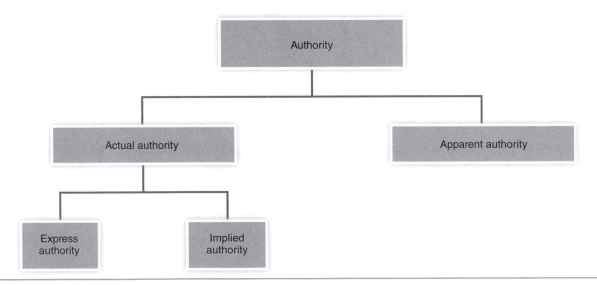

Figure 4.1 Levels of authority.

FIGURE 4.2 Language from the NFL Players Association Standard Representation Agreement

In consideration of the mutual promises hereinafter made by each to the other, Player and Contract Advisor agree as follows:

1. General Principles

   This Agreement is entered into pursuant to and in accordance with the National Football League Players Association (hereinafter "NFLPA") Regulations Governing Contract Advisors (hereinafter "the Regulations") effective September 9, 2011, and as amended thereafter from time to time.

2. Representations

   Contract Advisor represents that in advance of executing this Agreement, he/she has been duly certified as a Contract Advisor by the NFLPA. Player acknowledges that the NFLPA certification of the Contract Advisor is neither a recommendation of the Contract Advisor, nor a warranty by NFLPA of the Contract Advisor's competence, honesty, skills or qualifications.

   Contract Advisor hereby discloses that he/she (check one): [ ] represents or has represented; [ ] does not represent and has not represented NFL management personnel, any NFL coaches, other professional football league coaches, or college coaches in matters pertaining to their employment by or association with any NFL club, other professional football league club or college. If Contract Advisor responds in the affirmative, Contract Advisor must attach a properly completed and signed SRA Coaches and NFL Personnel Disclosure Form (Appendix G of the Regulations).

3. Contract Services

   Player hereby retains Contract Advisor to represent, advise, counsel, and assist Player in the negotiation, execution, and enforcement of his playing contract(s) in the National Football League.

   In performing these services, Contract Advisor acknowledges that he/she is acting in a fiduciary capacity on behalf of Player and agrees to act in such manner as to protect the best interests of Player and assure effective representation of Player in individual contract negotiations with NFL Clubs. Contract Advisor shall be the exclusive representative for the purpose of negotiating player contracts for Player. However, Contract Advisor shall not have the authority to bind or commit Player to enter into any contract without actual execution thereof by Player. Once Player agrees to and executes his player contract, Contract Advisor agrees to also sign the player contract and send a copy (by facsimile or overnight mail) to the NFLPA and the NFL Club within 48 hours of execution by Player. (NFL Players Association, 2012, appendix D)

Reprinted, by permission, from National Football Players Association. Available: https://nflpaweb.blob.core.windows.net/media/Default/PDFs/Agents/2012_NFLPA_Regulations_Governing_Contract_Advisors.pdf.

accomplish the agent's express responsibilities as provided in the **agency agreement** (either oral or written). Implied authority must be consistent with the express authority granted within the agency agreement, but implied authority will not be specified within the agreement, because unforeseen situations often arise that force the agent to take action for the benefit of the principal.

In the NFL Players Association Standard Representation Agreement shown in figure 4.2, the player agent is expressly authorized to "represent, advise, counsel, and assist Player in the negotiation, execution, and enforcement of his playing contract." Nothing within this language specifies that the agent has the authority to meet with a particular team or representatives of a team or to determine the exact manner in which the player will receive his salary. But any player would want the agent to do this. Therefore, the agent must have the implied authority to be able to act in this way for the benefit of the player.

The focal point for determining whether an agent acted with implied authority is the agent's reasonable understanding at the time the agent took action. If a court finds that the agent's interpretation of the agency relationship was unreasonable and that the agent lacked authority to perform an act, then the improper act falls outside the scope of the agent's authority. Actions that fall outside the scope of an agent's authority are considered *ultra vires*. From a risk management standpoint, agents and principals alike should try to limit the potential for *ultra vires* acts. The easiest way to avoid these acts is to include detailed written language within the agency agreement that describes all the ways in which the agent may act.

Apparent Authority

In situations in which it is unclear whether the agent has actual authority, the agent may have what is termed **apparent authority**. In these situations, because of the behavior of the principal, a third party may believe that the agent is acting with actual authority. As a result, if the principal allows a situation to exist that may mislead others about the actual authority of the agent, apparent authority may exist and a third party may be able to rely on the agent's actions to hold the principal accountable.

The power found in apparent authority is based on a third party's reasonable belief that the agent has the authority to act on behalf of the principal based on the action or inaction of the principal. Simply put, the principal created an appearance of authority through conduct or behavior that misled the third party into reasonably believing that the agent had the authority to act on behalf of the principal.

For an example of apparent authority, consider Patty, a professional billiards player who was highly marketable after winning six professional tournaments in a row. Patty attended a party with her friend and manager, Anton. Anton was not Patty's agent but had assisted her in some billiard-related sponsorship contracts. While at the party Patty was approached by Tom, a representative of a major motion picture studio who wanted to make a movie about Patty's life and career. Patty dismissed Tom's conversation about making the film and said, "Talk to Anton; he handles my business."

Patty had no intention of ever making a movie and believed that Anton knew that she was just blowing off the idea by leaving him to discuss the matter with Tom. Anton, however, decided that a movie would be good for Patty and set up a meeting with studio representatives for the next day. At that meeting Anton reached an agreement to have Patty's story made into a film. After finding out what Anton had done, Patty contacted the studio and cancelled the project. The studio had already purchased the rights to the story from Anton and decided to enforce its rights to Patty's story through a lawsuit. A reviewing court might find that when Patty told Anton to speak to Tom, she gave Anton the apparent authority to act on her behalf. If the court found that Tom's reliance on Patty's statements was reasonable, then Patty might be bound to honor the agreement or pay the studio damages. The rationale behind apparent authority is based on the idea that the third party is innocent and has reasonably been misled by the principal into believing that the agent has authority to act.

Ratification

When an agent acts without authority and the doctrine of apparent authority does not apply, then the principal is generally not legally bound by the agent's acts. However, if a principal affirms acts performed by an agent who lacked authority, then those acts are as legally binding for the principal as if the agent acted with actual authority in the first place. This affirmation is known as **ratification**.

To be ratified, an agent's actions must be those that the principal can delegate and that the agent can perform. For example, testifying in court and voting are not delegable acts. Ratification does not apply when third parties intend to deal with the agent in the agent's individual capacity and do not intend to deal with the principal. If no agency relationship exists at all, then ratification cannot occur. In addition, a principal cannot ratify something that had no legal effect in the first place. For instance, a principal cannot ratify a contract if no consideration was provided in the first place; no contract exists because the contractual element of consideration was not present.

Although not commonly used in the sport world, the principle of ratification can be extremely beneficial for the principal. This circumstance is most evident in the world of player agents. Some players allow their agents to negotiate on their behalf, without the players' being present or taking any part in the negotiations. This arrangement is common with successful players who are in high demand. The agent can negotiate on the player's behalf with the team that offers the best salary. Imagine that NBA star Dwyane Wade leaves all dealings with teams to his Chicago-based agent Henry Thomas by instructing Thomas to find Wade the best salary. Thomas talks to several teams and eventually gets the highest salary offer from the New York Knicks. Thomas comes to a tentative agreement with the Knicks on Wade's behalf because they will pay Wade $3 million more per year than any other team. Wade would likely ratify the contract with the best salary offer that Thomas developed for him.

A player will not always wish to ratify an agent's actions. During game 4 of the 2007 Major League Baseball World Series, Alex Rodriguez' agent Scott Boras announced that Rodriguez would opt out of his contract with the New York Yankees. This statement was important because the Yankees had stated publicly that they would not negotiate a new contract with Rodriguez if he opted out of his current contract. Almost immediately, Rodriguez refused to ratify his agent's move and contacted the Yankees to negotiate directly. He eventually signed a 10-year, $275 million deal without Boras' direct involvement (Feinsand & Madden, 2007).

Duties

An agency relationship is considered a fiduciary relationship, meaning that the agent has the **fiduciary duty** to act primarily for the benefit of the player in all matters connected to the agency relationship. In addition, this fiduciary relationship establishes several duties that the agent and the principal must uphold within the relationship. Often the agency agreement specifies the duties that each party has within the agency relationship. Each party, however, owes some general duties to the other.

Agent Duties to Principal

The agent owes several duties to the principal, including the duty to exercise reasonable care and skill and to provide information related to the agency relationship if the principal requests it. The duty of loyalty and the duty of obedience are also important.

Duty of Loyalty

The agent's primary duty is the **duty of loyalty**. This means that the agent must act solely and completely for the benefit of the principal. An agent is prohibited from competing with the principal in anything related to the subject matter of the agency unless the principal has expressly agreed to allow the agent to compete (*Restatement [Third] of Agency*, § 8.04, 2006). Furthermore, the agent may not, without the principal's consent, act on behalf of one with interests adverse to those of the principal in matters in which the agent is employed (*Restatement [Third] of Agency*, § 8.03, 2006). If an agent's interests become adverse to those of the principal, the agent must put the principal's interests first.

Agency law also prevents agents from using their status as agent to enter the principal into agreements that benefit the agent personally without first telling the principal of the agent's interest in the agreement. Even with the principal's consent, such a self-dealing transaction will be enforced by the courts only if the transaction is fair and reasonable.

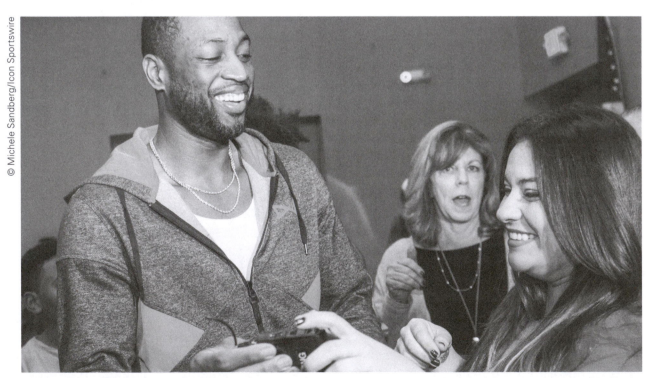

© Michele Sandberg/Icon Sportswire

Agency law makes it clear that agents cannot make even fair and reasonable decisions or agreements for an athlete without the athlete's consent.

For example, Anne represents Parker, a swimmer who has won two Olympic gold medals. Anne knows that now is the time to capitalize on Parker's success to maximize her income potential. Besides representing swimmers, Anne co-owns a company that manufactures swimwear. Anne would benefit if Parker would agree to be sponsored by Anne's swimwear company. The fiduciary duty of loyalty, however, prevents Anne from negotiating a deal with the company without first telling Parker about her interest in the company. If Anne neglects to tell Parker about her interest in the company and enters into a transaction with the company on behalf of Parker, then the transaction may be nullified by Parker. Furthermore, even if Anne informs Parker about the interest she holds in the company, the transaction could still be nullified if a court finds that the deal is not fair and reasonable for Parker.

In addition, during the agency relationship, an agent might have access to the principal's personal property or private information. The fiduciary duty of loyalty prevents the agent from using certain things—the principal's property, the agent's position, or nonpublic information acquired by the agent while acting within the **scope of employment**—for the agent's own purposes or for the benefit of another without first seeking the principal's agreement (*Restatement [Third] Of Agency*, § 8.05, 2006). This duty holds true even after termination of the agency relationship. Therefore, agents cannot use information obtained during the agency for personal gain after the termination of the agency relationship.

Duty of Obedience

The agent is under a duty to follow all reasonable instructions given by the principal, but this duty is not absolute. For example, consider a situation in which an agent represents a motocross athlete. The agency relationship covers all sponsorship and appearance contracts. If the agent and the athlete decide to pool their funds to create a separate company that will design, manufacture, and sell motorcycles, the agent's **duty of obedience** does not extend to dealings with the athlete within the new company. Because the agent has a legal interest in the company as a part owner, this interest supersedes the duty of loyalty in this situation.

If the principal provides instructions to the agent to do something that might harm only the principal's interests, then the duty of obedience requires the agent to perform the task as ordered. The agent should inform the principal that the desired actions could be harmful, but if the principal still desires the course of action, the agent should do as the principal instructs. This situation can be problematic because principals often have short memories and might blame the agent for any harm incurred because of the agent's actions. A good way for an agent to manage this risk is to document the communication that informs the principal of the harmful potential. Such communication should make it clear to the principal that the agent has advised against the course of action but will act according to the principal's wishes.

Conflicts of Interest

Many potential conflicts of interest can occur in the athlete–agent business. For example, suppose that a sport agent represents two shortstops who compete in Major League Baseball and both are up for the same job opening. The interests of these two players are adverse, but they have the same agent. How can an agent represent both players and fulfill his fiduciary duties of obedience and loyalty to them? This situation is especially problematic in leagues that contain salary caps (discussed in chapter 10) that restrict the amount of money the team can pay out in player salaries. Even after informing his clients of the situation and potential conflict, the agent may decide that he cannot responsibly represent both players and may terminate one of the relationships so that he can focus on one client. If the agent does not terminate one of the representations, he must exercise caution and represent both clients with the same degree of competence and vigor.

Principal Duties to Agent

Principals owe agents a duty to compensate them fairly for the work performed and to reimburse them for all expenses they incur on behalf of the principal. Principals owe agents a duty to compensate them for any losses suffered and to cooperate with agents by not working counter to or interfering with their efforts. The principal also has a duty of good conduct, which means that the principal should not do anything that would demean the agent or damage her reputation (Gregory, 2001).

Contract Liability

Under contract law, lawsuits often arise in which a court must determine who is liable for the performance of a contract: the principal, the agent, or both parties. Sometimes contracts are breached because the goods are damaged, because they don't conform to certain expectations (express and implied warranties), or for various other reasons. If an agent has acted within the scope of his authority in executing a contract, the issue becomes who should be held liable for a breach of the contract (the principal or the agent). The key issue in cases in which an agent contracts with a third party is whether the identity of the principal was known to the third party at the time the contract was made. Three situations might arise when a contract is made,

and three outcomes are possible regarding liability for performance of a contract.

In the first situation, an agent contracts with a third party and the third party knows the identity of the principal and knows that the agent is acting on behalf of the principal when the contract is made (executed). In this type of scenario, we have a **disclosed principal**, and the principal is liable for the performance of the contract. The agent is not liable.

In the second situation, an agent contracts with a third party and the third party knows that the agent is acting for someone (a principal), but the third party does not know the identity of the principal. In this case, we have a **partially disclosed principal**, and the principal is liable for the performance of the contract. In most states, the agent is also liable for performance of the contract.

In the third situation, the agent contracts with a third party who has no knowledge that the agent is acting in the capacity of an agent; that is, the third party does not know about the existence of the principal. In this case, we have an **undisclosed principal**, and both the principal and agent are liable for performance of the contract. The agent may, however, be given the opportunity to seek compensation from the principal if the agent is forced to pay the third party for damages.

To avoid the time and trouble of legal entanglements, the agent who is acting on behalf of another (the principal) should inform the third party of the existence and identity of the principal.

Tort Liability

Under tort law, the principal may be liable when torts are committed during the **scope of employment** or scope of agency. This type of liability extends to employers (the principal) under the doctrine of **respondeat superior**. Under this doctrine, the employer (as principal) potentially can be held liable for the acts of an employee (agent) committed while the agent is acting on behalf of the principal during the course of the agent's job. Under the doctrine of respondeat superior, the agent does not need to be found personally liable. If an agent or employee injures another, a court will look to a number of factors in determining whether a principal will be liable under the doctrine of respondeat superior. The key issue is whether the agent acted within the scope of employment when someone was injured because of an act committed by the agent. A court would consider the following factors:

- Whether the agent committed an act (resulting in injury to another) that was authorized by the principal

- The time, place, and purpose of the act

- Whether the act was commonly performed by employees on behalf of their employers

- Whether the employer's interest was enhanced by the act

- The extent of involvement of the employee's private interests

- Whether the employer furnished the means by which the injury was inflicted

- Whether the employer had reason to know that the employee would perform the act in question (whether the agent had done it before)

- Whether the act involved the commission of a serious crime

When determining liability, a court would not need to find that all eight factors weighed in favor of liability, only that liability could be inferred from an analysis of some combination of those eight factors.

Regulation of Athlete Agents

The most scrutinized career for an agent is representation of athletes. The highest-profile athlete agents represent athletes in the NFL, NBA, NHL, and MLB. Some agents also represent athletes within virtually all other sports as well, including boxing, motor sports, tennis, soccer, volleyball, and swimming. Athlete agents might work alone and represent a stable of clients, like well-known agents Scott Boras in baseball or Drew Rosenhaus in football, but athlete agents also work for larger companies like Octagon and IMG, in which groups of agents, lawyers, marketing representatives, and others jointly represent multiple athletes.

Athlete agents generally focus on helping their clients find teams to play for or events to play at. Some agents also represent athletes in dealing with the media, advertisers, sponsors, event organizers, and authorities. An agent must be a jack-of-all-trades, understanding more than merely how to get the athlete a position with a team. Because of the extensive knowledge base needed, many agents have advanced degrees in law or business, and many professional sports unions require certification of skills and registration for any agent who wants to represent their players.

The competition is intense. An agent's livelihood often depends on the success of the players who she represents. As a result, many agents act in unscrupulous ways, which has led to several types of regulations, from state and federal laws to professional union regulations.

These regulations affect and regulate only agents who represent professional athletes. Other types of agents within the sport industry, such as an agent who represents a television station in negotiations with a sports league or an agent who represents an event in negotiations with a television station, are not subject to these regulations.

Focusing on the regulation of athlete agents is interesting because it is an example of the way in which the government and private organizations can impose regulations on individuals in sport. In addition, one reason for extensive regulation of athlete agents is that their actions can negatively affect the young athletes involved and the universities and high schools where these athletes participate in sport.

Effect on Athletes

A high-profile example of agent abuse at the University of Southern California (USC) showed that agents try to influence athletes as well as their families and friends to persuade an athlete to sign with an agent. In September 2005 allegations surfaced that former USC running back Reggie Bush and his family accepted benefits worth more than $100,000 from marketing agents while Bush was still a student. These benefits were supplied by two groups that were attempting to sign Bush as a client. Bush's agents—Mike Ornstein, Michael Michaels, and Lloyd Lake—had attempted to launch an agency called New Era Sports & Entertainment, pursuing Bush as their first client. Bush himself received two hotel stays, one in Las Vegas and another in San Diego, and $13,000 to purchase and modify a car. Bush's family received airfare to the 2005 Heisman Trophy ceremony, hotel stays, suits for Bush's stepfather and brother to wear during the ceremony, a makeover for his mother for the event, and limousine transportation. In addition, Bush's family was allowed to live in a house in Spring Valley, California, that was owned by Michaels, without paying rent. Amid ongoing investigations, Bush asserted that

he and his family had done nothing wrong. Ornstein denied giving Bush or his family any benefits while Bush was still at USC and described any travel arrangements for the Bush family made by his employee as loans that were paid back (Robinson & Cole, 2006).

In a similar situation, former USC basketball player O.J. Mayo allegedly received thousands of dollars in cash, clothes, and other benefits during the 2007–2008 academic year from Rodney Guillory, a 43-year-old Los Angeles event promoter. While Mayo was in high school, Guillory received monthly payments from Bill Duffy Associates (BDA), a Northern California sport agency. BDA provided Guillory with around $200,000 before Mayo even arrived at USC. In exchange for payments and gifts from Guillory, Mayo entered a verbal agreement to allow BDA to represent him when he became a professional athlete. Mayo insists not only that he was a struggling university student and did not receive any money but that Guillory was a positive influence and a strong African American male presence in his life (Katz, 2008).

In neither situation did the athlete involved suffer serious negative consequences; both have gone on to highly lucrative professional careers. Instead, the university suffered serious sanctions under NCAA rules. In 2012 the NCAA added a new definition of *agent* to its bylaws (figure 4.3). Figure 4.3 shows that NCAA bylaws relate specifically to athlete ineligibility attributable to contact with an agent. For each bylaw, the specific part related to conduct causing the athlete to become ineligible is emphasized.

Because of these rules, an eligible university student-athlete cannot receive benefits from or enter into a verbal or written agreement with an agent, even if the agreement is related to working with the athlete after his

FIGURE 4.3   NCAA Bylaws Relating to Amateur Status and Agents

12.02 Definitions and Applications.

12.02.1 Agent. An agent is any individual who, directly or indirectly: (Adopted: 1/14/12)

(a) Represents or attempts to represent an individual for the purpose of marketing his or her athletics ability or reputation for financial gain; or

(b) Seeks to obtain any type of financial gain or benefit from securing a prospective student-athlete's enrollment at an educational institution or from a student-athlete's potential earnings as a professional athlete.

12.02.1.1 Application. An agent may include, but is not limited to, a certified contract advisor, financial advisor, marketing representative, brand manager or anyone who is employed or associated with such persons.

12.1.2 Amateur Status. An individual loses amateur status and thus shall not be eligible for intercollegiate competition in a particular sport if the individual . . . (g) enters into an agreement with an agent.

12.3.1 General Rule. An individual shall be ineligible for participation in an intercollegiate sport if he or she ever has agreed (orally or in writing) to be represented by an agent for the purpose of marketing his or her athletics ability or reputation in that sport. Further, an agency contract not specifically limited in writing to a sport or particular sports shall be deemed applicable to all sports, and the individual shall be ineligible to participate in any sport.

12.3.1.1 Representation for Future Negotiations. An individual shall be ineligible per Bylaw 12.3.1 if he or she enters into a verbal or written agreement with an agent for representation in future professional sports negotiations that are to take place after the individual has completed his or her eligibility in that sport.

12.3.1.2 Benefits from Prospective Agents. An individual shall be ineligible per Bylaw 12.3.1 if he or she (or his or her relatives or friends) accepts transportation or other benefits from

(a) Any person who represents any individual in the marketing of his or her athletics ability. The receipt of such expenses constitutes compensation based on athletics skill and is an extra benefit not available to the student body in general; or

(b) *An agent*, even if the agent has indicated that he or she has no interest in representing the student-athlete in the marketing of his or her athletics ability or reputation and does not represent individuals in the student-athlete's sport (National Collegiate Athletic Association, 2014).

Reprinted, by permission, from NCAA, *2014–15 NCAA division I manual* (Indianapolis, IN: National Collegiate Athletic Association).

eligibility to participate has expired. This practice, known as *postdating an agreement*, has been a standard ploy of unscrupulous agents who have tried to convince athletes that they will not become ineligible because the relationship will not begin until after their playing careers have ended.

For the student-athlete, the result of violating these rules is that she becomes ineligible to participate in athletics for her university. For some high-level athletes, this is not a problem because they have already decided that they are ready to try their hand at a career in professional sports. The school where the athlete played, however, may not be so lucky. Article 19 of the NCAA bylaws provides for the enforcement process that schools must face when rule infractions occur on their campus. If an athlete signs with an agent, she has broken the rules listed previously and her school may face serious sanctions.

One university that has faced numerous sanctions related to violations of the NCAA bylaws regarding athlete agents is California State University, Fresno. In 2002 a *Fresno Bee* report revealed that basketball player Tito Maddox had accepted illegal benefits from an athlete agent. As a result, the school put itself on 2 years of probation and lost three scholarships within the basketball program (Pugmire, 2008). But the story didn't end there. In 2003 the NCAA Committee on Infractions found that a representative of an agent had provided several members of the team with $20 to $100 cash after home games and wired $200 to $250 cash to players at other times (NCAA Division I Committee on Infractions, 2003). The agent also sent money to some players' relatives to cover the cost of their lodging and transportation to the Western Athletic Conference tournament. Although the infractions review also involved allegations of fraud, improper recruiting, and

improper distribution of financial aid, the sanctions imposed on the university are most telling because they evidence what can happen when a university violates NCAA rules, even if it has no direct control of the situation that caused the violation. It is incredibly difficult for an athletic department to monitor a student-athlete at all times, and these problematic contacts with agents often happen on the student's own time. In the situation just described, the university faced numerous sanctions:

- The university was placed on probation for 4 years.
- The men's basketball team was barred from participating in postseason competition for 1 year.
- The university was forced to reduce the number of scholarships available to the program by three for 2 years.
- The university forfeited all wins in games in which the players involved participated.
- The university had to return 90% of the money it received from participating in the 2000 NCAA tournament (NCAA Division I Committee on Infractions, 2003).

Obviously, the financial effect on a university can be huge when athlete agents are involved. Perhaps even more harmful is the severe negative publicity that the university will face within its community, among other schools, and with future recruits.

Because of these and other problems with unscrupulous athlete agents, various entities have tried to regulate the conduct of these agents. The focus of these regulations has been on state and federal laws and regulations by professional players unions.

State Law and the Uniform Athlete Agents Act

Regulation of agents began in California in 1981 with the Miller-Ayala Athlete Agent Act, based on California's Talent Agencies Act and focused on protecting athletes from unscrupulous agents (Miller-Ayala Athlete Agent Act, Cal. Bus. & Prof. Code §§ 18895 et. seq., 2015). Until 2000 the focus of the regulation of athlete agents remained at the state level. Many states had laws that regulated the way in which athlete agents could interact with athletes, often focusing on specific regulations for registering as an athlete agent with the state, certain ways in which an agent could communicate with an athlete, and payment of fees to a state body to be able to work as an agent in that state. The problem was that these state laws were not consistent, so an agent often had to act in different ways depending on where he was doing business or where the athlete lived or worked.

Consider an agent who represents an NBA player who is with the Milwaukee Bucks. The agent's residence and office are in San Francisco, California. The player lives in Miami, Florida, in the off-season. As an NBA player, the player plays in 30 different cities during the year (not to mention possible foreign locations in certain years), and each city may have a different tax structure that affects any salary the player makes for playing in that city. Before 2000 the agent had to determine whether she would need to be licensed as an athlete agent in each location, possibly paying multiple fees, and had to determine what procedures the particular players union had in place (discussed in the next section). This process became cumbersome, and many agents avoided registration requirements altogether.

In 2000 this landscape changed. The National Conference of Commissioners on Uniform State Laws (NCCUSL) is a group of lawyers and law professors who put together uniform laws that states can incorporate into their statutes so that multiple states will follow the same basic law. An example of a uniform law created by the commissioners is the Uniform Commercial Code (2012). In the late 1990s, working with the NCAA, the professional sports leagues, and others, the commissioners developed the **Uniform Athlete Agents Act** (National Conference of Commissioners on Uniform State Laws, 2000). The main purpose of this act was to provide for uniformity in registration and certification of athlete agents among the states. The act defines a student-athlete as "an individual who engages in, is eligible to engage in, or may be eligible in the future to engage in, any intercollegiate sport" (National Conference of Commissioners on Uniform State Laws, § 2(12)). The act thus focuses on an agent's interaction with student-athletes, which could include high school or university athletes. The act also provides that athlete agents who sign contracts with student-athletes must provide notice to the particular university and must make clear to the student-athletes that the agency agreement may affect their eligibility to participate in athletics while attending the university. In addition, the act provides civil remedies for a school that has suffered NCAA sanctions because an athlete signed an agency contract.

Because of continued agent abuses, a committee was appointed in 2012 to review the UAAA and determine whether it could be modified to provide better protection to student-athletes and the schools that they attend. As of April 2015 the committee had not finalized any revisions to the act. It focused on more clearly defining who is covered and expanding potential penalties for violating the UAAA. In addition, some states have begun to bring charges for agents who violate the state version of the UAAA. Agent Terry Watson was indicted in

North Carolina for alleged violations of that state's agency law for giving players money while they were still eligible to play college football (Pryor, 2013).

The easiest way to understand the Uniform Athlete Agents Act is by looking at a state statute from a state that has adopted the act. The Wisconsin Uniform Athlete Agents Act is found in section 440.99 of the state statutes. As with other states' versions of this act, the Wisconsin statute begins with agent registration. Under the statute an agent must register by filing a seven-page application with the Wisconsin Department of Safety and Professional Services and paying a $75 initial credential fee (Uniform Athlete Agents Act, Wis. Stat. §§ 440.99-440.999, 2013). The registration must be renewed each year and can be used to register in any other state that also has adopted the act.

The act also focuses specifically on the agency agreement that an agent would sign with an athlete. It requires that an agent specifically disclose the amount he will be paid and method that will be used to determine the amount, the exact expenses that the athlete will reimburse the agent for, and the exact services that the agent will provide the athlete. In addition, any agency agreement must include the following language:

> Warning: If you sign this contract
>
> 1. you may lose your eligibility to compete as a student-athlete in your sport;
>
> 2. if you have an athletic director, within 72 hours after entering into this contract, both you and your athlete agent must notify your athletic director; and
>
> 3. you may cancel this contract within 14 days after signing it. Cancellation of this contract may not reinstate your eligibility. (Uniform Athlete Agents Act, Wisc. Stat. § 440.994(3), 2013)

This provision is intended to notify any student-athlete of the risk of signing an agreement with an athlete agent. It also places a responsibility on the agent to notify the athletic director at the particular school. Perhaps most interesting, a student-athlete can cancel the agreement within 2 weeks after it is signed. If this happens, the agent cannot sue under the contract to have the athlete return any sort of gifts or other compensation the agent may have provided and cannot sue the athlete for breach of contract.

Finally, the act defines certain types of conduct that an agent cannot engage in. An agent cannot make false promises or provide misleading information about her services to induce the athlete to sign with the agent (Uniform Athlete Agents Act, Wis. Stat. § 440.996, 2013). This is an especially slippery slope for new agents who want to sell their services and persuade athletes to work with them. Agents must be careful not to exaggerate their skills in a way that might be misleading. In addition, an agent cannot contact student-athletes unless she is already registered under the statute, and the agent must always include the required language within any agency agreement signed. In effect, any athlete agents who represent athletes in states like Wisconsin that have adopted the Uniform Athlete Agents Act must create an express agreement with the athlete that contains all these conditions in writing.

As of April 2015, 40 states and Washington, D.C., had adopted the Uniform Athlete Agents Act into their state statutes (see table 4.2). Three states (California, Iowa, and Ohio) have alternative statutes that regulate athlete agents, and seven other states (Alaska, Maine, Massachusetts, Montana, New Jersey, Vermont, and Virginia) have no statutes that regulate athlete agents.

Table 4.2 State Regulations of Athlete Agents

State	Regulation (unless otherwise noted, each is known as the particular state's Uniform Athlete Agents Act)
Alabama	Code of Ala. §§ 8-26A-1–8-26A-31 (2015)
Alaska	No regulation
Arizona	Ariz. Rev. Stat. §§ 15-1761–15-1776 (2015)
Arkansas	Ark. Code Ann. §§ 17-16-101–17-16-123 (2014)
California	Cal. Bus. & Prof. Code. §§ 18895–18897.97 (2015)
Colorado	Col. Rev. Stat.§§ 23-16-101–23-16-219 (2014)
Connecticut	Conn. Gen. Stat. §§ 20-559–20-559s (2014)
Delaware	24 Del. Code §§ 5402–5420 (2015)
District of Columbia	D.C. Code §§ 47-2887.01–47.2886.18 (2015)
Florida	Fla. Stat. §§ 468.451–468.457 (2015)
Georgia	Ga. Code Ann. §§ 43-4A-1–43-4A-20 (2014)
Hawaii	Haw. Rev. Stat. §§ 481E-1–481E-19 (2015)
Idaho	Idaho Code §§ 54-4801–54-4820 (2015)
Illinois	225 ILCS 401/1–401/215 (2014)
Indiana	Burns Ind. Code Ann. §§ 25-5.2-1-1–25-5.2-2-16 (2015)
Iowa	Iowa Code §§ 9A.101–95A.119 (2013)
Kansas	Kan. Stat. Ann. §§ 44-1516–44-1536 (2014)
Kentucky	Ky. Rev. Stat. §§ 164.6901–164.6935 (2014)
Louisiana	La. Rev. Stat. §§ 4:420–4:433 (2014)
Maine	No regulation
Maryland	Md. Business Regulation Code Ann. §§ 4-401–4-416 (2014)
Massachusetts	No regulation
Michigan	A combination of various statutes, including, MCL §§ 390.1501–390.1504, §600.2968, and MCLS §750.411e (2014)
Minnesota	Minn. Stat. §§ 81A.01–81A.21 (2015)
Mississippi	Miss. Code Ann. §§ 73-42-1–73-42-39 (2014)
Missouri	Mo. Ann. Stat. §§ 436.215–436.272 (2014)
Montana	Statute repealed in 2007 because of lack of licensed agents
Nebraska	Neb. Rev. Stat. Ann. §§ 48-2601–48-2619 (2015)
Nevada	Nev. Rev. Stat. Ann. §§ 398.400–398.620 (2014)
New Hampshire	N.H. Rev. Stat Ann. §§ 332-J:1–332-J:15 (2015)
New Jersey	No regulation
New Mexico	N.M. Stat. Ann. §§ 61-14F-1–61-14-19 (2015)
New York	N.Y. CLS Gen. Bus. §§ 899–899-s (2014)
North Carolina	N.C. Gen. Stat. §§ 78C-85–78C-105 (2014)
North Dakota	N.D. Cent. Code §§ 9-15.1-01–9-15.1-16 (2015)
Ohio	ORC Ann. §§ 4771.01–4771.99 (2015)
Oklahoma	70 Okl. Stat. §§ 821.81–821.99 (2014)
Oregon	Or. Rev. Stat. §§ 702.005–702.165 (2015)
Pennsylvania	5 Pa. Cons. Stat. §§ 3101–3320 (2014)
Rhode Island	R.I. Gen. Laws §§ 5-74.1-2–5-74.1-20 (2015)

(continued)

Table 4.2 *(continued)*

State	Regulation (unless otherwise noted, each is known as the particular state's Uniform Athlete Agents Act)
South Carolina	S.C. Code Ann. §§ 59-102-10–59-102-190 (2014)
South Dakota	S.D. Codified Laws §§ 59-10-1–59-10-20 (2015)
Tennessee	Tenn. Code Ann. §§ 49-7-2101–49-7-2123 (2014)
Texas	Tex. Occ. Code §§ 2051.001–2051.006 (2013)
Utah	Utah Code Ann. §§ 15-9-101–15-9-119 (2015)
Vermont	No regulation
Virginia	No regulation
Washington	Wash. Rev. Code §§ 19.225.010–19.225.904 (2015)
West Virginia	W. Va. Code § 30-39-1–30-39-21 (2015)
Wisconsin	Wis. Stat. §§ 440.99–440.999 (2013)
Wyoming	Wyo. Stat. §§ 33-44-101–33-44-114 (2014)

Federal Law

Several attempts were made in Congress to pass legislation regulating sport agents. None of these attempts were successful until 2004 when the Sports Agent Responsibility and Trust Act (SPARTA) was passed (15 U.S.C. §§ 7801–7807, 2015). The goal of the act is to protect student-athletes and universities from unscrupulous sport agents by prohibiting agents from making false or misleading promises or providing gifts, cash, or anything of monetary value to student-athletes and those associated with student-athletes. Similar to the Uniform Athlete Agents Act, SPARTA requires agents to give students written disclosures informing them that they could lose their eligibility to play university sports if they sign an agency contract. Agents and student-athletes are required to notify, within 72 hours, the student's athletic director of any agency agreement reached by the student and the agent. If an agent fails to make a timely report, the agent can be fined as much as $11,000 per day. Additionally, the act allows schools to bring civil actions against violating agents if their residents have been adversely affected by an agent's actions.

Interestingly, SPARTA does not provide for any federal registration for agents. Therefore, although SPARTA mirrors the Uniform Athlete Agents Act adopted by many states, its effect is unclear. The Federal Trade Commission is the government agency that is named to enforce SPARTA, but without any sort of registration procedure, it is unclear how the commission would find agents to regulate their behavior. Instead, SPARTA seems to be a redundant version of the Uniform Act that does not add much to the overall regulatory scheme.

Union Regulations

The final level of athlete agent regulation is with the players unions in the four major professional sports leagues: the National Football League Players Association, the National Basketball Players Association, the National Hockey League Players Association, and the Major League Baseball Players Association (see table 4.3). The unions in these four professional sports leagues regulate athlete agents who represent the unions' players. Agents who represent athletes in individual performer sports such as swimming and tennis are not regulated to

Table 4.3   Internet Information on Players Association Agent Regulations

Players association	Agent regulations' Internet address
MLB Players Association	www.mlb.com/pa/info/agent_regulations.jsp
NBA Players Association	Limited information available at http://nbpa.com/nbpa-agent-application-package
NFL Players Association	www.nflpa.com/agents
NHL Players Association	www.nhlpa.com/inside-nhlpa/certified-player-agents

the same extent. The reasons for the regulation in team sports are that the players in these leagues have long histories of strong representation by their players unions and that the athletes in these leagues make the highest average salaries of any athletes. In addition, each union requires that its members hire only agents who are certified under the union's rules and that teams agree to negotiate only with certified agents.

A good example of an agent certification program is the *NFLPA Regulations Governing Contract Advisors* (NFL Players Association, 2012). Under these regulations, an agent must do the following to represent NFL players:

- Submit an application fee of $2,500
- Have an undergraduate and postgraduate degree (master's or law degree) from an accredited university
- Submit to a background investigation
- Attend an NFL Players Association educational seminar each year
- Complete a written exam that covers the collective bargaining agreement, salary cap, player benefits, NFL Players Association regulations, and other issues related to player representation

The regulations include the NFL Players Association Standard Representation Agreement that all agents must sign with their players to establish the agency relationship. Perhaps most important, the regulations set out the exact fee that an NFL agent can charge:

The maximum fee which may be charged or collected by a Contract Advisor shall be three percent (3%) of the "compensation" . . . received by the player in each playing season covered by the contract negotiated by the Contract Advisor. (p. 11)

Each of the other professional team sports leagues has similar rules.

As described in the disputes that are discussed later in this chapter, agents can violate these rules in many ways. (See the Court Upholds Authority of Union to Discipline Agent sidebar for an example of an agent who attempted to sue to stop a union from enforcing its rules.) The examples describe several agents who breached contracts and were convicted of crimes. Such agents are quickly decertified by the appropriate players union, and they can no longer represent athletes within that sport. But litigation is not always necessary. If an agent engages in any of the prohibited conduct barred by the union's regulations, he will lose the ability to represent athletes in that sport but may not face litigation. For instance, under the *NFLPA Regulations Governing Contract Advisors* 31 prohibited activities could cause an agent to be decertified, such as representing a player when the player has not entered into the NFL Players Association Standard Representation Agreement with the agent or failing to comply with the maximum fee provisions contained in the regulations (NFL Players Association, 2012, section 3(B)).

IN THE COURTROOM

Court Upholds Authority of Union to Discipline Agent

Black v. NFL Players Association (2000)

NFL agent William "Tank" Black was first licensed as an NFLPA contract advisor in 1995. In 1998, as part of his application to continue as a certified contract advisor, he agreed to be bound by NFLPA player agent regulations. In 1999 the NFLPA revoked his certification because of his mismanagement of a player's funds and other illegal actions he took as an agent. Under the regulations, this decision could be challenged only before a designated arbitrator. Instead, Black sued, claiming that the union's actions deprived him of his livelihood as a sport agent.

As the court explained, pursuant to the National Labor Relations Act, the NFLPA is the exclusive bargaining representative for NFL players, and it permits agents, or contract advisors, to represent its player members in negotiations with NFL teams. All contract advi-

sors agree to abide by the regulations put forth by the NFLPA. These regulations provide that all disputes between the NFLPA and its contract advisors must first go through arbitration. The court agreed that Black consented and agreed to these regulations, so he should have first taken his dispute to arbitration.

Black also argued that by disciplining him, the NFLPA tortuously interfered with his contracts with his players (because after the discipline he could no longer represent any NFL players and the contracts he had with them would be void). The court disagreed, finding that the NFLPA's regulations under which Black was disciplined were created in conformance with the collective bargaining agreement between the NFL and NFLPA, so any contractual claims of this nature were preempted by federal labor law.

In the end, the court found that Black could bring no claims against the union, because he agreed to follow the contract advisor regulations and the NFLPA was merely enforcing those rules.

Consolidation

The future of sport agency seems to be a focus on consolidation. Since the 1990s many large sport agencies such as IMG, Octagon, and SFX have expanded their businesses by purchasing the businesses of smaller sport agents. This expansion is often an effort to allow the larger agency to provide more services to a wider variety of clients. Consolidation can allow smaller agents or agencies to increase their fees by giving them the ability to increase the range of services they offer. These consolidations can benefit athletes, who will have access to larger agencies that can offer financial

planning, investment, and marketing services and may even help the athletes enter other areas in the entertainment business, including movies and television.

A famous example of consolidation involves agent Arn Tellem. In 1999 Tellem sold his athlete agent business to SFX, only to reacquire it in 2000. In 2006 he then sold his business to the Wasserman Media Group (www.wmgllc.com), which at the time represented about 50 action sports athletes. Adding Tellem's and other agents' business gave Wasserman about 100 NBA and MLB players, making the group one of the largest player agencies at the time (Davis, 2007).

Disputes

Given the extensive regulation of agents by states, the federal government, and professional sports players unions, it might be surprising to some that agents still run into many problems and end up in court. One of the most famous disputes involved agents Norby Walters and Lloyd Bloom. These agents offered athletes cash, loans, clothing, insurance policies, limousines, and other benefits to entice them to sign with the agents. When some of the athletes tried to get out of their agency agreements with Walters and Bloom, the agents "reminded them that they needed their legs to carry their bodies on the field and threatened to involve their organized crime associates to carry out the threats" (Greenberg & Gray, 1998, p. 1026). To enable the athletes, many of whom were still participating in university athletics, to sign with them, Walters and Bloom had the athletes lie to their universities and sign postdated contracts that would become effective when the athletes' eligibility was up. Walters and Bloom were eventually charged by federal prosecutors with allegations of mail fraud, conspiracy, and racketeering (*United States v. Walters & Bloom*, 1990). In 1992 Walters was sentenced to a year and a half in prison, fined $25,000, and ordered to complete 250 hours of community service. Bloom was sentenced to 5 years of probation and 500 hours of community service (Greenberg & Gray, 1998, p. 1032).

The behavior of Walters and Bloom may be the extreme for unscrupulous sport agents, but they are not alone. Agents also may find themselves in disputes involving other areas of law.

Breach of Contract

The basics of a breach of contract claim are discussed in chapter 5. A recent high-profile case focusing on breach of contract involved famous sport agents Leigh Steinberg and David Dunn. Steinberg claimed that Dunn breached his contract with their firm Steinberg, Moorad, and Dunn by removing trade secrets and confidential client information and using this information to divert high-profile athletes (including NFL stars Reggie White and Drew Bledsoe) to Dunn's new agency, Athletes First (*Steinberg, Moorad & Dunn, Inc. v. Dunn*, 2002). The trial court found that Dunn breached his contract with Steinberg, Moorad, and Dunn, a 5-year agreement worth $7 million, because the contract included a clause that prohibited Dunn from competing with Steinberg, Moorad, and Dunn. Steinberg was awarded $44 million in damages, and soon afterward the NFL Players Association suspended Dunn for 2 years for violating the NFL Players Association's agent regulations (Wolohan, 2007).

Tort Law

Other disputes focus on allegations that the agent made misrepresentations to the athlete or mishandled the agent's funds. Besides breach of contract claims, these lawsuits include tort claims of fraud and misrepresentation (further discussion of tort law can be found in chapter 2).

A highly publicized case involved William "Tank" Black, the former chairman and CEO of Professional Management, Inc. Black involved his player clients in major financial scams. For example, as president of Black Americans of Achievement (BAOA), a company that produced a board game regarding the accomplishments of African Americans, Black arranged for the athletes to promote the board game in exchange for free stock in the company. The players were not informed of this arrangement and did not agree to it. Regardless, Black told BAOA that his players had promoted the game and were entitled to the stock. As a result, BAOA issued two million shares of free stock in the names of the players and sent the stock certificates to Black, who then sold the stock to the players for $1,240,000, far above the stock's market value. The payments went to a shell company that Black had created, and he then transferred the money to his personal account.

The players eventually sued Black, alleging breach of fiduciary duty, negligence, and breach of contract (*Hilliard & Taylor v. Black*, 2000). Black was sentenced to 60 months in prison and ordered to pay $12 million in restitution to his athlete clients. He also was decertified as an NFL Players Association agent (Sharp, Moorman, & Claussen, 2007). See the Court Upholds Authority of Union to Discipline Agent sidebar (page 90) for more about Black's lawsuit attempting to stop the NFLPA from also disciplining him.

LEARNING AIDS

Summary

Many relationships in sport can be understood as a relationship between a principal and an agent. Although the most prominent sport agents represent athletes, sport agents also work with sponsors, facilities, events, equipment manufacturers, merchandisers, ticket sellers, and other entities. An agency relationship can exist any time that one person or entity (the principal) agrees to have another person or entity (the agent) work on her behalf.

The agency law principles discussed in this chapter apply to any agency relationship within sport. A formal contract is not needed to establish these types of relationships; any agreement reached orally or in writing can establish an agency relationship. The important issues involve the type of authority the agent has as he works for the principal. In addition, both agents and principals have fiduciary duties that they must uphold as they work with each other. Agents must work for the benefit of the principal, and the principal must then do whatever she can to make sure that the agent has the ability to perform his duties.

Athlete agents are unique because they are highly regulated. Most states have adopted the Uniform Athlete Agents Act, which, along with the federal law and SPARTA, requires athlete agents to follow strict registration requirements and include standard language in their agreements with players. In addition, athlete agents who represent players in the four major professional team sports must follow strict union regulation.

Many agents have engaged in unscrupulous activities when they have avoided their fiduciary duties and acted in their own self-interest or attempted to coerce players to sign with them. With the money involved in sport today, agents are unlikely to stop engaging in this type of conduct.

Discussion Questions

1. Provide a hypothetical example of the agency relationship: agent, principal, and third party.

2. Explain what is meant by the term *fiduciary duty*.

3. Describe the purpose and scope of the Uniform Athletes Agents Act.

4. Explain the issue of scope of employment in the context of agency and tort liability.

5. What types of regulations are agents subject to and why?

6. Provide your own hypothetical example (not in the book) of a potential conflict of interest for a sport agent.

7. Explain the difference between express and implied authority.

When Is an Agent Acting as an Agent?

Tommy was a new employee of Big Glove Sports, a manufacturer of sporting goods and sports equipment. A key product for Big Glove was its line of baseball gloves. The gloves were sold by Big Glove's agents and employees throughout the United States and Canada. The products were recognizable by the letters *BGS* emblazoned on the side of each glove produced by the company. After his mandatory training, Tommy was provided with a list of 20 local retailers to contact during his first month as a salesperson for BGS. Tommy visited most of the retailers in that first month, but none were interested in buying BGS gloves or other products. Tommy, fearing that he might lose his job if he returned without a sale, decided to visit his second cousin, Jake, who owned a successful sporting goods store. Tommy believed that with his family connections, he might be able to make a sale.

Tommy explained to Jake that he was selling baseball gloves and asked Jake whether he was interested in buying. Jake said that he was in good shape with his line of gloves but would buy extra from Tommy because he was a family member. Tommy didn't have a company contract written up for Jake, so he used a generic contract that Jake had on hand. Tommy signed the contract and left several boxes of gloves with Jake. Tommy was so excited about the sale that he forgot to mention that he worked for BGS and did not refer to BGS in the contract. They shook hands on the deal, and Tommy headed for his next appointment, happily daydreaming about a grand reception on his return and his possible future promotion. While preoccupied with those thoughts, Tommy failed to see a red stop light and a Good Samaritan (GS) helping a little old lady (LOL) across the street. Tommy collided with them, seriously injuring the GS and LOL. To make matters worse, back at the store Jake opened the box to see that the gloves had been damaged and could not be used or sold. The GS and LOL sued Tommy (as an agent of BGS) and BGS (the principal) for negligence. Jake sued Tommy (as an agent of BGS) and BGS (the principal) for breach of contract.

Contract Law

Chapter Objectives

After reading this chapter, you will know the following:

- The elements of a valid contract
- Common provisions within sport contracts
- The many types of contracts found in the sport industry
- The issues that arise when a sport contract is breached

From employment agreements to player contracts, from ticket sales to sea t licenses, sport managers encounter many forms of contracts every day. This chapter covers contract law and provides examples of the many types of contracts that sport managers may encounter:

- University and professional coaching contracts
- Player contracts
- Endorsement agreements
- Agent representation agreements
- Collective bargaining agreements
- Scholarships and letters of intent
- Ticket agreements
- Sponsorship agreements
- Concession agreements
- Lease agreements
- Seat license agreements

Contracts are involved at every level of the sport industry. This chapter focuses on the issues that can develop concerning breach of contract issues and damages and remedies for breach.

After reading this chapter, you will better understand the agreements that you might make with organizations and individuals within the sport industry. By having this knowledge, you can protect yourself and the organization that you work for.

Basics of Contract Law

To understand the principles that apply to a sport contract, you must understand the way in which the law defines a contract, the elements of a contract, and some typical provisions that can be found in all contracts. Contract law is often understood by reference to the Restatements of the Law. Written by legal scholars who are members of the American Law Institute, the Restatements explain what the law is in a certain area and how it is changing. Courts often rely on the Restatements to provide consistent explanations of certain areas of law. According to the *Restatement on Contracts*, a contract is "a promise, or set of promises, for breach of which the law gives a remedy, or the performance of which the law in some way recognizes a duty" (*Restatement [Second] of Contracts*, § 2, 1990). By entering into a contractual agreement, one party promises to do something in exchange for something that the other party promises to do. As shown later in this chapter, if one party does not live up to these obligations, a court may intervene to provide a remedy.

Contracts are either bilateral or unilateral. **Bilateral contracts** contain two promises. The first promise is in the **offer**, which is always a promise, and the second promise is in the **acceptance**. Any time an offeree accepts an offer by a promise to perform, the contract is bilateral. For example, in May 2008 MLB National League's 2007 Rookie of the Year Ryan Braun agreed to a new contract with the Milwaukee Brewers. The contract was bilateral because according to the agreement, the Brewers would pay Braun approximately $45 million over the next 7 years, for which Braun promised to play for the Brewers during the term of the agreement.

In a **unilateral contract** only one party makes a promise. The other party makes no promise but instead performs some act in exchange for the first party's promise. An insurance contract for an athlete is a unilateral contract because the athlete promises to pay a premium, and in return the insurance company agrees to pay out premiums (i.e., perform) if something should happen to make the insurance policy come into play.

Elements

To be enforceable, a contract must contain several elements. The three required elements are an offer, acceptance, and consideration. The absence of just one of these elements may prevent the formation of a contract.

Offer

An offer is a conditional promise to do or refrain from doing something in the future (*Restatement [Second] of Contracts*, § 24, 1990). An offer is made by one party, called the *offeror*, to another party, called the *offeree*. The most important aspect of an offer is that it creates a power of acceptance in the offeree. The term *power of acceptance* means that the party to whom the offer was made has the power to bind the offeror to the contract.

A statement may appear to be an offer, but if it does not create a power of acceptance, it is probably not an offer. Such statements are common in negotiations and are often used to determine whether another party is willing to either entertain an offer or make an offer. For example, Jill may ask Frank whether he would like to purchase a Super Bowl ticket. If Frank answers in the affirmative, does that conversation result in a contract? Specifically, did Jill create a power of acceptance in Frank's favor so that Frank could bind Jill to a contract through his acceptance? Given these limited facts, we have no way of answering the question. Jill's statements to Frank could have been more detailed if she truly wanted to sell her ticket to Frank.

The more detailed the statement is, the more likely it is to result in an offer, because statements that include details like price, quantity, and time for acceptance are more likely to create a power of acceptance. An offer should include the parties and subject matter involved, the way in which the subject matter will be performed, and the consideration (a term that will be defined in more detail later in this chapter). The more detailed the purported offer is, the more likely it is that a reviewing court will find the existence of an offer.

Going back to the Super Bowl hypothetical, suppose that the statement was more specific. Let's say that Jill asked Frank whether he would purchase a Super Bowl ticket that she owned for $2,000. In this hypothetical we have a statement that lists a particular thing (the Super Bowl ticket) that is to be purchased and a price for that thing ($2,000). The statement is not asking whether Frank would like to purchase the ticket but instead whether Frank will purchase the ticket. This second hypothetical statement is more detailed and is therefore more likely to be deemed an offer.

Acceptance

After an offer is made by one party, a contract can be created only if another party accepts the offer. Acceptance of an offer must be made in some positive manner, whether by words or by conduct. Notice of acceptance must be communicated to the offeror, and courts generally do not infer acceptance from silent parties.

An interesting example occurred in the NBA in 2004. Carlos Boozer left the Cleveland Cavaliers and signed a 6-year, $68 million contract with the Utah Jazz. The Cavaliers claimed that Boozer had already accepted their contract offer to remain a Cavalier. Boozer answered that he had never agreed to remain a Cavalier; in other words, he had never accepted their contract offer. Instead, he accepted the Jazz' contract offer and was a successful member of the Jazz until he joined the Chicago Bulls in 2010.

The offer may also provide the method in which acceptance must be communicated. If so, then acceptance must be communicated in the manner directed by the offer. If the offer is silent as to the method in which acceptance must be communicated, then any reasonable method of communication will suffice.

Relatively recent technological advances have changed the way that people communicate. Instant message services, text message services, listservs, and e-mail have become common methods of communication in both personal and professional settings. For the purpose of acceptance, the reasonableness of the communication method selected to communicate the acceptance will depend on the circum-

stances. For important transactions, the offeree should select a means that will provide proof (i.e., a copy or receipt) that the offeror received notice of the acceptance.

Consideration

After there is an offer and an acceptance, for a contract to be legally enforceable there also needs to be consideration. **Consideration** is the exchange of value or benefit that each party agrees to give up because of the contractual agreement. Simply put, consideration is what each party gets in return for the contractual performance.

The best way to understand the concept of consideration is to focus on the requirement that each party must get something in exchange for her performance. Thus, gifts cannot serve as valid consideration because a giving party does not receive anything in exchange for the given service or item. Similarly, items or services given for past performance cannot serve as a basis for consideration. Past performance is not consideration because the party that rewards the performance does not receive anything in exchange. After all, that party already received the performance. Had payment been made at the time of performance, that payment would serve as consideration.

For example, Chris is a general manager for a professional baseball organization. At Chris' retirement ceremony, he is given a gold watch by the organization for 20 years of loyal service. The watch breaks, however, and Chris wants the organization to provide a new watch, but the organization refuses. Chris sues the organization, claiming that the watch was given in consideration for 20 years of loyal service. Unfortunately for Chris, his contractual claim for a new watch may fail because the watch was given in consideration for services that were already rendered. Therefore, the watch resembles a gift more than consideration. After all, the baseball organization had already received the services and was not getting anything in exchange for the watch. Furthermore, Chris was paid a salary for his services during the 20 years he served as manager for the organization, and that payment was consideration.

Illegal acts cannot serve as consideration. If a party agrees to pay another for an illegal service, that agreement is not enforceable by the courts because it lacks consideration. But if one party agrees to do or refrain from doing something that causes him or her harm, that service can be deemed consideration as long as it does not violate the law. For example, one person could pay another not to try out for the football team. By not trying out for the team, the accepting party suffers a detriment for which compensation could be provided.

Legality and Legal Capacity

Even if an offer, acceptance, and consideration are valid, a contract is not formed if the underlying transaction is illegal. Courts will not enforce contracts that are based on an illegal promise or transaction. Suppose that a player enters into a contract with a bookie to drop a pass in the end zone, thereby causing the point spread that the bookie wants to remain in place. If the bookie fails to pay the player for this service, the player cannot ask a court to help him get his money from the bookie because the transaction itself, gambling, is illegal in most jurisdictions in the United States.

In addition, certain classes of people lack the ability, competence, or capacity to enter into binding contracts. Therefore, people who are mentally incompetent and those under the legal age for adulthood, which is 18 in most jurisdictions, cannot enter into valid contracts.

Oftentimes in sports, minors are involved in contracts. A contract between a minor and an adult usually is voidable by the minor but binding on the adult. The term **voidable** in this context means that the minor, unlike the adult, has the power to walk away from the contract. But some exceptions to this rule exist. For example, contracts that provide necessities for the minor may be enforced by adults against minors. Also, adults usually can enter into binding contracts with minors if the minor's parents or legal guardians have authorized the agreement.

For example, the National Letter of Intent (NLI) is a contract signed by high school athletes in which they agree to attend a university on an athletic scholarship. The standard language from the NLI states, on behalf of the student, that

> At the time I sign this NLI, I must receive a written offer of athletics financial aid for the entire 2013–14 academic year from the institution named in this document. The offer must list the terms, conditions and amount of the athletics aid award. (A midyear football two-year college transfer student-athlete must receive a written offer of athletics financial aid for the remainder of the 2012–13 academic year. If the institution does not renew the athletics aid for the following academic year, the student-athlete must be released of the NLI.) In order for this NLI to be valid, my parent/legal guardian and I must sign the NLI and I must also sign the offer of athletics aid (see institutional policy for parent/legal guardian signature) prior to submission to the institution named in this document, and any other stated conditions must also be met. If the conditions stated on the financial aid offer are not met, this NLI shall be declared null and void. (National Letter of Intent, n.d.)

As is clear from the language of the NLI, a large number of athletes are minors, so their parents or legal guardians are also required to sign these contracts before they can be enforced against the minor.

Typical Provisions

Contracts do not need to be written to be valid. Oral contracts can be legally enforceable if a valid offer, acceptance, and consideration are present. Specific considerations dealing with oral contracts are discussed in the section Contract Law Issues later in this chapter. Regardless of the validity of an oral contract, you are best advised to enter into written contracts to ensure that you protect your own rights and the rights of your employer.

Written contracts in sport come in many varieties, which are discussed in the next section. Some general provisions, however, are common to many types of sport contracts: party designations, term, warranties and representations, obligations and duties, and termination. These provisions are found in most sport contracts, so we discuss them in detail next.

Party Designation

A written contract must clearly identify the parties, typically by the full name of the individual or organization involved. For example, the NBA Uniform Player Contract starts by listing the team and player by name:

> THIS AGREEMENT made this _____ day of _____, 20____ by and between _____ _____ (hereinafter called the "Club"), a member of the National Basketball Association (hereinafter called the "Association") and _____ whose address is shown below (hereinafter

called the "Player"). (National Basketball Association, 2011, exhibit A)

Terms of the Agreement

Another basic provision of any sport contract is a clause providing the term of the agreement. The term is the defined length of time that the contract will exist. The language setting the term of the contract could be as basic as "This Agreement shall commence upon execution and remain in full force and effect through _____" or more detailed, as provided in the license agreement between the Atlanta Falcons and the Georgia Dome: "This Agreement shall expire upon the later of (a) June 30 of the License year in which occurs the Maturity Date of the Revenue Bonds issued by the Authority, or (b) June 30 of the twentieth (20th) License Year" (Miller & Anderson, 2001, p. 48). As this example shows, a contract does not have to specify the exact term of the agreement as long as the contract includes methods that can be used to calculate the exact term.

Warranties and Representations

A typical sport contract includes a section of warranties or representations by the parties. Warranties or representations are legal promises that certain facts are true. In most lease agreements for professional sports teams, the team must warrant that it is a valid member of the particular league. For example, within the team's lease agreement for Ralph Wilson Stadium, the Buffalo Bills warrant that the team will

> (i) keep and maintain the Team as a member in good standing of the NFL;
>
> (ii) keep and maintain the Franchise in good standing with the NFL . . . ;
>
> (iii) keep and maintain the Stadium as the facility designated to and by the NFL as the home facility for the Team; and

(iv) continuously operate the Team at the Stadium in accordance with NFL Rules and Regulations. (Miller & Anderson, 2001, p. 25)

Obligations and Duties

A sport contract typically includes a section that describes the duties and obligations of the parties involved. This section should specifically set out all the duties that each party has agreed to assume and the time at which the parties will undertake the actions necessary to fulfill those duties. The following contractual language provides a boxing promoter's duties within an agreement with a sponsor.

1.   THE FIGHTS: At Promoter's expense, Promoter agrees to perform all acts necessary for the holding of at least (*enter number of fights*) boxing Fight cards on the dates and at the locations to be mutually determined by the parties. Each Fight card will include at least (*enter number of bouts*) preliminary professional boxing bouts. Promoter warrants that it will produce the Fights in accordance with the following specifications:

(a) The Fights will be televised on (*enter television channel*) in (*enter city, state*). (Promoter will use its best efforts to televise the Fights on other network and cable channels in addition to Channel (*enter channel number*).

(b) The starting time of each Fight card shall be communicated to a Miller representative at least *forty-five (45)* days prior to the Fight card.

Contracts must cover many areas, such as the parties who will sign, the warranties and representations that are at play, and the obligations and duties of the parties.

(c) All Fights will be produced in a first class manner in accordance with prevailing professional, ethical and business standards, with the utmost regard for the safety of all persons, property, the environment and Miller's goodwill, will be contested in good faith, and will be sanctioned by all required state regulatory bodies.

(d) All Fights will be planned, designed and executed in compliance with *California* alcoholic beverage laws and regulations and in accordance with any conditions imposed by the *California Alcoholic Beverage Control Board*.

(e) In that all arrangements for the Fights and related Promoter organized activities (and any financial loss relating thereto) shall be solely Promoter's responsibility, Miller shall have no obligation to pay any amounts to Promoter or others as a result of the Fights or related Promoter organized activity, except the amounts payable to Promoter which are specified in Clause 7 below.

(f) All payments for boxers, judges, ring officials, ring girls, announcers, medical personnel, site rentals, a.v. equipment, electricians, stage hands, special security and police, clean-up personnel, ushers, tickets, ticker sellers, ticket takers, box office employees, truck loaders and unloaders, licenses, taxes, advertising and publicity services of every type required, lights, microphones and prop equipment and all other expenses of the Fights shall be the responsibility of Promoter. By way of specification (and not limitation), a Promoter shall perform all obligations imposed under worker's compensation, unemployment compensation insurance, disability benefits, boxing licensing, social security, withholding tax laws and union contracts.

Termination Provision

The final part to any sport contract is the termination provision. This clause sets forth each party's right to terminate the contract under certain circumstances. Termination usually occurs either at the expiration of the contract term or when a party breaches the agreement in some way that causes the contract to be terminated. For example, in a standard licensing agreement between an apparel company and a professional football player, the termination clause provides the following:

9.   Termination and Post Termination Right

a. Licensor shall have the right to terminate this Agreement upon thirty (30) days written notice in the event Licensee defaults on any of its obligations hereunder, including without limitation the obligation to pay royalties in a timely manner as set out herein, provided Licensee does not cure its default 'Within the thirty (30) day notice period.'

Licensor shall have the right to immediately terminate this Agreement in the event that Licensee:

i. files a petition in bankruptcy or is adjudicated a bankrupt or insolvent, or makes an assignment or arrangement for the benefit of creditors, or discontinues its business, or has a receiver appointed.

ii. breaches the provisions of this Agreement relating to unauthorized use of, or assertion of rights in, the

Smith Attributes, or challenges the validity or ownership of the Smith Attributes.

Sport Contracts

Various types of contracts are used within the sport industry. The next section discusses employment agreements, contracts with professional athletes and student-athletes, and agreements connected to sport facilities.

Student-Athletes

As mentioned earlier, a student-athlete who signs the National Letter of Intent enters into a contract with the school that also signs the letter. The NLI will be void and no longer a contract if the school does not admit the student or the student does not meet NCAA initial eligibility requirements. The student-athlete must also receive a scholarship offer from the school that represents the financial aid portion of the agreement. The NLI and the financial aid scholarship make up the contractual agreement between the student-athlete and the school that binds the school to provide the student-athlete with financial aid and a chance to participate in athletics, in exchange for the student-athlete's commitment to attend the school and remain eligible to participate in athletics. Until recently these contracts could last for only 1 year, but in 2012 NCAA rules were modified to allow multiyear scholarships for athletes not to exceed 5 years in length (National Collegiate Athletic Association, 2015, 15.3.3.1). A hypothetical scholarship offer is shown in figure 5.1.

Several cases have agreed that the NLI and scholarship constitute a legal and binding contract, starting with *Taylor v. Wake Forest University* (1972). (See more about this case in the accompanying e-book, *Case Studies in Sport Law, Second Edition* [Pittman, Spengler, & Young, 2016].) In this case, Taylor entered into a scholarship to play football at Wake Forest University. After participating in football for one semester and performing badly academically, he decided to stop participating in football. As a result the school terminated his scholarship. He then sued the school, claiming that it owed him for the money he had to pay to continue to go to school after the scholarship was terminated. The court agreed that there was a contract between Taylor and the school but also found that under the scholarship contract, he had agreed to maintain his athletic eligibility, physically and academically. Although his improved academic performance met the appropriate standards, when he refused to meet the physical requirements of the scholarship by refusing to participate in football, in the absence of any injury or excuse other than to devote more time to studies, he was not upholding his part of the contract.

The NCAA manual lays out the specific details of the grant-in-aid offered to student-athletes within the scholarship. A school can only give a student financial aid that does not "exceed the cost of attendance that is normally incurred by students enrolled in a comparable program at that institution" (National Collegiate Athletic Association, 2015, 15.01.6). The cost of attendance includes the "total cost of tuition and fees, room and board, books and supplies, transportation, and other expenses related to attendance at the institution" (15.02.2). These scholarships can be granted for up to five years and cannot be terminated on the basis of skill or performance on the field of play. As long as the student-athlete remains eligible to participate in athletics at the university, the university must provide that student-athlete with financial aid for the year in question.

FIGURE 5.1   A Hypothetical Scholarship Offer to a Student-Athlete

Dear Student-Athlete:

Enclosed you will find two copies of this scholarship letter and two copies of the National Letter of Intent. You and one of your parents should sign all copies on or after _____, keep one of the scholarship letters and one of the letters of intent for yourself, and return the other signed copies.

Also enclosed is a copy of the NCAA 2012 Graduation Rates Report. Important information about the NCAA's list of banned substances can be found online, and I have included information regarding initial eligibility requirements. Make sure that you have registered with the NCAA Clearinghouse.

By signing this Financial Agreement Letter, pending your qualification under NCAA initial eligibility standards and formal acceptance to the university, you will receive an athletic scholarship estimated at a value of $_____ for the _____ school year.

Under NCAA legislation, this scholarship may be renewed for up to 5 years as long as you remain eligible to participate. You may lose this scholarship if you fail in your academic endeavors, do something against university rules that would require your dismissal, fail to adhere to team rules as set up by your coach, or voluntarily withdraw from the team.

Once you sign the scholarship letter, qualify under initial eligibility legislation, and are accepted to the university, you will receive notification from the financial aid office.

Employment

A sport manager will come across many different types of employment contracts. Two of the most interesting types of sport contracts involve athletes and coaches.

Athletes

The contract that is the foundation for the legal relationship between players and management within any team sport is the **collective bargaining agreement (CBA)**. The CBA is the contract negotiated between the union (known as *players associations* in professional sports) and management (team owners) in major professional team sports. CBAs are typically hundreds of pages long because they include all the terms and conditions of employment for players, such as salaries, codes of conduct, drug-testing provisions, amateur draft rules, and grievance procedures.

Most leagues' CBAs are available on the Internet on either the players association or league website. For example, the current NFL Collective Bargaining Agreement can be found on the NFL Players Association's website: https://nfllabor.files.wordpress.com/2010/01/collective-bargaining-agreement-2011-2020.pdf. As with all sport CBAs, the NFL's CBA contains a uniform player contract that all players must sign. Some of the most interesting provisions of the NFL Uniform Player Contract (which are common in uniform player contracts) are provided in figure 5.2.

FIGURE 5.2 Sample Provisions of an NFL Player Contract

THIS CONTRACT is between _____, hereinafter "Player," and _____ a corporation (limited partnership) (partnership), hereinafter "Club," operating under the name of the _____ as a member of the National Football League, hereinafter "League." In consideration of the promises made by each to the other, Player and Club agree as follows. . . .

2. EMPLOYMENT AND SERVICES

Club employs Player as a skilled football player. Player accepts such employment. He agrees to give his best efforts and loyalty to the Club, and to conduct himself on and off the field with appropriate recognition of the fact that the success of professional football depends largely on public respect for and approval of those associated with the game. Player will report promptly for and participate fully in Club's official mandatory minicamp(s), official preseason training camp, all Club meetings and practice sessions, and all preseason, regular season and postseason football games scheduled for or by Club. If invited, Player will practice for and play in any all-star football game sponsored by the League. Player will not participate in any football game not sponsored by the League unless the game is first approved by the League.

3. OTHER ACTIVITIES

Without prior written consent of the Club, Player will not play football or engage in activities related to football otherwise than for Club or engage in any activity other than football which may involve a significant risk of personal injury. Player represents that he has special, exceptional and unique knowledge, skill, ability, and experience as a football player, the loss of which cannot be estimated with any certainty and cannot be fairly or adequately compensated by damages. Player therefore agrees that Club will have the right, in addition to any other right which Club may possess, to enjoin Player by appropriate proceedings from playing football or engaging in football-related activities other than for Club or from engaging in any activity other than football which may involve a significant risk of personal injury.

4. PUBLICITY AND NFLPA GROUP LICENSING PROGRAM

(a) Player hereby grants to Club and the League, separately and together, the right and authority to use, and to authorize others to use solely as described below, his name, nickname, initials, likeness, image, picture, photograph, animation, persona, autograph/signature (including facsimiles thereof), voice, biographical information and/or any and all other identifying characteristics (collectively, "Publicity Rights"), for any and all uses or purposes that publicize and promote NFL Football, the League or any of its member clubs in any way in any and all media or formats, whether

(continued)

analog, digital or other, now known or hereafter developed, including, but not limited to, print, tape, disc, computer file, radio, television, motion pictures, other audio-visual and audio works, Internet, broadband platforms, mobile platforms, applications, and other distribution platforms. Without limiting the foregoing, this grant includes the right to use Player's Publicity Rights for the purpose of publicizing and promoting the following aspects of NFL Football, the League and/or any of its member clubs: brands, games, ticket sales, game broadcasts and telecasts, programming focused on the NFL, one or more NFL clubs and/or their games and events (e.g., coaches shows, highlight based shows such as Inside the NFL, behind-the-scenes programming such as Hard Knocks), other NFL-related media offerings (e.g., branded content segments featuring NFL game footage and other programming enhancements), media distribution platforms (e.g., NFL.com, NFL Mobile, NFL Network), official events (e.g., NFL Kickoff, NFL Draft), officially sanctioned awards programs (e.g., Rookie of the Year), and public service or community oriented initiatives (e.g., Play60). For purposes of clarity, the foregoing grant of rights includes the right and authority to use, and to authorize affiliates or business partners to use, after the term of this Agreement any Publicity Rights fixed in a tangible medium (e.g., filmed, photographed, recorded or otherwise captured) during the term of this Agreement solely for the purposes described herein. Notwithstanding anything to the contrary, the foregoing grant does not confer, during or after the term of this Agreement, any right or authority to use Player's Publicity Rights in a manner that constitutes any endorsement by Player of a third-party brand, product or service ("Endorsement"). For purposes of clarity, and without limitation, it shall not be an Endorsement for Club or the League to use, or authorize others to use, including, without limitation, in third party advertising and promotional materials, footage and photographs of Player's participation in NFL games or other NFL events that does not unduly focus on, feature, or highlight, Player in a manner that leads the reasonable consumer to believe that Player is a spokesperson for, or promoter of, a third-party commercial product or service.

Player will cooperate with the news media, and will participate upon request in reasonable activities to promote the Club and the League. . . .

5. COMPENSATION

    For performance of Player's services and all other promises of Player, Club will pay Player a yearly salary as follows:

    $_____ *   for the 20____ season;

    $_____ *   for the 20____ season;

    $_____ *   for the 20____ season;

    $_____ *   for the 20____ season;

    $_____ *   for the 20____ season;

    (*designates the compensation Club will pay player if the player is not on Club's Active/Inactive List)

In addition, Club will pay Player such earned performance bonuses as may be called for in this contract; Player's necessary traveling expenses from his residence to training camp; Player's reasonable board and lodging expenses during preseason training and in connection with playing preseason, regular season, and postseason football games outside Club's home city; Player's necessary traveling expenses to and from preseason, regular season, and postseason football games outside Club's home city; Player's necessary traveling expenses to his residence if this contract is terminated by Club; and such additional compensation, benefits and reimbursement of expenses as may be called for in any collective bargaining agreement in existence during the term of this contract. . . .

11. SKILL, PERFORMANCE AND CONDUCT

Player understands that he is competing with other players for a position on Club's roster within the applicable player limits. If at any time, in the sole judgment of Club, Player's skill or performance has been unsatisfactory as compared with that of other players competing for positions on Club's roster, or if Player has engaged in personal conduct reasonably judged by Club to adversely affect or reflect on Club, then Club may terminate this contract. In addition, during the period any salary cap is legally in effect, this contract may be terminated if, in Club's opinion, Player is anticipated to make less of a contribution to Club's ability to compete on the playing field than another player or players whom Club intends to sign or attempts to sign, or another player or players who is or are already on Club's roster, and for whom Club needs room.

12. TERMINATION

The rights of termination set forth in this contract will be in addition to any other rights of termination allowed either party by law. Termination will be effective upon the giving of written notice, except that Player's death, other than as a result of injury incurred in the performance of his services under this contract, will automatically terminate this contract. If this contract is terminated by Club and either Player or Club so requests, Player will promptly undergo a complete physical examination by the Club physician. . . .

17. ASSIGNMENT

Unless this contract specifically provides otherwise, Club may assign this contract and Player's services under this contract to any successor to Club's franchise or to any other Club in the League. Player will report to the assignee Club promptly upon being informed of the assignment of his contract and will faithfully perform his services under this contract. The assignee club will pay Player's necessary traveling expenses in reporting to it and will faithfully perform this contract with Player.

Reprinted, by permission, from National Football Players Association, *Collective bargaining agreement*, August 4, 2011.

Perhaps most interesting to some are the assignment, other athletic activities, and termination clauses. Under paragraph 17 the team is allowed to assign the player's contract to another team. This provision allows teams to trade players under contract. Under paragraph 3, players are restricted from engaging in many other activities that could harm their ability to perform as an NBA basketball player, including hang gliding, bungee jumping, and driving a motorcycle. Finally, the contract contains a detailed section on termination that allows the team to terminate the player for many reasons, including the player's failure to conform his personal conduct to standards of citizenship and good sporting behavior.

Because players in professional team sports must sign these uniform player contracts, the players are able to negotiate only over their salary, and in most leagues, salaries are subject to both a rookie scale and a **salary cap**. The NBA's rookie salary scale is set in article VIII of the collective bargaining agreement (National Basketball Association, 2011). The salary cap for nonrookie contract players is found in article VII. The salary cap is provided as a percentage of basketball-related income (BRI), which includes gate receipts (from regular season, exhibition, and playoff games), broadcasting revenues, novelty and concession sales, proceeds from in-arena signage and luxury suite sales, naming-rights proceeds, and proceeds from premium seat licenses (National Basketball Association, 2011, Art. VII). The current NBA CBA runs from 2011 until 2021. The salary cap was $58.044 M for 2011–2012, 44.74% of BRI. In 2012–2013 and after that, the cap remains at 44.74% of BRI each year with numerous adjustments in the future.

Endorsement

Professional athletes in all sports enter into agreements with endorsers and sponsors. These contracts allow the athletes to receive compensation beyond their salary from the team itself (see table 5.1).

Endorsement contracts grant a sponsor or endorser the right to use the athlete's name, image, or likeness in connection with advertising the sponsor's or endorser's product. Many athletes in individual performer sports like golf and tennis enter into endorsement deals with equipment and apparel manufacturers that make products for their sport. Team sports athletes often enter into agreements to sponsor shoes, gloves, or other equipment and apparel.

Table 5.1   Highest Compensated Athletes

Rank	Player	Sport	Salary	Endorsements	Total
1	Floyd Mayweather	Boxing	$105,000,000	$0	$105,000,000
2	Cristiano Ronaldo	Soccer	$52,000,000	$28,000,000	$80,000,000
3	LeBron James	Basketball	$19,300,000	$53,000,000	$72,300,000
4	Lionel Messi	Soccer	$41,700,000	$23,000,000	$64,700,000
5	Kobe Bryant	Basketball	$30,500,000	$31,000,000	$61,500,000
6	Tiger Woods	Golf	$6,200,000	$55,000,000	$61,200,000
7	Roger Federer	Tennis	$4,200,000	$52,000,000	$56,200,000
8	Phil Mickelson	Golf	$5,200,000	$48,000,000	$53,200,000
9	Rafael Nadal	Tennis	$14,500,000	$30,000,000	$44,500,000
10	Matt Ryan	Football	$42,000,000	$1,800,000	$43,800,000

Adapted from The world's highest-paid athletes: 2014 rankings (n.d.). www.forbes.com/athletes/list/2/#tab:overall.

The provisions and amounts of money involved in an endorsement agreement vary with the popularity of the athlete and the resources of the sponsor. Of course, athletes who are nationally or internationally known, like Tiger Woods, are able to command more money in endorsements, and endorsers line up to get them to advertise their products.

Figure 5.3 provides sample language from a shoe endorsement agreement for a professional basketball player. Under the agreement, the athlete grants the company the exclusive right to use his name and likeness in the marketing of the company's products. The athlete also agrees that he will not endorse any competitor's products and agrees to use the company's products during events.

FIGURE 5.3 Sample Wording for an Endorsement Contract

THIS AGREEMENT is made as of _____ by and between _____ ("Company"), and _____ ("Athlete").

Recitals: Athlete is a well-known professional athlete whose endorsement has commercial value. Company desires to obtain the worldwide right to use Athlete's endorsement and services in connection with its products and services, and Athlete desires to grant such rights to Company.

NOW, THEREFORE, in consideration of the foregoing and the mutual promises set forth in this Agreement, Company and Athlete agree as follows:

1. DEFINITIONS. When used in this Agreement, the following terms will have the meaning set forth below unless the context requires otherwise:

    1.5 Endorsement: "Endorsement" includes the following or any part thereof. (a) Athlete's name, nickname, likeness, voice, live or recorded performance, photograph, signature or facsimile thereof, and biographical materials; (b) any and all trademarks, service marks, trade names, domain names, rights of publicity, copyrights and designs owned by or on behalf of Athlete; and (c) all other materials or indicia relating to or identifying Athlete. . . .

    1.10 Products: "Products" means all (a) footwear; (b) athletic, athletically-inspired and casual apparel, headwear and accessories; (c) eyewear, watches and performance measurement devices; (d) sports and fitness equipment; (e) posters; and (f) inflatables.

    1.11 Territory: "Territory" means the entire world. . . .

3. LICENSE TO COMPANY: Subject to and in accordance with the terms and conditions of this Agreement:

(continued)

3.1 Exclusive License: Athlete grants to Company the exclusive right and license during the Term and throughout the Territory to use the Endorsement in connection with: (a) the production, distribution, marketing, advertising, promotion and sale of Products; and (b) the design, development, creation, manufacture, production, distribution, marketing, advertising, promotion and sale of Licensed Products.

3.2 Exclusivity of Endorsement: Athlete agrees that during the Term he will not participate in any activity for the purpose of advertising or promoting a Competitor. Athlete specifically agrees that he will not permit the use of the Endorsement either in connection with any Product other than a Company Product or by or for the benefit of a Competitor. Athlete warrants and represents that he has disclosed to Company the details of any and all conflicts, potential conflicts, and disputes of which he is or reasonably should be aware which might compromise or restrict Company's ability to utilize the Endorsement or produce Licensed Products as intended by this Agreement. . . .

6. ATHLETE SERVICES:

6.1 Use of Company Products: Athlete warrants that he uses Company Products and agrees to use Company Products exclusively during all athletic workouts, practices, tournaments, games, events, exhibitions, media interviews and during all public activities where it is appropriate to wear Products ("Public Activities"). Athlete further agrees to use Company Products in the same condition as received from Company with any Company trademarks visibly displayed and with no other trademarks, trade names, logos or symbols affixed thereto. Athlete acknowledges that he has tested and worn Company Products and that Company Products are satisfactory for his use in professional competition and training. Athlete agrees that he will advise Company in writing if he experiences any difficulty with the fit, durability or comfort of Company Products and acknowledges that his failure to so advise Company will constitute an ongoing affirmation of his satisfaction with Company Products. Company agrees to provide ***sufficient*** quantities of Company Products for Athlete's professional use at no cost to Athlete.

Athlete Agent

Athletes in many sports enter into contracts with agents who will represent them in negotiations with teams, endorsers, or events. Many professional leagues have developed standard representation agreements or other rules that agents must follow in these situations. Further details on athlete agents and the agreements they sign with players can be found in chapter 4.

Coaches

The contracts that coaches sign are often for incredibly high salaries in both university and professional sports (see table 5.2).

Table 5.2 Highest Paid Coaches in Select College and Professional Sports

Coach	Team	Annual compensation
COLLEGE FOOTBALL		
Nick Saban	Alabama	$7,160,187
Mark Dantonio	Michigan State	$5,636,145
Bob Stoops	Oklahoma	$5,058,333
Kevin Sumlin	Texas A&M	$5,006,145
Charlie Strong	Texas	$5,000,270
Urban Meyer	Ohio State	$4,536,640
Les Miles	Louisiana State	$4,369,582
James Franklin	Penn State	$4,300,000
Kirk Ferentz	Iowa	$4,047,000
Steve Spurrier	South Carolina	$4,016,900
PROFESSIONAL FOOTBALL		
Sean Payton	New Orleans Saints (NFL)	$8,000,000
Bill Belichik	New England Patriots (NFL)	$7,500,000
Andy Reid	Kansas City Chiefs (NFL)	$7,500,000
Pete Carroll	Seattle Seahawks (NFL)	$7,000,000
Jeff Fisher	St. Louis Rams (NFL)	$7,000,000
John Harbaugh	Baltimore Ravens (NFL)	$7,000,000
Glenn Rivers	Los Angeles Clippers (NBA)	$7,000,000
Mike Shanahan	Washington Redskins (NFL)	$7,000,000
Tom Coughlin	New York Giants (NFL)	$6,800,000
Chip Kelly	Philadelphia Eagles (NFL)	$6,500,000

Information from Reevy (2014) and Berkowitz et al. (n.d.).

Drafting a contract for a university coach has become an art form; besides earning a base salary, these coaches now receive revenues from speaking engagements, summer camps, endorsement deals, television and radio shows, appearance fees, and many other revenue streams. For example, head basketball coach Kelvin Sampson earned a base salary of $500,000 per year at Indiana University. In addition, his employment agreement with the university provided him many fringe benefits:

- Standard university employee benefits
- Reasonable travel expenses associated with his work as coach
- Two cars
- Eight season tickets to regular home games and up to 22 single-game tickets
- Reimbursement for moving expenses
- Outside, marketing, and promotional income associated with his work promoting the basketball program: $600,000 during the first year of the contract and escalating to $1,150,000 in the final year of the contract
- Commercial endorsements
- Pay for summer camps (Indiana University, 2007)

Sampson was also eligible to earn supplemental compensation in the event that his team won the Big Ten regular season conference championship, won the Big Ten Tournament, or played in the NCAA tournament, as follows:

Article V—Supplemental Compensation

5.01. Supplemental Compensation for Big Ten Conference Regular Season Conference Championship, Big Ten Tournament Championship, and NCAA Men's Basketball Tournament Play

A. If the University men's basketball team which is under the direct supervision of the Employee wins "outright" or "ties" the regular season (not post-season tournament) conference men's basketball championship, the Employee will receive an additional amount of Twenty Thousand Dollars ($20,000).

B. If the University men's basketball team which is under the direct supervision of the Employee wins the conference men's post-season tournament basketball championship the Employee will receive an additional amount of Forty Thousand Dollars ($40,000).

C. If the University men's basketball team which is under the direct supervision of the Employee advances to the NCAA Division I Men's Basketball post season Tournament round of sixteen (16) teams, the Employee will receive an additional amount of Twenty Thousand Dollars ($20,000).

D. If the University men's basketball team which is under the direct supervision of the Employee advances to the NCAA Division I Men's post-season Basketball Tournament round of four (4) teams, the Employee will receive an additional amount of Twenty Thousand Dollars ($20,000).

E. If the University men's basketball team which is under the direct supervision of the Employee wins the NCAA Division I Men's Basketball post season Tournament Championship (National Champions), the Employee will receive an additional amount of One Hundred Thousand Dollars ($100,000).

F. If Employee is named the NCAA Coach of the Year, the Employee will receive an additional amount of Twenty Five Thousand Dollars ($25,000). (Indiana University, 2007)

When Indiana hired Sampson, he was already on probation for violating NCAA rules related to permissible phone calls to recruited student-athletes. Early in his tenure at Indiana, the school found that he had violated the rules again and took away a potential $500,000 bonus. In February 2008 the NCAA sent a Notice of Allegations to Indiana alleging five major infractions of NCAA rules involving Sampson (National Collegiate Athletic Association, 2008). Although Sampson's original employment agreement contained strong language allowing the university to terminate him because of any "significant, intentional, or repetitive violation of any law, rule, regulation, constitutional provision, bylaw or interpretation of the . . . NCAA" (Indiana University, 2007, p. 11), Sampson would not admit to any wrongdoing. Before the NCAA finished its investigation, the university and Sampson agreed to a separation agreement that terminated the employment agreement, and the university paid him a $750,000 settlement and recorded his agreement to resign (Separation Agreement, 2008). As a supplement to this agreement, both the university and Sampson agreed to release all potential legal claims against each other related to his employment at Indiana University.

Because of the strength of employment contracts of most coaches, universities find it difficult to fire them. Jim O'Brien was hired as the head basketball coach at Ohio State University for the 1997–1998 season. After several amendments, his contract paid him an annual salary of approximately $800,000 until 2007. According to his contract, he could only be terminated for cause as provided in section 5.1:

> Termination for Cause—Ohio State may terminate this agreement at any time for cause, which, for the purposes of this agreement, shall be limited to the occurrence of one or more of the following:
>
> a. a material breach of this agreement by Coach, which Coach fails to remedy to OSU's reasonable satisfaction, within a reasonable time period, not to exceed thirty (30) days, after receipt of a written notice from Ohio State specifying the act(s), conduct or omission(s) constituting such breach;
>
> b. a violation by Coach . . . of applicable law, policy, rule or regulation of the NCAA or the Big Ten Conference which leads to a "major" infraction investigation by the NCAA or the Big Ten Conference and which results in a finding by the NCAA or the Big Ten Conference of lack of institutional control over the men's basketball program or which results in Ohio State being sanctioned by the NCAA or the Big Ten Conference. (*O'Brien v. The Ohio State University*, 2007, ¶ 15)

In June 2004 the university fired O'Brien because it found that he had violated NCAA rules in 1998 by providing a $6,000 loan to a Serbian basketball player. O'Brien argued that he gave the money to the player to help his family, not to recruit him to play for the university. The player, Aleksander Radojevic, was a 7-foot 3-inch (221 cm) center who eventually played for the NBA's Utah Jazz.

Radojevic was eventually ruled ineligible to participate in university basketball because he had played professionally in Europe.

The university had the option to terminate O'Brien without cause; but if it did so, section 5.2 of the contract would come into play and the university would owe O'Brien the majority of his salary for the full term of his contract. In February 2006 O'Brien sued the university, claiming that his termination was in violation of the just cause provision of his contract. The court agreed, finding that O'Brien's conduct was not a material breach of his employment contract, so the school could not terminate him (*O'Brien v. The Ohio State University*, 2006). The court then awarded O'Brien $2.5 million under the termination-without-cause provision of his contract. The school appealed but lost again (*O'Brien v. The Ohio State University*, 2007). After reviewing the factors for material breach used by the trial court, the appellate court concluded that the trial court's finding that O'Brien did not materially breach his contract was consistent with the evidence provided.

What can be learned from the Sampson and O'Brien situations? Universities, lawyers, and sport managers must draft coaching contracts carefully and must understand how they apply in every situation. As the Ohio Court of Appeals said in *O'Brien*,

> OSU was the drafting party. OSU is not lacking in sophistication, and has only been prejudiced as a result of being held to its own bargain. OSU entered into this agreement with O'Brien having more-than-adequate knowledge and awareness of the risks and liabilities appurtenant to competing in NCAA Division I university sports. The Radojevic matter was not the first problem to hit the OSU campus. The tradition

and legacy of OSU and its sports team, however, has survived, and will continue to do so. (2007, p. 95)

Game and Event Contracts

In planning games and events for sport organizations, sport managers may also come across many contracts related specifically to the event itself. Game contracts are entered into to facilitate an individual game or contest between two sport organizations (i.e., athletes, teams, clubs, associations) (McMillen, 2007). Sport managers who work for sport facilities must take great care in entering into these contracts when scheduling games at a certain facility, because such scheduling will affect the ability to host any other events at the facility. Many considerations come into play when game contracts are developed, including the date and time of the event; ability to use and display the trademarks, names, and logos of the organizations competing; television and radio rights; travel expenses; and security and concessions.

Event-specific contracts, although similar to game contracts, may relate less to hosting a particular game and more to hosting an overall sporting event like the Super Bowl or a combination of events like the NCAA basketball tournament (McMillen, 2007). An event contract may include a game contract along with agreements related to the facility lease, concessions, corporate sponsorships, marketing, and television or other media contracts. Figure 5.4 is a hypothetical contract that includes many of the clauses seen in a typical event contract, such as the host's responsibility for planning the event, printing programs, providing meeting space, providing the necessary ticket sellers and vendors, and providing the exact financial arrangement and term for the agreement.

Waivers

Another type of sport contract is a **waiver**. Sport organizations often use waivers to protect themselves and their business from the financial effects of lawsuits that might occur when people are injured at an event or facility. A waiver is a contract between the sport organization and the participant; it is signed before participation in a sporting event. Waivers are especially important in recreational and club sports and in health and fitness organizations because the organization may not be able to withstand payments for injuries that could occur at its facility.

The waiver must meet the essential elements of a contract to be valid. These elements were discussed previously in this chapter but are provided here again in the context of waivers. To have a valid and enforceable contract (waiver), one that will legally bind the parties to an agreement, a valid offer and acceptance must be present. As such, a contract represents an exchange. It is an agreement to *offer* a product, service, or experience that requires *acceptance* of the terms of that offer. With a waiver, there is an offer to provide a sport experience (the offer to allow a person to participate) in exchange for an acceptance of the terms of the waiver (an agreement to absolve the sport organization from liability for injuries that she suffers as a result of participation). As you recall, the thing of value that is exchanged is called *consideration*. The consideration in waiver agreements is somewhat different from ordinary contracts for the sale of goods, for example, in which tangible objects are exchanged (e.g., money for a car). With waivers, the consideration is intangible: the exchange of a right (to participate) for a promise (not to hold the sport organization liable for injury).

Two overriding concepts form the basis for an enforceable waiver: fairness and

FIGURE 5.4 Sample Event Contract

National Association of Athletics: 2007 and 2008 NAA Men's and Women's Swimming National Championships

AGREEMENT

The National Association of Athletics (hereinafter referred to as the "NAA") and the Community College District (hereinafter referred to as the "Host") agree to the following conditions relative to the organization, management and administration of the 2007 and 2008 NAA Men's and Women's Swimming National Championships (the "Championships") to be held at the College Natatorium, March 2–5, 2008.

I. APPROVAL AND ACKNOWLEDGEMENTS

A. The NAA hereby approves College as the official host of the Championships. The Championships shall consist of those individuals and relay teams that meet the required qualification standards. The official schedule and time shall be mutually agreed upon by the Host and the NAA.

B. The Championships shall be conducted under the direct control and supervision of NAA, including implementation of policies established by the NAA Swimming Association (the "NSA"). Policies regarding format of the Championships are subject to change by the NAA Council (the "NC") and the NSA. The NAA shall approve the designation of the Host's Championships coordinator, who shall work with the NAA national administrator in organizing and conducting the Championships.

C. Corporations with business interests beyond the local area of the Championships site shall not be solicited for financial support without the prior written approval of the NAA. Further, no business or corporations shall be identified or receive recognition as a title sponsor of the Championships without prior written approval from the NAA.

D. Alcoholic beverages and tobacco products of any form shall not be advertised, sold, disbursed, or brought onto the site of the Championships.

E. The Host shall honor all NAA credentials issued to authorized player, coaches, officials, and media for admittance to the Championships. NAA membership cards presented will be honored for a complimentary ticket to the Championships.

F. The NAA, in consultation with the Host, shall be responsible for any and all negotiations for radio and television broadcast rights. Any Internet broadcast or website by the Host must be approved in writing by the NAA.

G. The name National Association of Athletics, initials NAA, logo, and other NAA symbols and insignia (the "NAA Marks") are the exclusive property of the NAA. The Host is awarded limited rights and privileges in using the NAA Marks to promote, advertise, and market the Championships.

(continued)

II. RESPONSIBILITIES OF THE PARTICIPATING INSTITUTIONS

A. The participating institutions shall pay the established entry fees, which must accompany the official entry form, made payable to the Host. Entry fees shall be $5.00 per individual for each event entered and $20.00 for each relay entry.

B. Participating institutions shall pay for the cost of transportation, housing, and meals (with the exception of the Championship banquet) in route to and from, and while at the Championships. All teams must stay at the assigned hotel.

C. Participating teams shall attend and participate in the Championships Banquet and any awards presentations as deemed necessary by the NAA.

III. NAA RESPONSIBILITIES

A. The NAA, in cooperation with the Host, shall coordinate and administer the Championships, including, but not limited to, the qualification of individuals and teams and schedule of events. The NAA Men's and Women's Swimming Rules Committee shall be responsible for hearing protests and enforcing rules of competition.

B. The NAA shall order and ship all approved awards for the Championships, but all costs of the relating to such awards shall be the financial obligation of the Host.

C. The NAA shall print and provide credentials for use by participants, coaches, authorized media, and officials.

D. The NAA shall be responsible for the cost of printing and postage of all entry information and related materials.

E. The NAA and the Host shall have final approval of the agenda for the Championship Banquet. The Championship Banquet agenda shall be carefully controlled by the Host and the NAA in regard to time.

IV. HOST RESPONSIBILITIES

A. The Host shall provide the Natatorium for practice and meet competition March 2–5, 2008. This includes use of the pool for practice a day before the Championships. Use of the pool complex shall include all facilities and equipment necessary to administer the Championships, including, but not limited to, spectator seating, lights, scoreboards, computerized timing system, computer program for all heating and seeding, public address system, parking lots, restrooms, dressing rooms, meeting rooms, ticket booth, concession and souvenir stands, press room, team benches, signage, water coolers, and all normal preparation and maintenance of such facility.

B. The Host shall provide all Championships personnel necessary to conduct the Championships, including, but not limited to, ticket sellers and taker, adequate security or police, concession vendors, maintenance crew, hospitality workers, public address announcers, and computer operators.

C. The Host shall provide travel, housing, and meals for the Championship officials and Head Official. Officials' ground travel shall be reimbursed at the rate established by the Internal Revenue Service at the time of the Championships. The NAA in consultation with the Host will select and assign the Head Official. The Host in consultation with the Head Official will select and assign the official starters, meet referees and certified officials necessary for the supervision and conduct of the Championships, including, but not limited to, timers, turn inspectors, stroke and turn judges, and diving judges from the local swimming and diving officials association.

D. The Host shall provide a press room and financial support for travel and housing for one (1) media representative. The site shall be equipped with the necessary equipment to meet the standards and approval for the NAA. Specific needs include: three (3) telephone lines, one (1) high speed copier, one (1) on-line work station with Internet access and an e-mail account for use by NAA authorized personnel, one (1) laser printer, and one (1) facsimile (fax) machine.

E. The Host shall provide the Championships Vendor with a covered area to market and sell NAA merchandise at the site, hotel headquarters, banquet area, and registration area. Each sales area shall be equipped with tables, chairs, electricity, and a phone line. The Host shall provide a sales staff (normally two (2) full-time equivalents) to market and sell merchandise at the locations previously listed. In exchange for providing the aforementioned sales areas and staff, the Host shall receive ten percent (10%) of gross sales (total receipts less any applicable taxes) in such areas.

F. The Host shall provide travel, housing, and meals or meal expenses up to $25.00 per diem for a maximum of two (2) NAA representatives.

G. The Host shall provide a certified trainer to cover all sessions of the Championship including the operation and administration of training room. The trainer must be NAA approved.

H. The Host shall have medical assistance reasonably available for the Championships to include a physician and an ambulance service on-site or on-call throughout the Championships, through volunteers provided by the Sports Foundation. Onsite medical equipment should include, but is not limited to, AEDs (automated external defibrillators), backboards, crutches, splints and braces, and biohazard containers. The Host shall not be held responsible for any errors, omissions, or other acts of any personnel supplied pursuant to this section or for any damages resulting from use of the medical equipment (including but not limited to malfunction).

I. The Host shall be responsible for arranging an opening banquet for all players, coaches, and Championships officials.

J. The Host shall negotiate the best possible rates for team housing to include a room block of not less than 150. Rooms should be double-double, non-smoking. The Host shall provide complimentary hotel rooms for the NAA representatives.

(continued)

K. The Host shall provide the necessary meeting room space during the course of the event at the event headquarters hotel or on campus. These rooms shall be used for coaches' business meeting, diving coaches' meeting, rules committee meeting, executive committee meeting, and pre-Championships general coaches' meeting. The Host shall provide meeting and hospitality space at the competition venue as deemed necessary by the NAA.

L. The Host shall produce the championships souvenir program in consultation with the NAA and shall be responsible for all expenses related to printing of all programs.

M. The Host shall print and provide an informational press packet for the media covering the event. The NAA and the Host will work together to discuss what information will need to be provided to the media.

N. The Host shall be responsible for the printing of event tickets and the management of all Championships admissions. NOTE: Approval of the copy for the front and backside of Championships tickets and the cost of admissions must be approved by the NAA Administrator.

O. The Host shall be responsible for the advance publicity and promotion of the Championships to include any paid advertising, posters, flyers, and related expenses.

   A. The Host shall be responsible for all expenses related directly to the administration of the Championships, including, but not limited to, printing, postage, telephone calls, and supplies.

   B. The Host shall provide general commercial liability insurance for the event at a minimum of $1,000,000 per occurrence, naming the NAA as an additionally insured party. Host shall provide the NAA with a copy of said coverage thirty (30) days before the event.

   C. The Host shall provide the official photographer and photography services to include reproduction, sales, and distribution covering the banquet, Championships, and awards ceremonies.

V. FINANCIAL AGREEMENT

A. The Host shall submit an estimated budget of income and expenses to the NAA at least sixty (60) days before the beginning of the Championships.

B. A financial report of all income and expenses related to the Championships shall be sent to the NAA within sixty (60) days of the conclusion of the Championships.

C. The Host shall submit an economic impact, attendance, and room pick-up report to the NAA National Office within sixty (60) days of the conclusion of the Championship.

D. The NAA Administrator will invoice the Host immediately following each of the Championships for the expenses incurred by the NAA that are the financial responsibility of the Host under this Agreement.

E. The Host shall be responsible for all authorized Championships expenses and shall have the right to retain all income derived from the Championships. If the event expenses exceed income, the Host shall be responsible for the deficit. If the event income exceeds expenses, the net income shall be divided between the Host and the NAA on a 50-50 percentage basis.

VI. LENGTH OF AGREEMENT

A. The length of this Agreement shall cover the 2008 NAA Men's and Women's Swimming National Championships.

the ability of the person or organization to understand the terms of the waiver that they are signing. Factors that influence ability to understand the language of a waiver come from several sources, namely, the characteristics of the person agreeing to the terms of the waiver and the way that the waiver is written. What factors might make it difficult for someone to understand the terms of a waiver? One that probably comes to mind is the age of the person. Waivers signed by a minor (a person under the age of either 18 or 21, depending on the state) are unenforceable. The law uses the term *capacity* to describe the ability of a person to understand the terms of a contract. The perception is that a person younger than the state-mandated legal age of majority does not have the capacity to enter into a waiver and therefore should not be held to the contract. Other situations in which a person might lack the capacity to understand the terms of a waiver are intoxication and disability. Mental status can be influenced by health status and disability or by being under the influence of alcohol or drugs. Where a person cannot understand the terms of a waiver because of intoxication or disability, the waiver likely will not be enforceable and therefore will not offer protection from liability for the sport organization. Therefore, when implementing waivers, the sport manager needs to understand the mental state and age of the person signing the waiver.

A second issue that relates to the ability to understand a waiver is the way that the waiver is written. For example, a waiver written in confusing language or with legalese may be difficult for the average person to understand. The size and font of lettering should be easily readable. A waiver is an example of a contract in which the language is very important.

The fairness of the contract is also an overriding principle that governs the enforceability of waivers. The term *equal bargaining power* is often used in determining whether a waiver was fair between the contracting parties. This term means that one party should not be overwhelmed or unduly intimidated by the other party's status and power. Some large organizations and governments, for example, stand in positions where they have far superior bargaining power. A situation might arise in which one party stands in a position of having no choice but to accept the terms of a waiver, given the power that another party has over the first party. In these cases unequal bargaining power might be brought up as an argument against the enforceability of a waiver. Another issue of fairness involves whether a party has voluntarily entered into a waiver agreement. Waivers may be deemed unenforceable if one side is forced or tricked into signing the waiver. We should be free to enter contracts as we choose. Sport managers should be aware of situations in which people believe that they have lost their choice in entering into a waiver agreement.

Further, fairness may be an issue in which a sport organization attempts to avoid any liability in a waiver, even that amounting to acts of gross negligence. Most jurisdictions will not uphold waivers that attempt to relieve the organization from any form of liability. Waivers are generally intended to relieve the sport organization only of liability for ordinary negligence. So, when dealing with waivers, sport managers should be aware of the bargaining power of both parties, the characteristics of the person signing the waiver, and the clarity of the language of the waiver. All these considerations (those relevant to contracts) should be taken into account and discussed with a competent attorney when waivers are drafted and administered.

A waiver clause for a participant in a swimming meet might look like this:

> In consideration of the acceptance of this entry, I, for myself and for my executors, administrators, and assigns, waive and release any and all claims against United States Swimming, U.S. Masters Swimming, Wisconsin Swimming Inc., the Swim Club, and any of their staffs, officers, officials, volunteers, sponsors, agents, representatives, successors, or assigns and agree to hold them harmless from any claims or losses, including but not limited to claims for negligence for any injuries or expenses that I may incur at this meet or while traveling to and from this meet. I am a bona fide amateur athlete, am registered with United States Swimming and U.S. Masters

Swimming, or am swimming and competing independent of any affiliation and am eligible to compete in all events I have entered.

Lease Agreements

A lease agreement is a contract entered into between a facility owner (lessor) and a party that wants to use the facility for a defined amount of time (lessee). Under any sport lease agreement, the party that owns a facility (lessor) promises to allow another party to use the facility (lessee) for some designated amount of time in consideration for some form or payment, whether the lessee makes actual financial payments in the form of rent or whether the lessee promises to use the particular facility and no other facility for the duration of the lease contract.

In professional sports, the lessor often is not simply one entity; instead, it is the community itself and some other organization (usually known as a *facility district*) created to assist in the funding of the facility. Therefore, anyone working for the team must understand the exact nature of the lessor to understand the rights that the team has under the lease agreement. For example, the Green Bay Packers entered into a lease agreement with the Green Bay–Brown County Professional Football Stadium District and the City of Green Bay (joint owners of Lambeau Field and the property that the field stands on) to allow the Packers to lease "the entirety of the Site and the Existing Facility, together with the rights appurtenant to the Site and the Existing Facility, and all of the City's Ownership Interest in and to the Lambeau Field Complex" (Lease Agreement, 2001).

Professional team facility leases have many detailed and unique provisions that define the relationship between the parties.

The New York Yankees lease Yankee Stadium from New York City.

These lease agreements often run hundreds of pages and include many subagreements or separate agreements that lay out funding, development schedules, construction agreements, facility management agreements, and other contracts important to understanding the entire lease agreement.

Although the media often focus on the enormous public investment in sport facilities, teams and sport organizations from the lowest level to the professional leagues often make commitments under the lease agreement. These commitments are the consideration necessary to create an enforceable contract. Often this consideration is in the form of rental payments. For example, the Milwaukee Brewers Baseball Club agreed to pay rent in the following amounts to the Southeast Wisconsin Professional Baseball Park District during the 30-year term of their lease (Amended and Restated Lease Agreement, 2004):

Lease Year	Annual Rent
1–10	$900,000
11–20	$1,200,000
21–30	$1,208,401

Annual rental payments are in addition to most teams' agreements to pay the costs associated with maintenance, operations, security, and facility improvements. As a result, most teams promise to make significant financial commitments within the lease agreement.

One of the most interesting provisions of a modern lease agreement is a direct answer to the franchise relocation issues discussed in the chapter about antitrust (chapter 10). City administrators worry that teams will leave their facilities during the term of the lease agreement. As a result, many lease agreements contain clauses that relate to retaining the team in the event that it attempts to break the lease agreement. These provisions are typically called *nonrelocation agreements* because by entering into these contracts, the team agrees that it will not relocate to another facility during the term of the lease agreement. The Amended and Restated Lease Agreement (2004) contains a separate agreement (although acknowledged within the full lease agreement) that makes clear that both parties encouraged each other to enter into the nonrelocation agreement:

> E.   As an inducement to the Team to continue to cause the Milwaukee Brewers to play their Baseball Home Games in the City, the District, the State and the Team have agreed to cause the "Stadium Project" and "Infrastructure" . . . to be constructed pursuant to that certain Construction Administration Agreement. . . .

> F.   As an inducement to the District and the State to assist the Team in causing the Stadium Project and Infrastructure to be constructed, the Team has agreed to enter into this Non-Relocation Agreement. (Amended and Restated Non-Relocation Agreement, 2004, p. 1)

Under the nonrelocation agreement, the team agreed to play all its home games for each season at Miller Park. If the team breaks this agreement, the state and ballpark district can immediately terminate the lease, go to court to stop the team from leaving the stadium, and force the team to fulfill its obligations under the lease.

Seat License

Another interesting type of facility contract that has become important in university and professional sports is a seat license. Often referred to as a *personal seat license*, *permanent seat license*, *seat deposit*, or *PSL*, a seat license provides a buyer with the option to purchase tickets for a small fee. The license does not pay for the tickets or guarantee that certain seats or other options will be available. Instead, by paying the seat license fee, the purchaser is given some level of priority and the ability to buy tickets before other purchasers.

Many professional sports teams' season ticket packages now include seat deposits that act in the same way and must be paid above and beyond the normal price for the tickets. Universities also have begun to incorporate seat licenses and deposits within their season-ticket selling schemes. Teams and schools create seat licenses to raise funds that are often used for renovations or facility construction. As long as demand for the particular tickets is high, fans have continued to pay these fees. For example, the Green Bay Packers recently added a deposit to their season-ticket package to help the team pay for the costs associated with rising player salaries and the renovation of Lambeau Field. In 2013 new season-ticket holders, many of whom were placed in one of the 7,000 seats added by that year's stadium renovation, had to pay seat user fees of $2,100 for a seven-game package or $900 for a three-game packages (Imig, 2013). Few have complained. Packers' season tickets have been sold out since 1960, so if fans want to keep their tickets, they have to pay the seat deposit.

Contract Law Issues

With any contract, issues can arise, from the contract being breached by one party to a court having to interpret the contract to assess damages or remedies in a particular situation. This section provides an overview of these issues.

When one party does not meet its obligations under a contract, that party may be found to have breached the contract. The Parole Evidence Rule and the Statute of Frauds are common law rules that assist in understanding the contract when it is breached. In addition, the nonbreaching party can seek several remedies to compensate for its loss.

Parole Evidence Rule

The **Parole Evidence Rule** provides that when contracting parties express their full intentions in writing, no other evidence can be introduced in a court of law that contradicts the terms of the written agreement. If one party breaches a written contract, the Parole Evidence Rule stops either party from looking to prior written or oral statement that might contradict the terms of the written agreement. Simply put, the Parole Evidence Rule prevents litigants from asserting facts that existed before contract formation that are inconsistent with or contradict the existing written contract.

Sport managers should be cautious when material terms or conditions are omitted from a written agreement, because a court may view the written agreement as fully integrated, meaning that the parties intended the written agreement to be final and complete. If the contract is viewed as fully integrated, then a court will not hear any evidence pertaining to any material terms or conditions that are not included in the original written agreement. In contract negotiations, many drafts may be circulated among the parties before a final written contract is completed. Each party must ensure that the final contract represents exactly what the party bargained for.

Statute of Frauds

Common law usually does not require contracts to be in written form. But when parties enter into an oral contract, problems may arise involving ambiguity, mistakes, or even fraud, and the common law allows parties to assume these risks for many types of agreements. In addition, some contracts must be in written form according to the legal principle known as the **Statute of Frauds**. According to this principle, three types of contracts must be in written form: (1) contracts concerning the sale, mortgage, or lease of an interest in land; (2) contracts that cannot be performed within 1 year of their making; and (3) contracts for the sale of goods that have a value in excess of $500. These three types of contracts are most relevant to sport managers. Accordingly, lease agreements for stadiums and arenas, long-term coach or player contracts, and contracts for sport apparel that exceed $500 are examples of contracts that require a written document to be enforced.

Remedies

When a party breaches the terms of a legally enforceable contract, the party that suffers from the breach can seek compensation from the courts. The compensation awarded by courts of law for breach of contract is called damages. Damages are awarded in contract cases to put the aggrieved party in an economic position identical to that which the party would have been in had the contract been performed.

Compensatory Damages

Compensatory damages consist of money necessary to make up for whatever monetary loss a party has suffered attributable to the breach of contract. For instance, if an athlete has agreed to pay an agent an hourly rate for work that the agent does and then the athlete breaches the agency contract to sign with another agent, the agent could sue and ask for compensation equal to the per-hour rate in the contract for the time of the agent's work.

Consequential Damages

Consequential damages are monetary relief for a party's economic losses that were caused indirectly by the original breach of contract. In the example of the athlete who signs with another agent, if this action caused other athletes to leave the original agent, the agent may sue asking for consequential damages relating to this extra loss.

Liquidated Damages

Liquidated damages are specific amounts of damages that the parties agreed to within the contract itself. When the parties negotiate the details of a contract, they agree to an amount that must be paid by the breaching party. This provision has become standard within facility lease agreements, because cities want to protect themselves in the event that a team breaches the lease agreement. For example, the former Charlotte Hornets' lease agreement to play in the Charlotte Coliseum included a liquidated damages clause stating that if the team

> fails or refuses to play its Team Home Games in the Coliseum . . . [the team] shall pay to Authority as liquidated damages the sum of $3 million for each Basketball Season or portion thereof in which Team Home Games are not played in the Coliseum as required by this Agreement. (Miller & Anderson, 2001, pp. 363–364)

Similar provisions can be found in many other types of sport contracts. These provisions are important when there is no remedy or other amount of damages that the nonbreaching party will find sufficient to compensate for its loss. Therefore, if you believe that the loss of a team, coach, or high-profile event will cause significant damage above what a court will be able to reimburse you for in a breach of contract action, you should consider including a liquidated damages clause within your contract.

Specific Performance

At times, no amount of monetary damages will be sufficient to compensate the non-breaching party. In these situations, the nonbreaching party may seek to have the breaching party forced to uphold its obligations under the contract. In these rare situations, courts can issue an injunction to order parties to carry out their contractual duties; this remedy is called **specific performance**. Specific performance provisions are rare. In sport, they are typically applied only in situations that involve unique items, not in employment contracts involving athletes or coaches. An interesting situation involving specific performance can be found in the Granting a Specific Performance Claim sidebar; in this case, the court granted the plaintiffs specific performance claim, giving them tickets to the Sugar Bowl.

Duty to Mitigate

A party that is harmed by another party's breach of contract is under a duty to mitigate, or reduce, its damages. The duty to mitigate damages prevents wronged parties from doing nothing while damages accumulate. Courts enforce the duty to mitigate by limiting a party's ability to recover for damages that were caused by a breach of contract if the party that was harmed could have prevented the harm without undue risk, burden, or humiliation (*Restatement [Second] of Contracts*, § 350, 1990).

For example, say that Marcus is the head groundskeeper for a professional baseball stadium. Marcus hires Billy's company to replace the irrigation system for the sta-

Granting a Specific Performance Claim

Levert v. University of Illinois (2003)

In *Levert v. University of Illinois* (2003), a group of people ordered tickets through the University of Illinois Athletic Ticket Office for the January 1, 2002, Nokia Sugar Bowl Game in New Orleans, Louisiana. This Sugar Bowl game featured Louisiana State University (LSU) versus the University of Illinois (UI).

Tickets were a hot commodity for LSU fans because the Sugar Bowl game was the first Bowl Championship Series game for LSU and was going to be played in LSU's home state. The plaintiffs, who were LSU fans, thought that they might improve their chances of securing tickets by attempting to purchase some of the 15,000 tickets that had been allotted to the University of Illinois. The Illinois ticket office began selling these tickets during December 2001, and each plaintiff ordered a number of tickets through a website and by calling the ticket office.

For the online transactions, the plaintiffs alleged that the Illinois ticket office charged each purchaser's card and then sent a confirmation e-mail. In at least one telephone transaction, a ticket office representative assured the caller that tickets would be mailed.

Several days later, the Illinois ticket office informed the plaintiffs that it would not honor their ticket requests because of the high demand for Sugar Bowl tickets. The plaintiffs sued, asking the court to force the ticket office to give them the tickets.

The trial court ordered the University of Illinois to provide the plaintiffs with a designated number of Sugar Bowl tickets. The plaintiffs secured their tickets and were able to attend the game. This case provides an example of the use of specific performance in a sport setting where no substitute was available for the LSU fans to cheer for the team in the first Bowl Championship Series game.

---

dium. Billy's company does not perform the job as requested in the contract. Because of this, the sprinklers burst hours before a game, causing the field to collect water. Billy's crew is not on site, so they cannot stop the flooding. Marcus' stadium is now under a duty to mitigate the damages. Although the water collection was caused by a breach of contract by Billy's company, because Marcus and his employees did not take steps to prevent the field from flooding, a court will reduce the amount of damages that Marcus' stadium will be able to recover from Billy's company. A court will determine the point at which the stadium could have limited the harm and cap the recoverable amount at that point.

Alternative Dispute Resolution

Sport contracts are increasingly including clauses that focus on alternative dispute resolution (ADR) methods so that the parties involved can attempt to solve their disputes without going to court. Parties turn to ADR to reduce the costs, in time and money, of litigation.

Several forms of ADR are used. **Arbitration** is a process in which a neutral third party (the arbitrator or panel of arbitrators) renders a decision after a hearing at which both parties are given a chance to be heard and to present evidence. The value of arbitration as a form of ADR is that arbitration decisions are typically final and binding on the parties and can be enforced by a court.

Perhaps the most well-known form of arbitration in sport involves athletes in international competitions. Each international federation has agreed that all disputes involving its sport must be submitted to arbitration before the Court of Arbitration for Sport (CAS), an international arbitral body based in Switzerland. Each national governing body that regulates a sport within a particular country agrees to follow the international federation rules as part of its membership in the Olympic movement. Athletes who participate in international sport for that country agree to follow the rules of the national governing body and therefore must submit any disputes related to their competition to CAS. CAS is not a typical court; it is made up of hundreds of arbitrators who form panels that hear and resolve disputes. Lists of arbitrators, the guidelines for arbitration before CAS, and recent arbitration decisions can all be found at www.tas-cas.org.

According to the contract they sign when they agree to join the national governing body in their particular country, athletes must first submit disputes related to international competitions to arbitration. For example, Floyd Landis lost his Tour de France title after appealing the results of a drug test. The CAS panel that heard his dispute found that although some discrepancies occurred in the testing used on Landis, he still violated the international doping standards (*USADA v. Landis*, 2007).

Another form of ADR is mediation. **Mediation** (sometimes called *facilitation*) is a private, informal process in which a neutral third party (the mediator) helps the parties in a dispute reach an agreement. Although the mediator can help the parties reach a decision, the mediator's decision is not binding on the parties. Instead, the parties are responsible for upholding the agreement. Mediation provisions are less common in sport, although some sport leases have mediation clauses that allow the parties to submit disputes to mediation. CAS allows mediation to be used in limited ways.

Some sport lease agreements contain provisions that allow mediation and arbitration. For example, the Carolina Hurricanes' lease agreement mandates that the parties must initially attempt to negotiate to settle any dispute. If they are unable to come to a resolution, they must submit the dispute to mediation. If they are unable to settle the dispute within 60 days using mediation, they must submit the dispute to arbitration (Miller & Anderson, 2001, pp. 353–354).

LEARNING AIDS

Summary

Sport managers deal with many kinds of contracts during their careers. Understanding employment agreements, collective bargaining agreements, and endorsement and event contracts is essential to protect the sport manager and the sport organization.

All contracts must include a valid offer, acceptance, and consideration. Although oral contracts are legally enforceable, sport managers are advised to prepare written contracts that include all the details of the agreement to protect themselves and their organizations in the event the contract is disputed.

Most sport contracts have common features. Even student-athletes sign contracts in the letters of intent and scholarship letters they enter into with a university. Professional athletes often sign contracts in the form of endorsement deals, uniform player contracts, and agreements with athlete agents. Coaches at the university and professional levels enter into contracts with escalating salaries. Every sporting event involves contracts: the agreement detailing the event itself, the lease agreement for the facility, and the seat license agreement for the tickets that customers purchase. Waivers are also common within sport as event organizers attempt to protect themselves from liability.

Business relationships often go sour, and a contract may be breached. In these situations, you may want to seek damages or other remedies, including asking the court for specific performance of the breaching party's obligations under the contract. Contracts are increasingly including alternative dispute resolution provisions that call for arbitration or mediation as alternatives to lengthy and expensive litigation.

Discussion Questions

1. Explain what is meant by the term *capacity* and the conditions in which a person might be held to lack legal capacity to enter into a contract.

2. Is a gift considered valid consideration in a contract? Why or why not?

3. Explain the difference between a bilateral contract and a unilateral contract; give an example in the sport context.

4. Explain the Statute of Frauds and provide a hypothetical example in the sport context.

5. Describe several key issues that arise when a college coach's contract is breached.

6. What is the purpose and function of a waiver? Is it "worth the paper it is written on"? Why or why not?

7. Provide a hypothetical example of how the remedy of specific performance might apply in the sport context.

Use of a Waiver for a Sporting Event

Samantha Slowpitch, a sophomore transfer student at Topten University, was a skilled softball player who truly loved the game. The first thing that Samantha did when she arrived at school was to form a coed intramural softball team from among people who came highly recommended as good players. The long-awaited first game finally came, and Samantha and her team showed up early to warm up. During warm-ups, an intramural department staff member approached Samantha and told her that she and her teammates needed to sign up. She was handed a double-sided piece of paper with spaces for player names and ID numbers on one side. At the bottom of the page, in 10-point font, was the statement "Exculpatory agreement on reverse side." Samantha signed her name and glanced at the back side of the paper. At the top, it read "Waiver" followed by what she later recalled as "something that looked like a waiver." She recalled bits and pieces of the document such as "hold harmless," "acts of negligence," "occurring during the game of softball," "in consideration for," and some reference to "turf" and "thrown or batted balls." She did not read the document carefully, given that she was excited about playing her first game and didn't want to waste time reading a full page of small print.

After signing her name on the roster side of the paper, Samantha handed the roster to the rest of the team for them to sign. No other members of the team read the waiver language on the reverse side of the paper. Samantha and her team then took the field for their first game of the semester. They had the game well in hand, winning 6 to 1, when Samantha ran to catch a routine fly ball. As she was running toward the ball, Samantha stepped into a six-inch-deep (15 cm deep) depression in the turf and severely injured her ankle. The depression was caused by a utility truck that had parked there earlier in the day to repair a damaged outdoor flood light atop a pole in the outfield. Samantha was carried off the field and taken to the hospital, where it was determined that she would not be able to play softball for the remainder of the year. Samantha was severely upset and emotionally distraught. In addition, her ankle was broken and some ligament damage had occurred. Samantha sued Topten University and the intramural department for negligence for failing to maintain the turf in proper condition. The university and intramural department defended their case based solely on the waiver.

Employment Law

Chapter Objectives

After reading this chapter, you will know the following:

- Key legal issues in employment for sport managers

- Relevance of the doctrine of employment at will

- Primary issues in employment discrimination

- Key legal issues relevant to sexual harassment

- The main elements of federal employment legislation

Case Studies in Sport Law Connection

Check out the following case studies related to this chapter in the accompanying e-book, *Case Studies in Sport Law, Second Edition* (Pittman, Spengler, & Young, 2016):

Burkey v. Marshall County Board of Education

Hegener v. Board of Education of City of Chicago

Moore v. University of Notre Dame

Perdue v. City University of New York

Stanley v. University of Southern California

Employment law encompasses a wide range of issues concerning people and their relationships at work. The work environment in sport may refer to traditional jobs such as managing staff and facilities or planning events, but it also refers to athletes' jobs. Lawsuits arise over many situations in the employment context: An employee is fired or passed over for promotion, a qualified job applicant is not hired, an employee is sexually harassed while on the job, or an employee injures herself or others while on the job. Employment cases in sport are often the subject of much commentary, debate, and legal action. The issues discussed in this chapter are diverse and useful from a practical standpoint in that they pose various situations in which employment-related issues may arise. In this chapter, we discuss the employment relationship, discrimination, sexual harassment, and federal employment laws.

Employment Relationship

A good starting point for discussing employment issues in sport is the employment relationship. Parties involved in a legal conflict must be able to prove that an employment relationship exists. Employees, as agents of an organization, have certain rights and

obligations when acting on behalf of the organization. For example, a sport manager employed by a sports team has the authority to enter into a contract with a sports equipment company to buy helmets for the team. An organization might be liable for torts committed by its players, such as situations involving player–player and player–fan violence at sport events, if those actions were committed within the scope of employment. State and federal employment laws provide certain rights to employees and obligations to employers, but an employment relationship must be proved. These laws govern important issues such as Social Security payments, insurance plans, withholding taxes, workers compensation, unemployment compensation, workplace safety, and employment discrimination (e.g., the Civil Rights Act of 1964). For those and other reasons, determining whether an employment relationship exists is important. After this determination is made, the topics discussed later in this chapter become highly relevant.

The employment relationship is usually formed by contract between an employer and an employee. The contract spells out the nature of the employment along with the rights and responsibilities of the parties (e.g., salary, work duties, benefits). Situations arise, however, in which there is no express agreement in the form of an employment contract and the employment relationship is not clear. In thinking about the employment relationship, ask yourself whether a university scholarship athlete should be considered an employee of a university.

At the time of this writing, athletes playing for university teams were not considered employees under the law. Interestingly, an early case found otherwise. In 1953 the Colorado Supreme Court upheld a determination by the state Industrial Commission that a football player at the University of Denver was an employee within the meaning of the Colorado workers' compensation statute. The university was treating the athlete as an employee and therefore was responsible for providing workers' compensation for his football injuries. Not long afterward, however, the NCAA popularized and used the term *student-athlete*, and the tide turned against considering athletes to be employees. In 1983 a Michigan court held that student-athletes were not considered employees under the law (see the Athletes and the Employment Issue sidebar). Recent legal actions by Northwestern University football players and the National College Players Association, backed by the United Steelworkers union, seeking to unionize college athletes may result in employee status and collective bargaining status for college athletes.

The employment relationship is typically governed by the common law doctrine of **employment at will**. According to this doctrine, either the employer or employee may terminate the employment relationship at any time and for any reason. As with all legal doctrines, however, there are exceptions.

One important exception is that if an employment contract exists, the terms of that contract govern when and why an employee might be terminated. Also, when discrimination is the reason for terminating

an employee, something must be available to protect people from this unfair treatment. That *something* is state and federal law (statute). Certain laws, as discussed later in this chapter, prohibit an employer from firing an employee when a state or federal statute has been violated (e.g., when an employee has been fired in a discriminatory manner). Hiring and retention issues and the relevant laws that govern these matters are discussed next.

Discrimination

All sport managers have the job of hiring, promoting (or deciding not to promote), and firing employees, coaches, or players. The work goes beyond difficult and is often unpleasant when the manager must tell people that they didn't get the job, they don't deserve a promotion or a raise, or, worst of all, they are fired. The financial burden and associated stress on notice of termination can be devastating and difficult for individuals and families. Worse yet, some people are not hired, are fired, or are not promoted for subjective discriminatory reasons that are unethical and violate state or federal law. Most hiring, retention, and promotion decisions have the potential for actual or perceived discrimination. Consider the following hypothetical situation in the context of making employment decisions.

You own and operate a sport and fitness club. The club boasts a variety of services, from supervised sport instruction to personal fitness training and nutrition counseling. Your business has been in operation for more than a year, and membership has expanded rapidly. You have 20 employees on your payroll. Although you are enjoying the success of your business, you are also concerned about legal issues relevant to employment, particularly discrimination.

IN THE COURTROOM

Athletes and the Employment Issue

Coleman v. Western Michigan University (1983)

Coleman, a football player for Western Michigan University, was injured while playing football for the university. He received his scholarship for the entire year following his injury, but the scholarship was revoked the following fall because of "cutbacks in the university's scholarship program" (p. 36). He sued the school, claiming that he was an employee and, as such, was entitled to the rights and benefits of an employee. He wanted to keep his scholarship. Coleman argued that he was an employee as defined by the Michigan's Worker's Disability Compensation Act, in which an employee is defined as "every person in the service of another, under any contract of hire, express or implied" (p. 37).

The court applied the "economic reality" test to determine whether an employment relationship existed. Four factors were examined as a part of this test:

1. The proposed employer's right to control or dictate the activities of the proposed employee
2. The proposed employer's right to discipline or fire the proposed employee
3. The payment of "wages" and, particularly, the extent to which the proposed employee is dependent on the payment of wages or other benefits for his daily living expenses
4. Whether the task performed by the proposed employee was "an integral part of the proposed employer's business" (p. 38)

These factors would have to be considered together, as a whole, to determine whether an employment relationship was present. The court considered all these factors and determined that no employment relationship existed.

As for the first factor, although the university could control Coleman's actions on the field, the university had no more control over Coleman than it did over other students. This idea applied to discipline as well. As to the wages portion of the test, the court agreed that Coleman's scholarship constituted wages. "In return for his services as a football player, plaintiff received certain items of compensation which are measurable in money, including room and board, tuition and books" (p. 40). But as for the fourth factor, the court concluded that Coleman did not perform an integral part of the employer's business. Playing football, reasoned the court, was not an integral part of the university's business; rather, the business of the university was education. Taking all these factors into account, the court determined that no employment relationship existed between the university and Coleman.

Your full-time employees are a group of excellent people—3 Hispanic, 4 African American, 2 Asian American, and 11 Caucasian employees (9 are females, and 11 are males). All are of the age of majority; possess the requisite certifications, training, and skills; and are highly qualified for their jobs. Your work has increased to the point that you must hire an assistant manager to help with administrative duties and teach some of the sport and fitness classes. You have a diverse applicant pool in terms of age, gender, and race and ethnicity. You also posted a job announcement to hire someone to supervise and referee basketball league play at your facility; application for this position is now closed, and you have only three applicants. The only applicant who is qualified by way of experience and knowledge of the game uses a wheelchair for mobility. You have heard about federal laws that prohibit discrimination in matters of employment. Federal law recognizes several protected classes to which discrimination laws apply:

- Race, color, and national origin
- Gender
- Religion
- Age
- Disability

We now look at several employment discrimination issues, using this hypothetical example to walk us through the issues.

Title VII of the Civil Rights Act of 1964

The first three categories of protected classes (race, color, and national origin; gender; and religion) are offered protection from discrimination under the Civil Rights Act. **Title VII of the Civil Rights Act** and its amendments apply to governmental agencies, federal government employees, labor unions, and employers with 15 or more employees. Section 2000e defines employers to whom the law applies.

> The term "employer" means a person engaged in an industry affecting commerce who has fifteen or more employees for each working day in each of twenty or more calendar weeks in the current or preceding calendar year, and any agent of such a person, but such term does not include (1) the United States, a corporation wholly owned by the Government of the United States, an Indian tribe, or any department or agency of the District of Columbia subject by statute to procedures of the competitive service (as defined

in section 2102 of title 5), or (2) a bona fide private membership club (other than a labor organization) which is exempt from taxation under section 501(c) of title 26, except that during the first year after March 24, 1972, persons having fewer than twenty-five employees (and their agents) shall not be considered employers.

This law applies to our sport and fitness club, which, as you recall, has 20 employees. This law governs the first three categories listed: race, color, and national origin; gender; and religion. Your hiring decision with regard to applicants therefore must be made with respect to Title VII. As such, you should also know about the **Equal Employment Opportunity Commission (EEOC)**, the U.S. governmental agency that monitors compliance with Title VII. If one of your applicants is qualified and believes that he has been discriminated against in the hiring process, he would first file a claim with the EEOC. The EEOC would then decide whether to investigate the claim and take action. If not, the person may bring a lawsuit against you and the organization directly.

When you have a diverse applicant pool, an issue to avoid is a potential discrimination claim based on race, color, or national origin. Discrimination claims can be brought on the basis of either intentional or unintentional acts of the employer. Unintentional discrimination is termed **disparate-impact discrimination**. In this situation, the employer's workforce does not mirror the percentage of those in protected classes in the local labor market. You know that your policy on employment decisions does not discriminate against applicants on the basis of color, race, or national origin, given that the diversity of your workforce mirrors that in the local job market. In fact, your workforce is more diverse than the local labor market.

Decisions on hiring, promotion, and retention must be based solely on job-related qualifications and cannot reflect discriminatory practices. This point is the basic requirement in Title VII and is stated as follows:

Sec. 2000e-2. Unlawful Employment Practices

(a) Employer practices

It shall be an unlawful employment practice for an employer—

> (1) to fail or refuse to hire or to discharge any individual, or otherwise to discriminate against any individual with respect to his compensation, terms, conditions, or privileges of employment, because of such individual's race, color, religion, sex, or national origin; or

> (2) to limit, segregate, or classify his employees or applicants for employment in any way which would deprive or tend to deprive any individual of employment opportunities or otherwise adversely affect his status as an employee, because of such individual's race, color, religion, sex, or national origin.

Also, your personal ethics dictate that you treat all applicants equally and do not intentionally discriminate against anyone. Suppose, however, that a member of a protected class is not hired and argues that she has been discriminated against. If she believes that she has been intentionally discriminated against, she has to prove three things:

- She is a member of the protected class (e.g., by race, color, or national origin).
- She is qualified for the job.
- The job remained open or was offered to someone not in the protected class.

This type of discrimination (intentional discrimination) is termed **disparate-treatment discrimination**. If a case for disparate-treatment discrimination can be shown, the burden of proof rests on the business, which must defend its actions (i.e., you have to defend your actions). One type of defense is the **bona fide occupational qualification (BFOQ)** defense. This defense arises when a particular trait is necessary for a particular job (e.g., only females are hired for the job of female locker room attendant). Race, however, is not considered a BFOQ. But gender, as illustrated, might be considered a valid BFOQ.

Title VII also covers discrimination based on religion, another issue you want to know more about in relation to the hiring process. You understand that certain religions observe days of rest or days on which observers are prohibited from working. This circumstance could make it difficult to schedule work duties and cover sport and fitness classes. Under Title VII, however, you cannot base your decision to hire solely on these potential time conflicts when they stem from an applicant's sincerely held religious beliefs. The manager must reasonably accommodate the religious practices of employees. The exception would be when this accommodation places undue hardship on the functioning of the business.

You also have a concern regarding gender discrimination. To this point, you have hired an almost equal numbers of males and females. You made some of your female hires because of the need to hire an instructor for women's-only fitness and conditioning classes held in a private area of the facility. Your facility restricts some fitness classes to women because of high demand for this service. Female participants in these programs were unanimous in their desire to have a female instructor. Gender, in these instances, is essential to the job. Therefore, selecting only females for this

When hiring a new employee, at any level of sport, you need to understand the many areas of potential employee discrimination, including race, color and national origin, gender, religion, age, and disability.

hire was OK. But the assistant manager's position does not involve teaching the women's-only classes, and no other issue makes a particular gender essential to the job function. Therefore, applicants for this position cannot be discriminated against and selected on the basis of their gender. Your plans are to advertise the position and hire the most qualified person regardless of gender. See chapter 8 for further discussion of gender discrimination.

Affirmative Action

Besides making efforts to avoid discrimination, you have heard about affirmative action. **Affirmative action** is a proactive process whereby employers actively seek out, hire, and promote qualified people in protected groups. This approach is designed to reduce or eliminate discriminatory practices in hiring, promotion, and retention of employees by providing increased employment opportunities to people in protected classes, and to ensure equal opportunity in employment. The purpose of affirmative action is to eliminate or remedy the present effects of past discrimination. Although affirmative action is not a requirement under Title VII (and is not recognized in some states), you should consider affirmative action requirements when advertising and writing descriptions and applications for job positions. A sample affirmative action statement is shown in figure 6.1.

FIGURE 6.1   Sample Affirmative Action Statement

_____ (*your organization*) actively seeks and encourages nominations of and applications from individuals who are members of underrepresented groups.

_____ (*your organization*) is an equal provider of services and an equal opportunity employer—Civil Rights Act of 1964 and American with Disabilities Act 1990. We actively seek candidates from diverse backgrounds.

_____ (*your organization*) is an equal opportunity–affirmative action employer. Women, minorities, veterans, and people with disabilities are strongly encouraged to apply.

_____ (*your organization*) is committed to ensuring equal opportunity to all persons and does not discriminate on the basis of race, color, sex, religion, ancestry, national origin, age, applicable disability, or sexual orientation in its employment practices as required by Title IX of the Educational Amendment of 1972, section 504 of the Rehabilitation Act of 1973, the Americans with Disabilities Act, and other applicable statutes.

Another important issue with regard to affirmative action is the provision of advertisements (job position announcements) in publications, online sources, and venues specific to protected groups.

Age Discrimination in Employment

Most of your employees are young and fit, which is mainly a function of the types of applicants who were interested in working in a sport and fitness club. In addition, you are located in a university town, so most of your potential employees are university age. You should be aware of the federal law governing age discrimination. Enacted in 1967, the applicable law is the **Age Discrimination in Employment Act (ADEA)**. This law prohibits employment discrimination on the basis of age for people at least 40 years old. The law applies to businesses with 20 or more employees and whose activities influence interstate commerce. An employer to whom the law applies is defined as follows.

Sec. 630. Definitions. . . .

(b) The term "employer" means a person engaged in an industry affecting commerce who has twenty or more employees for each working day in each of twenty or more calendar weeks in the current or preceding calendar year: Provided, that prior to June 30, 1968, employers having fewer than fifty employees shall not be considered employers. The term also means (1) any agent of such a person, and (2) a State or political subdivision of a State and any agency or instrumentality of a State or a political subdivision of a State, and any interstate agency, but such term does not include the United States, or a corporation wholly owned by the Government of the United States.

Commerce is defined as follows:

> The term "commerce" means trade, traffic, commerce, transportation, transmission, or communication among the several States; or between a State and any place outside thereof; or within the District of Columbia, or a possession of the United States; or between points in the same State but through a point outside thereof.

The ADEA applies to organizations that are involved in interstate commerce. The fitness center advertises nationally (through the Internet), has members who cross the state line to participate in sport and fitness classes, and is accessible to the state and interstate highway system. As such, it is likely that the activities of the fitness center affect interstate commerce. The business also has 20 or more employees. Therefore, if a qualified applicant is 40 years old or older, you must ensure that no implication of discrimination occurs in the hiring process. This obligation is true for promotion and termination as well. A claim brought by someone who thought that he was being discriminated against would come either through the EEOC, as with other types of discrimination, or directly through a private lawsuit against the club.

Earlier, we discussed intentional and unintentional discrimination. Suppose that a 75-year-old man applied for the job of weight room supervisor, a job that would require him to spot the bench press and other heavy weight activities. A 25-year-old man was selected, and the 75-year-old man sued for discrimination. Suppose that the older man accused you of unintentional discrimination (disparate-impact discrimination), claiming that the club hired more young people to work in the weight room than other clubs in the local area. If the club required, as a condition of employment, that applicants be able to bench press at least 200 pounds (91 kg), then the club might raise the **business necessity** defense. This defense asserts that a hiring practice with a discriminatory effect is a business necessity. For example, the requirement of being able to bench press 200 pounds has had the effect of having younger people work in the weight room of the club. If the club could prove that a definite connection exists between job performance and the (legitimate) strength requirement, then the club would likely succeed in the business necessity defense.

An example of an age discrimination lawsuit in which the ADEA was at issue is *Moore v. University of Notre Dame* (1998). Moore, a 60-year-old football coach for the University of Notre Dame, was fired. He sued, among other things, for age discrimination under the ADEA. He found employment after his discharge, coaching at another school, but for less money. He sought certain remedies available under the ADEA, which included reinstatement (getting his job back), back pay (salary lost from Notre Dame while out of the job), and front pay. Front pay is

> a lump sum representing the discounted present value of the difference between the earnings an employee would have received in his old employment and the earnings he can be expected to receive in his present and future, and by hypothesis, inferior, employment. Front pay is awarded for a reasonable amount of time, until a date by which the plaintiff, using reasonable diligence, should have found comparable employment. (p. 900)

The court denied reinstatement but did award front pay, given that the coach used due diligence to find another job, along with the presumption that his chances of finding a job with comparable pay at his age were slim.

Discrimination Based on Disabilities

Besides having the preceding concerns, you seek fairness in the hiring process for the assistant manager and for the basketball referee. For both jobs, the applicable law is the **Americans with Disabilities Act of 1990 (ADA)**. The ADA was passed to prohibit, on a national scope, discrimination against people with disabilities (42 U.S.C. §§ 12101 et seq., 2008). The ADA is divided into seven parts, called titles, several of which are applicable to employment. The ADA furthers the protections provided by the Rehabilitation Act of 1973, which prohibits discrimination against people with disabilities by government agencies that receive federal funds (Rehabilitation Act of 1973, 219 U.S.C. § 794).

If someone believes that she has been intentionally discriminated against because of a disability, the process is similar to that for allegations of discrimination under the Civil Rights Act. The plaintiff must prove three things:

- She has a disability.
- She is qualified for the job.
- She was denied the job because of her disability.

Title I of the ADA applies to employees of sport organizations (with 15 or more employees) who are disabled and can demonstrate that they are otherwise qualified for the job. In other words, if they can show that they have the necessary skills, experience, and education and can perform the essential functions of their job with or without some form of accommodation to their disability, the employer cannot discriminate against them. In your hiring decision, you as an employer are under a legal obligation to make a reasonable effort to accommodate the work-related needs of an employee with disabilities. This accommodation requirement would apply to job applicants as well. The term **reasonable accommodation** means that an employer finds work responsibilities and environments that allow employees with disabilities to be successful in performing their job functions. Title I of the ADA applies to both job applicants and employees of sport organizations who have disabilities and can demonstrate that they are otherwise qualified for the job. If the person with a disability can show that he has the necessary skills, experience, and education and can perform the essential functions of the job with or without some form of accommodation to his disability, the employer cannot discriminate against him. In other words, the applicant must be qualified for the job. The employer must provide certain accommodations to allow the person to work as long as those accommodations do not force an undue burden on the employer.

For the assistant manager position in the fitness club, it might mean providing access to the basketball courts for the applicant who uses a wheelchair or technological assistance for the assistant manager in her use of computers or other electronic devices. Many types of accommodations are relatively simple and inexpensive to implement. In these situations, making accommodations is of prime importance.

For the basketball referee hire, an issue of concern is safety. A referee who officiates basketball games obviously must be able to move around the court. You are concerned that a person in a wheelchair might pose a safety hazard both to players and to himself. The ADA, however, requires accommodation and prohibits discrimination against people with disabilities. Concerns over the safety of participants (e.g., someone colliding with the wheelchair) must be weighed in light of the employment, participation, and accessibility requirements of the ADA. A person with a disability cannot be dismissed out of hand, and an employer cannot make blanket requirements such as never allowing wheelchairs on a basketball court under any conditions. Decisions must be made case by case. Some guidance is provided from *Anderson v. Little League Baseball Inc.* (see the Inclusion in Sport Activities sidebar), although the case involved a volunteer coach rather than an employee.

This case provides a good example of an application of the ADA in sport as well as an example concerning accommodation. In all employment decisions relevant to hiring, promotion, and retention, managers must be aware of and avoid potential discrimination.

The ADA might apply to employment in another context. Professional athletes make their living performing in their respective sports. In essence, their role as a professional athlete is their job. The ADA has been applied to professional sports when athletes have requested and required accommodations based on their disabilities. The claim is that without the accommodation, they are unable to participate, resulting in the loss of their job as a professional athlete.

Title III of the ADA bars discrimination against disabled people "in the full and equal enjoyment of the goods, services, facilities, privileges, advantages, or accommodations of any place of public accommodation by any person who owns, leases (or leases to), or operates a place of public accommodation" (Prohibition of Discrimination by Public Accommodations, 42 U.S.C. § 12182(a), 2008). The statute specifically includes gymnasiums, golf courses, and other places of exercise and recreation as places of accommodation covered under this part. Many forms of discrimination are banned under Title III. Perhaps most impor-

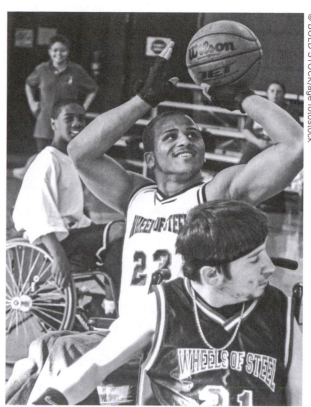

Sport facility managers must balance safety for referees and players along with requirements from the ADA on a case-by-case basis.

tant in connection to sport and recreational activities are barring people with disabilities from enjoying the goods and services of the place of public accommodation; failing to make reasonable modifications, unless such modifications would "fundamentally alter the nature" of the goods and services of the place of public accommodation; and failing to remove structural and other facility barriers to people with disabilities.

Perhaps the most well-known and influential professional sport case involved professional golfer Casey Martin. Martin was born with Klippel-Trenaunay-Weber syndrome, a rare disorder that caused a progressively worsening muscle and bone condition in his right leg and resulted in severe pain when he walks. He started playing golf

IN THE COURTROOM

Inclusion in Sport Activities

Anderson v. Little League Baseball Inc. (1992)

In *Anderson v. Little League Baseball Inc.* (1992), a father who was paraplegic and used a wheelchair was the coach of his son's Little League baseball team. The father attended games and coached from the third-base coaching box. He had been coaching his son's team for three years without injuries or incidents. He was unexpectedly told by Little League that he could no longer coach his son's team. The league cited safety concerns. Little League created a policy banning wheelchairs from the field because of a perceived threat of injury to the players. The policy was absolute without consideration made to the circumstances of each activity or individual case. The coach sued Little League, claiming discrimination under the ADA. The federal district court found in favor of the plaintiff, struck down the policy disallowing wheelchairs, and determined that cases were to be decided individually. The court also found, contrary to the claims of Little League, that the coach did not pose a direct threat to the health and safety of the players. The court stated

> In determining whether an individual, such as plaintiff, poses a direct threat to the health or safety of others, a public accommodation must make an individualized assessment, based on reasonable judgment that relies on current medical knowledge or on the best available objective evidence, to ascertain: (1) the nature, duration, and severity of the risk; (2) the probability that the potential injury will actually occur; and (3) whether reasonable modifications of policies, practices, or procedures will mitigate the risk (28 C.F.R. § 36.208(c)). (p. 345)

at age six, won junior championships in Oregon, and then went to Stanford University, where he was the captain of the 1994 team that won the NCAA championship. After leaving Stanford, he walked for two years on the Hooters Tour, though he also played on the Tommy Armour Tour because it allowed carts. He then entered the PGA Tour's qualifying school tournament in the hopes of making the PGA or Nike Tour. He made it through the first two stages of the tournament using a cart, as allowed under the rules, but was barred from using a cart in the third stage. He then sued the PGA Tour, claiming that the no-cart rule failed to make tournaments accessible to people with disabilities and was in violation of the ADA (*Martin v. PGA Tour, Inc.*, 1998). The district court granted an injunction allowing Martin to use a cart in the third stage, and the PGA lifted the no-cart rule for the third stage. Martin was also allowed to use a cart in two tournaments on the Nike Tour. The PGA then returned to court, contending that it was not subject to the ADA.

Initially, the court noted that golf courses are specifically covered under Title III of the ADA. The PGA argued that allowing Martin to use a cart would fundamentally alter the nature of PGA golf by providing him with an unfair advantage over golfers who had to walk. Deeming that walking does not add much to the fatigue of a typical golfer, the court disagreed and held that allowing

Martin to use a cart would not fundamentally alter the game. Therefore, in accord with the ADA, the PGA had to provide Martin with the reasonable accommodation of a golf cart when he competed in events.

The immediate backlash was staggering. Commentators, other golfers, and armchair quarterbacks everywhere criticized the decision, most believing that even though Martin was obviously disabled he should be forced to walk a golf course as every other golfer does. Few seemed to recognize that Martin could not compete unless he used the cart and that, regardless of this accommodation, he would soon lose all use of his leg because of his disability.

Of course, the PGA appealed the initial decision (*Martin v. PGA Tour, Inc.*, 2000). The appellate court focused on whether Title III of the ADA even applied to the PGA. The PGA argued that although the ADA applies to golf courses in general, the areas roped off for PGA Tour events are not open to the public, so it is not a place of public accommodation under the ADA. The court disagreed because no matter how selective a facility is in giving access (i.e., only allowing the best golfers to play), it still is a place of public accommodation. Therefore, because it was a place of public accommodation covered under Title III, the PGA Tour had to provide some form of reasonable accommodation to Martin. The court again found that allowing Martin to use a cart would merely provide him with access and not fundamentally alter the game of golf, especially when walking is not a requirement specifically found in the official rules of golf.

The PGA would still not give up and appealed to the Supreme Court (*PGA Tour, Inc. v. Martin*, 2001). Substantially agreeing with every decision of the earlier courts, the Supreme Court also found that modifying the rules to provide Martin with a cart during competition would not fundamentally alter the PGA's tournaments. Because the walking rule is not an essential aspect of the game of golf and because Martin did not gain any advantage over other golfers by using a cart, his use of the cart was a reasonable modification of PGA golf.

Even after this decision, many in the sport world believed that the decision would cause courts to intervene in their sports, forcing them to modify their rules in bizarre ways to accommodate people with disabilities. Some speculated that sports leagues would have to allow wheelchair basketball players or prosthetic tennis rackets, but none of this has occurred. Instead, the ADA will force professional sport organizations to modify what they do only when such modifications will not fundamentally alter the nature of their competition.

Keep in mind that even Casey Martin had to prove that he was an otherwise qualified person with a disability. He had to demonstrate that he could compete at the highest level of golf even though he had a disability. The ADA would not allow him to show that he could compete at the highest level only if he was given an accommodation. The ADA cannot force sports leagues to find ways to make people with disabilities into high-quality competitors. Instead, it provides high-quality competitors who happen to have disabilities with the same chance to participate as anyone else.

Sexual Harassment

An issue that is closely associated with gender discrimination is **sexual harassment**. Points regarding sexual harassment derived from EEOC guidelines and the courts are as follows. Sexual harassment (a) consists of unwelcome sexual advances, (b) is not desired by the employee (victim), (c) creates a hostile or abusive work environment, and (d) can arise from either verbal or physical conduct.

Sexual harassment, therefore, is conduct that is sexual in nature and can occur with any combination of gender (including same gender). It is conduct that is not consensual between both parties, meaning that one party does not want, or agree to, the sexual conduct. Physical conduct may first come to mind, but verbal conduct can amount to sexual harassment as well. The determination of a hostile and abusive work environment is the central issue in many sexual harassment claims. A **hostile and abusive work environment** is one in which someone is so affected by the sexual conduct and finds it so offensive or intimidating that it negatively affects the person's job performance. The working environment becomes filled with intimidation, ridicule, and insult.

In addition to determining sexual harassment by the finding of a hostile work environment, the courts have also used another context. Sexual harassment has also been classified as *quid pro quo* (Latin for "something in exchange for something else"). This type of sexual harassment occurs when sexual favors are demanded in return for things like raises, promotions, a better office, and better opportunities. If a lawsuit for sexual harassment is made, the facts of the case are reviewed in light of these legal considerations.

Sexual harassment litigation often arises after an employee has been fired, quits, or claims that she has been constructively discharged from her job. Constructive discharge occurs when an employee claims she can no longer work at a place of business because the work situation is intolerable. Sexual harassment can occur because of interactions with coworkers, supervisors, and nonemployees of the same or opposite gender. Sexual harassment is a critically important issue for sport managers from both an ethical and a legal standpoint. Guidance on sexual harassment comes primarily from Title VII of the Civil Rights Act as amended in 1972, the EEOC, and court decisions. Some sport organizations have staff attorneys who use bulletins, online sources, and short courses to explain to managers the important points regarding sexual harassment. Sport managers should educate themselves about sexual harassment using a valid and reliable source. Sport organizations should have zero tolerance for abusive and objectionable behavior.

The key for the sport manager is to avoid sexual harassment lawsuits in the first place. This means having a plan in place and promoting a work environment where all employees are treated with dignity and respect and where everyone knows that sexual harassment will not be tolerated. Managers should also take every sexual harassment claim seriously and initiate the proper agency protocol for handling the situation. Think about the following scenario:

Allie, just out of college, takes a job working for a minor league baseball organization. Soon after she starts her job, her immediate supervisor, Bob, begins asking her out on dates. He does this repeatedly, and she refuses every time. Bob then makes harassing remarks and touches her inappropriately. He also tells Allie that if she sleeps with him, he will give her easy tasks and look the other way if she wants to go home early some days. If not, he tells her that she will be spending a lot of time cleaning toilets. Allie is disgusted and speaks to the upper-level manager (Steve) about her situation. She expresses that she is deeply concerned and troubled by her supervisor's abusive comments. Steve tells her that this is baseball, so she should suck it up and deal with it. Steve also says that Bob probably doesn't mean anything by his comments. Allie leaves his office crying and continues working. Bob hears of her complaint and increases his abusive behavior toward her. He also makes Allie stay late, beyond normal working hours, and do all the dirty jobs (e.g., cleaning bathrooms, washing towels, and picking up trash), which eventually make up more than 90% of her working day. Allie goes to the manager again, complaining of the abusive behavior. She is told that she should just make the best of her situation. Allie cannot take the abuse any longer and decides to quit her job. Jobs are difficult to find, and she is now unemployed with a college loan and many bills to pay. Allie hires a lawyer and brings suit against all responsible parties.

What issues do you think the court would rely on to determine whether there was liability on the part of the minor league baseball organization? The scenario certainly raises serious ethical concerns. From a legal standpoint, however, a court would likely consider the following issues in determining whether sexual harassment existed:

- **Quid pro quo** harassment—sexual favors are demanded in exchange for better working conditions.
- Hostile work environment—intimidation and insult alter the work environment.
- The existence of sexual harassment policies and procedures—plans should be put in place to correct and prevent any sexually harassing behavior.
- Whether sexual harassment policies and procedures were followed—formal complaints must be taken seriously, and remedial action should be taken as necessary against the supervisor.

An employer might also be liable if managers knew, or should have known, of harassment perpetrated by a coworker or customer, or if in response to a complaint of sexual harassment, immediate and effective action is not taken to stop the harassment. Protection extends to situations in which employees are harassed by supervisors, coworkers, or people of the same gender.

Other issues to consider include knowing who in the chain of command should be legally notified and knowing the proper procedures for interviewing both the victim and the accused. If no one in your agency or organization is responsible for providing guidance on sexual harassment, a competent outside source should be consulted. Remedies available to a claimant of sexual harassment include lost wages (back pay), benefits, punitive damages (if the employer acted with malice or "reckless indifference"), and attorney's fees. The proper handling of sexual harassment claims protects both the manager and the organization from liability and is the right thing to do. Consult the web for organizations that may help you develop protocols for sexual harassment. See chapter 8 for additional discussion of sexual harassment in the sport context.

Federal Employment Laws

The health and safety of employees are critical concerns for the sport manager. Sport managers owe an ethical duty to their employees to provide a reasonably safe work environment. Aside from an ethical duty, a legal duty is placed on employers to protect those under their care and at their place of employment. Legislators have stepped in to pass federal and state laws that protect employees from the risk of accidental death, injury, or disease that occurs while on the job.

Occupational Safety and Health Act

The most common and arguably most important law providing for the safety of employees is the **Occupational Safety and Health Act**. This federal law, enacted in 1970, has a twofold purpose: (1) to require employers to meet certain specific, federally mandated, safety standards and (2) to impose a general duty on employers to keep their workplaces safe. Several enforcement agencies—the Occupational Safety and Health Administration, the National Institute for Occupational Safety and Health, and the Occupational Safety and Health Review Commission—take part in developing and enforcing standards set by this act and have oversight responsibilities for safety and health in the work environment. Table 6.1 provides web addresses for these organizations.

Employees face many health hazards in the work environment:

- Sudden cardiac arrest—coaches and sport supervisors
- Heat-related illness—coaches and sport supervisors
- Carpal tunnel syndrome—office workers
- Heavy equipment–related injury—turf and field maintenance workers
- Blunt trauma—batting coaches
- Chemicals—aquatics personnel
- Blood-borne pathogens—sport and fitness personnel

Blood-borne pathogens (BBPs) pose an especially significant health concern for employees in sport. Fitness personnel, coaches, lifeguards, sport supervisors, athletic trainers, and those who might be required to perform CPR (which would include many in the sport profession) are at risk from BBPs. BBPs are microorganisms in human blood that can cause disease in humans. The BBPs of major concern include but are not limited to the hepatitis B virus (HBV) and the human immunodeficiency virus (HIV). A single exposure incident could result in infection, subsequent illness and, in some cases, death (Spengler, Connaughton, & Pittman, 2006). OSHA has created standards for BBPs, the basic components of which are as follows:

1. Employers are responsible for identifying job classifications that entail occupational exposure to BBPs (these include the previously mentioned

Table 6.1 **Enforcement Agencies for the Occupational Safety and Health Act**

Organization	Purpose	Website
Occupational Safety and Health Administration (OSHA)	"To assure safe and healthful working conditions for working men and women; by authorizing enforcement of the standards developed under the Act; by assisting and encouraging the States in their efforts to assure safe and healthful working conditions; by providing for research, information, education, and training in the field of occupational safety and health; and for other purposes." (OSH Act of 1970, Pub. L. No. 91-596)	www.osha.gov
National Institute for Occupational Safety and Health (NIOSH)	Through the Centers for Disease Control and Prevention, NIOSH provides national and world leadership to prevent work-related illnesses and injuries.	www.cdc.gov/niosh
Occupational Safety and Health Review Commission (OSHRC)	The OSHRC is an independent federal agency created to decide contests of citations or penalties resulting from OSHA inspections of American workplaces. The review commission, therefore, functions as an administrative court and has established procedures for conducting hearings, receiving evidence, and rendering decisions by its administrative law judges.	www.oshrc.gov

jobs as well as lifeguarding and athletic training).

2. Employers must minimize employee exposure to blood-borne pathogens through proper planning, education, and record keeping.

3. Employers are required to establish a written exposure control plan that lists the tasks, procedures, and job classifications with which occupational exposure may occur.

4. The employer must provide at no cost to employees appropriate personal protective equipment, such as gloves and pocket face masks.

5. The employer must offer, at its own expense, voluntary HBV vaccinations to all employees who have occupational exposure.

This information can be obtained from various sources and should be implemented in consultation with qualified legal professionals. You can obtain a brochure and fact sheets about BBPs by writing to OSHA Publications, 200 Constitution Avenue, NW, Room N3101, Washington, DC 20210 or by calling 202-219-8148.

OSHA regulations relevant to sport business include the following:

- Employers with more than 11 employees must keep records of occupational injury and illness for each employee:
  - Employers must report to OSHA the occurrence of any work-related injury or disease.
  - Employers must report to the Department of Labor the occurrence of any work-related accidents resulting in death or any one incident that causes five or more employees to be hospitalized. Employers must submit this report to the Department of Labor within 48 hours or the employer will be fined.
  - Subsequent inspection of premises is mandatory.
- Sport facilities can be inspected by OSHA compliance officers.
- Employees can file complaints about workplace health and safety.
- Employees cannot be fired if they complain or refuse to work in a dangerous area where bodily harm or death may reasonably result.

Employee safety in the sport setting must be approached in a thoughtful and thorough manner. Laws and regulations relevant to employee health and safety must be followed, preferably with the advice and consultation of competent professionals familiar with federal, state, and local requirements.

Fair Labor Standards Act (FLSA)

Although organizations can legally hire children and youth (minors) to work in the sport industry, an important law called the **Fair Labor Standards Act (FLSA)** regulates child labor practices. The FLSA was enacted to protect children from abuses in employment. The primary concerns addressed by the legislation are the hours of work, wages, and labor (employment) conditions of children and youth. Some important provisions include prohibitions against children working under the following conditions:

- Before 7 a.m.
- After 7 p.m. (after 9 p.m. in the summer)
- More than 3 hours on a school day
- More than 8 hours on a nonschool day
- More than 18 hours during a school week
- More than 40 hours during a nonschool week
- For less than minimum wage
- In certain occupations (those with particular health and safety risks)

Family and Medical Leave Act (FMLA)

Employees may have family health issues, either their own or those of a family member, that require them to be absent from work for an extended time. The birth of a child, illness, or the death of a family member might all qualify as legitimate health issues. Under the **Family and Medical Leave Act (FMLA)**, organizations are required to provide employees with up to 12 weeks (at any time of the year) of leave to attend to health issues. Although required to provide leave time, the organization is not required to provide paid leave. It is required, however, to continue the worker's health care coverage while the employee is on leave. When the worker returns, the employer must allow the employee to resume employment at the same or similar position, unless he is considered a key employee (one whose pay falls within the top 10% of the organization's workforce).

COBRA

Under the **Consolidated Omnibus Budget Reconciliation Act (COBRA)**, employees retain the rights to insurance coverage under their employer's health plan even after their employment has been terminated (either voluntarily or involuntarily). This provision means that employees can keep their cover-age (although they have to pay the premiums) for a certain length of time after they have left the job. The types of coverage protected include medical, dental, and optical. Former employees who choose to continue coverage may do so for up to 18 months after leaving the job. Former employees with disabilities may continue coverage for up to 29 months. Those who were fired because of gross misconduct are not protected by COBRA.

Health Insurance Portability and Accountability Act (HIPAA)

The **Health Insurance Portability and Accountability Act (HIPAA)** does not require employers to provide insurance coverage but instead provides rules for employers that do choose to provide a health plan for employees. The law says that an employer cannot exclude coverage to employees who have preexisting medical conditions for which medical advice, care, or treatment was provided within 6 months before coverage would begin. The act also requires employers to do what is reasonably necessary to ensure that employees' health information is not available to those without permission to have it. Some ways in which this can be accomplished include personnel training and information relevant to the communication of privacy issues and information.

Table 6.2 outlines the federal laws discussed in this text.

Table 6.2   Federal Employment Laws

Employment issue	Applicable law
Leave for medical and family reasons	Family and Medical Leave Act (FMLA)
Employee safety and health	Occupational Safety and Health Act
Wages and compensation, child labor	Fair Labor Standards Act (FLSA)
Employee insurance and health plans	Consolidated Omnibus Budget Reconciliation Act (COBRA) and the Health Insurance Portability and Accountability Act (HIPAA)
Discrimination in employment based on race, color, national origin, gender, or religion	Civil Rights Act of 1964
Discrimination in employment based on age	Age Discrimination in Employment Act (ADEA)
Discrimination in employment based on disability	Americans with Disabilities Act (ADA)

LEARNING AIDS

Summary

Discrimination can occur in hiring, promoting, and firing employees, so employers should put safeguards in place to eliminate or reduce the likelihood that a person will be discriminated against. Categories of discrimination include race, color and national origin, gender, religion, age, and disability. The ADEA, Title VII of the Civil Rights Act, other state and federal laws, the EEOC, and court decisions all influence issues of discrimination in the workplace. The sport manager should also be familiar with affirmative action, a concept closely associated with discrimination.

Sexual harassment is a violation of Title VII of the Civil Rights Act. Sexual harassment should never be tolerated by a sport organization (or any organization), and policies and procedures must be put in place and implemented to ensure that abuses do not occur. This right allows employees to argue their case and tell their side of the story before being terminated. Finally, the sport manager should be aware of employee health and safety issues and the relevant laws and regulations.

Discussion Questions

1. Make an argument supporting the unionization of college athletes (in the employment context).

2. Make an argument against the unionization of college athletes (in the employment context).

3. From the sexual harassment scenario in the text, address the key legal arguments and issues.

4. Provide a real-life example of the application of the Occupational Safety and Health Act.

5. Explain what is meant by *BFOQ* and give a hypothetical example in the sport context.

6. Explain the concept of disparate-treatment discrimination and provide an example in the sport context.

Sexual Harassment in the Sport Context

Carl was the women's tennis coach at the University of Wewilsu. He was considered one of the top tennis coaches in the country, having led Wewilsu to three national championships in his 10-year tenure at the university. Carl was well liked and respected by most people.

Last year, he hired a new assistant tennis coach, Cari Tenpro. Cari was an accomplished player who had had an excellent coaching career so far, although she had not been coaching long. She was also one of three assistant coaches, the other two having similar skills but more coaching experience. Veronica, an African American, was the head assistant coach. She had the highest pay of all the assistants and had the most responsibility. Susan, a Latin American, was the assistant in training and was second to Veronica. Susan was paid slightly less than Veronica was, but she earned more than the lowest level. Cari was hired as an assistant in training.

After several weeks at her new job, Cari began to notice some seemingly odd behavior from Carl. He would make jokes about women that made her uncomfortable and was insistent on numerous "friendship" hugs. She put up with this, thinking that Carl was just a bit quirky. One day, Carl made a highly suspicious comment. He told Cari that she was doing an outstanding job and deserved a promotion. He told her that she was a great colleague and friend and that he was looking forward to more friendship hugs in the future. In fact, he asked whether she would like to come over to his condominium that evening to strengthen their friendship. After all, he said, love is part of the score in tennis. Cari was extremely upset but needed the job and promotion. She told Carl that she valued their friendship and would take him up on his offer the following week. Carl seemed very excited and promoted Cari immediately to the head assistant position with a pay raise effective immediately.

The next day, Carl called Veronica into his office and told her that she would have to find another job or move back to the assistant in training position. Veronica was furious. Carl told Veronica that Cari was better suited for the head assistant position and that she was a fast learner. He could not give Veronica any more specific reasons. Veronica refused to take the assistant in training position, and Carl fired her. She told Susan what had happened. Susan shared her concern and was angry with Carl as well. The next week, Carl asked Cari over to his place again. Cari made up an excuse, but Carl would not accept no for an answer. He told Cari that if she came over to his place that night then they could get to know one another better—which he was certain would lead to more job perks and pay raises for Cari in the near future. Cari asked, "Do you mean if I sleep with you, you will let me keep my job and get these benefits?" Carl said, "I knew you were a smart one." Cari turned in her resignation that hour, even though she desperately needed the job. She then complained to the athletic director, but the athletic director told her that she should give Carl another chance. Cari was deeply upset and could not face Carl again. Carl was not disciplined. Cari, Veronica, and Susan all brought lawsuits against Carl and the university.

Constitutional Law

Chapter Objectives

After reading this chapter, you will know the following:

- How the United States Constitution applies to private and public sport entities

- The free speech and freedom of religion protections provided by the First Amendment

- How the First Amendment regulates religious prayers and activities in sport settings

- What substantive and procedural due process are and how their requirements apply to sport organizations

- How the Equal Protection Clause of the Constitution affects sport-related affirmative action plans

Case Studies in Sport Law Connection

Check out the following case studies related to this chapter in the accompanying e-book, *Case Studies in Sport Law, Second Edition* (Pittman, Spengler, & Young, 2016):

Blair v. Washington State University

Denis J. O'Connell High School v. The Virginia High School League

Doe v. Taylor Independent School District

Hall v. University of Minnesota

Hill v. National Collegiate Athletic Association

Jager v. Douglas County School District

Menora v. Illinois High School Association

National Collegiate Athletic Association v. Tarkanian

Palmer v. Merluzzi

Schaill by Kross v. Tippecanoe County School Corporation

Tinker v. Des Moines Independent Community School District

University of Colorado v. Derdeyn

Vernonia School District 47J v. Acton

The constitutional rights and amendments that most often apply to the sport industry typically involve issues regarding freedom of speech and religion, due process, equal protection, and the right from unreasonable search and seizure. These rights and protections are found in the First, Fourth, Fifth, and Fourteenth Amendments (see table 7.1). A major portion of this chapter addresses these issues and amendments as they relate to interscholastic and intercollegiate student-athletes. Constitutional law usually is not applicable to professional sports, for two major reasons. First, athletes in professional sports are parties to a collective bargaining agreement.

Table 7.1 Constitutional Law as It Applies to Sport

Amendment	Protections	Applicability to sport
First	Congress shall make no law respecting an establishment of religion, or prohibiting the free exercise thereof; or abridging the freedom of speech, or of the press; or the right of the people peaceably to assemble, and to petition the Government for a redress of grievances.	• Public school–based prayer • Freedom of expression, such as wearing arm bands • Freedom of association, such as forming leagues and associations (e.g., NCAA, Little League teams)
Fifth	No person shall . . . be deprived of life, liberty or property without due process of law.	• Recruiting rules violations resulting in firing a coach • Failed drug test that causes an athlete to lose a scholarship • Due Process Clause, which ensures fairness and impartiality before the government denies people their life, liberty, or property
Fourteenth	No state shall make or enforce any law which shall . . . deny to any person within its jurisdiction the equal protection of the laws.	• No discrimination based on race, gender, or ethnicity • Access of sport administration jobs to minority groups • Affirmative action

When a players union agrees to a collective bargaining agreement, certain individual rights are relinquished, including freedom of expression. For example, a professional athlete who makes disparaging and insensitive remarks about minority groups may be suspended by the commissioner for his remarks. Second, professional sports leagues are not state actors but private entities (Wong, 2010).

The U.S. federal government and all 50 states have separate written constitutions that set forth the basic organization, powers, and limits of their respective governments. Constitutional law is the law as expressed in these constitutions. State constitutions often vary; some are modeled after the U.S. Constitution, and others provide even greater rights to their citizens. The U.S. Constitution was adopted in 1787 by representatives of the 13 newly formed states. Initially, people expressed fear that the federal government might abuse its power. To alleviate such concerns, the first Congress approved 10 amendments to the U.S. Constitution, commonly known as the Bill of Rights, which were adopted in 1791. The Bill of Rights limits the powers and authority of the federal government and guarantees many civil (individual) rights and protections.

Although the Bill of Rights does not directly apply to the states, the U.S. Supreme Court has held that the Fourteenth Amendment includes many of the principal guarantees of the Bill of Rights, thereby making them applicable to the individual states. Therefore, neither the federal government nor state governments can deprive individuals of those rights and protections. But the rights provided by the Bill of Rights are not absolute. Many of the rights guaranteed by the Bill of Rights are described in broad terms. For instance, the Fourth Amendment prohibits unreasonable search and seizures, but it does not define what an unreasonable search and seizure would entail. Ultimately, the U.S. Supreme Court interprets the Constitution, thereby defining our rights and the government's boundaries.

The majority of the rights and protections afforded by the U.S. Constitution and its amendments apply only to governmental, or state, action. **State action** consists of any action of the federal or state governments or their subdivisions, such as city or county governments or agencies. Only the Thirteenth Amendment, which abolishes slavery, applies to the actions of private individuals. All other protections regarding individual rights apply only to governmental, or state, actors.

Action taken by private entities may constitute state action if the state exercises coercive power over the challenged private action, has substantially encouraged the action, or was significantly involved in the action (Mann & Roberts, 2010). For example, in *Brentwood Academy v. Tennessee Secondary School Athletic Association* (2001), the U.S. Supreme Court, in a 5-4 decision, found state action in this athletic association's regulatory activity attributable to the pervasive involvement of state school officials in its structure. In this case, the court specifically pointed out

To the extent of 84% of its membership, the Association is an organization of public schools represented by their public officials acting in their official capacity to provide an integral element of secondary public schooling. There would be no recognizable Association, legal or tangible, without the public school officials, who do not merely control but overwhelmingly perform all but the purely ministerial acts by which the Association exists and functions in practical terms. (*Brentwood*

Academy v. Tennessee Secondary School Athletic Association, 2001)

Historically, courts have considered the action of public schools, state universities, or any of their officials to be state action. High school interscholastic athletic associations have also been declared as state actors by most courts. Since the mid 1980s, national organizations that govern university athletics, including the National Collegiate Athletic Association (NCAA), typically have been found not to be state actors (*Arlosoroff v. NCAA*, 1984; *Cureton v. NCAA*, 1999; *National Collegiate Athletic Association v. Tarkanian*, 1988).

First Amendment

The First Amendment to the U.S. Constitution states

> Congress shall make no law respecting an establishment of religion, or prohibiting the free exercise thereof; or abridging the freedom of speech, or of the press; or the right of the people peaceably to assemble, and to petition the Government for a redress of grievances.

The major elements of the First Amendment that often apply to sport include religious issues, predominantly public school–based prayer, freedom of expression, and freedom of association.

Religious Issues

The first part of this amendment, referred to as the **establishment clause** and the **free exercise clause**, deals with religious freedom. The establishment clause bans the government or its agencies from establishing a state-sponsored religion, promoting (endorsing or aiding) a specific religion, or favoring one religion over another. This concept is referred to as *separation between church and state*. The free exercise clause bans the government or its agencies from interfering with anyone's religious belief. In other words, the government cannot interfere with an individual's practice of his religious beliefs.

The U.S. Supreme Court has established three tests to determine whether religious practices challenged under the First Amendment are unconstitutional:

- Lemon test—a three-part test used to determine whether a government (religious) practice is constitutional. To be constitutional, (1) the practice must be secular in purpose, (2) the practice's primary effect can neither advance nor inhibit religion, and (3) the practice must avoid excessive entanglement with religion (*Lemon v. Kurtzman*, 1971). Although the Lemon test has received criticism from legal scholars (Esbeck, 1990; Marshall, 1986) and the court for "not providing adequate standards for deciding Establishment Clause cases" (*Wallace v. Jaffree*, 1985), it remains an option for the courts.

- Endorsement test—a test used to consider whether the government endorses a particular religion or disproves of any religion. The government cannot endorse, favor, or disprove any religion or practice (*Lynch v. Donnelly*, 1984).

- Coercion test—a test that examines a religious practice to determine whether people are pressured or coerced to participate. The government may not coerce individuals to participate in religion or its exercise (*Lee v. Weisman*, 1992).

Religious practices, such as pregame prayers, have been common at U.S. sporting events for many years. Several recent law-suits have forced the courts to determine whether such practices, particularly in public schools, are constitutional. In *Santa Fe Independent School District v. Doe* (2000), Texas high school students held elections to vote on whether a prayer would be said before the start of home football games and, if so, who would deliver the prayer over the public address system. The U.S. Supreme Court agreed with the Fifth Circuit Court of Appeals and held that the public school district's policy allowing student-initiated and student-led prayer at public high school football games is unconstitutional.

In *Adler v. Duval County School Board* (2001), the school board's policy that allowed prayer at graduation ceremonies was challenged. The school board's guide-lines allowed graduating seniors to decide (1) whether to have a brief opening or closing message at graduation, (2) which student volunteer would give a message, and (3) what the content of the message would be. School officials were not involved in the decision-making process, and the content of the message was solely up to the individual student who would deliver the message. The 11th Circuit Court held that the school board's policies regarding student-led prayer were constitutional. The court stated that the school board policy promoted freedom of speech by allowing the volunteer student to speak on any subject of her choice and presenting a message that could be religious or secular. The court held that the school board policy was neutral, did not determine the content of the message, and did not establish any religion. This case example demonstrates an issue concerning freedom of religion in a public school that would also likely apply in public interscholastic sport.

In *Borden v. School District of Township of East Brunswick* (2008), Marcus Borden, the head football coach at East Brunswick

High School, engaged in pregame prayer activities that occurred at the team dinners and while taking a knee in the locker room. Over the years he served as head coach, Coach Borden, a local minister, and players said the pregame dinner prayer. In addition to authorizing the prayer before the team dinner, Coach Borden led his team in a prayer just before the game after discussing game tactics and strategy. The team partic-ipated in this tradition for the 23 years that Borden was head coach.

After complaints about the prayers were filed by parents, the school district directed Coach Borden not to lead the team in prayer and informed him that all prayer needed to be student initiated. Additionally, the district provided Coach Borden with guidelines, stemming from and coinciding with previous court decisions, regarding faculty participation in student-initiated prayer. Angered that that the district and the guidelines prevented him from bowing his head at the pregame meal prayer and taking a knee with his team during the pregame locker room prayer, Borden sued the superintendent, district, and board of education, claiming that the district's policy was unconstitutional and violated his First Amendment rights. The Third Circuit Court of Appeals upheld the district's policy and, in fact, held that it was necessary for the district to avoid establishment clause vio-lations. Furthermore, the court held that Coach Borden's silent acts (bowing his head and taking a knee during prayer) con-stituted an unconstitutional endorsement of religion. Considering the 23 years that Borden organized, participated in, and led prayer, the court found that a reasonable observer would conclude that Borden is endorsing religion (*Borden v. School District of Township of East Brunswick*, 2008).

Certain religious beliefs may require dress standards that can contradict policies set forth by athletic administrators, as seen in *Menora v. Illinois High School Association* (1982). In this case, an association bylaw prohibited students from wearing any headwear, except a sweatband, while participating in basketball. The bylaw was challenged by a student-athlete who was Jewish. He claimed that the bylaw was unconstitutional because it prohibited Jewish student-athletes from wearing yarmulkes, a requirement of their Jewish faith. Although the court sympathized with the student-athlete, the appeals court affirmed the trial court's decision in favor of the high school association. The appeals court concluded that the plaintiff must decide whether in fact the Jewish faith requirements did not allow his participation in the voluntary sport of basketball and whether his headwear is not appropriate for the sport of basketball.

Freedom of Expression

Also included in the First Amendment is the **free speech clause**, which provides us the right to say what we want without government intervention. Not all speech, however, is protected. The government may impose restriction on the time, place, and manner in which we express ourselves. Some types of speech, such as obscenity, receive no protection. Most types of speech, however, are protected by the strict or exacting scrutiny standard. These standards require the existence of a compelling government interest to justify restricting speech (Mann & Roberts, 2010; Miller, Cross, & Jentz, 2011).

For example, in *Bethel School District v. Fraser* (1986), Matthew Fraser, a high school senior, gave a speech to the student body that was filled with sexual innuendo. The speech created uproar among the students; some yelled during the speech, whereas others were embarrassed and bewildered. The speech prompted disciplinary action from the school administration, which sus-pended Fraser from school for 3 days and did not allow him to speak at his graduation ceremony. The U.S. Supreme Court upheld the suspension and found that the school district's policy did not violate the First Amendment. The court stated,

> Surely it is a highly appropriate function of public school education to prohibit the use of vulgar and offensive terms in public discourse. The schools, as instruments of the state, may determine that the essential lessons of civil, mature conduct cannot be conveyed in a school that tolerates lewd, indecent, or offensive speech and conduct such as that indulged in by this confused boy. The pervasive sexual innuendo in Fraser's speech was plainly offensive to both teachers and students—indeed to any mature person. We hold that petitioner School District acted entirely within its permissible authority in imposing sanctions upon Fraser in response to his offensively lewd and indecent speech.

Vulgar and offensive trash talking by athletes or coaches at a public school sport event may be restricted for similar reasons. For example, in *Dambrot v. Central Michigan University* (1995), a basketball coach was terminated after using the N-word in a halftime speech to his team. Claiming that he was attempting to motivate his team, he subsequently sued and argued that the termination violated his First Amendment rights. Although the court affirmed the ruling in favor of the plaintiffs (Coach Dambrot), finding that Central Michigan University's discriminatory harassment policy violated the First Amendment, they upheld the university's termination of Coach Dambrot's employment.

The First Amendment to the U.S. Constitution provides citizens of the United States with freedom of expression, but protection does not extend to all types of expression, such as obscenity.

A democratic government cannot survive unless the people can freely express their political views and opinions as well as criticize governmental policies and actions. Freedom of speech, especially political speech, is an important right, and the courts have traditionally provided strong protection for this right. Symbolic speech, which encompasses nonverbal conduct (articles of clothing, gestures, and other forms of expressive conduct), is also protected under the First Amendment, as shown in the Freedom of (Symbolic) Speech sidebar.

An interscholastic athlete who wishes to symbolically express herself by wearing something attached to the traditional uniform (like a sticker or ribbon) may be permitted to do so under the First Amendment but would likely be restricted by league or association rules. Although the *Fraser* and *Tinker* cases are not sport related, these two U.S. Supreme Court landmark cases are frequently cited in legal disputes and cases involving free speech in a public school.

Another form of speech, known as **commercial speech**, can be defined as expression that is related to the economic interests of the speaker and his audience. This form of speech would include advertisements for a product or service. Although commercial speech is protected by the First Amendment, it is afforded less protection than political speech is. Commercial speech is protected because of the interest such communication has for the advertiser, consumer, and public. Advertising conveys essential information for the proper and efficient distribution of resources in our free market system. The government, however, may restrict certain types of advertising, for instance, in the interest of protecting the public from being misled by certain advertising practices (Mann & Roberts, 2010; Miller et al., 2011).

IN THE COURTROOM

Freedom of (Symbolic) Speech

Tinker v. Des Moines Independent Community School District (1969)

Petitioner John F. Tinker, 15 years old, and petitioner Christopher Eckhardt, 16 years old, attended high schools in Des Moines, Iowa. Petitioner Mary Beth Tinker, John's sister, was a 13-year-old student in junior high school. In December 1965 a group of adults and students in Des Moines held a meeting at the Eckhardt home. The group determined to publicize their objections to the hostilities in Vietnam and their support for a truce by wearing black armbands during the holiday season and by fasting on December 16 and New Year's Eve. Petitioners and their parents had previously engaged in similar activities, and they decided to participate in the program.

The principals of the Des Moines schools became aware of the plan to wear armbands. On December 14, 1965, they met and adopted a policy that any student wearing an armband to school would be asked to remove it, and if he refused he would be suspended until he returned without the armband. Petitioners were aware of the regulation that the school authorities adopted.

On December 16, Mary Beth and Christopher wore black armbands to their schools. John Tinker wore his armband the next day. They were all sent home and suspended from school until they would come back without their armbands. They did not return to school until after the planned time for wearing armbands had expired—that is, until after New Year's Day.

This complaint was filed in the U.S. district court by petitioners, through their fathers, under section 1983 of Title 42 of the United States Code. It requested an injunction restraining the respondent school officials and the respondent members of the board of directors of the school district from disciplining the petitioners, and it sought nominal damages. Ultimately, the Supreme Court, in a 7-2 decision in favor of Tinker, ruled that students retain their constitutional right of freedom of speech while in public school and had the right to wear armbands to protest the Vietnam War.

The U.S. Supreme Court has made it clear that certain types of speech will not be afforded protection under the First Amendment. For example, defamatory speech, that which disgraces or diminishes a person's reputation by communicating a false statement, is not protected. Speech that violates criminal laws, such as pornography or threatening speech, is also not protected (Mann & Roberts, 2010; Miller et al., 2011).

Right of Association

Sport and recreation associations are common, such as Little League Baseball Association, the Amateur Athletic Association, and the National Collegiate Athletic Association (NCAA). Some associations are formed with the purpose of promoting a specific sport or activity by location, such as "Anytown" Youth Football Association, the Florida Recreation and Parks Association, or the National Intramural and Recreational Sports Association. Besides promoting sport, some associations protect the interests of athletes and participants. Individuals have the right to form associations, thereby choosing with whom they wish to associate and socialize. This basic right is guaranteed by the First Amendment, provided that the association does not commit criminal activities or violate an individual's civil rights related to race, gender, age, religion, or national origin.

Other elements of the First Amendment that often involve athletes are **equal protection** and **due process**. Equal protection, contained in the Fourteenth Amendment, guarantees that laws will be applied in an equal and nondiscriminatory manner. Due process rights are contained in both the Fifth and Fourteenth Amendments as well as in many state constitutions. Due process guarantees that a person cannot be deprived of life, liberty, or property without a fair process or hearing.

Fourteenth Amendment

The Fourteenth Amendment of the United States Constitution provides that "no State shall make or enforce any law which shall . . . deny to any person within its jurisdiction the equal protection of the laws." This sentence is commonly referred to as the Equal Protection Clause (EPC). The EPC, like the Thirteenth, Fourteenth, and Fifteenth Amendments, was enacted at the close of the Civil War and secured free and equal treatment of former slaves.

The EPC has been used to impose a general restraint on governmental inequality based on classifications. The EPC is triggered any time people are classified and treated differently on the basis of classifications. Although people can be classified or distinguished in countless ways, the classifications that receive the most restraint involve immutable characteristics—characteristics with which people are born, such as a race, ethnicity, and gender. A history of discrimination based on race, ethnicity, and gender exists in American sport, so sport managers must be mindful to avoid possible EPC violations. For example, before the civil rights movement, African Americans were not allowed access to university and high school sports teams in many parts of the country. This circumstance has changed, but questions remain concerning the degree of access that African Americans and other minority groups have in seeking sport administration and coaching positions.

Strict Scrutiny

The type of classification assigned to a person affects the way a court scrutinizes the legality of the classification. In this sense, *scrutiny* means the way in which a court analyzes whether state action should be condoned or rejected. So how does strict scrutiny work? Think of scrutiny as the degree to which someone analyzes an issue (figure 7.1). For example, teachers scrutinize the work of their students regularly. If a teacher lightly scrutinizes a student's assignment, then that teacher is giving the student leeway in terms of accomplishing the goals set for the assignment. Conversely, if the teacher scrutinizes the assignment strictly, the student has little or no room for error. Similarly, courts that use strict scrutiny give the government no room for error in convincing them that the classification is necessary. Thus, strict scrutiny is the most rigorous degree of scrutiny. After a court decides that strict scrutiny is the appropriate standard, then the court will uphold the state action only if it is necessary to achieve a compelling governmental interest (*Grutter v. Bollinger*, 2003).

Courts use strict scrutiny in EPC cases any time state action uses a suspect classification or a classification linked to a fundamental right (Lockhart, Kamisar, Choper, & Shiffrin, 1991). Classifications based on race or national origin are suspect classifications, so state action that classifies people based on their race or their national

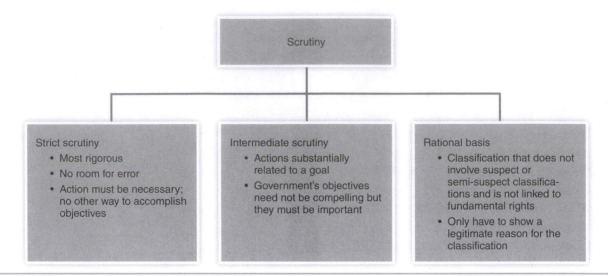

Figure 7.1 Various types of scrutiny used when courts rule on Equal Protection Clause cases.

origin will be subject to strict scrutiny. For example, state high school athletic associations in the U.S. South once separated African American high schools from white high schools, and the two types of athletic programs were prohibited from competing against each other. Any state action that separates competitors today based on race or national origin will be subject to strict scrutiny.

The other way that strict scrutiny applies concerns a classification that is linked to a fundamental right (Lockhart et al., 1991). If the court concludes that state action has a material effect on a fundamental right or interest, the action must survive strict scrutiny. There are not many fundamental rights. Those rights that have been deemed fundamental by the courts include the right to vote, the right to criminal appeal, and the right to interstate travel. So if a community limited the right to vote to those who have lived in that community for more than 10 years, strict scrutiny would apply. Although time span of residence does not involve a suspect classification per se, the classification is tied to the fundamental right to vote, which is why strict scrutiny is applicable.

As previously stated, when strict scrutiny is applied the court will allow the governmental action to survive only if it is necessary to achieve a compelling governmental interest. To grasp the concept of strict scrutiny, we need to understand what courts mean by the words *necessary* and *compelling.* For the purpose of EPC analysis, *necessary* means that there is no other way to accomplish the government's objective. Courts often use the phrase *narrowly tailored* when describing what is intended by *necessary.* This phrase provides a visual example of what the courts expect from governmental action that triggers strict scrutiny. Specifically, a narrowly tailored suit is one that fits tightly; likewise, the means to accomplishing the compelling governmental objective must also fit tightly. That is, in accomplishing the compelling governmental interest, the government must do only what is absolutely necessary. Any unnecessary classification or regulation based on a classification will be found unconstitutional.

The second key term used in strict scrutiny analysis is the word *compelling.* This term means that the objective sought through the state action must compel the court. A court is compelled when the court believes that the action must be taken. This notion goes beyond the idea that the regulation is important or that it is a good idea. Instead, a high level of justification is needed for the discriminatory classification to survive. As society changes and evolves, so does the law. What a court may find compelling one day may be unthinkable later.

In *Louisiana High School Athletic Ass'n v. St. Augustine High School* (1968), the Fifth Circuit used strict scrutiny in analyzing the need for a segregated high school athletic association. In doing so, the court found no necessity for maintaining a segregated high school athletic system. The court found that the evidence presented in the case supported an inference that race was the basis for the exclusion of St. Augustine (a predominantly African American high school) from the association, and this reason did not compel the court to allow the association's discriminatory denial of access to the school.

Intermediate Scrutiny

An intermediate level of scrutiny is available to courts to analyze state action that discriminates against people on the basis of gender, illegitimacy, and alienage (Lockhart et al., 1991). Thus far, race and national origin are the only two classifications that courts have deemed suspect. But courts have recognized that these three groups deserve added equal protection. Although these classes do not rise to the level of suspect, thus resulting in strict scrutiny, they have been labeled semisuspect by the courts. When the government makes distinctions between people based on semisuspect classifications, then the government's actions are subjected to intermediate scrutiny.

Intermediate scrutiny is not as rigorous as strict scrutiny (Lockhart et al., 1991). For a classification to survive strict scrutiny, the government must show that the classification was substantially related to achieving an important governmental interest. Instead of showing that its actions were necessary, the government need only show that its actions were substantially related to its goal. Thus, the government's actions can survive intermediate scrutiny if there are other, less discriminatory means of accomplishing the government's objectives as long as the means chosen were substantially related to the goal.

Furthermore, the government's goal or objective need not be compelling, although it must be important. The difference between *compelling* and *important* can be described as the difference between *must* and *should*. For example, a person must eat to survive but should eat healthily to live longer. Objectives used to justify semisuspect classifications do not have to be so vital that they must be accomplished. Instead, they need only be the type that should be accomplished.

A good example of a court using intermediate scrutiny can be found in *Ludtke v. Kuhn* (1978). This case involved a challenge against the New York Yankees' policy of excluding female sport reporters from the baseball team's locker room in a stadium owned and operated by the government. Ludtke, the female reporter challenging the policy, named the mayor of New York, Yankee Stadium, the Yankees, and the commissioner of Major League Baseball in her lawsuit. The defendants argued that the policy was substantially related to the important goals of (1) protecting the privacy of those players who are undressed or who are in various stages of undressing and getting ready to shower, (2) protecting the image of baseball as a family sport, and (3) preserving the traditional notions of decency and propriety (*Ludtke v. Kuhn*, 1978). The court recognized that fresh-off-the-field interviews are important to the work of sport reporters because these interviews give a competitive advantage to reporters who have access to the ballplayers at that time. The court also recognized that several less-sweeping alternatives could be used rather than simply banning women from the locker rooms. The defendants admitted that players could undress in their cubicles in the clubhouse and could be shielded from the "roving eyes" of any female reporters by a curtain or swinging door on each cubicle. In addition, towels were available to players who wished to maintain privacy after showering or changing out of their uniforms. Based on these findings, the court held that the policy of banning female reporters from the locker rooms at Yankee Stadium was not substantially related to an important governmental interest and therefore did not survive intermediate scrutiny (*Ludtke v. Kuhn*, 1978).

Rational Basis

The rational basis standard is a type of scrutiny that applies to all classifications not covered by strict or intermediate scrutiny (i.e., all those that do not involve suspect or semisuspect classifications and are not linked to fundamental rights). The courts are charged with ensuring that people are afforded equal protection under the law, so governmental decisions that classify and differently treat groups of people must be scrutinized. But the standard for all other classifications is much lower in that the government need show only a rational basis for its action. The government has to show only a legitimate reason for the classification, proving that the basis for the classification is rationally related to a legitimate governmental interest. The

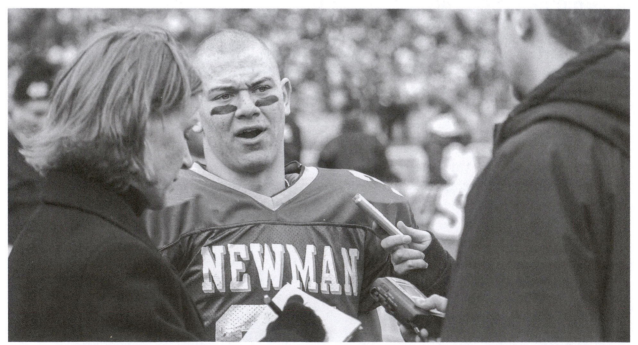

Is it legal to exclude female sport reporters from men's locker rooms? Intermediate scrutiny was used to answer such a question in *Ludtke v. Kuhn*.

court does not even have to agree with the rational basis asserted by the government as long as the basis is rational. The rational basis standard is the same standard used by courts in evaluating substantive due process claims. It is not the role of the court system to micromanage governmental decisions. Courts interfere with governmental decisions only when the government cannot justify its decision rationally.

Types of Discrimination

Two types of discrimination can lead to an EPC challenge. The first is called **de jure discrimination**; roughly translated, this phrase means "discrimination by law" (Lockhart et al., 1991). De jure discrimination exists any time a law or policy has a discriminatory purpose. For example, a rule that forbids African Americans from competing in high school sports with white athletes would be de jure discrimination because the purpose for the law is discriminatory. The second type of discrimination is called **de facto discrimination**. This type of discrimination exists when the law or policy lacks a discriminatory purpose but has a discriminatory effect (Lockhart et al., 1991). For example, a high school sport association delineates districts in such a manner that the districts divide groups of people based on race. Although no discriminatory purpose may be behind the creation of sport districts, challengers may demonstrate that the division results in discrimination.

Affirmative Action

Affirmative action is a term given to programs designed to reverse the effects of past and current discrimination. Affirmative action programs often involve hiring or admittance policies that assist people who are members of a group or classification of people who have been discriminated

against. The goal of affirmative action is to provide a springboard to those who need assistance because they are disadvantaged in the hiring or admittance process because of their classification. The concept of affirmative action is controversial because discrimination cannot be reversed without treating people differently based on the same criteria on which past discrimination was based (i.e., race, gender, national origin, and alienage). Thus, affirmative action has been labeled by some as reverse discrimination (Cohen & Sterba, 2003). The courts, however, have upheld proper applications of affirmative action under the opinion that such applications result in benign (meaning harmless) discrimination.

The EPC applies to affirmative action programs that have been implemented by state actors. Accordingly, affirmative action plans are subject to the same scrutiny that would be used to analyze other discriminatory programs, rules, or regulations. Any affirmative action plan that uses race or national origin as a criterion for advancement must survive strict scrutiny. The U.S. Supreme Court has repeatedly held that the goal of reversing past discrimination is a compelling governmental interest. Affirmative action plans, however, don't always satisfy the necessary requirement of strict scrutiny. Specifically, affirmative action plans must still be narrowly tailored in that they must do only what is necessary, and if less discriminatory means are available, then those means must be used.

Narrowly tailored affirmative action plans are those that are properly administered. Proper administration means that employers develop minimum requirements for the position and first obtain a qualified candidacy pool before using race, national origin, or gender as a consideration. Affirmative action plans should not use quotas, and employers or selection committees should not enter a search with the goal of hiring someone based on suspect or semisuspect class status. Hiring or admitting unqualified applicants based on their racial, ethnic, or gender classification is not proper application of affirmative action.

A good example of how to use an affirmative action plan can be found in the case of *Grutter v. Bollinger* (2003). Although this case is not directly related to sport, it provides insight into how courts handle EPC cases that challenge affirmative action programs. The case involved a white law school applicant who accused the University of Michigan School of Law's affirmative action plan of being responsible for the rejection of her application to the school. The applicant filed a lawsuit against the university, alleging that the school's diversity policy violated the Equal Protection Clause. The school required applicants to submit an essay stating how they would benefit the school's policy aimed at developing diversity in its student body. The school evaluated each student to determine how she would promote the school's diversity policy. The essay was considered only after it was determined that the applicant satisfied the school's minimum grade point average and LSAT score requirements. The case ultimately reached the U.S. Supreme Court, where Justice Sandra Day O'Connor held that (1) the law school had a compelling interest in attaining a diverse student body and (2) the admissions program was narrowly tailored to serve its compelling interest in obtaining the educational benefits that flow from a diverse student body and thus the university's policy did not violate the Equal Protection Clause (*Grutter v. Bollinger*, 2003). The court held that the school's policy was narrowly tailored because the school followed proper application of affirmative action. The school did only what was necessary and no more to promote diversity. The application process consisted of first obtaining a qualified candidacy pool and only then considering race.

Sport organizations, leagues, teams, and university athletic programs have used affirmative action programs primarily to promote diversity in coaching hires. The National Football League (NFL) requires each team to interview at least one minority candidate before hiring a head coach. The NFL's rule is controversial because some believe that it promotes needless interviews in situations where it is obvious that a team already has its next coach in mind. Others, however, argue that the rule opens doors that would otherwise remain closed, because it forces teams to consider those who ordinarily would not be considered. The NFL's program doesn't exactly comply with proper administration of affirmative action; the NFL is not subject to constitutional review for its affirmative action program because the league is not a state actor.

Conversely, university athletic associations at state-run schools are vulnerable to EPC review for their hiring practices. Athletic directors at such schools must use care in adopting affirmative action plans for hiring coaches. They are advised to use *Grutter v. Bollinger* as a roadmap in developing an affirmative action plan: Use race as a consideration, but do so only after establishing a qualified pool of candidates. An athletic program should decide up front what minimum criteria job candidates must possess. Do candidates need head coaching experience? Is a master's degree required? Should the coach have experience in the region or conference in which the athletic program competes? Suspect or semisuspect class status should be considered only after the athletic association's minimum job requirements are satisfied. Affirmative action is used to promote diversity for all suspect and semisuspect classifications, which means that proper administration of affirmative action assists all groups of people who have been subject to past discrimination. These groups include but are not limited to African Americans, Hispanics, Asians, and women.

Fifth Amendment

Sometimes the government or state actors restrict persons in their actions, in their professions, or in regard to their possessions. In sport, governmental restrictions can cause a coach to lose his job for violating rules governing recruiting or cause an athlete to lose her scholarship for failing a drug test. Even when the government is justified in its restrictions, it must still afford those restricted some form of process before the restrictions are enforced.

The rule requiring process from the government can be found in the Due Process Clause (DPC) of the U.S. Constitution. The DPC is found in the Fifth Amendment of the Constitution and provides that "no person shall . . . be deprived of life, liberty or property without due process of law." The Fifth Amendment applies only to federal state actors, but the Fourteenth Amendment extends the DPC to the states. Most state constitutions also include due process guarantees. Due process exists to protect people from arbitrary, capricious, and unreasonable governmental restriction. In other words, the DPC exists to ensure fairness and impartiality before the government denies people of life, liberty, or property.

Life, Liberty, and Property Interests

To trigger the DPC's application, the government must attempt to deny persons of a life, liberty, or property interest. The government denies people of life interests when it denies people their lives, as in when the government punishes someone for a capital offense, meaning an offense that is punishable by death. This aspect of the DPC is not very applicable to sport. But life interests can also be restricted when the government incarcerates people for crimes. We often see news stories of sport

personalities and athletes who are accused of criminal activities. Before any criminal penalty can be imposed, the government owes the accused due process.

Although life interest is fairly specific, liberty interest is not. Liberty interest includes all privileges recognized as essential to the orderly pursuit of happiness. In sport, the term *liberty interest* is typically used to describe damage to a person's reputation when he is fired from a job. A person who is fired is not deprived of a liberty interest when the employer alleges merely improper or inadequate performance, incompetence, neglect of duty, or malfeasance (*Siegert v. Gilley*, 1991; *Stanley v. Big Eight Conference*, 1978). Likewise, a charge or allegation that merely makes a person less attractive to other employers but does not prevent the person from getting another job does not constitute a liberty deprivation (*Chilingirian v. Boris*, 1989). To activate the DPC, the employer must have made a statement in the course of the employee's discharge that might seriously damage the employee's standing in her profession (*Board of Regents v. Roth*, 1972). In doing so, the employer places a stigma on the employee that damages her career. The stigmatizing statements or charges must be made public, and the employee must claim that the chargers were false (*Codd v. Velger*, 1977). If these requirements are met, the employee is entitled to notice and an opportunity to be heard through a name-clearing hearing. The employee must request such a hearing (*Gillum v. City of Kerrville*, 1993). A name-clearing hearing does not have to adhere to any formal procedures to be valid.

A good example can be found in *Ludwig v. Board of Trustees of Ferris State University* (1997). In this case, the coach of a men's basketball team at a public university brought a DPC action in state court against the university's board of trustees and various other officials, alleging that the coach was deprived of due process in connection with disciplinary proceedings. One of the coach's claims was that the university deprived him of a liberty interest when school officials made comments in the local newspaper alleging that the coach used racial slurs. Although the court recognized that the coach's reputation had been harmed by the statements made by school officials, the coach had failed to request a name-clearing hearing and this prevented him from successfully prevailing on his DPC claim.

A person's interest in property is the third interest protected by the DPC. Courts have defined *property interest* broadly in that the term includes all valuable interests that can be possessed outside of oneself, that have exchangeable value, or that add to a person's wealth or estate (*Board of Regents v. Roth*, 1972). In sport, a property interest can take many forms, ranging from an owner's interest in a professional franchise to a university athlete's interest in a scholarship. Although the term *property* is broadly defined, courts require that people actually have an interest in the thing for which they claim they are being deprived. To have a property interest, a person must have more than an abstract need or desire for what he claims. More than a unilateral expectation must be present; instead, there must be a legitimate claim of entitlement (*Board of Regents v. Roth*, 1972).

Price v. Univ. of Alabama (2004) provides a good example of what courts expect of those who allege that the government deprived them of an interest in property. Mike Price was hired as head football coach at the University of Alabama in January 2003. In May 2003 he was fired for alleged inappropriate conduct committed while he was representing the school at a charity golf event in Florida. Price claimed that the university fired him without any real process or hearing and thus deprived him of a property interest in his employment contract with the university. But Price and the university had yet to complete the contract, and the university claimed that Price was an at-will employee who could be fired at any time. At-will employment includes no property interest (*Green v. City of Hamilton Hous. Auth.*, 1991). In Alabama, agreements to agree in the future to terms of an employment contract are not contracts (*Price v. Univ. of Alabama*, 2004). The court found that Price did not have a property interest in an enforceable contract with the university simply because the two parties had plans to enter into a contract in the future. Therefore, Price did not have a valid property interest that could be protected by the DPC.

Substantive Due Process

Two types of due process are required under the DPC: substantive due process and procedural due process. Substantive due process concerns the actual rule or regulation in question—that is, the substance of the rule. When a person alleges a violation of substantive due process, that person is challenging the content and application of the rule. The DPC protects people from unreasonable rules and regulations. If a rule is unfair or arbitrary in either content or application, then that rule may violate the DPC of the U.S. Constitution.

For example, a university athletic department has a rule that any student-athlete accused by law enforcement officials of using drugs or performance-enhancing substances will be stripped of her scholarship. Dani, a volleyball player and student at the university, is accused of drug possession after police find drugs in a car in which Dani was a passenger. On notification of the incident, the athletic department suspends Dani's scholarship with no opportunity for appeal. Dani could allege a DPC violation on the basis that the department's substance abuse policy violates substantive due process. Dani must establish that she is being deprived of a life, liberty, or property interest by a state actor. The university is a public university, so she could probably establish state action. The depriving governmental entity is a branch of state government rather than the federal government, so Dani would rely on the Fourteenth Amendment's DPC protection. Furthermore, Dani is being deprived of a property interest through the termination of her university scholarship, something that has real value.

Dani could challenge the content and application of the rule to her case on the basis that it is unfair. Dani was accused of possessing drugs merely because she was in a vehicle where drugs were found. It could be later discovered that Dani was walking home from practice when some students she recognized from school offered to give her a ride to her dorm. Dani accepted the ride mere minutes before campus police pulled the car over for a traffic violation. During a legal search, the police found two marijuana cigarettes in the glove compartment of the car. Dani was in the backseat of the car and did not know that the cigarettes were in the car. Had the rule not been so strict to include mere accusations of drug abuse and had Dani been given a chance to defend herself through a hearing, she would have been able to clear her name and keep her scholarship.

The government can survive a substantive due process challenge if it can show a rational basis for the rule or regulation that is being challenged. The rational basis standard is the lowest standard of court scrutiny. Rational basis is also the standard required of the government to overcome equal protection challenges for discriminatory practices that do not affect suspect or semisuspect classifications or involve fundamental rights. The reason that courts have placed a relaxed standard on the government in substantive due process challenges is that courts do not like to interfere with the rule-making function of the government without good cause.

The United States has three branches of government, and the judicial branch is not charged with the responsibility of passing laws and making regulations. Those duties were given by our Constitution to the legislative branch. Furthermore, judges are not always equipped with the expertise to interfere with the decisions of governments and governmental agencies. Let's go back to the hypothetical situation involving Dani and the drug possession charge. Who is in a better position to make decisions and rules affecting university athletes: athletic directors or judges?

A reviewing court will not strike down the university's substance abuse policy if the university can provide a rational basis for its stringent rule. Dani could argue that the rule is unfair because it allows the university to terminate an athlete's scholarship based on mere accusations and provides no hearing for the athlete. But the university could argue that the policy is needed because the school has a strong drug culture and student-athletes are the leaders of said drug culture. The university could argue that a strict, no-nonsense drug policy is necessary until the drug culture is curbed and drug abuse is reduced. Does the school's argument provide a rational basis for the rule? Keep in mind that a rational basis is the lowest standard; the university only has to provide a reason for its policy. The court does not even have to agree with the university's rule. How do you think a court would answer these arguments? Would the court side with Dani or with the university?

Procedural Due Process

Procedural due process concerns the procedures used to enforce a rule or regulation. The primary distinction between substantive and procedural due process is that persons alleging violations of procedural due process are not challenging the rule's content, just the way the rule was applied to them. In procedural due process suits, typically a person alleges that he was not given enough process. This concern brings up a question: Just how much process is due?

The amount of process owed to a person who is about to be deprived of a life, liberty, or property interest varies on the basis of the severity of the violation and the severity of the sanction to be imposed. Two extreme examples demonstrate this concept. The first concerns a parking violation on a university campus. When someone violates a parking ordinance, usually that person is punished by receiving a parking ticket that states the fine imposed and the date by which it is to be paid. The process afforded to someone charged with a traffic violation is called *minimum due process*.

Minimum due process is the process that is minimally due before someone is deprived of a life, liberty, or property interest (Lockhart et al., 1991). Minimum due process includes the following:

- A statement of the specific violation
- Notice of the sanctions that will be imposed
- An opportunity for the accused to comment

Minimum due process should be used only in situations in which the offense is minor and the sanction to be imposed is equally minor. A parking ticket typically includes a statement of the violation committed, notice of the fine owed for the offense, and information on what the offender can do to contest the ticket.

The second example includes someone who is being punished for committing multiple murders in a state that has the death penalty. This offense is probably the most severe offense that can be committed in any jurisdiction, and the punishment (either life in prison or the death penalty) is equally severe. For a person charged with committing murder, notice of the violation and the penalty that will be imposed is insufficient; more process is due. Such a person is granted what is called *maximum due process*.

Maximum due process requires (a) written notice of a hearing, (b) a written statement of the charges, (c) provision of an adversarial hearing (a hearing or trial where both sides can present arguments and have the matter heard by one or more neutral and detached decision makers), (d) a written or audiotaped record of the proceedings, and (e) the right to appeal. In a murder trial, an accused person is afforded all the aforementioned process. Maximum due process is required whenever the offense and sanction are severe (Lockhart et al., 1991).

The two examples provided, the parking violation and the murder case, are close to extreme cases. Most situations fall somewhere between those extremes. For this reason, the DPC is flexible in its procedural requirements and depends on the facts of each case. For example, if a coach is accused of misconduct with an athlete and is likely to be fired, then something akin to maximum due process is probably required. Conversely, if an athlete breaks curfew before a big game and is punished by being made to sit out the first quarter of the game, something closer to minimum due process is in order.

The case of *Jennings v. Wentzville R-IV School Dist.* (2005) provides a good example of the flexibility of due process. In *Jennings*, two students were accused of being intoxicated at a football game and were suspended from school for 10 days. The court in *Jennings* held that school suspensions trigger the DPC because a student's right to education is a property interest. Thus, some form of process was required of the district before it could suspend the students, even if the procedure afforded did not rise to the degree of maximum due process. Courts have consistently held that when students face suspensions of 10 days or less, they are entitled to oral or written notice of the charges against them and, if the students deny the charges, an explanation of the evidence the authorities have and an opportunity to present their side of the story (*Goss v. Lopez*, 1975). No delay is required between the time notice is given and the time of the hearing.

LEARNING AIDS

Summary

The equal protection requirements of the U.S. Constitution demand that all people be treated equally under the law. Any time the government discriminates between classes of people, it runs the risk of violating the Equal Protection Clause. Courts will review discriminatory cases to determine whether the government's discriminatory policies are justified. If the policy discriminates based on race or national origin, then the government will have the heavy burden of satisfying the court's strict scrutiny standard. Policies that discriminate on the basis of gender will have to overcome intermediate scrutiny, and all other forms of discrimination require a rational basis to survive. Affirmative action is a discriminatory program that is often used by sport organizations. To survive strict scrutiny, an affirmative action program must be narrowly tailored to achieve the compelling interest of reversing the effects of past discrimination.

Due process is an aspect of constitutional law that all sport management professionals will deal with during their careers. Countless situations may arise in which a sport manager may either implement process or argue for more process. Whether a sport manager is firing a coach or assistant or sanctioning an athlete for misconduct, some form of process is due. Sport managers must be careful when developing rules and regulations that could restrict someone's life, liberty, or property interests. By understanding what is due in terms of process, sport managers can protect themselves in claims that their actions conflict with the Constitution.

Discussion Questions

1. Suppose that you are an athletic director of a large public high school. (a) The women's basketball coach approaches you and asks whether you would permit allowing fans a ticket discount if they present their church's weekly bulletin. The coach believes that this promotion would increase attendance at games. (b) The football coach, who is heavily involved in his local church, would like to invite a minister from his parish to speak and pray with the team in the locker room before games. What issues may be involved in making such decisions? What legal options may exist? How would you proceed in making such decisions?

2. Provide an example of restriction of an athlete's freedom of expression. Is the practice constitutional? How may a court decide?

3. In an equal protection case, when will the court use strict scrutiny? Intermediate scrutiny?

4. Provide and discuss a recent example involving an athlete being disciplined for posting something on a social media site. What legal issues may be involved in such cases involving high school, college, and professional athletes?

5. How can a sport organization implement a constitutionally acceptable affirmative action program?

6. What governmental deprivations trigger due process protection?

7. Provide and discuss a recent sport-related case law example in which the plaintiff alleged a due process violation.

8. What is substantive due process and how does it differ from procedural due process?

9. Why have state high school athletic associations typically been declared state actors?

10. Suppose that you are an athletic director at a major, public university. A transgender student has expressed interest in participating in athletics. How would you address this request? What legal and policy issues may this request involve? Consult the following resource for guidance: *NCAA Inclusion of Transgender Student-Athletes*.

MOOT COURT CASE

A Violation of Constitutional Rights

Paul was a football player for a public university. He was the first member of his family to attend a university and was proud of his athletic scholarship. Paul made decent grades and, unlike most of his teammates, generally stayed out of trouble. After a game against the university's in-state rival, Paul posted comments about his decreasing amount of playing time and the coaching staff's alleged lack of leadership, which had resulted in lower team morale. The university president was so infuriated by Paul's negative comments that he terminated Paul's scholarship. To make matters worse, Paul did not find out about the termination of his scholarship until he tried to enroll the following semester. Paul was confused by the president's decision because he did not violate a university rule or policy and did not receive an opportunity to challenge the president's ruling. Paul sues the university, claiming that his constitutional rights were violated.

Gender Equity

Chapter Objectives

After reading this chapter, you will know the following:

- The various federal gender equity laws and how they apply to sport

- The history of Title IX, how it has been interpreted, and how it is applied today

- The definition of sexual harassment and how it is regulated in sport

- The various types of employment discrimination laws

Case Studies in Sport Law Connection

Check out the following case studies related to this chapter in the accompanying e-book, *Case Studies in Sport Law, Second Edition* (Pittman, Spengler, & Young, 2016):

Davis v. Monroe County Board of Education

Favia v. Indiana University of Pennsylvania

Franklin v. Gwinnett County Public Schools

Gebser v. Lago Vista Independent School District

Jackson v. Birmingham Board of Education

Kelley v. Board of Trustees

Roberts v. Colorado State Board of Agriculture

Perhaps no area of sport law is more controversial than the laws concerning gender equity. These laws were created to combat discrimination in all areas of education. Title IX has been used to focus on athletics at the high school and university level because the government and the courts have found athletics to be a valuable part of the educational mission of high schools and universities.

Athletic administrators are often caught in the difficult situation of deciding how to allocate resources within their athletic programs properly and fairly. At issue is the allocation of scholarship funds, roster spots, travel funds, equipment and supplies, and facilities and practice space. These decisions often come down to finances. Because football and men's basketball are the primary, if not the only, revenue-producing sports in many athletic programs, athletic administrators find it difficult to balance a budget while also providing opportunities to female athletes.

This chapter explores federal gender equity laws and their effect on athletics. It discusses the legal framework of gender equity and the historical development and modification of this framework. The analysis begins with the federal laws, regulations, and guidelines that make up gender equity law. The focus then shifts to areas of athletics that are subject to gender equity laws, including participation, scheduling, and facilities. This chapter also focuses on conduct within athletics that can be actionable under gender equity laws, including harassment and employment discrimination.

Title IX

In the late 1960s and early 1970s, few athletes at the high school or university level were female. Women who participated received little support from athletic department budgets. With the enactment of Title IX, women began to see exponential gains in athletic participation at the high school and university levels.

The legislative impetus for Title IX was the Civil Rights Act of 1964. Its framework, which forced schools and employers to honor the civil rights of minority students and employees, also forced schools and employers to recognize the rights of women. Title IX of the Education Amendments of 1972 (20 U.S.C. §§ 1681 et seq., 2015) provides the following:

No person in the United States shall, on the basis of sex, be excluded from participation in, be denied the benefits of, or be subjected to discrimination under any education program or activity receiving Federal financial assistance.

Simply stated, Title IX prohibits programs that receive federal funding from excluding people from participating in the programs or denying people access to the benefits that the programs might provide. The focus of Title IX is to prohibit discrimination against the underrepresented sex, which historically has been women.

Although the law's prohibition of discrimination seems clear, many questions remain. Title IX says nothing about athletics; instead, its focus is on educational programs. But courts quickly understood that athletic participation is a benefit within an overall educational program. As a result, the focus of Title IX litigation has been athletic departments and organizations.

There has also been confusion over what programs or activities receive federal financial assistance and therefore come under Title IX. At first, courts determined that the law applied only to programs that received federal funding. Therefore, athletic departments were not covered unless it was clear that the department itself directly received federal funding. In fact, in 1984 the U.S. Supreme Court found that only the specific department receiving federal funding should be required to comply with Title IX (*Grove City College et al. v. Bell*, 1984).

In the case of *Grove City College*, a private liberal arts college refused to agree to Title IX's nondiscrimination provisions as required by the Department of Education. As a result, the Department of Education pulled grant and loan money for students. The school sued so that it could get the funding back. The Supreme Court agreed that the Department of Education could pull the funding because the school did not comply with Title IX, but the court limited its decision to the specific programs at the school that received federal financial assistance.

The results of this case were staggering. Because most universities have separate financial aid offices that provide student financial aid, athletic departments could avoid review under Title IX because the athletic departments themselves did not receive direct federal financial aid. But 3 years later Congress passed the Civil Rights Restoration Act (2015), overturning the Supreme Court and making clear that as long as any part of a program or activity receives federal financial assistance, Title IX applies (20 U.S.C. § 1687, 2015). As a result, because virtually every American university and high school receives some form of federal funding, Title IX applies to all schools.

Although Title IX applies to virtually every school, it does not apply directly to every athletic organization. For instance, the Supreme Court has held that the National Collegiate Athletic Association (NCAA) is not subject to Title IX because the organization does not directly receive federal funds (*NCAA v. Smith*, 1999). Renee Smith sued the NCAA because its rules barred her from participating in volleyball at one institution after she had already graduated from another institution. The Supreme Court found that the NCAA only indirectly received federal funds from the dues paid by its member schools and that this was not enough to force the NCAA to be subject to Title IX. Regardless, the NCAA has voluntarily agreed to work toward compliance with the law and has been at the forefront of providing equitable opportunities for women.

There was also early confusion over who could bring a lawsuit to push for equitable opportunities under the law. Title IX does not provide any specific way for an individual to sue to enforce the law. But in 1979 the Supreme Court held that there is an implied private right of action under Title IX (*Cannon v. Univ. of Chicago*, 1979). In *Cannon*, a female student who was denied admission to a medical school sued the school for violating Title IX. The Supreme Court found that an individual can sue under Title IX even though this right is not spelled out in the language of the statute itself. After this case, private individuals, from students to coaches, could sue, arguing that a school or program violated Title IX.

For many years it was unclear what a successful plaintiff could receive if she won a Title IX lawsuit. The law provides that federal funding can be pulled from any school that violates Title IX (20 U.S.C. §1682, 2015), but this punishment has never been imposed. In 1992 the Supreme Court ruled that monetary damages could be available to people who were successful in lawsuits alleging intentional violations of Title IX (*Franklin v. Gwinnett County Public Schools*, 1992). (See more about this case in the accompanying e-book, *Case Studies in Sport Law, Second Edition* [Pittman, Spengler, & Young, 2016].)

The regulation and enforcement of the law were left to the then Department of Health, Education and Welfare, which is now the Office for Civil Rights (OCR) within the Department of Education. In 1975 the department passed regulations that spelled out how the law affects athletics. The regulations initially focused on equal opportunity (Athletics, 34 C.F.R. 106.41, 2015). They began by repeating Title IX's prohibition of discrimination more specifically within any high school, intercollegiate, club, or intramural athletic program. The regulations mandated that high school and university athletic programs provide equal opportunity for members of both sexes within several program areas, including provision of equipment and supplies, scheduling of games and practices, provision of locker rooms, and provision of practice and competitive facilities (Athletics, 34 C.F.R. 106.41(c)(2–10), 2015). Next, the inter-

ests and abilities of both genders and the selection of sports for both must be effectively accommodated (Athletics, 34 C.F.R. 106.41(c)(1), 2015). The regulations also call for equivalency in the administration of financial assistance (Financial Assistance, 34 C.F.R. 106.37(c), 2015). Although meant to explain in more depth the requirements and enforcement of Title IX, the regulations did not accomplish this goal because they did not provide any way for a school to measure whether it was in compliance with Title IX.

After the regulations were in place, advocates began to sue athletic programs that they perceived were not providing equal opportunities to female athletes. In 1979 the government attempted to provide further clarification with its policy interpretation (Policy Interpretation, 44 F.R. 239, 1979). The interpretation was designed specifically for university athletics but applies equally to high school, club, and intramural athletic programs. The interpretation is divided into three areas.

- Part 1 deals with financial assistance and requires that such assistance be allocated equally to male and female athletic participants.

- Part 2 deals with equality in the other program areas provided in the regulations, such as facilities and equipment.

- Part 3 deals with **effective accommodation** of the interests and abilities of both sexes to provide equal athletic opportunity for members of both sexes. This area has seen the most litigation.

The interpretation is not law, but courts have repeatedly deferred to it because it is the interpretation of the law provided by the federal agency responsible for enforcing Title IX.

Female athletes have always been and continue to be the underrepresented sex, but they have made exponential gains in participation, even though their participation is still not equal to that of male athletes. For instance, at the high school level, according to the National Federation of State High School Athletic Associations (NFHS), during the 2013–2014 season, 3,267,664 girls participated in high school sports, an all-time record. At the same time 4,527,994 boys participated, the highest total ever for boys (National Federation of State High School Associations, 2014). At the university level, even though women make up 57% of all undergraduate students (National Center for Education Statistics, 2013), they represent only 43.2% of university athletes (National Collegiate Athletic Association, 2012a, p. 5). During the 2011–2012 season, 195,657 women and 257,690 men participated in collegiate athletics (National Collegiate Athletic Association, 2012a, p. 79). Therefore, girls and women still do not participate at levels equal to boys and men and are underrepresented in athletics. As a result, the specific enforcement mechanisms applied by the OCR and the courts focus on bringing female athletes up to a level of participation equal to that of male athletes.

Since these regulations were put in place, gender equity disputes have focused on the areas that are discussed in the next sections of this chapter, including participation issues, such as the **three-part test**, separate teams, and claims by athletes from discontinued male teams; scheduling of sports and facilities for each sex; harassment of students by coaches or other athletes; employment discrimination; and federal reporting requirements. Sport administrators must be familiar with how the courts have interpreted the law and regulations by using the interpretation. Much of the interpretation has been further clarified by the OCR in the past 2 decades, as discussed later in this chapter.

Participation

No one can deny that since the implementation of Title IX, and especially since 1979 when the policy interpretation was developed and the *Cannon* case was decided, athletic opportunities for women have increased exponentially. Before passage of the law, approximately 16,000 university female athletes participated on varsity teams. By 2014 there were 9,581 women's university teams, representing 8.83 women's teams per school, the highest number of female teams ever (Carpenter & Acosta, 2014, p. 1). Still, the nature of these increases continues to be debated.

Lawsuits under Title IX are rare occurrences. Although many schools would not be considered in compliance with Title IX for many reasons, student-athletes are not necessarily looking to sue these schools. A lawsuit usually is not the first thing on the minds of high school and university athletes. Indeed, many female student-athletes appreciate the opportunities they have and do not focus their participation in athletics on comparisons to their male counterparts. Still, because the OCR is understaffed and its role is to enforce the law rather than monitor schools' compliance with the law, most changes are made only when student-athletes raise the issues and initiate a lawsuit. Schools must be vigilant in keeping track of participation opportunities by sex, not only to make sure they comply with the law but also to be prepared if their best efforts are met with legal claims by disgruntled student-athletes.

Although some female advocacy groups believe otherwise, most athletic administrators are not focused solely on providing opportunities to men. Lawyers, courts, and even the OCR staff themselves have struggled for years to understand, apply, and enforce Title IX. Often, situations arise when well-intentioned athletic administrators make painful budgetary decisions and do not understand the effect on gender equity compliance. The days when athletic administrators intentionally engaged in discriminatory conduct are long gone. Nonetheless, most athletic departments still do not comply with all aspects of the federal gender equity law. The problem is even worse at the high school level, which has not yet been the focus of extensive evaluation or litigation.

Claims brought in connection with presumed participation issues typically focus on the three-part test created in the regulations and policy interpretation used to implement Title IX, separate teams for athletes of separate genders, and claims by athletes from discontinued male teams.

When administrators and managers analyze participation opportunities for athletes, the focus must start with the regulations. As mentioned earlier, the regulations mandate equal athletic opportunity for both sexes and the effective accommodation of the interests and abilities of both sexes. The policy interpretation sets out a three-part analysis, called the three-part test, to assess whether these interests and abilities are being equally accommodated by the provision of equal athletic opportunities (Policy Interpretation, 1979):

1. The first part looks at whether participation opportunities for male and female students are provided in numbers substantially proportionate to the school's undergraduate enrollment.

2. The second test focuses on whether the institution can show a history and continuing practice of program expansion responsive to the developing interests and abilities of the members of the underrepresented sex.

3. The third test looks to whether an institution can demonstrate that the interests and abilities of the members of that sex have been accommodated fully and effectively by the present program. To determine whether these interests have been accommodated, schools must survey their students to determine their interests and abilities.

This analysis begins with a look at whether participation opportunities for male and female students are in proportion to a school's undergraduate enrollment. This first test has often been known as a **safe harbor**, because courts and the OCR have determined that schools that can demonstrate that the numbers of women and men who participate in athletics are proportionate to the numbers of women and men in the student body will have met the requirements of Title IX. In other words, if a school's enrollment is 50% men and 50% women, there should be close to 50% men and 50% women participating in its athletic program.

The second test focuses on whether the school has continuously expanded programs to meet the interests and abilities of women. In the past, many schools complied with Title IX under this test. Four decades after the enactment of Title IX, it is hard to believe that schools will still be able to use this test as a defense against a Title IX claim if they have not expanded their athletic programs during this time.

The third test looks to whether a school has fully and effectively met the interests and abilities of female athletes. To determine whether these interests have been accommodated, schools must survey their students to determine their interests and abilities. Courts and commentators do not agree on whether only enrolled students must be surveyed or whether schools must also survey applicants or admitted students. Schools must rely on their attorneys or the advice of experts who are up to date on the law and its effect on athletics.

To provide athletic programs that comply with the three-part test, athletic administrators and their attorneys (i.e., university general counsels or outside legal representatives) can look to several cases that have interpreted the test (see, for example, the A Court's Review of a School Under the Three-Part Test sidebar). Although the law and its regulations have been in place since the early 1970s, the interpretation of this law and its enforcement have developed over time (particularly over the past 2 decades). An administrator or manager must be constantly vigilant to remain up to date on new court decisions and governmental interpretations of gender equity laws.

A 1996 clarification memorandum by the OCR reiterated that the three-part test gives schools three ways to comply with Title IX (Office for Civil Rights, 1996). Under the first part, schools must ensure that the numbers of male and female athletes receiving benefits (e.g., scholarships, tutoring aid, athletic training) from the school are proportional to the school's total numbers of male and female students; proportionality is required, however, only if there are enough athletes to make a viable team in a particular sport.

Under the second part, schools must be responsive to projected female interests and the interests of enrolled students. To comply with this part, schools must be able to demonstrate that they continuously expand opportunities in sport in response

IN THE COURTROOM

A Court's Review of a School Under the Three-Part Test

Cohen v. Brown University (1992)

Several members of the women's teams at Brown University sued the university for violating Title IX (*Cohen v. Brown University*, 1992). In 1991 Brown funded 31 teams, 16 for men and 15 for women. Those teams included 894 athletes—566 (63.3%) men and 328 (36.7%) women. That year, 2,951 men (52.4%) and 2,683 women (47.6%) were enrolled at Brown. In response to a university directive to cut 5% to 8% from the budget, the school eliminated funding for men's golf and water polo and women's gymnastics and volleyball.

The court began by looking at the first part of the three-part test and found it clear that the university was not in compliance. Although 48.2% of enrolled students were female, they represented only 36.6% of the athletes at the school, a 12% difference. For the second part of the test, Brown failed to show a history of

expanding opportunities for women since 1977. And finally, because Brown was cutting varsity opportunities for women, the school was not effectively accommodating the interests and abilities of its female students as required in the third part. The court ordered the university to restore the women's teams with funding, coaching, and other benefits comparable with the men's teams (*Cohen v. Brown University*, 1992).

The case eventually returned to the First Circuit in 1996 (*Cohen v. Brown University*, 1996). The school attempted to show that female students were not interested in sport and thus the school was in compliance with the third part of the test. Pointing to the 1996 clarification, the court noted that when a school cuts a viable women's team, it is not effectively accommodating the interests and abilities of the female students on that team.

to women's interests. Cuts to male sports that increase the proportionate participation of women, although allowed under the first part, are not allowed under the second part.

As to the third part, the OCR made clear that a school must effectively accommodate the interests of all admitted and enrolled students. In reviewing a school, the OCR will consider whether there is unmet interest, whether this interest will sustain a viable team, and whether such a team would likely have opportunity to compete in the region where the school is located. A 2010 clarification required that schools periodically assess student interest to make sure they are meeting the accommodation goal (Office for Civil Rights, 2010b). As with the second part, schools cannot cut women's teams under this part because the presence of a team is a clear indication of interest and ability in that team.

A clarification from OCR in 2003 reiterated that each of these parts provides a sufficient means for complying with Title IX (Office for Civil Rights, 2003). As a result, schools have options in how to provide athletic opportunities to their students.

A case that focused on the three-part test was *Boucher v. Syracuse University* (1998). The case, which involved members of the women's club lacrosse and club softball teams at Syracuse University, focused on the application of the three-part test. In 1971 the university established its women's athletic program with basketball, fencing, swimming, tennis, and volleyball teams. Field hockey replaced fencing in 1972. Women's crew was added in 1977, and indoor and outdoor track were added in 1981. The OCR performed a Title IX compliance review from 1980 to 1982 and found the school to be in compliance. In 1996 the school added a women's soccer team, and in 1997 it added a women's lacrosse team. During the time of the litigation the school had 10 men's and

11 women's teams, and it planned to start a women's softball team in the 1999–2000 season. All other sports were club sports, meaning that the student participants raised the necessary funds.

The student-plaintiffs alleged that the university was in violation of Title IX because it did not provide effective accommodation of their interests and abilities. The plaintiffs claimed that because they were members of successful club teams, the university should recognize their participation as the interest and ability necessary to warrant varsity status and to receive all the benefits and university funding that varsity teams received.

Pointing to the policy interpretation, Syracuse argued that it complied with Title IX under part 2—that it had a history and continuing practice of program expansion for women. In reviewing this defense, the court found that although no new women's teams were added from 1982 to 1995, the number of female varsity athletes increased during that time and that the addition of new teams since 1995 demonstrated a history of expanding opportunities for women. The court also noted that although the university did not have a formal policy of monitoring the interests of its students to expand athletic opportunities for them, the athletic director informally monitored this interest by reviewing club sport participation and sport-related interests at the national and regional levels. Therefore, the expansion in the 1990s was in direct response to the interests and abilities of female students. As a result, the court found that Syracuse met the second part of the three-part test.

For many, the results of this case were disconcerting. Although the university had begun to expand opportunities for women, this occurred only after a 15-year lapse and did not take into account thriving club sports teams that offered clear indications of interest by female students. Many athletic programs have similar patterns of growth, showing large gains for women in the 1970s and little gain after 1980. But this case is clear evidence that courts do not want to impose their judgment over that of athletic administrators. When evidence indicates that administrators have made their best efforts to meet the interests of female students, courts typically allow the administrators to meet those interests in the manner they see fit.

Separate Teams

Although many advocates have argued that one way to ensure equity in participation is to have teams made up of both sexes, the regulations do allow separate teams. Specifically, schools may sponsor separate teams for members of each sex when the selection of team members is based on athletic skills or the activity involved is a contact sport (Athletics, 34 C.F.R. 106.41(b), 2015). This

language has led to what some call the **contact sport exception**, an argument that contact sports such as football should not be taken into account concerning a school's compliance with Title IX. However, courts have consistently found that there is no contact sport exception, so football and other contact sports must be counted when evaluating a school's compliance with Title IX.

Many schools run into problems with this issue. No other sport can compare with football in team roster size. Therefore, no other sport will receive benefits, from scholarship aid to facilities, that can compare with the benefits received by a football team. At the same time, because of revenues associated with larger crowds and bowl games at the highest level of football, no sport produces as much revenue for an athletic department as football does. Still, universities must include the football team in any calculations involving the three-part test or other parts of Title IX. As a result, the number of

Schools with large football rosters must still comply with all aspects of Title IX. The number of football players must be factored into Title IX compliance.

teams at a school can be misleading if one of those teams is a football team. If a school has 12 male teams and 12 female teams, an outside observer may believe that the school is in compliance. The football team, however, may be equivalent to four or five female teams, so compliance may still be a problem.

Another interesting situation occurs when an athlete is allowed to participate on a team of another gender. For example, Heather Mercer, an all-state kicker in high school, tried out for the Duke University football team. In her first year she practiced with the team but did not play in a game until an annual intrasquad game, when she kicked the winning field goal. After that game she was featured on ESPN, and the coach told her she had made the team. The next year she again did not participate in any games, but she was listed on the team roster and practiced with the team. During that year, however, she faced various forms of discrimination including offensive comments from the coach. At the beginning of the next season she was dropped from the team.

Mercer sued, arguing that the decision to cut her from the team was discriminatory because other less qualified walk-ons were kept on the team (*Mercer v. Duke University*, 1999). Relying on the contact sport exception, the district court dismissed her claim. The appellate court reviewed the language of the regulations and the prohibition against discrimination in all circumstances, and found that after an institution allows a member of one sex to try out for a team operated for the other sex, even in a contact sport, the institution cannot discriminate against that person. Subsequently, a jury awarded Mercer $1 in compensatory damages, $2 million in punitive damages, and attorney's fees. The university appealed, and the court vacated the punitive damage

award, finding that punitive damages are not available for private actions to enforce Title IX (*Mercer v. Duke University*, 2002).

What did Heather Mercer get by winning her case? Not much. She received $1 in damages from the university and was reimbursed for the attorney's fees she paid. The university was not forced to reinstate her on the team, but it could not have done so even if it had wanted to because she had graduated by the time the litigation ended in 2005.

Although the court made clear that there is no specific contact sport exception as previously understood, the result of the case means that allowing female athletes to try out for men's teams is risky because cutting those athletes from the team for any reason will be difficult. Instead, universities are better served by keeping separate teams as allowed under the regulations.

Cutting Teams

Since the 1970s a consistent criticism of the application of federal gender equity laws is that they have resulted in the cutting of many male teams, especially at the university level. In the 1980s and 1990s many schools decided that to come into compliance with Title IX, they had to eliminate men's baseball, swimming, golf, and wrestling teams. Much of the focus of this litigation has been on the proportionality test contained in the first part of the three-part test. Advocates for men's sports have claimed that this test has forced schools to cut male teams or that schools that seemingly do not provide proportionate opportunities actually do. One problem is that the OCR has never set a ratio that can be seen as proportionate. Therefore, schools do not know whether a 10% difference between the percentage of enrolled female students and the percentage of female students who participate in athletics is close enough to satisfy the test. Courts are left to interpret the facts case by case.

In 1993 the University of Illinois decided to cut men's swimming and fencing, and men's and women's diving. The decision was made mainly in response to a large athletic budget deficit. But since 1982 the OCR had determined that the university was not in compliance with Title IX. In 1993, although women made up 44% of the student body, they represented only 23.4% of the school's athletes. Therefore, even with the cuts, the percentage of women participating was still substantially lower than the percentage of men participating and the percentage of women enrolled. Members of the men's swimming team claimed that the decision to cut the team was illegal because the regulations and policy interpretation violated Title IX and the three-part test mandated a quota system whereby schools had to push constantly for numerical equality in athletics. The court disagreed, finding not only that the university had to defer to the agency rules but also that its decision to cut the men's teams was specifically an effort to comply with the law. Therefore, the male athletes' claims were dismissed (*Kelly v. Board of Trustees*, 1994).

Of course, the story didn't end there. Male athletes continued to sue universities when their teams were cut. In fact, in 2001, the secretary of education's Commission on Opportunity in Athletics argued that the proportionality test in part 1 of the three-part test has caused schools to cut men's teams. The OCR disagreed, however, pointing out that although men's teams could be cut so that universities could come into compliance with the law, this method of compliance is not only disfavored but also contrary to the spirit of the law in providing opportunities for all (Office for Civil Rights, 2003). Predictably, the lawsuits by male

athletes and advocacy groups over these cuts have continued.

In another case, former members of the disbanded male tennis, wrestling, and soccer teams at Miami University of Ohio sued the school, claiming that by cutting their teams the university violated Title IX's prohibitions against eliminating programs on the basis of sex (*Miami Univ. Wrestling Club v. Miami Univ.*, 2002). The school had worked hard to come into compliance, but by 1997, although female students were 55% of enrollment, they represented only 47% of athletes participating in sport. Under the first prong of the three-part test, the university interpreted that this disparity would not be seen as providing proportional opportunities to both sexes. The university also knew that interests among women were unmet in equestrian, crew, golf, lacrosse, and water polo. After conducting a fiscal analysis, the university administrators realized that they could not afford to add all these new teams. Therefore, the administrators determined that the only way the university could come into compliance with Title IX was by cutting four men's teams. Reviewing the situation, the court noted that the policy interpretation recognizes that Title IX can lead to difficult choices because universities do not have unlimited funds. Dismissing the male athletes' claims, the court found that gender equity laws provide only members of the underrepresented sex with rights; they do not provide males, part of the overrepresented sex, with any such protection. Therefore, cutting men's opportunities was a reasonable way for the university to comply with Title IX.

This decision has not satisfied male athletes who have lost their opportunity to participate or advocacy groups such as the College Sports Council, which posits that cutting men's teams is a form of prohibited discrimination. In answer to this, Congress asked the U.S. General Accounting Office (GAO) to research why universities had cut men's teams. The 2001 report found that from the 1981–1982 to 1998–1999 seasons, opportunities for women increased from 90,000 to 163,000 and women gained 3,784 teams (U.S. General Accounting Office, 2001). At the same time, male opportunities stayed at a higher level as the number of male participants increased from 220,000 to 232,000 and men gained 36 teams (U.S. General Accounting Office, 2001). Overall, 386 male teams and 150 female teams were cut. In most cases, when women's teams were added, no cuts were made in men's teams; instead, these schools relied on revenue from other sports or outside sources to fund the new teams. The report found that teams were added to respond to female students' interests in particular sports and to meet gender equity requirements, whereas men's teams were cut for several reasons, including lack of student interest, budget concerns, and the need to comply with gender equity laws. The report found that for most schools, female participation increases were not at the expense of men's teams.

In 2007 the GAO (which had since been renamed the Government Accountability Office, still GAO) released another report finding that both men's and women's participation in intercollegiate athletics increased from 1991 to 2005. Although men's participation increased 21% over this time and women's participation increased 63%, men's overall participation in university athletics was still higher than women's (U.S. Government Accountability Office, 2007). Overall participation in most male sports still increased during this time, except in wrestling, which had significant declines in participation.

Advocates for men's sports continue to disagree with the GAO reports and with the use of Title IX, blaming the law and particularly the three-part test for the cuts in their sports. In 2004 the National Wrestling Coaches Association (NWCA) sued the Department of Education, trying to get the department to rescind the three-part test, claiming that its misapplication had caused the illegal cuts in men's teams (*National Wrestling Coaches Assoc. v. Department of Educ.*, 2004). The NWCA argued that the GAO report showed that the teams were cut because of the application of the three-part test. The court disagreed, finding instead that the report was inconclusive about the primary reason for these cuts and that many schools had decided to cut male teams because of their own budgetary decisions. Similar to decisions by other courts addressing claims brought by men from cut teams, the decision by the court was that because the school's own actions led to the cuts, the NWCA could not sue the federal government under Title IX.

Until 2011 no court had supported this type of claim. But in a case brought before the U.S. Court of Appeals for the Fourth Circuit, the court found that an advocacy group may have standing to sue the federal government because its members are former athletes and the university involved claimed that they made the cuts to male teams only to comply with federal law (*Equity in Athletics v. Department of Education*, 2011). If this decision is upheld, it could pave the way for men to have a new claim against schools that cut their sports opportunities.

Athletic administrators face many difficult choices. Even non-revenue-producing sports can cost a lot of money to maintain. Although we want to believe that a school can continue to add women's teams in an effort to provide opportunities for women, this goal is often unrealistic because of the financial costs involved. Therefore, honest

Many schools are faced with cutting men's teams to comply with Title IX.

and fair-minded athletic and university administrators must make difficult decisions and often have to cut men's teams to comply with the law. The following example provides some perspective.

If a school has an 80% representation of male athletes among all of its athletic programs and females represent 80% of all enrolled students (but only 20% of the school's athletes), the school does not have to cut opportunities for males to comply with the law unless it follows part 1 of the three-part test. If it follows part 1, the school will have to work hard to ensure that the level of female participation in sport approaches 80%—the proportion of female enrolled students. The university does have options, however, because it can comply with Title IX under the second part of the test by showing a history of program expansion for female students. Alternatively, it can follow the third part and comply by demonstrating that it is meeting the interests and abilities of its students.

Although schools can cut male teams and opportunities to come into compliance with Title IX, the reverse is not true. In the early 1980s, the OCR conducted a compliance review at Colorado State University (CSU), finding that opportunities for men and women were not proportional to enrollment. During the 3 years reviewed, the differences between women enrolled and women athletes were 7.5%, 12.5%, and 12.7%. In 1992 CSU announced that it was cutting the varsity women's fast-pitch softball team and men's baseball. Similar to the male athletes mentioned previously, the women sued, claiming that the school violated Title IX when it cut the women's team (*Roberts v. Colorado State Board of Agriculture*, 1993). (See more about this case in the accompanying e-book, *Case Studies in Sport Law, Second Edition* [Pittman, Spengler, & Young, 2016].) At the time the disparity between enrolled women and participating women was 10.5%, and the court found that this percentage was unacceptable even though it was a lesser disparity than before the teams were cut. Turning to the second part of the three-part test, the school could not show any history and continuing expansion of opportunities for female athletes. As to the third part of the test, the fact that CSU was cutting a softball team that played a competitive schedule and had interested and able participants was evidence that the school was not meeting the interests and abilities of the underrepresented sex. Therefore, the court ordered the school to reinstate the team and to provide it with the benefits associated with varsity status.

The *Roberts* court acknowledged that most schools facing budgetary constraints would not be able to comply with Title IX by continuing to expand opportunities for female athletes. In addition, schools cannot claim that cutting large men's teams, such as lacrosse, which has a 40-man roster, somehow results in expanded opportunities for women. Although the percentage of athletes who are women may increase because of cuts in men's teams, such cuts do not add any opportunities for women.

So what can a university do? Faced with financial difficulties and compliance with federal law, a university can cut a men's team to meet the first part of the three-part test. This option is not preferred or favored, but it is one way for a university to meet its obligations. A university cannot cut women's teams at the same time even if those cuts would alleviate financial concerns. But the issue is not this cut and dried. Creative budgetary planning and support of viable athletic programs can allow a university to avoid cutting opportunities for anyone. A university has many options when it comes to complying with Title IX, and administrators who complain that their only option is to cut opportunities may not be running financially efficient athletic departments in the first place.

What Is a Sport?

Sports administrators often struggle to determine what activities can count as a sport in their efforts to comply with Title IX. The federal government has provided guidance on this question, but the definition of sport for Title IX purposes continues to evolve.

The 1996 Clarification provided that athletic opportunities offered to comply with Title IX requirements must be "real, not illusory," but such general statements have not added much clarity (Office for Civil Rights, 1996). In 2000, in two letters to high school athletic administrators, OCR tried to provide further clarity. Initially, an April 2000 letter explained that in judging whether an activity can count as a sport, the focus will start with whether "the primary purpose of the activity is athletic competition" and whether athletes are "engaging in sports at the intercollegiate or interscholastic level of competition" (Office for Civil Rights, 2000, April 11). As a result, club and intramural athletes cannot be counted to meet Title IX requirements. The letter also reinforced that OCR presumes that drill team, cheerleading, and similar activities are not sports. One month later OCR clarified this guidance by further specifying that cheerleading includes competitive and sideline cheer and that similar activities like danceline, skateline, and pep squads are presumed not to be sports (Office for Civil Rights, 2000, May 24).

A Dear Colleague Letter in 2008 from OCR provided further guidance for sport administrators who were trying to determine what activities could count as sports. In this letter OCR laid out in detail factors that it uses to determine whether an activity is a sport, including team preparation, structure, administration, and competition (Office for Civil Rights, 2008). In addition,

OCR introduced another presumption by explaining that if a school is part of an athletic association like the NCAA, the association has its own requirements for determining what a sport is, and the school follows the association's requirements, then OCR will also find that the activity is a sport.

This all matters because schools are constantly seeking to create new sport activities, perhaps to comply with Title IX but also to respond to student interest in a particular activity. For example, within the NCAA, only new sports for women can be created. Since 1991 the NCAA has added new, emerging sports for women including rowing, bowling, water polo, and ice hockey (National Collegiate Athletic Association, 2012b). Cheerleading has never been sanctioned as a sport. Most recently, following the letters discussed earlier, the United States Court of Appeals for the Second Circuit affirmed a district court ruling that Quinnipiac University could not count competitive cheerleading as a sport (*Biediger v. Quinnipiac University*, 2012).

The district court did leave the door open a bit, noting that "once competitive cheer is better organized and defined, and surely in the event that the NCAA recognizes the activity as an emerging sport—competitive cheer will be acknowledged as a bona fide sporting activity" (*Biediger v. Quinnipiac University*, 2010, p. 101). If cheerleading or similar activities can be counted as sports, the landscape of high school and college athletics may change irrevocably. For example, according to the National Federation of State High School Athletic Associations, for the 2011–2012 season 122,875 girls were participating in the sports of competitive spirit squad, dance and drill, and drill team, and another 99,977 were participating in the activity of cheerleading (National Federation of State High School Associations, 2012). If these activities were all counted as sports, an additional 222,852 girls would immediately be participating in high school sports. Before long, more colleges may be providing opportunities to continue participation in these activities. Some universities have already done so by sponsoring acrobatics and tumbling through the National Collegiate Acrobatics & Tumbling Association. And perhaps someday the NCAA will sanction such activities as sports.

Facilities and Scheduling

As mentioned earlier, the regulations enforcing Title IX discuss other program areas. Although these program areas have not been the subject of extensive litigation at the university level, two areas have been the subject of litigation at the high school level: the scheduling of games and practices and the provision of locker rooms and practice and competitive facilities. For these program areas, the policy interpretation sets out a complicated scheme of enforcement.

The governing principle of the policy interpretation is that male and female athletes should receive equivalent treatment, benefits, and opportunities. The interpretation created a four-part analysis of these program areas:

1. Assessment of benefits and treatment
2. Analysis of nondiscriminatory factors
3. Additional factors to analyze from the regulations
4. Overall determination of compliance

The first step is the assessment. This assessment compares the benefits and treatment given to both sexes to see whether they are comparable. For example, if both male and female soccer teams participate in the same season, they are comparable in the assessment of the scheduling program area.

Second, the provision of these program areas can differ if the differences in what is provided to male and female athletes are attributable to nondiscriminatory factors. Therefore, because of the nature of football, schools can have football programs for male athletes that provide more roster spots, larger practice facilities, and other unique benefits, as long as the overall athletic program benefits provided to both male and female athletes are equivalent.

Third, the interpretation provides additional factors that must be analyzed to assess compliance with the 10 factors provided in the regulations. For example, the regulations mandate that athletic programs provide equal opportunity in scheduling of games and practice times for male and female athletes (Athletics, 34 C.F.R. 106.41(c)(3), 2015). The interpretation then explains that the assessment of whether the scheduling of male and female sports is equal must look at the number of competitive events per sport, the number and length of practice opportunities, the time of day when competitive events are scheduled, and the opportunity to engage in preseason and postseason competition (Policy Interpretation, 1979).

Fourth, an overall determination of compliance is made. If school policies related to the program areas are discriminatory, the school will not be in compliance with Title IX. If benefits provided to members of opposite sexes are significantly different—for instance, if all male teams have better practice facilities than female teams and women do not have an advantage over men in any other benefits provided to them—the school will not be in compliance. Finally, if one benefit provided to male athletes is substantial—for instance, if male athletes receive significantly higher levels of financial aid—it may be enough to deny equal opportunity to female athletes.

This complicated area of the law can best be understood by looking at a sample case. In *McCormick v. School District of Mamoroneck* (2004), two Olympic-level female soccer players sued several New York school districts because girls' soccer was scheduled in the spring and boys' soccer in the fall. The districts put girls' soccer in the spring in response to a survey showing that most female soccer players preferred to play in the spring. This scheduling allowed girls' field hockey, a highly popular sport, to be played in the fall. But because girls' soccer was scheduled in the spring, girls could not participate in the regional and state soccer championships, which took place in the fall. In addition, university coaches recruit female soccer players in the fall season, so girls who played in the spring may have missed out on scholarship opportunities.

In reviewing the girls' claim, the court focused on the fact that girls who participated in soccer could not participate in postseason competition, a specific factor provided in the policy interpretation to assess compliance. The district argued that it would be costly to move girls' soccer because there were not enough coaches or enough field space and scheduling soccer in the fall would negatively affect other female sports. The court found this rationale unpersuasive and found that this one disparity was enough to show that the scheduling of girls' soccer in the spring was a violation of Title IX. As a result, even though the majority of the girls preferred the scheduling of soccer as it was, the school districts had to change the schedule and move soccer to the fall season with boys' soccer.

When dealing with program areas such as scheduling, athletic administrators cannot rely on what they perceive as serving the interests of the majority. Instead, they must consider the effect of the schedule on participants of both sexes and make sure that the schedule is set to provide equivalent benefits to both sexes.

The issue is the same in relation to practice and competitive facilities. The policy interpretation sets out other factors that must be analyzed, including the quality and availability of the facilities, exclusivity of use of the facilities, availability and quality of locker rooms, and maintenance and preparation of those facilities. Schools have encountered problems when the facilities used by their teams are not comparable.

High school girls and boys in Minnesota have historically participated in the state hockey tournament in different facilities. The girls' tournament began in a 3,400-seat facility, but because the seating was insufficient for attendance, the tournament moved to the State Fair Coliseum, which seats 5,200. The boys' tournament is held at the XCEL Energy Center, the home of the NHL's Minnesota Wild, which seats 17,000. The OCR began to review the tournament in 2000. The Minnesota State High School League asked for bids to host the girls' tournament, but the professional sport facility was not interested. The league told the OCR that it was moving the girls' tournament to the brand-new Ridder Arena on the campus of the University of Minnesota, a newer facility than the XCEL Center but one that seats only 2,700. The OCR approved the move. The 2002 girls' tournament drew 15,551 fans, whereas the boys' tournament drew 120,000 fans. In reviewing the organization of the state hockey tournaments, the court noted that differences in the provision of competitive facilities are allowed only if those differences do not limit the potential for women's athletic events to increase in spectator appeal (*Mason v. Minnesota State High School League*, 2004). The court found that restricting the girls to a smaller facility could restrict the growth of the girls' hockey tournament and necessarily restricts the spectators, who can add to the success of the tournament.

At the university level, with the exception of some successful women's basketball teams, female athletes are often forced to practice or play in facilities that are not comparable to those available to male athletes. Even if men and women are in the same facility, male athletes often have the better time slots for practice (morning or afternoon) and competition (weekends or prime time on weekdays); female athletes often suffer through early morning practices and play in the middle of the week when spectators cannot easily support them. Female university athletes may eventually claim that their practice and game schedules and the facilities they use for practice and games are not comparable with those of men. Sport administrators must ensure that female athletes are given equal priority in scheduling games and practices and are allowed to play in facilities that are comparable with those of male athletes. Administrators who cannot ensure equity in these areas must increase benefits to female athletes in other areas, such as providing better equipment and supplies or better locker rooms, to offset this disparity.

Similar problems have been seen at the high school level when comparing girls' softball teams with boys' baseball teams. In one case, high school boys' baseball was provided with an electronic scoreboard, batting cage, concession stands, lighting for night games, and quality bleachers. Girls' softball received none of those benefits and played before smaller crowds because of dilapidated bleachers. In another high school, the boys played on baseball fields on campus that had all the amenities just listed, including a large storage area for their equipment. The girls played at public fields designed for boys' softball that contained a single small shed for their equipment. In both situations, the court found that the disparities in facilities and scheduling were violations of Title IX (*Daniels v. School Board of Brevard County*, 1997; *Landow v. School Board of Brevard County*, 2000).

The school board argued that it provided equal funding to each team so it could not be responsible for the inequities. Each team raised its own funds through a booster club, and the boys' teams were able to raise more funds for their facilities. Equality in funding, however, is a responsibility of the athletic administration, so it was the board's responsibility to put a system in place that ensured equal opportunity in the athletic facilities for baseball and softball. The board attempted to remedy the problem by taking away some of the benefits provided to the boys, such as by taking away the scoreboard for baseball. Although cutting boys' teams can bring a school into compliance with the effective accommodation requirements of the three-part test, imposing disadvantages on boys without improving benefits provided to girls does nothing to lead to equality.

Someday universities will face similar scrutiny. The focus could be university basketball programs, in which men typically play in better facilities that have higher seating capacities than do women. Universities may claim that they cannot bear the cost to provide similar opportunities for female basketball players, but such financial considerations are not legitimate reasons for otherwise discriminatory behavior. Intent to discriminate is not the issue: The law makes clear that the assessment is of the program factor, such as scheduling or the facility. The reasons for inequalities (e.g., women are forced to play in an inferior facility or under a less favorable schedule) need not constitute some form of intentional discrim-

ination. The differences may be enough to show that the school or university is in violation of Title IX.

Schools cannot hide the details about what is provided to their male or female athletes. The Equity in Athletics Disclosure Act of 1998 (Pub. L. No. 105-244, 1998) requires all universities that receive federal student aid and have intercollegiate athletic programs to prepare reports that track financial aid, athletic revenues, and other resources. These reports are provided to the public on the Office of Postsecondary Education's website at http://ope.ed.gov/athletics. The purpose of this reporting is to provide students and their parents more information about the schools that the students may attend.

Schools must also be careful in dealing with coaches or other employees who complain about differences in treatment between male and female sports. In 2005 the Supreme Court recognized that it is illegal for schools to retaliate against a coach or other employee who complains of inequalities that may be violations of Title IX (*Jackson v. Birmingham Board of Education*, 2005). In this case, the coach of the girls' basketball team complained that his team was not given funding or access to practice facilities and equipment comparable with the boys' team. He never claimed that anyone discriminated against him. He was soon fired as coach, but he kept his job as a physical education teacher. Although Title IX does not provide a way for a coach to sue unless he is the subject of discrimination, the court found that retaliation against a coach who complains of inequalities in an athletic program is also a form of discrimination.

Most Title IX issues are brought forth because of people, like the girls' basketball coach, who complain about inequalities. Athletes, especially at the high school level, may not notice the differences between girls' and boys' sports or may simply accept that things have always been that way. These students may not realize that "the way things have always been" is illegal.

Sexual Harassment

Another area of concern relates to conduct that athletes face that may cause them serious harm and discomfort and that may affect the nature of their participation. Many athletes have faced **sexual harassment** by coaches or fellow players that has not only harmed them physically and emotionally but also damaged their chances to participate in athletics. (See chapter 6 for a discussion of sexual harassment in the employment context.) Unfortunately, not until 1992 did the courts clearly show that sexual harassment by coaches was barred under Title IX.

Christine Franklin was a high school student subject to continued harassment from a coach who was also her teacher. The coach asked her about her sex life, asked whether she would sleep with older men, and forcibly kissed her in the school parking lot. After she complained, the school investigated the coach but did not dismiss him. In fact, the school discouraged her from pressing charges until the coach resigned at the end of the year. She complained to the OCR, which found that the school had allowed her to be subject to sexual harassment but agreed to let the school remedy the situation by putting together a grievance procedure to deal with similar situations in the future. Finding that this did nothing to help her, Franklin sued. The Supreme Court found that Title IX places a duty on schools to stop teachers and coaches from discriminating against students in any school activities (*Franklin v. Gwinnett County Public Schools*, 1992). In addition, because sexual

harassment is a form of discrimination, it is also barred. Because of this case, all victims of sexual harassment or other intentionally discriminatory conduct under Title IX can sue for monetary damages.

The OCR attempted to clarify the requirements that schools must follow with its 1997 and 2001 *Sexual Harassment Guidance* (Office for Civil Rights, 1997, 2001). A student can always sue the coach or teacher who harassed her or him. But the real issue in athletics is determining when a school can be liable for the harassing conduct of its teachers and coaches. Schools typically have more financial resources than individual coaches or teachers do, so a plaintiff will most likely attempt to sue the school to receive a higher level of damages. Because sexual harassment is a form of prohibited sex discrimination under Title IX, schools must have procedures in place to assist students who face such conduct. The procedures must cover both male and female students who participate in any sport or other extracurricular activity, whether the activity takes place at school or off campus. A school may be liable for damages for the harassing conduct of a coach who tells a player that he or she must submit to the coach's advances to make the team (i.e., liable for quid pro quo sexual harassment). A school might also be liable if the coach's overall conduct is so severe, as in *Franklin,* that it constitutes **hostile environment sexual harassment**, which is harassment that interferes with the athlete's ability to perform. Factors used to determine whether an environment is hostile include the degree to which the conduct affects one or more students; the type, frequency, and duration of the conduct; the identity of and relationship between parties; the number of people involved; the age and sex of the alleged harasser; the size of the school or program; the location and context of the incidents; other incidents at the school; and incidents of gender-based nonsexual harassment. Schools have the chance to respond to harassment and fire or discipline a coach, but if they do not take immediate steps to remedy the problem, they will be liable under Title IX.

In 2010 OCR released a letter focused on harassment and bullying reiterating much of the *Guidance* and making clear that schools must eliminate hostile environments and ensure that harassment caused in these environments does not recur (Office for Civil Rights, 2010a). In 2011, in a letter focused on harassment in the form of sexual violence, the OCR provided further guidance related to an institution's responsibilities in response to allegations of sexual harassment (Office for Civil Rights, 2011). Schools are required to distribute clear notices that such conduct is prohibited, designate an employee who will coordinate the school's efforts to comply with Title IX, and adopt clear grievance procedures that will resolve issues promptly and equitably. Schools also must be proactive, working to prevent sexual harassment and violence. All this guidance was explained in detail in a Dear Colleague Letter sent to the University of Montana in 2013 (Office for Civil Rights, 2013). This letter is now considered the blueprint for schools to follow to comply with Title IX regulations related to sexual harassment.

The challenge with sexual harassment cases is determining the level of harassment that would cause a school to be liable. The OCR regulations state that harassment must be severe, persistent, and pervasive, and these rules provide many factors to ascertain whether conduct rises to this level. But each situation is different. Although some athletes can laugh off or shrug off the advances of their coaches, others will find such conduct debilitating. The best policy is for schools to make clear that any conduct that could be interpreted as possibly harassing (such as a male coach hugging female players) will be monitored and should be avoided.

Another issue is that a student may sue a school for harassment only when she or he can also show that a school official in a position of authority knew that something was happening and failed to act (*Gebser v. Lago Vista Independent School District*, 1998). (See more about this case in the accompanying e-book, *Case Studies in Sport Law, Second Edition* [Pittman, Spengler, & Young, 2016].) As a result, a student who has been harassed must first notify the proper administrative authorities in the athletic department or at the university or school. According to the courts and the OCR guidance, potential responsibility for sexual harassment begins when school officials first learn of the conduct. If a school administrator knows of the problem and does nothing to remedy the situation, the school itself may be liable for the conduct of its employees. The courts and regulations have named this type of behavior **deliberate indifference**, but courts have struggled to define the term.

Students can also sue a school because of harassing conduct by classmates or teammates. In one situation, a fifth-grade student kept telling her teacher that a boy was constantly picking on her by making sexual comments. The teacher supposedly told the principal, but neither did anything that stopped the boy's behavior. As a result of this situation, the Supreme Court found for the first time that a student could sue a school because of harassment by another student (*Davis v. Monroe County Board of Education*, 1999). (See more about this case in the accompanying e-book, *Case Studies in Sport Law, Second Edition* [Pittman, Spengler, & Young, 2016].) The court found that peer sexual harassment is prohibited under Title IX when the school acts with deliberate indifference and the harassment is so severe and pervasive that it bars the victim's access to an educational opportunity. When the fifth-grade boy's harassment ruined the fifth-grade girl's ability to achieve in the classroom, the conduct was considered severe and was prohibited under Title IX.

At the university level, sexually harassing conduct is often even more severe. A 2014 White House report found that one in five women have been sexually assaulted while in college, but only 12% report those incidents (White House Council on Women and Girls, 2014). To support efforts to stop sexual violence in educational institutions, President Barack Obama created the White House Task Force to Protect Students from Sexual Assault. The task force launched the website www.notalone.gov as a clearinghouse for information about combatting sexual assault. Still, as of April 2015, 106 schools were under investigation by the Office of Civil Rights for mishandling sexual assault allegations (Rios, 2015).

Since 1995 several female students at the University of Colorado have complained that they were sexually assaulted by football recruits and players. One such student was Lisa Simpson. She alleged that several football recruits and current players sexually assaulted her at a party at her apartment. She reported the incidents to the university, and its Office of Judicial Affairs charged several of the football players with violations of the school's code of conduct. Although the district attorney's office charged several of the players with felonies, the school would not pursue sexual assault charges against them and none of the players lost any eligibility to play football. Simpson sued the school under Title IX, claiming that the school allowed a sexu-

ally hostile environment to exist on campus that led to her assault. The trial court found that even though the school was aware of earlier incidents, it was not put on notice of the specific type of severe harassment that she faced. This lack of knowledge was not the required deliberate indifference, so it was unclear whether the school could have prevented what happened to Simpson (*Simpson v. University of Colorado*, 2005).

Simpson appealed, and the appellate court focused on whether the university violated Title IX specifically within its official policies. The court discussed a great deal of evidence of sexual harassment involving football players in football programs throughout the country and specifically at Colorado. This harassment often took place during recruiting visits. The court found that the football coach at Colorado knew of these problems but did not supervise the recruiting program to avoid these issues even though he was repeatedly told of the need to do so; the court also found that the coach discouraged women from complaining about sexual harassment, and he always supported players in these situations. After reviewing all the evidence, the appellate court reversed the trial court and found that the need for more or different training of player hosts within the recruiting program was so obvious and the inadequacy of the program was so likely to result in Title IX violations that the coach was deliberately indifferent to the harassment that Simpson suffered (*Simpson v. University of Colorado*, 2007).

Before the case returned to court to discuss any possible damages for Simpson, the university settled. Still, there were no real winners in the situation. Simpson received $2.85 million from the university 6 years after she was raped. The university spent approximately $3 million on the litigation, and 11 of 12 top university administrators either were fired or left, including the president, two chancellors, and the athletic director. The case is clear evidence that university athletic administrators must supervise their programs at all times, not merely on the practice and playing fields. This approach will protect the university from potential liability, and, more important, protect students at the university from potential harassment.

Employment Discrimination

Another important area of gender equity law concerns employment discrimination faced by female employees in athletics. (See chapter 6 for discussion of employment discrimination as it relates to employment law.) In the United States in 1972, 90% of the coaches of women's teams and administrators of women's programs were women. By 2014 only 43.4% of those coaching jobs and 36.2% of all administrative positions were held by women. At the same time, only 3% of men's teams were coached by women, 23% of all teams had a female head coach, roughly 33% of head athletic trainers were female, and 12% of sports information directors were female (Carpenter & Acosta, 2014). Overt discrimination against women may not be the only reason for those numbers, but unfortunately the gains women have made in participation in athletics have not been mirrored by gains in employment within university athletics.

Although the focus of employment discrimination litigation in sports has been in intercollegiate athletics, the lack of female representation in employment is not restricted to university sports. In 2013, 26.5% of senior administrators in Major League Baseball were women, essentially no change from the previous year. At the team level in 2013, 23 of 30 teams had at least one female vice president and 27% of team professional administrators were women (Lapchick, May 2014). In 2013-14, women held 40.9% of the professional positions in the National Basketball Association league office. At the same time, two teams had female presidents, and women made up 16.6% of team vice presidents, 21.4% of team senior administrative positions, and 34.7% of team professional administrative positions (Lapchick, June 2014).

Women who believe that they are being discriminated against because of conduct they are forced to endure while on the job or because of inequities in salary or other work-related benefits can file two possible claims, the first under the Equal Pay Act of 1963 (EPA) (29 U.S.C. § 206(d), 2015) and the second under Title VII (42 U.S.C. § 2000e-2, 2015).

The Equal Pay Act prohibits discrimination in wages between employees on the basis of sex for **equal work** on jobs that require equal skill, effort, and responsibility, under similar working conditions. To be considered to entail equal work, two jobs don't have to require identical skill, effort, and responsibility; instead, the two jobs must be substantially equal except for the fact that one employee is paid more even though the jobs are basically the same.

Marianne Stanley was a highly successful women's basketball coach at the University of Southern California (USC), a team that had won a national championship. She complained because her salary of $60,000 with a $6,000 housing allowance was much less than the salary of men's basketball coach George Raveling, who was making between $130,000 and $150,000. After extensive negotiations, Stanley was offered a raise to $96,000, but eventually the university withdrew the offer after she continued to complain that she should be paid as much as Raveling was. Stanley sued USC under the EPA, claiming that she was denied equal pay for equal work (*Stanley v. University of Southern California*, 1999).

To start an EPA claim, Stanley had to pick another person employed by the same employer in a substantially similar job. Obviously, because both Stanley and Raveling were basketball coaches, this choice was simple. The analysis then shifted to the differences between the jobs. Raveling had significant public relations and promotion responsibilities that resulted in 90 times more revenue per year for the men's team compared with the women's team. He was involved in 12 outside speaking engagements, had been a coach for 31 years, had an extensive marketing background, had written two novels, and was a significant public relations representative on behalf of USC. In Stanley's 17 years as coach, her teams were much more successful than Raveling's, but Stanley was not required to engage in the same intense level of promotional and marketing activities. The court noted that these significant job differences resulted in a difference in responsibilities and justified different levels of pay (*Stanley v. University of Southern California*, 1999).

Sports employers may reward employees for greater professional experience and education, as Raveling possessed, without violating the EPA. Employers may also consider an employee's marketplace value and pay a more valuable employee at a higher level. Raveling was a nationally known and renowned coach, and the market for coaches at his level in men's basketball justified a higher salary for him. The point is that employers can legitimately take these types of considerations into account when assessing salaries. Paying people more because of their experience, education, and marketplace value will not be found discriminatory. What is discriminatory is

paying a man more than a woman in a similar job, simply on the basis of the sex of the person involved.

At USC the men's team generated higher attendance (men 237,950, women 41,917), more media interest, larger donations (men $98,000, women $828), and substantially more revenue (men $4 million, women $59,918) per year. These team-related factors also justified a higher level of pay for Raveling. Stanley argued that because the school did not allocate funds to the women's team, revenue and attendance for women's games were lower. The court disagreed, finding that USC made a business decision and could not be responsible for societal discrimination and stereotyped notions of women's sports that cause most people to prefer to watch men's and not women's sports. The court also found that revenue generation is an important factor in determining whether responsibilities and working conditions are substantially equal. In this case, the differences showed that they were not.

The differences between Raveling's job and Stanley's job showed that Raveling had to put in more effort and had a higher level of responsibility than Stanley did. In addition, his marketing background and extensive coaching career put him at a higher skill level. Therefore, Raveling and Stanley were not similar, and USC was justified in paying Raveling a higher salary.

In 1997 the Equal Employment Opportunity Commission (EEOC), the agency in charge of enforcing employment discrimination law, published a notice related specifically to sex discrimination in the compensation of coaches (U.S. Equal Employment Opportunity Commission, 1997). The notice discussed affirmative defenses available to a school when it has been sued for violating the law. In addition to discussing valid seniority and merit systems, the notice also mentioned several factors other than sex that can justify salary differences. These factors mirrored some of what was discussed in *Stanley*, including production of revenue, marketplace value, experience, and education. USC used precisely those factors to rebut Stanley's claims. In the end, unless a female coach is hired at the same time as a male coach, has the same level of experience, and has been given the same responsibilities by the athletic department, a female coach is not likely to bring a successful EPA claim against a school.

The notice made clear that in addition to making claims under the EPA, coaches may be able to bring a separate claim under Title VII. Title VII prohibits discrimination against any employee based on his or her sex in compensation and other benefits associated with employment. Title VII is different from the EPA because an employee does not have to show that she or he performed equal work; the employee merely has to show some negative job action, such as termination or a reduction in pay, that was taken because of the employee's sex (see table 8.1).

An example case involved assistant coach Robin Murphy, who claimed that the University of Cincinnati discriminated against her in violation of Title VII when the head swimming coach fired her after she complained about the way she was treated.

She claimed that the head coach did not provide her with enough responsibility or seek her advice in running the team. Although she was fired by the head coach, she could not prove that she was qualified for the job because she would not follow the head coach's instructions and so did not meet his legitimate expectations. Also, she could not show that a similarly situated male coach was treated better. In addition, although she showed that the coach made some rude, off-color comments to her, none of this demonstrated that she was fired because of her gender (*Murphy v. University of Cincinnati*, 2003).

Several reasons can account for differences in pay between male and female coaches and other athletic personnel, some of which are illustrated in the case studies in this section. But these justifications do not mean that women can be paid less merely because they are not men. The work that men and women perform and the responsibilities they are given must be legitimately different for their pay to be different.

Although an important part of gender equity law, employment discrimination laws have done little to change the landscape of sport and provide more employment opportunities for women. Although professional sports seem to be taking the lead in providing more opportunities for women, university sports are falling short and

Table 8.1 Statutory Requirements for Title VII and the Equal Pay Act

	Title VII	Equal Pay Act
Prohibitions	Prohibits discrimination against any employee on the basis of sex in compensation and other benefits associated with employment	Prohibits discrimination in wages between employees on the basis of sex for equal work on jobs that require equal skill, effort, and responsibility, under similar working conditions
Requirement	Plaintiff merely has to show some negative job action, such as termination, that was taken on the basis of the employee's sex	Plaintiff must show equal work, that is, work that is substantially equal except for the fact that one employee is paid more even though he or she performs basically the same job

seem to provide less overall opportunities each year. No gender equity laws mandate equality of opportunity in employment for women, and existing laws have not been successfully used to push for equality for women in this area.

LEARNING AIDS

Summary

Sport administrators in high schools, universities, and athletic associations must understand Title IX and its effect on athletics. Because the participation rate in athletics for women continues to lag behind that of men, any athletic program may be subject to an analysis under the three-part test. Such an analysis would be conducted if female athletes complain that your athletic program discriminates against them in the way in which it provides participation opportunities to men and women.

The law also can be used to review the specific ways in which you run your athletic program, such as scheduling games and practices, building facilities, and providing equipment and supplies. All these aspects of your program must be equitable to both sexes, which demands constant vigilance by administrators, coaches, and athletic departments.

Sport administrators must create environments that protect athletes from possible sexual harassment. Although still underreported by victims, sexual harassment by other players, recruits, coaches, and others remains a serious problem within athletics. By creating programs to address this problem, you will protect yourself and your institution from the liability that may attach to harassment. More important, you will protect your students or athletes from harassment.

Serious disparities in employment remain because women still do not have the same opportunities as men do in athletics. Unfortunately for women, neither the Equal Pay Act nor Title VII has solved this problem by forcing sport organizations to provide more opportunities for women.

Discussion Questions

1. What was the original purpose of Title IX? Was Title IX focused solely or primarily on sport when it was first passed as a law?

2. What is the three-part test, and how is it used to determine whether a school complies with Title IX?

3. Should cheerleading be considered a sport under Title IX? Explain your answer, drawing on the discussion in the text.

4. What types of comparisons must an athletic administrator make to determine whether an athletic program provides equal opportunities for boys and girls?

5. Describe the two remedies available to women who believe they have been discriminated against because of conduct they were forced to endure while on the job or because of inequities in salary or other work-related benefits.

6. Explain the factors that would show that a student-athlete was in a hostile work environment.

University Budget Cuts Cause Title IX Issue

SACB University is a small public university that has a tradition of having successful teams in men's and women's tennis, men's lacrosse, and women's softball. The university is federally funded and thus subject to the mandates of Title IX. In 2000–2001, SACB had 10,793 students: 4,790 men and 6,003 women. Thus, approximately 55% of the students were female and 45% were male. The percentage of genders in athletics, however, was quite different: 37% of athletes were female and 63% were male. In fiscal year 2000–2001, the university faced a budget crisis. Both state and federal aid to the school fell substantially, and as a result the university administration advised its various departments that they had to reduce their budgets. The Department of Athletics was instructed to reduce its budget by $500,000. The athletic director had to make some difficult decisions and knew that he would be forced to eliminate some programs. In August 2001 he announced that the women's softball and tennis teams and the men's soccer and water polo teams would be eliminated beginning with the 2002–2003 school year. The athletic director believed that the best approach was to eliminate an equal number of men's and women's teams. The teams to be eliminated brought the school prestige but were expensive to maintain because of the costs for trainers, travel, equipment, and supplies. At the time of the 2001 cutbacks, SACB had 12 varsity teams (6 male and 6 female). Because of the elimination of the four teams, SACB now had four teams per gender. The athletic director claimed that it was his intent, and the intent of the university, to replace the women's tennis team with a lower-budget women's club tennis team, create a women's club gymnastics team, and reinstate the women's softball program in the future when more money was available to the university. Several of the female athletes who played on the softball and tennis teams brought a lawsuit against the university, claiming that the actions of the athletic director and the university violated Title IX.

Intellectual Property Law

9

Chapter Objectives

After reading this chapter, you will know the following:

- The areas of intellectual property law that apply to sport

- The types of trademarks that are used in the sport industry

- Ways that a sport organization can protect itself when its trademarks, copyrights, or patents are used by others who are not authorized to do so

- The value that athletes have in their personal right of publicity

Case Studies in Sport Law Connection

Check out the following case studies related to this chapter in the accompanying e-book, *Case Studies in Sport Law, Second Edition* (Pittman, Spengler, & Young, 2016):

Boston Athletic Association v. Sullivan

Dallas Cowboys Cheerleaders, Inc. v. Pussycat Cinema, Ltd.

Lyons Partnership v. Giannoulas

National Football League v. McBee & Bruno's, Inc.

San Francisco Arts & Athletics, Inc. v. United States Olympic Committee

University of Pittsburgh v. Champion Products, Inc.

The success of a sport event often depends on the revenues derived from the event. Although revenues for university and professional sports teams often come from sales of merchandise, tickets, and concessions, some of the revenues come from intangible sources. These revenues include the sale of player or team names and likenesses, sponsorship of events and facilities, sales of merchandise with particular names and logos, or other sources that come under the umbrella of intellectual property law.

In addition, the sources of revenue for professional and university sports differ. In professional sports, teams often make revenue from ticket sales, but the bulk of their revenue comes from television contracts that sell the broadcasts of their games, sales of merchandise with the team name and logo, and sponsorships within their home stadium or arena. University-level sport is similar, although schools may depend more on revenues associated with ticket sales. Although universities sell merchandise with the university logo and nickname, this revenue is often for the school and does not go only to the athletic department. In addition, most university teams do not have lucrative television deals of their own, so they make significant revenue from television only if they participate in the men's basketball or football championships. Although professional teams are individual for-profit businesses that benefit from membership in professional sports leagues whose marketing and media arms make money for all teams, university teams are part of a university and often can be sustained only if the athletic budget allows.

This chapter uses cases and real-life examples to discuss the areas of intellectual property law that are important in sport. The focus is on some basic areas of intellectual property law that you need to understand: trademark, copyright, the right of publicity, and patent.

Each area of intellectual property law affects the sport industry in specific ways. Most of these areas are controlled by federal law, so you can use your knowledge about intellectual property law no matter where you work in the United States.

Trademark Law

Perhaps the most valuable asset that a sport or recreation organization has is its name, logo, or other defining characteristic that the public can recognize and associate with the organization. Because such defining characteristics can be extremely valuable, competitors often try to use these "marks" without permission, such as by copying them to put on their own products or events. Event and sport organizations must protect themselves by registering these marks to sell their own products and services. One of the strongest ways to gain this protection is by registering these characteristics as trademarks.

Federal Laws

The Federal Trademark Act of 1946, known as the Lanham Act, governs the law of trademarks and their registration and provides causes of action that protect trademark rights from infringement. The purpose of the Lanham Act is to protect the owner of a mark by preventing others from using the owner's mark without permission or in a way that will cause confusion about the actual source of the mark.

According to the act, a **trademark** includes

> any word, name, symbol, or device, or any combination thereof . . . used by some entity to identify and distinguish the services of one person, including a unique service, from the services of others and to indicate the source of the services, even if that source is unknown. (Lanham Act, 15 U.S.C. § 1127, 2015)

A trademark serves several important functions: It identifies a seller's goods and distinguishes them from those sold by others; it signifies that goods come from one particular source; it indicates that products are of a certain quality; and it advertises, promotes, and assists in selling the particular goods.

Because of these functions, trademarks are known by many different names (see figure 9.1). The strongest marks that an organization can have are **arbitrary or fanciful marks**. These marks have no direct relationship to the product itself, such as *NIKE* for sports apparel; instead, they are inherently distinctive because they indicate the source of the goods rather than describe the goods themselves. **Suggestive marks** may hint at the characteristics of the goods or services but require some imagination to understand the product they stand for. For instance, although some consumers would understand that *Hot Pockets* (a suggestive mark) refers to a warm food item, it takes a bit of imagination to understand that the name stands for a meal wrapped in a flaky crust.

Marks that are merely descriptive only identify a characteristic or quality of a good or service. For example, a golf ball that produces a loud screeching sound when hit is named the Screech Golf Ball, which is a **descriptive mark**. Descriptive marks can be given trademark protection only if they obtain secondary meaning. **Secondary meaning** applies when a mark has received widespread use and public recognition so that it indicates the source of the good or service instead of the good or service itself. For example, team logos and color schemes, although not inherently distinctive, can obtain secondary meaning after they have been associated with a particular team in the marketplace.

Generic marks do not receive trademark protection, because they refer to the name or class of the good or service and are so common that they do not clearly indicate the source of the good or service. Some companies that create distinctive names or logos eventually lose their trademark rights because these names or logos become so well known. The classic examples are *Kleenex* for facial tissue and *JELL-O* for gelatin. When the products were introduced, their names were merely the company

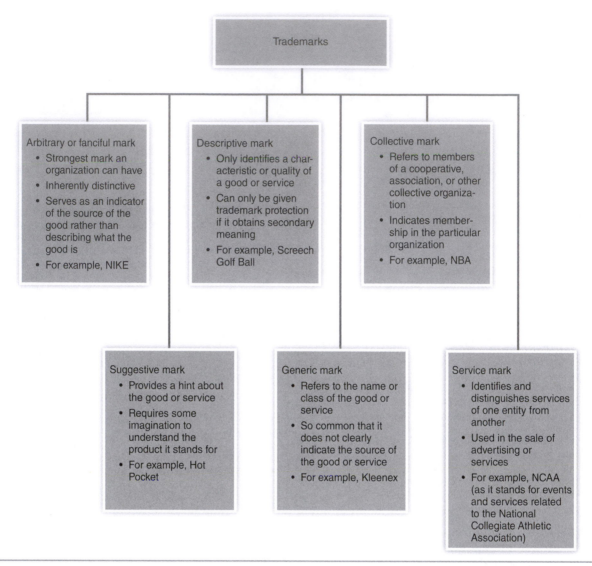

Figure 9.1   Various types of trademarks.

names for the particular brand of facial tissue and gelatin. Now both marks are so generic that people often refer to facial tissue as *Kleenex* and gelatin as *JELL-O* regardless of what particular brand they have purchased.

The Lanham Act also protects collective marks and service marks. A **collective mark** is a trademark used by the members of a cooperative, association, or other collective organization to indicate membership in that organization. Examples of collective marks in sport are widespread, from sports league initials such as *NBA* and *NHL* to college conference names such as *Big East* and *SEC*. A **service mark** is used in the sale or advertising of services to identify and distinguish the services of one entity from the services of others. Whereas a trademark identifies the source of a product, a service mark identifies the source and quality of an intangible service. For example, the mark

NCAA, because it stands for events and services related to the National Collegiate Athletic Association, is a service mark.

To create ownership rights in any of these types of trademarks, the trademark owner must be the first to use the mark in trade (i.e., by selling a product or service that displays the trademark). The owner also must make continuous, uninterrupted use of the mark after this first use on its products or within its services. After the trademark is used, consumers should be able to identify and distinguish the owner's unique goods or services from those of others in the particular industry. A valid trademark owner may also federally register the mark. Although federal registration extends rights to the trademark owner to use the mark throughout the United States and provides notice to other users of the mark's validity, registration extends trademark rights only across the United States; it does not necessarily extend internationally. A trademark owner must reregister the mark every 10 years to maintain exclusive use of the mark on her products and services.

Infringement

One of the main problems that a successful sport organization can face is an attempt by another organization to use the first organization's marks without its permission to capitalize on its success. This process can happen in simple ways. For example, fans may produce T-shirts or hats with team logos that they are not authorized to use, or students can make their own outfits using the school logo to support the team. For example, at Marquette University, student season-ticket holders for the men's basketball team traditionally create T-shirts using the school's logo, the Golden Eagle, and they often use the discontinued Warrior logo even though the university still owns

the trademark in that logo and has not authorized its use by the students. As with most universities, if the university administration is made aware of this unauthorized use, it will vigorously protect its mark by seeking a restraining order against the students or taking other actions to stop the sale of unauthorized products. No matter what the use is, if a person uses the properly registered trademark of another without the owner's consent, the use may be found to be a form of trademark infringement.

Trademark infringement can cause direct harm to the proper owner of the trademark in several ways. Money that might be spent on products produced by the sport organization itself is now spent on the infringing products, so the trademark owner loses revenues. In addition, a trademark used in a format that the owner would not approve of, such as on lower-quality goods, can reflect negatively on the quality of officially licensed merchandise. This practice often happens on college campuses. In the example at Marquette University, students may use the current Golden Eagle logo on low-quality T-shirts. Although the use itself could infringe on the university's trademark rights, even with permission the university may not want to have the logo displayed on low-quality T-shirts when its normal shirts are produced by sport apparel company Champion.

To establish trademark infringement, the trademark owner must first show that he has used and registered the mark as required and therefore has a protectable right in the trademark. Additionally, the owner must demonstrate that the other party's use of the mark is likely to cause confusion or deceive consumers about who is the true source of the trademark. A court evaluating a claim of trademark infringement will focus on the following factors when evaluating whether consumers would likely be confused by a possible infringing use of a trademark: the strength of the mark, similarity between the marks, evidence of actual confusion, consumer sophistication, quality of the alleged infringer's products, similarity between the products and the ways they are sold, likelihood that the owner will expand the use of her own marks in the future on other products, and whether the alleged infringer acted with good faith.

Individuals and companies are often sued for alleged trademark infringement. For example, in 1979 the Dallas Cowboys Cheerleaders sued Pussycat Cinema, a movie theater that began to show the pornographic movie *Debbie Does Dallas* (*Dallas Cowboys Cheerleaders, Inc. v. Pussycat Cinema, Ltd.*, 1979). (See more about this case in the accompanying e-book, *Case Studies in Sport Law, Second Edition* [Pittman, Spengler, & Young, 2016].) The cheerleaders sued, claiming that they had a trademark in their unique uniform and that the advertisements used for the movie showing its star in a uniform similar to the Cowboys cheerleaders' uniform infringed on their trademark. The defendants argued that even though the uniform worn in the movie closely resembled the actual cheerleaders' uniform, the public would not be confused, a requirement under the federal law. The court disagreed, explaining that the public's mere belief that the true trademark owner must have actually sponsored or approved of the use of the mark within the advertisements was enough to meet the confusion requirement. The court found that the use of a confusing mark in the movie would confuse consumers and injure the plaintiff's business reputation; it therefore affirmed the trial court's grant of an injunction stopping the particular confusing advertising and distribution of the film.

Often the infringement claim deals with the devaluing of the trademark itself. These disputes occur because a sport entity has signed an agreement to provide another entity with a license to produce products including the sport organization's trademark. A **license** is granted by its owner, known as the licensor, to a third party, the licensee. It permits the licensee to associate its goods, services, or business with the logos, names, and mascots of the licensor. Granting a license creates a contractual relationship between the licensor and the licensee. The licensor's aim is to gain additional public exposure, expand its business, and generate income by granting permission to the licensee to use its various images. The licensee hopes to increase the public's demand for its business, goods, or services by linking with a popular local, national, or even international entity. Problems can occur when entities other than the licensee attempt to use the licensor's images or when the licensor becomes unhappy with the licensee's use of the granted license. Consider the following case.

Mark Sullivan sold T-shirts and other merchandize that featured the mark *Boston Marathon*. The Boston Athletic Association (BAA) is a charitable organization that has conducted the Boston Marathon since 1897. BAA registered the name *Boston Marathon* with both the state and federal trademark offices. For several years, BAA has put together an exposition before the marathon where the organization sells shirts and other official apparel to defray some of the costs of the race. Although Sullivan originally provided merchandise to BAA, eventually BAA signed an exclusive licensing agreement and gave notice that any use of its trademarks by others would infringe on its rights. Sullivan continued to print shirts including the words *Marathon* and *Boston*.

The shirts were of lesser quality than BAA's merchandise.

BAA sued, claiming that Sullivan's use of the marks infringed on BAA's trademark rights (*Boston Athletic Association v. Sullivan*, 1989). (See more about this case in the accompanying e-book, *Case Studies in Sport Law, Second Edition* [Pittman, Spengler, & Young, 2016].) In analyzing BAA's complaint, the court focused on whether consumers would be likely to mistake Sullivan's T-shirts for BAA's. In looking at the eight factors previously mentioned, the courts found that the marks used by Sullivan were identical and were used on the same type of merchandise that BAA produced, that both parties sold and advertised their products in the same venues, that some consumers were confused about whether Sullivan's shirts were official BAA merchandise, and that Sullivan wanted to realize some profit from his use of marks associated with BAA. On this last factor, note that although BAA had only recently registered its marks, it had consistently used them on its products and events even before registration. Therefore, the court found that Sullivan clearly infringed on BAA's marks and that his infringement through the sale of inferior products had the potential to have a negative effect on the perception of the quality of the products produced by BAA.

As this case demonstrates, two issues often arise in a trademark infringement dispute. Initially, the focus will be on determining exactly what trademark rights the owner has. For instance, does a team have a trademark in only the team name, or does the mark extend to merchandise, the team color scheme, and the use of the name in the context of the particular sport? This issue is typically resolved by determining what was actually registered as the trademark and what forms of the mark have been used by the owner.

The focus of an infringement analysis then typically shifts to whether consumers will be confused by the use of a mark by another party. Simply saying that another party used the same words as those registered by the owner is not enough. If that were the case, there could not be a New York Giants in the NFL and a San Francisco Giants in MLB because the teams would not be allowed to have the same name. Instead, the factors previously mentioned must be reviewed to determine whether confusion is likely to occur, keeping in mind that courts typically look for evidence produced by surveys of consumers showing that they were in fact confused by the potentially infringing use of the marks.

Still, the trademark laws provide strong protection for sport organizations that continue to find many creative ways to profit from their own marks, from logo apparel to restaurants named after a particular team. This necessary connection between revenue production and the use of a trademark causes many high-profile professional and college sports teams and leagues to take steps to stop other organizations from infringing on their trademarks.

Fair Use or Parody

Trademark protection is not absolute and does not bar all possible uses of a trademark by those who do not own the trademark. Section 1115(b)(4) of the Lanham Act provides that when a trademark is used fairly and in good faith only to describe the goods or services involved, no trademark infringement has occurred. For example, a television station's use of the term *Boston Marathon* to describe the station's unlicensed broadcast of the marathon was not found to be trademark infringement even though another station was exclusively licensed to broadcast the event. The court

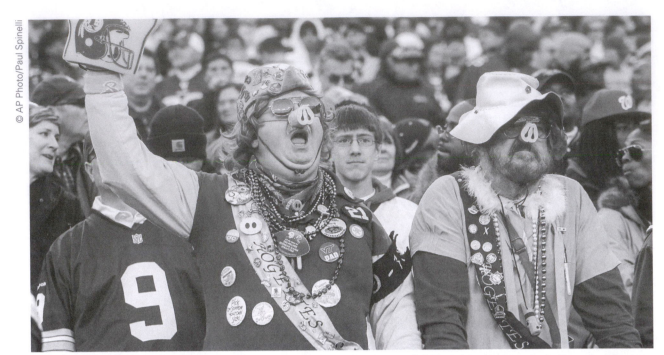

Trademark laws protect organizations so that they can develop and depend on the symbols they develop as a part of their marketing.

found that this use was merely descriptive of the event being broadcast and did not create viewer confusion about who was sponsoring the event (*WCVB-TV v. Boston Athletic Association*, 1991).

For the same reason, a parody of a trademark typically will not be held to be infringement. The classic sport case in this regard involved the Major League Baseball Players Association, which sued a parody baseball card maker claiming that the player caricatures on the cards infringed on trademarks that the association owned in player trading cards. The court found that the parody baseball cards did not create confusion regarding the source of the cards because they were merely meant to amuse the consumer who purchased them (*Cardtoons, L.C. v. Major League Baseball Players Assoc.*, 1996).

Dilution

With the introduction of the Federal Trademark Dilution Act of 1995, trademark owners were given another form of protection (15 U.S.C. § 1125(c), 2015). According to this act, **dilution** is the lessening of the capacity of a famous mark to identify and distinguish goods or services, regardless of either the presence or absence of competition between the parties or a likelihood of confusion, mistake, or deception. There are two types of dilution. Blurring occurs when a party uses or modifies a mark in such a way that the use creates the possibility that the original mark will lose its ability to serve as a unique identifier for the trademark owner. Tarnishment occurs where the mark is used in association with unwholesome or shoddy goods and services.

One of the best examples of a dilution claim in the sport industry involved the NBA. In 1999 Untertainment, a record label, planned to release a rap album titled *SDE Sports, Drugs, & Entertainment*. To promote the album, the company made a banner in New York City that included the NBA trademark with the player in the mark holding a gun. The company also sold the advertisement to several magazines. After seeing the advertisement, several people contacted the NBA to complain about its participation. In response, NBA Properties, the marketing and licensing arm of the NBA, sued, claiming trademark infringement and dilution (*Dream Team Collectibles, Inc. v. NBA Properties, Inc.*, 1997). The court found that the advertisements would create a negative association with the NBA logo; therefore, under the tarnishment theory of dilution, Untertainment was forced to stop using the advertisement.

A dilution claim could be important to a sport organization that is attempting to protect its trademark rights, specifically because the organization will not need to demonstrate a likelihood of confusion, as is necessary for a trademark infringement claim. The NBA case demonstrates this point clearly, because although some consumers were confused about the record label's use of the NBA mark, the typical consumer would not be. Instead, the offensive use of the mark could damage the NBA because the mark was associated with violence, so the NBA needed some other way to protect itself. The dilution claim was this other form of protection. Other trademark owners in sport can similarly protect themselves when their marks are diluted.

Olympic Marks

Perhaps the strongest trademark protection in the United States is provided to the United States Olympic Committee (USOC). Under the Ted Stevens Olympic and Amateur Sports Act (36 U.S.C. § 220501, 2015), the USOC has the exclusive right to use and license the Olympic marks (including the word *Olympic* and the five-ring Olympic logo) within the United States.

San Francisco Arts & Athletics (SFAA) promoted the Gay Olympic Games, to be held in 1982, by using those words on letterhead, merchandise, and various advertisements. After learning about this use, the USOC contacted the SFAA and requested that it terminate its use of the word *Olympic* in association with the event. When SFAA refused, the USOC sued to enforce its rights under the Stevens Act (*San Francisco Arts & Athletics, Inc. v. United States Olympic Committee*, 1987). (See more about this case in the accompanying e-book, *Case Studies in Sport Law, Second Edition* [Pittman, Spengler, & Young, 2016].) In finding that the USOC had the exclusive right to the use of the word *Olympic*, the court determined that the likelihood of confusion was not required, as would be the case with a normal trademark. Therefore, SFAA's mere use of the word in advertising for its event infringed on the USOC's strong trademark rights.

Although the USOC's trademark rights are incredibly strong, they are not absolute, so we often see the word *Olympic* used in many ways. The media can use the word *Olympic* when reporting on Olympic competitions and may include the Olympic marks within newspapers or other media when reporting about the Olympic Games.

But sport event organizers would be wise not to use the word *Olympic* or the Olympic marks in their events, no matter how tame the use may be. The USOC vigorously pursues those who use virtually any form of their protected marks.

Licensing

If you work for a successful sport organization, merchandisers, sponsors, advertisers, and others will want to associate with you so that they can take advantage of your success. To ensure that your organization also benefits from the relationship, you may wish to grant those businesses a license so that they can use your organization's trademarks for a fee.

Most professional sports leagues have created licensing programs that allow the league to capitalize on public demand for merchandise and apparel that displays the logos of the league and its clubs. Each of the four major professional team sports leagues (MLB, NBA, NFL, and NHL) has created a separate division, often known as *properties* (e.g., Major League Baseball Properties, Inc., and NFL Properties, LLC), that establishes procedures for sponsors, advertisers, and merchandisers to obtain licenses to use league and club trademarks on their products. Typically, the league divides the revenues created from these licensing agreements among the clubs that make up the league.

The players associations in these leagues (e.g., the National Football League Players Association) have also created licensing divisions to handle licensing for the athletes themselves. These divisions—such as Players, Inc., in the NFL and the MLBPA Players Choice Group Licensing Program in the MLB—work with merchandisers, advertisers, and sponsors that are interested in selling products bearing the names and likenesses of current and former players. Like the leagues, these programs typically divide any revenues generated among the players who are members of the particular players association.

Some players have even registered trademarks in their own names and likenesses. For example, current Green Bay Packers All-Pro quarterback Aaron Rodgers has registered his name as a trademark for endorsement services. If companies want to sell products bearing his name or image, they must first obtain a license from his representatives.

Licensing is also important at the college level. The NCAA has registered 68 trademarks and service marks that are associated with the organization, in particular with its championships in various sports (National Collegiate Athletic Association, n.d.). The NCAA has many types of licenses—from T-shirt and sporting goods licenses to licenses for key chains, coasters, backpacks, and concession cups. Each license is for a certain type of event: Some are for all NCAA championship events, some are for NCAA March Madness only, and some are sport specific, applying only to basketball or football, for example. The licensees are permitted to use the NCAA's marks on particular licensed products but cannot use the marks to promote their particular brands. Further information on the NCAA's licensing program can be found on the NCAA website at www.ncaa.org under the Championships tab in the section on marketing.

Approximately 200 schools have licensing programs for their names and registered trademarks, including team logos and nicknames. The Collegiate Licensing Company (CLC), a subsidiary of IMG College, is the licensing representative for the NCAA. CLC is responsible for administering the licensing program, including processing applications, collecting royalties, enforcing trademarks, and pursuing new market opportunities for the NCAA. CLC's goal is to increase the NCAA's overall merchandise sales through its apparel and nonapparel marketing divisions. The CLC also represents nearly 10 conferences, 24 bowl games, NCAA football, the Heisman Trust and the National Invitational Tournament, among others (Collegiate Licensing Company, 2015).

Nicknames

Most professional and university sports teams and even some high school sports teams have registered trademarks in their team name. Because the trademark is registered, these teams can sell or license exclusive apparel that includes their trademarked team name. Legal problems can

develop, however, when dealing with trademarked team names, particularly Native American nicknames.

At the professional level, the focus has been on Native American nicknames that some people find disparaging. Trademark protection can also be denied if a mark is shown to be immoral, deceptive, scandalous, or disparaging under section 1052(a) of the Lanham Act. In the late 1990s several Native Americans petitioned to cancel the trademark registrations for the marks *Washington Redskins* and *Redskins*, which were owned by Pro-Football, Inc., the owners of the NFL's Washington Redskins franchise (*Harjo et al. v. Pro-Football, Inc.*, 1999). The U.S. Patent and Trademark Office initially granted the petition to cancel the marks, finding that they were disparaging to Native Americans. The team sued to avoid the cancellation of the marks and the court

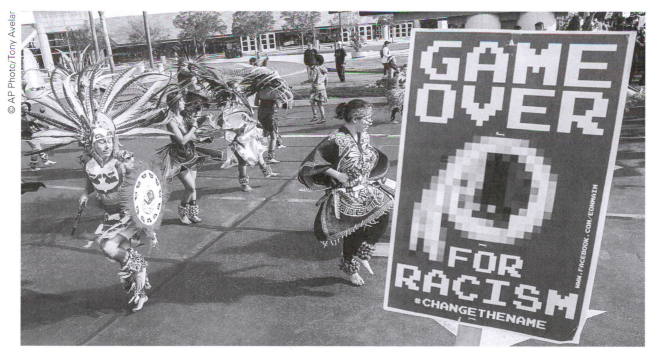

Sport team nicknames often can be protected under trademark law. But Native American nicknames, such as the Washington Redskins, often face tough opposition.

reversed the decision, finding that the petitioners did not present sufficient evidence that the marks were disparaging to Native Americans and that the claim was barred by the doctrine of laches. This doctrine holds that when a plaintiff waits too long to sue to protect a trademark, the court can find that the delay would harm the defendant and can rule in the defendant's favor. In this case, because a 25-year delay occurred in bringing the suit, the court found that the team would be harmed if the court allowed the Native Americans' claim. The case was appealed and remanded to the lower court, but the lower court again ruled in favor of the team. The defendants appealed, but the appellate court could find no abuse of discretion and affirmed the trial court's subsequent opinion.

Many universities, including the University of Wisconsin and the University of Iowa, will not schedule games against schools that use Native American nicknames or mascots. Under a controversial policy introduced by the NCAA in 2006, NCAA schools are prohibited from displaying hostile and abusive racial, ethnic, or national origin mascots, nicknames, or imagery at any of its championships. Institutions that currently use Native American nicknames are required to take reasonable steps to conceal the nicknames or may be prohibited from wearing them altogether. In 2004 the NCAA asked 33 schools to review their use of Native American mascots, and 15 immediately complied.

Several universities contested the NCAA rule and fought to keep their Native American nicknames. A complete list of the schools banned under the policy and current developments surrounding their mascots is available on the NCAA's website www.ncaa.org under Native American Mascot Policy—Status List. As discussed on that website, after an appeal, Florida

State University was allowed to continue to use the word *Seminole* because of its close relationship with the Seminole Tribe of Florida. The University of North Dakota (UND), however, lost a similar appeal over its nickname *Fighting Sioux* because it did not have the support of the three recognized Sioux tribes of North Dakota. Unlike many schools, UND sued the NCAA, denying that it has been hostile, abusive, or disrespectful toward Native Americans. In support of UND, the state board of higher education authorized the lawsuit, which was to be paid for by alumni and other donations. In November 2006 UND won a preliminary injunction that barred the NCAA from stopping the university from using the nickname and allowed the university to host an opening-round playoff game in the Division II football playoffs. The court specifically found that the school had met its burden of establishing irreparable harm to its reputation if it was characterized as an institution that allows a "hostile and abusive" environment to exist toward Native Americans (*State of North Dakota v. NCAA*, 2006). Soon after, in October 2007, the NCAA and the university settled the dispute. The university had 3 years to obtain approval from the Sioux tribes for the use of the nickname and related imagery. If UND did not get approval, it would transition to a new logo and nickname that did not violate the policy. In March 2011 the state legislature passed a bill requiring the university to use the logo, but the bill was quickly repealed. In 2012 over two-thirds of the population in North Dakota voted for the university to drop the nickname. Because of a provision in current law calling for a cooling-off period, the university will not be able to have a new nickname until 2015 (Smith, 2012).

Since the NCAA adopted the rule, many other organizations at all levels of sport have begun to review their use of Native American trademarks and nicknames.

Domain Names and the Internet

Use of the Internet to market sports teams, events, and merchandise has increased exponentially since the early 1990s, increasing the need for sport organizations to protect their intellectual property rights on the Internet. In the early 1990s, when teams and other sport organizations began to create websites, some organizations found that third parties not associated with the organization had already registered the organization's preferred domain name. These parties came to be known as cybersquatters because they would acquire domain names and then sit on them, waiting for the organization associated with the name to find out. These cybersquatters would then attempt to extort money from the true rights holder to buy back the domain name they had registered.

In 1999 Congress finally acted by passing the Anti-Cybersquatting Consumer Protection Act (ACPA), which amended the Lanham Act by creating a specific claim against cybersquatters. The act outlaws **cybersquatting**, which is described as the act of registering, with the bad faith intent to profit, a domain name that is confusingly similar to a registered or unregistered mark or that dilutes a famous mark. A legitimate trademark owner can sue under the act to stop a cybersquatter, even when the disputed owner of the name cannot be found or cannot be served in the United States.

A recent case dealing with a claim under the ACPA involved the domain name march-madness.com, the NCAA, and the Illinois High School Association (IHSA). The NCAA's first use of the phrase "March Madness" occurred in 1982 when CBS broadcaster Brent Musberger used it when discussing the NCAA men's basketball tournament. The IHSA, however, had begun using the phrase to refer to its boys' basketball tournaments in the 1940s. After some initial litigation concerning who owned the phrase, the NCAA and IHSA agreed to work together to protect their rights. They formed the March Madness Athletic Association (MMAA), and each retained a license to use the phrase in advertising its basketball tournament.

Claiming to be associated with the NCAA, Netfire acquired the domain name march-madness.com in 1996. MMAA sued, claiming that Netfire was engaging in cybersquatting in violation of the ACPA. The court agreed, finding that Netfire acted with bad faith in attempting to profit by using the trademarked phrase and that the domain name was identical or confusingly similar to the actual trademark in violation of the ACPA (*March Madness Athletic Assoc., LLC v. Netfire Inc.*, 2005).

The ACPA is not the only recourse for trademark owners who want to challenge a cybersquatter. The Uniform Dispute Resolution Process (UDRP) is administered by the Internet Corporation for Assigned Names and Numbers (ICANN). Under this process, a trademark owner must allege that its mark is identical or confusingly similar to the mark used by the cybersquatter, who has no legitimate rights or interests in the domain name, and that the cybersquatter registered and used the domain name in bad faith. The World Intellectual Property Organization's (WIPO) Arbitration and Mediation Center, based in Geneva, Switzerland, is authorized to hear disputes under the UDRP process. Information on this organization and particular disputes can be found at www.wipo.int/amc/en/index.html.

The NHL and the owners of the Pittsburgh Penguins franchise, specifically Mario Lemieux, sued a corporation that registered the domain name nhlpenguins.com and linked it to pornographic material while at the same time acting as a true cybersquatter by attempting to sell it back to the true trademark owners (*National Hockey League and Lemieux Group LP v. Domain for Sale*, 2001). After the defendants refused to stop using the domain name, the plaintiffs filed a complaint with WIPO's Arbitration and Mediation Center. The center found that the domain name was confusingly similar to the NHL's and Penguins' marks and that it was being used in bad faith to reroute customers to pornographic materials. Therefore, because the defendant was not making any legitimate use of the domain name, the panel ordered that the domain name be transferred to the plaintiffs.

Although organizations can use these processes to challenge unauthorized uses of their trademarks within domain names, often the only thing that the organizations get for winning these fights is a difficult-to-enforce decision from the courts or WIPO Arbitration and Mediation Center verifying their rights. Obtaining damages from cybersquatters is virtually impossible, especially when they cannot be located because they register domain names around the world. Moreover, most of these disputes become one sided because the cybersquatters never appear in court. To them the benefit is in merely infringing on the domain name for as long as possible, and often particular individuals or entities are repeatedly sued for this type of conduct.

Copyright Law

Sport organizations often want to protect the accounts of their events found in the media through television, media guides, radio broadcasts, newspapers, magazines, and other sources. These forms of expression are protected by **copyright** law. Unlike trademark law, copyright law does not protect intangible ideas; rather, it protects ideas or other items that can be identified on tape, on paper, or on screen.

The federal Copyright Act (17 U.S.C. §§ 101 et seq., 2015) provides for federal protection and registration of copyrights. As it explains, copyright protection extends to "original works of authorship fixed in any tangible medium of expression, now known or later developed, from which they can be perceived, reproduced, or otherwise communicated, either directly or with the aid of a machine or device" (§ 102). Copyright protection can be extended to the following "original works of authorship":

- Books and other literary works
- Music and musical works, including any accompanying words
- Dramatic works such as plays, including any accompanying music
- Pantomimes and choreographic works
- Pictorial (photographic), graphic, and sculptural works
- Motion pictures and other audiovisual works
- Sound recordings
- Architectural works (§ 102)

The owner of a copyright has the right to do or authorize others to do the following:

- Reproduce the copyrighted work in copies or phonorecords
- Prepare derivative works based on the copyrighted work
- Distribute copies or phonorecords of the copyrighted work to the public by sale or other transfer of ownership or by rental, lease, or lending
- Perform the copyrighted work publicly, in the case of literary, musical,

dramatic, and choreographic works; pantomimes; and motion pictures and other audiovisual works

■ Display the copyrighted work publicly, in the case of literary, musical, dramatic, and choreographic works; pantomimes; and pictorial, graphic, or sculptural works, including the individual images of a motion picture or other audiovisual work

■ Perform the copyrighted work publicly by means of a digital audio transmission, in the case of sound recordings (§ 106)

Under this federal law, copyright protection begins when a copyrightable work is created, and it extends for the life of the author plus 70 years. The U.S. government also provides a website with information for those interested in obtaining copyright protection for their work by registering it at www.copyright.gov. Although registration is not required, registering a copyright is necessary before bringing a lawsuit against someone for copyright infringement.

Businesses often include a copyright policy in their publications and company brochures or even on the company website. For example, the National Football League includes a statement affirming its copyright rights and prohibiting users from using NFL copyrights on NFL.com in a terms and conditions section of the website (NFL, 2013).

People who duplicate the copyrighted materials of others often are found to have infringed on the rightful owner's copyright. **Copyright infringement** is an unauthorized use of copyrighted material in a way that violates one of the owner's exclusive rights in the copyright. In most circumstances, copyright infringement is subject to a strict liability standard (the legal principle of strict liability is discussed in chapter 2), so the owner needs to show only that his pro-

tected copyright was copied to sustain his claim. If infringement is found, the copyright owner then has a variety of remedies available, from injunctive relief to the recovery of damages, which could include any profits that the infringer made from the owner's copyrights and attorney's fees.

Beyond clear infringement, some copyright material can be used without the copyright owner's permission. This concept is known as **fair use**. Copyrights can be used in this way for purposes such as criticism, comment, news reporting, teaching (including multiple copies for classroom use), scholarship, or research (Copyright Act, 17 U.S.C. § 107, 2015). If an organization attempts to defend its use of a copyright that it does not own by arguing that it was a fair use, the court will consider the purpose and character of the use, including whether it is of a commercial nature or for nonprofit educational purposes; the nature of the copyrighted work; the amount and substantiality of the portion used in relation to the copyrighted work as a whole; and the effect of the use on the potential market for or value of the copyrighted work.

Copyright issues in sport typically involve one of two areas: (1) who owns the copyright and who can use it in game statistics and accounts and (2) how much copyright protection extends to the Internet.

Game Accounts

With the rise of fantasy sports leagues and other forms of gambling on sport, the statistics produced by athletic participants and the accounts of the games played continue to grow in value. Media outlets, fantasy leagues, and even the public want access to these statistics and accounts, but copyright owners—more specifically, individuals or entities who believe that they are copyright owners—want to protect their rights to these statistics and accounts and profit from the licensing and distribution of permission to use them.

One of the earliest cases of this type in sport took place in the 1930s involving the Pittsburgh Pirates. The Pirates played their home games in Forbes Field and sold the exclusive rights to broadcast play-by-play descriptions or accounts of their games to General Mills. NBC then contracted with General Mills to broadcast these play-by-play game accounts over the radio. Another radio station, KQV, also broadcast game accounts provided by its own observers at Pirates games. The Pirates sued to protect their rights in the game broadcasts and to stop KQV from its unauthorized broadcast of Pirates games (*Pittsburgh Athletic Co. v. KQV Broadcasting Co.*, 1938). The court found that because the Pirates created the game, controlled the park, and restricted the dissemination of game accounts, the team had a protectable property right in these game accounts. In addition, the team had the right to control the use of this game information for a reasonable time after the games took place. Therefore, KQV violated the Pirates' copyrights by broadcasting their game accounts.

As the law evolved and sport expanded, further issues arose. For instance, leagues and teams wanted to know who owned the copyright in the actual broadcast of the game. Keep in mind that copyright protection depends on authorship; that is, a determination must always be made of who authored the work in question. But the Copyright Act also allows for joint or coauthorship (17 U.S.C. § 201(a), 2015). In the context of sport, this idea applies when teams and leagues (or schools and conferences on the university level, and schools and associations on the high school level) jointly create the broadcasts that are eventually seen. A case analyzing whether MLB

clubs own exclusive rights to the television broadcasts of their players defined these broadcast rights more clearly.

For years MLB and its players union argued over who owned the right to broadcast the performances of MLB players. In 1982 the union sent letters to each club and to television and cable companies stating that they were broadcasting the players without the players' consent and therefore had misappropriated each player's property rights in his performance. In response, the clubs went to court to seek a judicial declaration that they had an exclusive right to broadcast the games and exclusive rights in the telecasts themselves (*Baltimore Orioles, Inc. v. Major League Baseball Players Assoc.*, 1986). The clubs argued that the game telecasts were "works made for hire" as defined under the Copyright Act. Under section 201(b) of the act, if the telecasts are works made for hire, then the clubs that own the broadcasts would be considered to have authored the broadcasts as required for copyright protection. As a result, unless the clubs reached a separate agreement with the players, the clubs owned the right to the copyrights in the game accounts provided in the broadcasts.

To determine whether the clubs owned copyrights under the doctrine of work made for hire, the court began by noting that the various aspects of a game broadcast, such as camera angles, types of shots, use of instant replays and split screens, and shot selection, are all forms of authorship in the copyrightable telecast that are themselves audiovisual works covered by the Copyright Act. In addition, the players were employees of the clubs, and their employment terms included playing games before live and remote audiences. Finally, because no other formal agreements were made granting the players a copyright in the game broadcasts, the clubs were found to be the valid owners of the copyright.

Because of this reasoning and similar decisions in other courts, clubs and the leagues that they make up can bargain with each other to sell their copyrighted works to television networks. This pooling of rights is discussed further in chapter 10, within the discussion of the exemption of this activity from the antitrust laws as provided in the Sports Broadcasting Act.

Sport employers who hire players and then reach agreements with broadcasters to televise their games usually will be found to own the copyrights in the game broadcasts. Players and their unions can negotiate for those rights within the collective bargaining process, but typically they instead negotiate for a bigger percentage of the revenues derived from the sale of those broadcasts

to the networks. Currently, these values are astronomical (see table 9.1). For instance, the NBA's contract with ABC, ESPN, and TNT has been valued at $7.6 billion and runs from the 2008–2009 season through the 2015–2016 season. Additionally, MLB extended its contract with ESPN in 2012 to begin in 2014 and extend through 2021, combining all the TV, radio, digital, and international rights and providing ESPN with more flexibility.

Another issue related to game broadcasts involves attempts to broadcast games even when leagues have imposed a blackout. Most television contracts with the major professional sports leagues provide that games that are not sold out within a certain number of days or hours before the contest are blacked out; that is, they are not broadcast in the team's home region. The reasoning behind these blackout rules

Table 9.1 Broadcasting Agreements in Sport

Years	Network	Total	Per year
NATIONAL FOOTBALL LEAGUE			
2014–21	ESPN	$15.2 billion	$1.9 billion
2013–22	NBC	$8.55 billion	$950 million
2013–22	CBS	$9 billion	$1 billion
2013–22	Fox	$9.9 billion	$1.1 billion
MAJOR LEAGUE BASEBALL			
2014–21	ESPN	$5.6 billion	$700 million
2013–21	Fox	$4 billion	$500 million
2013–21	Turner	$6.8 billion	$850 million
NATIONAL BASKETBALL ASSOCIATION			
2008–09 until 2015–16 season	ABC/ESPN, Time Warner	$7.44 billion	$930 million
NATIONAL HOCKEY LEAGUE			
2010–11 season through 2020–21 season	NBC, Versus	$2 billion	$200 million
NASCAR			
2015–24	FOX, NBC	$8.2 billion	$820 million
NCAA			
2011–24	CBS, Turner	$10.8 billion	$771 million

is that a blackout in the team's home region will encourage ticket sales and therefore result in sellouts of team home games. If all home games were broadcast regardless of ticket sales in the home region, fans might not buy tickets and instead just stay home to watch their team. Of course, when local fans were barred from watching their team, litigation followed. A good example involved the NFL.

The NFL's blackout rule in the mid 1980s provided that games that were not sold out within 72 hours of game time were blacked out and not to be broadcast within a 75-mile (120 km) radius of the home team's playing field. Owners of restaurants within this radius of Busch Stadium (the home of the St. Louis Cardinals at that time) picked up the broadcast of blacked out Cardinals' home games to show in their restaurants. The NFL and the Cardinals sued to stop the restaurant owners from showing the blacked-out games, claiming that the broadcasts violated the NFL's and the Cardinals' copyrights (*National Football League v. McBee & Bruno's Inc.*, 1986). (See more about this case in the accompanying e-book, *Case Studies in Sport Law, Second Edition* [Pittman, Spengler, & Young, 2016].) Although the court recognized an exemption within the Copyright Act allowing the transmission of copyrighted material in a private home, the satellite receivers used by the bar owners were not similar to those in a private home, so the exemption did not apply. As a result, the restaurant owners were permanently barred from intercepting the game broadcasts.

Statistics

Other copyright issues have focused on the rights to the actual statistics produced by players and teams. Leagues and clubs often claim that they own the statistics produced

within their sports, whereas media outlets and other consumers argue that the statistics should not be subject to copyright protection. One of the seminal decisions in this area concerned the NBA.

Beginning in 1996 Motorola manufactured and marketed the SportsTrax paging device, which received game statistics from NBA games supplied by STATS. The statistical information was provided by STATS reporters watching the games on television or listening to them on radio and then keying the statistical information into their personal computers. The NBA sued Motorola, asserting that its activities infringed on the NBA's copyright in its game broadcasts, which the NBA argued were original works of authorship that the league had the exclusive right to republish and sell (*NBA v. Motorola*, 1997). The court determined that the NBA did not hold a copyright in the underlying games because the games are unscripted and the outcome is uncertain. Therefore, the games are not authored as required under the Copyright Act. Even though the broadcasts of the games were subject to copyright protection, the defendants did not infringe on the NBA's copyright in these broadcasts, because they only reproduced facts from the broadcasts, not a description of the game itself. According to this decision, sports leagues and teams do not own copyright in game statistics, so newspaper and other media outlets can reproduce statistics in their products. But a few years later, another decision added confusion to this area of law.

The PGA developed the Real-Time Scoring System (RTSS) to compile tournament scores for PGA events. Under this system, volunteer "walking scorers" followed each group of golfers on the course and tabulated the scores of each player. "Hole reporters" then relayed this information to a production truck that compiled the scores and transmitted them to electronic leaderboards, distributed along the golf course, as well as to the on-site media center and the website www.pgatour.com. Because the PGA prohibited the use of wireless devices by the press or public during tournaments, the RTSS was the sole source of compiled golf scores for the full list of tournament players. In addition, the PGA required media organizations to agree to other regulations to gain access to the media center, including mandated delays before publishing scoring information.

Morris Communications, a media company that publishes print and electronic newspapers, is a main competitor with the PGA in the market for real-time golf scores. Morris wanted to continue to sell real-time scores to several Internet publishers, so it sued the PGA to enjoin it from enforcing these regulations (*Morris Comm. Corp. v. PGA Tour*, 2000). Differentiating this case from the *Motorola* decision, the district court noted that Motorola, one of the defendants in that case, was able to gather its information simply by tuning in to a publicly aired television or radio broadcast that any member of the public could access. Morris, however, could obtain the real-time scores only by accessing information gathered throughout the golf course simultaneously and then compiling the information and generating the scores in a private media center through the PGA's system. Therefore, the real-time golf scores were the end product of a system that the PGA designed for itself. The court found that Morris was attempting to capitalize not just on the golf scores themselves but also on the PGA's system for simultaneously gathering and generating the scoring information. On appeal, the court focused on antitrust claims brought by Morris against the PGA and did not address the PGA's property right in the real-time scores (*Morris*

Comm. Corp. v. PGA Tour, 2002). The court concluded that the PGA had not illegally monopolized the market for real-time tournament scores and denied Morris' motion for summary judgment.

Because of these decisions, the NBA was found to have no property rights in any real-time game statistics, whereas the PGA was seemingly found to have a property right in its real-time scores. This issue is confusing, and only after careful analysis of the cases can the differences be found.

Initially, the *Motorola* court focused on the fact that the company used its own resources to pay for the collection of the scores. But Morris Communications had a free ride on the collection system that the PGA Tour created and did not invest any resources of its own in the collection of the information. In addition, although NBA game scores are readily available to the public in real time, scores from golf events are not so readily available to the public because the PGA's system does not allow scores to be immediately provided to the public. Of course, unlike the NBA, the PGA also claimed that it had a property interest in both the system it used to acquire real-time scores and the scores themselves, and it maintained control over the dissemination of these scores by maintaining its system of requiring the media to pay a license fee for access.

The appellate court in *Morris* specifically avoided discussing the potential copyright issues involved, focusing instead on the antitrust issues. The court merely mentioned that the PGA had a property interest in the scores in conjunction with the system it created; the court did not define this interest as a copyright. The answer is not clear, because the Supreme Court has yet to rule on the issue. See the First Amendment Protection for Use of Sport Statistics sidebar for another example of how the courts have

IN THE COURTROOM

First Amendment Protection for Use of Sport Statistics

C.B.C. Distribution & Marketing, Inc. v. MLB Advanced Media (2007)

In 1995 the Major League Baseball Players Association (MLBPA) granted C.B.C. Distribution & Marketing (CBC) a license to use the names of baseball players and their statistics in fantasy baseball games. In its games, CBC provided lists of MLB players for selection by participants who pay fees to play and to trade players. Before the start of the season, participants form their teams by drafting players. Participant owners then compete against other fantasy owners who have drafted teams. In 2002 the MLBPA renewed the license with CBC.

When the renewal expired in 2005, the MLBPA granted the exclusive right to use the players' names and statistics to MLB Advanced Media (MLBAM). After receiving the license from the players association, MLBAM proposed a license under which CBC could promote fantasy baseball games on MLB.com but could

not continue offering its own fantasy baseball products. CBC sued, asking the court to find that it could continue to use the names and statistics related to MLB players without a license from MLBAM.

The focus of the case was whether CBC's use of the players' information violated their right of publicity or whether any such violation was preempted because the use was protected by the First Amendment. The district court found that CBC did not infringe on the players' rights of publicity because it did not use their names as symbols of their identity to make a profit and that the First Amendment protected CBC's use of the information. The U.S. Court of Appeals for the Eighth Circuit affirmed, finding that although CBC violated the players' rights of publicity by using their names and identities, the First Amendment preempted the claim because the information CBC provided was readily available to the public and so was protected.

---

dealt with sport statistics as they relate to fantasy baseball games.

Right of Publicity

Closely related to copyright and trademark law is the right of publicity. The **right of publicity** has come to signify the right of any person to control the commercial use of her identity. This right is not produced under federal law; instead, many states have recognized the right by common law or included it in their state statutes. The right of publicity protects athletes' and celebrities' marketable identities from

commercial misappropriation by recognizing their right to control and profit from the use of their names and nicknames, likenesses, portraits, performances (under certain circumstances), biographical facts, symbolic representations, or anything else that evokes this marketable identity. But this right is not absolute. An athlete cannot use this right to prevent his name or picture from appearing in newspapers. Newspaper reproductions of this type are protected as free speech under the First Amendment. In addition, although most of the cases protect celebrities (including athletes), the right of publicity extends to everyone.

The phrase was coined in a 1953 case. Haelan Laboratories entered into a contract with baseball players that provided Haelan with the exclusive right to use the players' photographs on baseball cards sold in packets of gum. As part of the agreement, the players agreed not to grant any other gum manufacturer the right to use their pictures. Topps Chewing Gum then entered into a similar agreement with the players, who allowed it to use their pictures on its own cards. Haelan sued Topps, claiming that it illegally induced the players into breaching their contracts with Haelan (*Haelan Laboratories, Inc. v. Topps Chewing Gum, Inc.*, 1953). The case focused on what rights the players had in their own identity and picture and whether those rights were assignable at all. For the first time, the court recognized a property right in the publicity value of a person's identity, providing the players with a right to grant a company the exclusive right to publish their pictures.

Another illustrative case involved boxer Muhammad Ali. In its February 1978 issue *Playgirl* magazine included a cartoon of a nude black man seated in the corner of a boxing ring, with the caption "Mystery Man" and an accompanying reference to "The Greatest." Ali sued, claiming that the cartoon violated his right of publicity (*Muhammad Ali v. Playgirl, Inc.*, 1978). The court noted that Ali had regularly called himself "The Greatest" and that the media regularly identified him by that moniker. The court also noted that the features in the cartoon man were recognizable as Ali's features. Therefore, the court concluded that Ali's right of publicity had been violated.

In the *CBC* case discussed earlier, MLB Advanced Media also argued that CBC had violated the players' right of publicity in its litigation against the fantasy sports provider (*C.B.C. Distribution & Marketing, Inc., v. MLB Advanced Media*, 2006). The court explained that to prove a violation of this right, MLB had to show that CBC commercially exploited the players' identities without their consent and to gain a commercial advantage. Because it was clear that CBC used the players' identities without their consent, the court focused next on whether CBC did so to gain a commercial advantage. Nothing about CBC's fantasy games demonstrated or implied that the players were associated with or endorsed CBC, and CBC did not use the players in an effort to attract business from other fantasy sports providers. All such leagues use the same player information; therefore, the court found no evidence that CBC used the players' identities to gain a commercial advantage. The court also found that CBC used the players' names only in association with their playing statistics, and not their pictures, personality, or reputation. Finally, the court found that CBC's use of the players' names and records did not dilute the value of each player's identity. In the end, the court held that CBC did not violate the players' right of publicity. On appeal, the court found that CBC did not use the players' identity in its fantasy products for profit or to gain a commercial advantage (*C.B.C. Distribution & Marketing v. MLB Advanced Media*, 2007). The court allowed the players' claims for violations of their rights of publicity to continue. The court then balanced the players' rights against CBC's First Amendment rights and concluded that CBC's rights in providing fantasy baseball products outweighed the players' claims.

As a result, although all professional athletes have some recognizable right of publicity in their identity, this right does not extend to the use of their names or career statistics on the Internet. Still, the full extent of the right of publicity within sport remains to be determined. Technology continues to advance, and the numerous fantasy sports and sports gambling sites demonstrate new ways in which information related to professional athletes can be disseminated on the Internet. Presumably, players and leagues will continue to seek to receive revenue associated with the use of player information by new technologies.

At the college level, athletes have begun to bring lawsuits claiming that the use of their images and likenesses violates their right of publicity. In one such suit, former Arizona State quarterback Sam Keller led a lawsuit that sued the NCAA and EA Sports. He claimed that the use of his image and likeness in the NCAA Football video game violated his right of publicity. The initial lawsuit eventually became *In re NCAA Student Athlete Name & Likeness Licensing Litigation*. In July 2013 the United States Court of Appeals for the 9th Circuit rejected the claim of EA Sports that its use of Keller's and other players' images and likenesses in the video game was protected by the First Amendment (*Keller v. Elec. Arts Inc.*, 2013). A year later, EA Sports settled the lawsuit by paying the players $40 million, and

the NCAA similarly settled for $20 million (Dauster, 2014). The NCAA has since ended any relationship with EA Sports to create video games for NCAA competitions. As a result, the extent of the right of publicity that current players possess is still unclear.

Patent Law

A final area of intellectual property law that affects the sport industry is patent law. (See table 9.2 for a summary of the intellectual property laws discussed in this chapter.) Patent law is designed to advance science and inventions by providing protection to those who create new things. A **patent** is a document provided by the federal government that gives the owner the right to exclude others from reproducing the patented invention for 20 years. The patent itself specifically describes the invention in detail. An invention is patentable if it is a "new and useful process, machine, manufacture, or composition of matter, or any new and useful improvement thereof" (Patent Act, 35 U.S.C. § 101, 2015).

Table 9.2 Summary of Intellectual Property Laws

Law	Who or what it protects	Sport examples
Trademark law	Any word, name, symbol, or device used to identify and distinguish the services of one person from the services of others and to indicate the source of the services, even if that source is unknown	• Logos • Team names
Copyright law	Literary or artistic productions and the reproduction, publication, or sale of these productions	• Game accounts • Statistics
Right of publicity	The right of any person to control the commercial use of his or her identity	• Baseball cards • T-shirts
Patent law	Inventors of new things that receive federal protection providing the inventor with the right to exclude others from reproducing the invention for 20 years	• Equipment • Apparel design • Games

A patent can be awarded for any invention that is a new product, process, apparatus, or composition, including living matter. Abstract ideas, laws of nature, literary and artistic works, and inventions that are not considered useful cannot be patented. To obtain a federal patent, the inventor must submit an application to the U.S. Patent and Trademark Office within 1 year of the time the invention will be sold or in public use. The inventor must demonstrate that the invention is new (no one else invented it or applied for a patent for it), useful (it must serve some clear purpose), and nonobvious (an ordinary person would not have found the invention to be obvious in the particular field). Beyond these stipulations, the courts have allowed people to patent virtually anything (35 U.S.C. §§ 102–103).

Sport organizations have patents for everything imaginable—the equipment used to play the sport (balls, bats, gloves, clubs), designs for the apparel worn (shoes, shirts, jackets, cleats), and even certain games themselves (the Arena Football League owns a patent for that style of football). The patent for Arena Football League–style football, patent number 4,911,443, described as a "football game system and method of play," is registered as follows:

> A new game is disclosed, involving substantially the same rules as American football (e.g., NFL or NCAA) except that kicks or passes into the end zone may be deflected back onto the playing field as a playable ball by a rebounding assembly that surrounds the goalposts. Upon an attempted field goal, an errant kick will result in the ball hitting the rebounding assembly instead of passing between the vertical uprights of the goalpost. The reflected ball can be caught before it hits the ground by only players of the team defending the goal. Once caught, the defending team may advance the ball toward the opposite goal in accordance with the normal rules of American football. If the ball reflected off of the rebounding assembly hits the ground before it is caught by a player of the team defending the goal, the ball is free for players of either team to advance. In order to ensure that an errant kick results in the rebounding of the ball back into the playing field, the rebounding assembly is comprised of resilient material that returns much of the kinetic energy to the ball after it impacts the rebounding assembly. The rebound assembly for playing the game is comprised of a goal post substantially similar to that used in American football, with the exception that the instant goal is provided with a ball rebound net extending outwards from each side of the goal post, along the extremity of the end zone to substantially the entire width of the playing field.

Patents have begun to proliferate in fantasy sports games. One of the most recent such patents is patent number 8,821,291, granted on September 2, 2014, for a "system and method for conducting a fantasy sports competition":

> The present invention embodiments pertain to conducting fantasy sports or other competitions, where users select or draft an entirely new team of professional players each week (or at other suitable time interval). The competition types (including playoffs) include fee based and free. Each fee based competition has

a pre-determined entry fee, and prizes are awarded to the winner of that competition each week. The free competitions similarly include weekly prizes and further provide for a grand prize. Within each of the free and fee based types of competitions, users may compete in a "private" competition or a randomly composed "open" competition. Users within the free and fee based competitions may accumulate points that qualify for redemption to obtain prizes. These points are accumulated based upon the statistical performance of the drafted players for each team. The present invention embodiments further provide mechanisms for information sharing and interaction between users.

To find out what patents have been granted in the sport world, anyone can visit the U.S. Patent and Trademark Office website at http://patft.uspto.gov.

The main purpose of a patent is to give the inventor the right to exclude others from copying an invention for at least 20 years. Theoretically, if the patent is for items of value that can be sold in some market, the inventor will be able to recover any costs of developing the invention and potentially make a profit. Inventors usually market their inventions themselves so that they can make money from them. If they are unable to produce and market products using their patent, they sell licenses to others, granting them permission to use the patent and sell products themselves.

As with all intellectual property right claims, litigation focuses on potential infringement, in this case **patent infringement**. To show patent infringement, an inventor must show that someone else made, used, offered to sell or sold, or imported into the United States her patented material without her permission (35 U.S.C. § 271, 2015). An inventor can receive damages, attorney's fees, and injunctive relief if she succeeds in a claim of patent infringement.

Fantasy Sports Properties, Inc., patented a particular method of playing fantasy football on the Internet—patent number 4,918,603, for a "computerized statistical football game." Fantasy sued Sportsline.com, Yahoo!, Inc., and ESPN, claiming that their computerized fantasy football games infringed on this patent (*Fantasy Sports Properties, Inc. v. Sportsline.com, Inc.*, 2002). A court reviewing a claim of patent infringement must first determine the scope and meaning of the patent claims asserted and then compare those claims to the alleged infringing product. Here, the court analyzed Fantasy's patent specifically. Fantasy argued that its patent covered any scoring method that awarded any bonus points, whereas the court determined that the patent specifically related to bonus points that can be given in addition to standard points given for a particular play in an actual game, based on the difficulty of play. Therefore, Yahoo! did not infringe on the patent because its game awarded miscellaneous points only when a kicker scored a touchdown but still valued those points as a regular touchdown with an asterisk. In addition, ESPN's game did not infringe on the patent because its game did not award bonus points beyond the normal points awarded in a football game. But the court could not determine whether Sportsline.com's software tool awarded bonus points in violation of the patent, so the court remanded that issue to the trial court.

Ambush Marketing

As a sport administrator, you have the job of making sure that your organization can earn money from any sponsorship agreement it enters into. Unfortunately, other companies that have not entered into a written sponsorship agreement may attempt to create some sort of false association with your event or organization to profit from the association without paying for a sponsorship. A company that uses this practice, known as **ambush marketing**, creates an advertising or promotional campaign that confuses consumers and wrongly implies that the company is an official sponsor of an event. This practice harms companies that are official sponsors by weakening their relationship with the event.

These types of ambush marketing campaigns are particularly found with large-scale events such as the Super Bowl or Olympics that offer official recognition as event sponsors to companies and organizations that pay sponsorship fees in the millions of dollars. For example, worldwide Olympic sponsors (the highest level of sponsorship) for the 2012 Summer Olympic Games, including Coca-Cola, Acer, Atos Origin Dow, GE, McDonald's, Omega, Panasonic, Proctor & Gamble, Samsung, and Visa, paid an estimated $957 million combined between 2009 and 2012, which is more than 40% of Olympic revenues for the games. Companies that cannot afford to be official sponsors may try to associate with the event in other ways without paying for an official sponsorship.

An interesting example of an ambush marketing campaign connected with the 2012 Summer Olympics involved Paddy Power, a bookmaker that takes bets on various sporting events. The bookmaker put up large posters and billboards around London saying "Official Sponsor of the Largest Athletics Event in London this Year! There You Go, We Said it (Ahem, London France that is)." Paddy Power was not an Olympic sponsor, but it did sponsor an egg and spoon race in the town of London located in Burgundy, France. Arguing that this campaign illegally violated its rights, the London Organising Committee of the Olympic Games wrote to Paddy Power's owner, requesting them to remove the posters and billboards. Paddy Power refused, instructing its lawyers to seek a court order because it did not believe the campaign violated any laws (Hall, 2012). Eventually, the committee backed down and allowed the posters to stay up, likely to avoid negative media attention.

During the 2014 Winter Olympic Games in Sochi, Subway and Red Bull took advantage of the Games' viewership by creating commercials filled with images of athletes participating in winter activities such as skating and snowboarding. Because of the commercials depicting Olympic sports, both companies landed not only on a list of perceived sponsors of the Games by the public but also in the top five, alongside actual sponsors Proctor & Gamble, Samsung, and Coca-Cola (Goddard, 2014).

Sport organizations and event hosts are reluctant to go after ambush marketers because of the limited case law showing that this activity is illegal. In addition, ambush marketing campaigns are often short lived because companies put forth a campaign only in a short period close to the event itself. Sport organizations that want to take action often focus on trademark or copyright infringement claims against the ambushing company.

LEARNING AIDS

Summary

Intellectual property law provides the foundation for the protection of rights that an organization can sell to generate revenue. Trademark rights are perhaps most valuable because they allow an organization to generate revenue by licensing the use of its name and logo. Collective marks allow leagues to create new logos and nicknames that represent the entire group of member teams. The law provides specific ways for an organization to stop competitors who try to infringe on and dilute the organization's marks. With the protection provided by anti-cybersquatting laws and the Uniform Dispute Resolution Process, organizations can also protect their websites and domain names. This protection is especially important as sport organizations continue to find new ways to sell tickets and merchandise online.

Copyright law provides organizations with ways to protect their rights in television broadcasts, game accounts, media guides, newspapers, and magazines. Still to be decided are the exact rights that a league or team has to protect the statistics produced by players and teams. Although players can control and profit from the use of their identity because of the right of publicity, their playing statistics do not receive similar copyright protection.

Finally, many sport organizations create new and profitable styles of play, equipment, facilities, and products. All these inventions can be registered as patents, which exclude others from using an invention without permission for 20 years, a long time during which the patent holder can make a profit.

Discussion Questions

1. Create a hypothetical example of copyright infringement and a brief explanation.
2. Provide a hypothetical example of cybersquatting and explain why the domain would be considered cybersquatting.
3. Explain the key differences between a trademark, copyright, and patent.
4. Do you agree with the court's decision in *CBC v. MLBAM*? Explain.
5. Explain the circumstances under which trademark protection of a university team name might be denied.
6. Provide an example of a violation of the right of publicity for a professional athlete.
7. List and briefly describe 10 patents relevant to sport.
8. What types of marks can a sport organization seek legal protection for?

Team Use of Native American Nickname

A new professional baseball team was set to be established in southwest Florida, an area once populated by the Native American Seminole tribe. The name chosen for the team was the Florida Redskins. The U.S. Patent and Trademark Office granted permission to the new owners to use this name. The Florida Redskins enjoyed immediate success and popularity in southwest Florida. Native Americans living in Florida, however, were upset with the use of the nickname, which they believed to be disparaging to Native Americans and in violation of the Lanham Act. As a result, a group of Native Americans petitioned to cancel the trademark registrations for the marks *Florida Redskins* and *Redskins*, which were owned by the owners of the MLB's Florida Redskins franchise. The owners immediately brought suit to avoid the cancellation of the marks and to keep the team name.

Antitrust Law

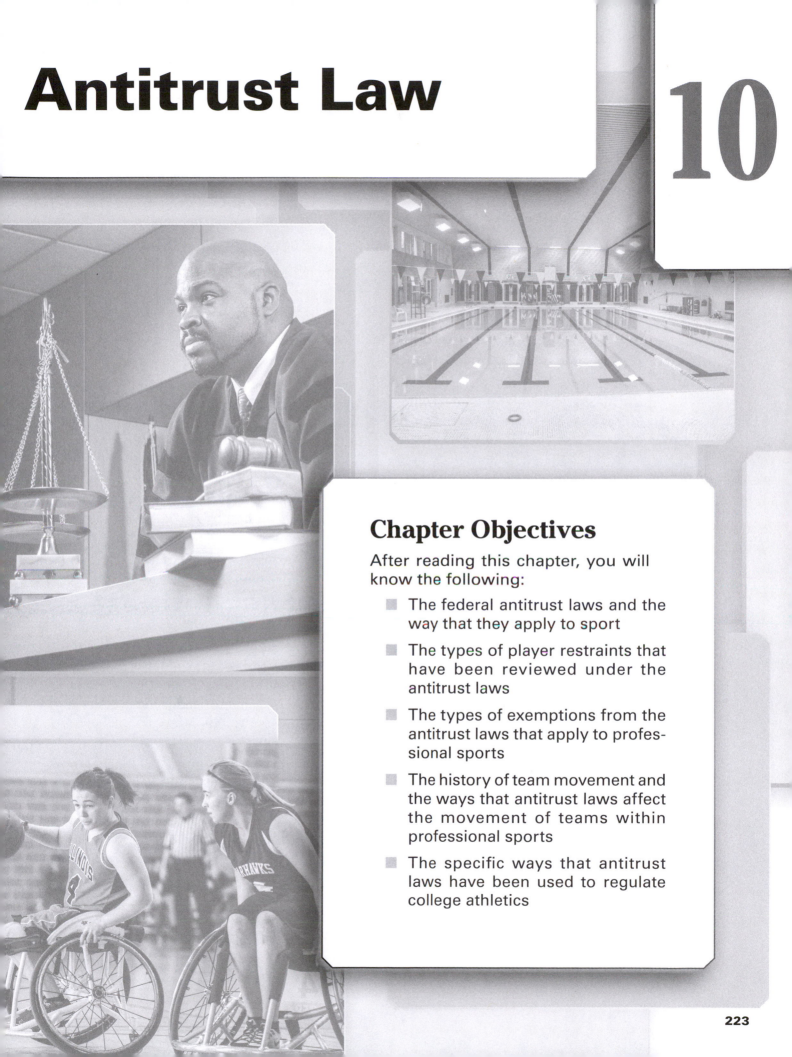

Chapter Objectives

After reading this chapter, you will know the following:

- The federal antitrust laws and the way that they apply to sport

- The types of player restraints that have been reviewed under the antitrust laws

- The types of exemptions from the antitrust laws that apply to professional sports

- The history of team movement and the ways that antitrust laws affect the movement of teams within professional sports

- The specific ways that antitrust laws have been used to regulate college athletics

Antitrust laws were implemented to promote competition and efficiency in the marketplace and to protect consumers from the growing **monopoly power** of big business. These laws were designed to maintain a high level of competition among producers so that consumers would be able to get products at affordable and reasonable prices. In sport, antitrust laws have been used by players, owners, universities, teams, and leagues in attempts to change conditions that these parties believe have caused them to suffer negative economic consequences. Such negative consequences include lower wages, the inability to relocate teams, unfair competition, and lower television revenues.

The application of antitrust laws in sport is most prominent in professional sports. This chapter discusses the interaction of antitrust laws with professional sports in several areas, including player restraints, franchise relocation, ownership issues, and disputes between leagues. Professional sports leagues have been found to operate outside the antitrust laws through various exemptions, and some leagues, such as Major League Soccer, have been created using single-entity structures that provide protection from certain forms of antitrust scrutiny.

Although antitrust has primarily been used to regulate professional sports, amateur sports have not been immune to review under the antitrust laws. In particular, the NCAA has faced numerous challenges under the antitrust laws, typically because people claim that NCAA regulations restrain trade.

Before discussing the effect that the antitrust laws have had on the sport industry, the chapter begins by discussing the federal antitrust laws themselves.

Federal Antitrust Laws

Federal antitrust laws, particularly the Sherman Antitrust Act, have a substantial effect on sport. This chapter focuses on federal law, but each state has adopted a form of antitrust law that mirrors the federal law. As a result, analysis under the federal law is similar to that under state laws. Passed in 1890, the Sherman Antitrust Act includes two major sections. Section 1 states that "every contract, combination in the form of trust or otherwise, or conspiracy in restraint of trade or commerce among the several states or foreign nations, is declared to be illegal" (15 U.S.C. § 1, 2015). To prove a violation of the Sherman Act under section

1, a plaintiff must satisfy three elements. First, the plaintiff must show that two separate parties have an agreement. Next, the plaintiff must show that the parties' conduct taken under the agreement unreasonably restrains trade because the conduct is anticompetitive. Finally, the activity must affect **interstate commerce**—that is, commerce that takes place between two or more states.

When looking at whether a sport organization's conduct violates section 1, a court analyzes the nature of the conduct under either the **per se rule** or the **rule of reason**. Conduct that is inherently anticompetitive, such as **price fixing** and **group boycotts**, is considered illegal per se and automatically violates the Sherman Act. This conduct is so destructive to competition that a plaintiff only has to show that these things happened; the plaintiff does not have to show that she was harmed by them.

The rule of reason analysis applies when the conduct is not inherently anticompetitive. Instead, the focus is on whether the challenged conduct unreasonably restrains trade. Under this analysis, a plaintiff must show that separate entities have an agreement, that this agreement negatively affects competition in a relevant market, and that the anticompetitive effects of the agreement outweigh any procompetitive effects. A defendant can defend conduct that might otherwise violate the rule of reason by showing that there is a legitimate business reason for the restraining conduct and that the methods used are the least restrictive means possible.

Section 2 provides that

> every person who shall monopolize, or attempt to monopolize or combine or conspire with any other person or persons, to monopolize any part of the trade or commerce among the several states, or with foreign nations, shall be deemed guilty of a felony. (15 U.S.C. § 2, 2015)

A **monopoly** is an organization that possesses exclusive control over the means of selling and producing a product. Because a monopoly's control is exclusive, it does not face competition from other organizations that might force it to lower its prices or provide better products to compete in the marketplace. To show a violation of section 2, a plaintiff must show that the organization possesses monopoly market power and has used unacceptable means to acquire or maintain this power.

The other important law dealing with antitrust issues is the Clayton Antitrust Act, passed in 1914 (15 U.S.C. § 15, 2015). This law provides that when a plaintiff proves that a breach of the Sherman Act has occurred, the damages that the plaintiff can recover are tripled. For example, in 1984 when Los Angeles Raiders owner Al Davis won his antitrust lawsuit against the NFL, the tripled damages amounted to more than $35 million.

Two other federal antitrust laws, the Sports Broadcasting Act and the Curt Flood Act, are discussed later in the chapter as they specifically relate to professional sports. See table 10.1 for a summary of the antitrust laws discussed in this chapter.

Application to Professional Team Sports

In professional sports, teams have long used different types of restraints to restrict player movement, such as free-agent compensation arrangements, option and **reserve clauses**, no-tampering rules, and the draft system. Players and their respective

Table 10.1   Summary of Antitrust Laws

Federal law	What it does	How it applies to sport
Sherman Antitrust Act, section 1	Regulates agreements that restrain trade Focuses on anticompetitive behavior Regulates only the activities that affect commerce between two or more states	Review of ownership rules in professional sports Review of participation eligibility rules in individual performer sports Review of salary restrictions in college sports
Sherman Antitrust Act, section 2	Regulates entities that exhibit some form of monopoly power by possessing exclusive control over the means of selling and producing a product	Review of franchise relocation rules in professional sports Review of television contracts in college sports Review of competition among leagues in professional sports
Clayton Antitrust Act	Allows for damages to be tripled when a court finds that there has been a violation of the Sherman Act	Referred to in all situations where a violation of the Sherman Act is found (e.g., the damages awarded to the Raiders were tripled from $11.5 million to $34.5 million when they proved that the NFL violated the Sherman Act when it tried to stop them from relocating)
Sports Broadcasting Act	An exemption from the Sherman Act, section 1 Allows professional hockey, football, baseball, and basketball to pool and sell their rights in game telecasts	Review of restrictions against individual team television contracts in professional sports
Curt Flood Act	Allows baseball players to sue MLB if they believe that some condition of their employment may violate the antitrust laws	Applies only to potential claims brought by baseball players against MLB

players associations repeatedly object to these practices because they limit player salaries and bolster profits for teams. On the other hand, management at both the club and league level views such restraints as necessary to maintain economic viability and competition, and clubs and leagues often are provided exemptions from the antitrust laws so that these restraints are allowed to continue. What follows is a brief analysis of the effect of the antitrust laws on professional team sports.

Player Restraints

Some of the earliest applications of antitrust law in sport focused on protecting player salaries from illegal restraints or unfair competition. These restraints have taken many forms over the years.

Player Drafts

One restraint that has seen a lot of litigation is the amateur player draft. Each of the major sports leagues uses an annual draft to select and allocate players to its member teams. Each league also sets out specific requirements related to the age of those who can be drafted, their completion or progress in high school or university, and their eligibility to be drafted by a member team.

In the early 1970s the NBA draft rule allowed players to be eligible only after 4 years had passed since they graduated from high school. Players did not have to graduate from college, but they were eligible only at a point 4 years past their high school graduation. Spencer Haywood, a talented basketball player playing for the American Basketball Association, wanted to play for the NBA but was barred from the draft because of this rule. He sued, arguing that this player restraint was a group boycott that violated the Sherman Act (*Denver Rockets v. All-Pro Mgt., Inc.*, 1971). The court agreed, finding that the NBA draft rule was a group boycott because the NBA conspired to avoid dealing with players who were not 4 years beyond high school graduation, and therefore the NBA was restraining trade in violation of the Sherman Act.

In a similar case 5 years later, James McCoy Smith sued the NFL, claiming that its draft system prevented him from negotiating a contract that would reflect the free market value of his services (*Smith v. Pro-Football, Inc.*, 1978). (See more about this case in the accompanying e-book, *Case Studies in Sport Law, Second Edition* [Pittman, Spengler, & Young, 2016].) Conducting a rule of reason analysis, the court found that the draft system was an unreasonable restraint of trade. The draft rule forced each seller (the player drafted) to deal with only one team, robbing the player of any bargaining power. The NFL argued that the rule was necessary to achieve competitive balance, to produce better entertainment for the fans, and to create higher salaries for all NFL players. The court found that these justifications had nothing to do with the market for players and held that the rule was an unreasonable restraint of trade.

Even after these decisions, both the NFL and NBA continued to use an amateur draft. Eventually, the NBA modified its draft rules to allow virtually any athlete to apply for the draft. As a result, even high school players became eligible, and in the 1990s teams began to draft increasingly younger players. Recently, as part of its newest collective bargaining agreement, the NBA modified its draft rule again, restricting eligibility to players who are 19 years of age or older. By 1990 the NFL had settled on eligibility rules that permitted a player to enter the draft three full seasons after that player's high school graduation. Although some speculated that these draft rules would also be found to be a restraint of trade, a recent case against the NFL (see the Legality of a Professional Sports League Player Draft sidebar) seems to show that courts will now uphold draft rules in certain situations.

Leagues can apparently maintain amateur drafts as long as they are created as a part of the collective bargaining process and, most likely, as long as they are included within the collective bargaining agreement. This practice makes sense because the agreement represents the terms and conditions of employment that have been agreed to by both players (as represented by their union) and management.

Restrictive Free Agency

Over the years several leagues have implemented rules that have restricted the ability of players to move freely to sign contracts with different teams and have forced teams to provide compensation of some form to another team if they sign that team's player. For example, under MLB's reserve system, each player was the property of his team for the extent of his playing career. At the time, each player contract contained a **reserve clause** that stipulated that if the player did not automatically sign a new contract with the team for the next season, all the provisions of his present contract would be automatically renewed. As a result, each team had the perpetual right to renew each of its own player's contracts. The player could still be

IN THE COURTROOM

Legality of a Professional Sports League Player Draft

Clarett v. NFL (2004)

Clarett v. NFL (2004) involved Maurice Clarett, who ran for 1,237 yards and scored 18 touchdowns during his freshman year at Ohio State University. Ohio State went 14-0, and Clarett scored the winning touchdown in the Fiesta Bowl, which gave his team the 2002 BCS National Championship.

Ohio State suspended Clarett for the 2003 season after he was charged with filing a false police report, received thousands of dollars in special benefits, and repeatedly misled investigators. He tried to enter the NFL draft, but he was barred because he was not three full seasons removed from his high school graduation. Clarett sued, claiming that the rule was an unreasonable restraint of trade in violation of federal antitrust law. The district court agreed and ordered that he be made eligible for the 2004 draft. The NFL appealed.

Clarett argued that NFL clubs are competitors for the labor of professional football players and that the rules violated antitrust laws. Note that certain concerted activity between labor and employer is beyond the reach of the antitrust laws because of the nonstatutory labor exemption. Typically, mandatory subjects of bargaining such as wages and working conditions have been protected from antitrust review by the exemption. Therefore, the court noted that NFL teams are permitted to engage in joint conduct with the union with respect to the terms and conditions of players' employment without risking antitrust scrutiny. The court held that the eligibility rules are mandatory bargaining subjects and are protected by the labor exemption. Therefore, Clarett could not contest these rules on antitrust grounds. The Second Circuit Court reversed the district court and remanded the case with instructions to enter judgment for the NFL.

traded or fired, but this would occur at the club's option. There was no **free agency**, so players were not allowed to negotiate with other teams for their services. At the same time, league rules prevented teams from negotiating with players on other teams and seeking their services.

Supported by baseball's **antitrust exemption**, the reserve clause remained in force until 1975. In that year, baseball players Andy Messersmith and Dave McNally played without a contract because they could not agree with their clubs on the renewal of their old contracts. At the end of the year, both players declared themselves free agents, arguing that the reserve clause affected them for only 1 year after the expiration of their contracts. Their clubs

disagreed, arguing that the reserve clause was perpetual and that the players were still under contract. As provided in the **collective bargaining agreement (CBA)**, the Major League Baseball Players Association filed a grievance on behalf of the players before a designated arbitrator (*Arbitration of Messersmith*, 1975).

Agreeing with the players, the arbitrator interpreted the reserve clause to mean that a player's contract was reserved for a team for only 1 year after his contract had expired. Therefore, Messersmith and McNally were free agents. The owners challenged the decision, but the challenge failed because the court determined that the designated arbitrator was the proper party to interpret the provisions of the players' contracts as dictated in the collective bargaining agreement. Because of this decision, each subsequent collective bargaining agreement has modified the player contract, stating that the player is bound to the team that drafts him for a defined period before he is eligible to become a free agent.

The NFL had a similar rule called the **Rozelle rule**. This rule required a team signing a veteran free agent to provide compensation to the team that was losing the player. The rule effectively stifled competition because teams did not want to pay this compensation; players were kept on the teams that drafted them and could not reap the benefits of free agency. The Rozelle rule stayed in place until 1975, when several players sued the NFL, claiming that the Rozelle rule was an illegal restraint on trade in violation of the Sherman Act (*Mackey v. NFL*, 1976). The court initially determined that because of the rule, players were not able

to sell their services on an open market so the salaries they were paid were lower than they would have been in an open market. The league argued that the rule was needed to promote competitive balance. Although the court was sympathetic to this argument and recognized that some restraints on free agency were necessary, it found that the Rozelle rule was an excessive restraint on competition.

Although each league still maintains some restrictions on free agency, each league also has some form of free agency. At some point during a player's career, the player is free to sign a contract with the team of his choice.

Salary Caps

Salary caps in sport set a limit on the amount of money a team can spend on player salaries (see table 10.2). These caps are set either as per-player limits or as a

Table 10.2 Recent Salary Caps in Professional Team Sports

Season	NBA	NHL	Season	NFL
2000–2001	$35.5 million	NA	2001	$67.4 million
2001–2002	$42.5 million	NA	2002	$71.1 million
2002–2003	$40.271 million	NA	2003	$75.007 million
2003–2004	$43.84 million	NA	2004	$80.582 million
2004–2005	$43.87 million	Cancelled	2005	$85.5 million
2005–2006	$49.5 million	$39 million	2006	$102 million
2006–2007	$53.135 million	$44 million	2007	$109 million
2007–2008	$55.63 million	$50.3 million	2008	$116 million
2008–2009	$58.68 million	$56.7 million	2009	$128 million
2009–2010	$57.7 million	$56.8 million	2010	Uncapped
2010–2011	$58.044 million	$59.4 million	2011	$120.375 million
2011–2012	$58.044 million	$64.3 million	2012	$120.6 million
2012–2013	$58.044 million	$70.2 million	2013	$123 million
2013–2014	$58.679 million	$64.3 million	2014	$133 million
2014–2015	$63.065 million	$69 million	2015	$143.28 million

Information taken from various league websites and collective bargaining agreements.

total limit that a team can pay its players. In 1983 the NBA became the first league to implement a salary cap, and since then the NFL and NHL have added some form of salary cap. Often the amount of the salary cap is a major issue in negotiations between owners and players over a collective bargaining agreement. The issue is important to many players because they believe that a salary cap will depress their ability to negotiate for a maximum salary. MLB players still have not agreed to a salary cap. As a result, teams like the New York Yankees continue to be unrestricted in paying huge salaries to their players ($218 million in 2015), and smaller-market teams that cannot pay these salaries often believe that they cannot compete. For example, the Houston Astros spent $70 million on player salaries in 2015, approximately one-third as much as the Yankees did.

Many players have challenged salary caps. For instance, Leon Wood sued the NBA, claiming that various provisions of the collective bargaining agreement, including the salary cap, violated the Sherman Act (*Wood v. NBA*, 1987). Wood was drafted by the Philadelphia 76ers in 1984 and was offered a 1-year contract for $75,000 under the salary cap. Arguing that he would be forced to sign a contract under his true market value, Wood sued to stop the NBA's use of its salary cap. The court rejected Wood's claim because it found that the salary cap was created within the collective bargaining agreement as a normal part of the negotiation process between management and labor.

Although many forms of player restraints, including salary caps and player drafts, have been upheld by the courts, the restrictive player restraints of years past are long gone and all players can become free agents at some point in their careers.

Exemptions

Exemptions from the antitrust laws typically provide a league, club, or other entity with immunity from scrutiny for conduct that might otherwise be found to be illegal. The most well-known exemption in sport is enjoyed by Major League Baseball.

Baseball

Since 1922 players have not been able to sue MLB by claiming that the league's policies violate the antitrust laws, even though such suits are possible in other professional sports leagues. By 1913 the National and American Leagues were well established, but they faced competition from the newly formed Federal League. Both the National and American Leagues offered Federal League owners considerable amounts of money to disband the new league. They also offered Federal League owners the right to purchase franchises in the National and American Leagues. The Baltimore club of the Federal League sued, claiming that this conduct violated the Sherman Act. Baltimore argued that the Federal League was destroyed by a conspiracy between the National and American Leagues. In a landmark decision, Justice Holmes stated that the antitrust laws did not apply to baseball because baseball was an "exhibition" and "not subject to commerce" (*Federal Baseball Club v. National League*, 1922).

Because of this case, players have been unable to sue MLB under the Sherman Act. This judicially recognized exemption has continued for decades, but not without challenge. In 1953 several players sued baseball, claiming that the standard reserve clause in their contracts violated the antitrust laws. As explained earlier, under the reserve system teams were allowed to renew a player's contract automatically at the end of each year. This provision created a continuous cycle that prevented players from marketing their services to other teams. The Supreme Court affirmed its decision in the *Federal Baseball* ruling, upholding the exemption, and leaving it to Congress to decide whether antitrust laws should apply to baseball (*Toolson v. New York Yankees*, 1953).

In 1972 baseball player Curt Flood challenged the exemption, arguing that baseball's reserve system violated the Sherman Act. He was unsuccessful (*Flood v. Kuhn*, 1972). (See more about this case in the accompanying e-book, *Case Studies in Sport Law, Second Edition* [Pittman, Spengler, & Young, 2016].) Although the Supreme Court finally recognized that as a business, baseball did engage in interstate commerce, the court also noted that Congress had not intervened in 50 years to change the exemption. Therefore, it again left the matter to be changed by Congress.

It was not until 1993 that courts began to be more vocal in their disagreement with baseball's antitrust exemption. Vincent Piazza and Vincent Tirendi formed a limited partnership to buy the San Francisco Giants and move the team to Tampa, Florida. When MLB did not approve of the purchase, Piazza and Tirendi sued, claiming that MLB's actions violated the antitrust laws (*Piazza v. Major League Baseball*, 1993). They alleged that MLB monopolized the market for baseball teams and placed restraints on the purchase, sale, and other forms of competition for these teams. The court found that baseball's antitrust exemption did not extend to the purchase of an existing team. Soon after the case, the Giants were sold to a local buyer.

Pursuant to a provision in the 1994 MLB collective bargaining agreement, the players and owners lobbied Congress to modify the baseball exemption. In 1998 Congress passed the Curt Flood Act (15 U.S.C. § 26(b), 2015) in commemoration of Curt Flood. The act allows baseball players to sue MLB if they believe that some condition of their employment may violate the antitrust laws. Other aspects of the business of baseball itself (i.e., ownership, management, relocation) are still protected by the antitrust exemption, as the City of San Jose found when it sued Major League Baseball for barring the Oakland Athletics from moving to San Jose. Finding that the exemption applied to franchise relocation, the United States Court of Appeals for the Ninth Circuit dismissed the city's claims (*City of San Jose v. Office of the Commissioner of Baseball*, 2015).

Nonstatutory Labor Exemption

The U.S. Supreme Court created the nonstatutory **labor exemption** so that when employers and employees have agreed to a collective bargaining agreement in good faith, neither of them can bring an antitrust challenge related to the terms of the agreement. As a result, terms and conditions that normally could be attacked as violations of the antitrust laws (such as salary caps and player restraints) are immune from antitrust scrutiny as long as they were negotiated for within collective bargaining. Although not created for sport, the nonstatutory labor exemption has been discussed in many sport-related cases.

Courts have developed a three-part test about when a league can use the labor exemption as a defense to claims brought by players or unions. Most challenges will be brought against the league, because it is the employer and enforces the terms and conditions of the player's employment contract. To use the labor exemption, a league must show that (1) the restraint of trade affects only the parties to the collective bargaining agreement; (2) the restraint is

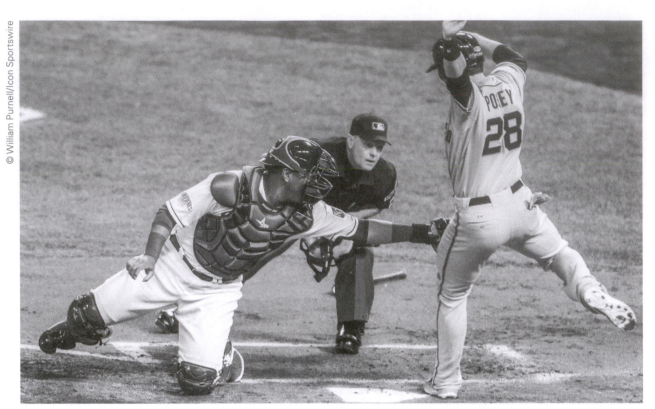

The Curt Flood Act modifies baseball's antitrust exemption, but the exemption still stands.

a **mandatory subject of collective bargaining** (these include wages, hours, and other terms and conditions of employment); and (3) the collective bargaining agreement is the product of arms-length bargaining, meaning that each party has an equally strong position to bargain from.

Although the nonstatutory exemption can allow employers to avoid antitrust liability in a manner similar to the baseball exemption, courts have struggled to understand its application. Two interesting situations developed out of the possible application of the exemption, the first after a player strike and the second in regard to developmental squad players.

In 1987, after the NFL's collective bargaining agreement expired, the league wanted to maintain the status quo on all the mandatory subjects in the expired agreement, including player salaries. When negotiations between the league and union soured, the players went on strike. The strike ended after 1 month, but the players and owners still could not reach an agreement, and the league insisted on implementing the conditions of the expired agreement. The players sued to stop the NFL from implementing the expired agreement and asked the court to determine whether the labor exemption protected the league's first refusal and compensation policy (*Powell v. NFL*, 1989). The court found that the labor exemption could be invoked even after the collective bargaining agreement expired. Although the union and owners were at **impasse** at this stage, there was still the possibility that they could reach an agreement in the future. In addition, because the rule at issue was a mandatory subject and because the parties were still negotiating over the terms of the next agreement, the exemption immunized the league's conduct from antitrust review.

How long the nonstatutory labor exemption can apply after the expiration of a collective bargaining agreement is still unclear. The *Powell* court hinted that the union would have to stop serving as the players' representative within negotiations before the exemption would expire. Therefore, for most conditions of employment related to salaries and free agency, as long as the parties are negotiating or can still negotiate to reach an agreement, the exemption still appears to apply. As a result, management typically can implement policies from the past agreement and maintain the status quo, even though the union disagrees, without violating the antitrust laws.

The second situation that developed out of the possible application of the exemption occurred in the 1990s when the NFL proposed a new plan in which up to six first-year free-agent players who failed to secure a roster spot with a team could be designated for a development squad. These players could play in regular practices and were to be paid approximately $1,000 per week. The players union rejected this idea, arguing that all players should receive the same benefits and protections. The union and management could not agree, and they reached impasse. Thereafter, the owners unilaterally implemented the developmental squad plan. Predictably, the players sued, claiming that the NFL's imposition of the policy violated the antitrust laws (*Brown v. Pro Football, Inc.*, 1996). (See more about this case in the accompanying e-book, *Case Studies in Sport Law, Second Edition* [Pittman, Spengler, & Young, 2016].) In analyzing whether the nonstatutory labor exemption applied, the court noted that the plan was created during collective bargaining and implemented immediately after impasse

was reached. It involved a mandatory subject of bargaining that had to be negotiated for, and it concerned only the parties to the agreement. Therefore, as with the *Powell* decision, the exemption immunized the league from claims that the imposition of the policy violated the Sherman Act.

Broadcasting Exemption

The Sports Broadcasting Act (15 U.S.C. §§ 1291 et seq., 2015) was enacted in 1961 to allow professional hockey, football, baseball, and basketball to pool and sell their rights in sponsored telecasts of games. Such pooling of rights to be sold to one buyer would be considered price fixing or monopoly behavior in most situations and would violate the antitrust laws. However, the Sports Broadcasting Act provides that the pooling of these television rights is exempt from section 1 of the Sherman Act. The purpose of the Sports Broadcasting Act was to enable clubs to put their separate rights together into one package so that the league can sell the package to one purchaser, such as a television network, in an effort to protect their home game ticket sales and to allow clubs to share television revenues. The focus on "sponsored telecasts" has been interpreted to ensure that free national and local televising of league games continues. As a result, paid broadcasts on cable and league agreements with cable broadcasters have not been covered by this antitrust exemption.

Teams in the NBA have jointly pooled and marketed some of their television rights through the league under the exemption granted by the Sports Broadcasting Act. In the early 1990s this agreement between the NBA and TNT provided each team with its single largest source of shared league revenues, at about $6.8 million. In 2014 the NBA signed its largest media rights deal ever for $24 billion with ESPN and Turner

Sports. Under this deal, starting in the 2016–2017 season, the league will receive approximately $2.6 billion per year.

Since about 1982, in an effort to maximize the value of the agreement, the league has also restricted local broadcasts by teams, especially local broadcasts on superstations. Superstations are independent broadcasters that broadcast in their local market and are carried in other parts of the county, like Chicago's WGN and Atlanta's WTBS. Over the years the NBA has limited the number of games that teams can air on superstations. The limit was 41 games in 1980 and was lowered to 25 in 1985. In 1990 the NBA's board of governors decided to change its rule, reducing the number of games a team could broadcast on a superstation from 25 to 20. At the same time, teams could televise up to half (41) of their regular-season games on local television stations located in their home territory. Most teams would do this because they were able to keep 100% of the revenues from these local deals. Games broadcast on a local superstation counted against this 41-game limit.

In 1990 the Chicago Bulls and WGN sued the NBA, claiming that the reduction from 25 to 20 games was a restraint on the team's ability to broadcast its own games and thus violated section 1 of the Sherman Act (*Chicago Professional Sports Limited Partnership v. National Basketball Association*, 1996). (See more about this case in the accompanying e-book, *Case Studies in Sport Law, Second Edition* [Pittman, Spengler, & Young, 2016].) The NBA argued that its superstation rules were exempt from antitrust scrutiny under the Sports Broadcasting Act. The court disagreed, finding that only agreements sold by the league (and not by an individual team) were exempt under the act and that under a rule-of-reason analysis the policy was an unreasonable restraint.

Among other arguments, the NBA argued that the rule was necessary to protect other teams and their local broadcasts. But the court explained that the antitrust laws protect competition and not individual competitors like the NBA teams, so this justification was not enough. The U.S. Court of Appeals for the Seventh Circuit agreed, finding that the Bulls and WGN would suffer irreparable harm because of the policy and that the NBA's justifications did not outweigh this harm.

League Versus Team

Leagues also have many rules that govern team owners. Leagues argue that the rules they put in place governing ownership are necessary to maintain financial stability, to improve or maintain the league's image, or to protect the product that the league is trying to put forth. Most leagues can be considered joint ventures because the teams that make up the league come together in the league entity so that they can undertake certain economic activities together, such as sharing revenues and expenses, negotiating with the players union on terms and conditions of employment, and forming joint broadcasting agreements. The rules that leagues put in place usually are meant to promote the development of the league as a whole.

Some leagues' rules have become the subject of antitrust litigation because of accusations that the rules are too restrictive. Rules preventing franchise relocation have faced the strongest challenges. Leagues create limits on franchise relocation for several reasons but primarily to protect the overall league product and to protect individual owners from losing revenues when a competing team moves into their geographic area. Often teams want to relocate because they seek stronger stadium or arena deals that will provide them with more revenue. In other cases, a new ownership group buys the team and wants to move it to a new city. All owners in a particular league must unanimously agree to allow a member team to relocate. Because of these rules, in the NFL, for example, no teams were allowed to relocate from 1963 until the 1980s. But one franchise owner would change these restrictive rules forever.

In 1976 the NFL's owners approved the move of the Los Angeles Rams to Anaheim. The Los Angeles Memorial Coliseum Commission immediately sought to replace the team with a new or existing franchise. At the same time, Al Davis, the owner of the Oakland Raiders, had reached an impasse in negotiations for a new lease with the Oakland Coliseum. As a result, he wanted to relocate to Los Angeles. Rule 4.3 of the NFL's constitution required that if a team wanted to move to the home territory of another team (a 75-mile [120 km] radius surrounding the home team), in this case the Rams, the owners had to agree unanimously. In 1980 the owners voted unanimously against the move.

Because of this vote, the coliseum commission sued the NFL, alleging that the franchise relocation rule violated section 1 of the Sherman Act (*Los Angeles Memorial Coliseum Commission v. National Football League*, 1984). Analyzing the rule under the rule of reason, the court found that the NFL's rule restricting franchise movement was anticompetitive because it gave each team a virtual monopoly in its home territory and the league could not show that the Raiders' move would harm the league in any way. Therefore, the Raiders were allowed to move, the team was awarded $11.5 million, and the coliseum commission was awarded $4.6 million (both tripled under the Clayton Act).

Although the case was in the Ninth Circuit and did not affect all jurisdictions throughout the United States, after this decision several leagues realized that they could not stop franchise relocation and modified their rules. In the NFL alone, six teams have moved since 1984 (Colts from Baltimore to Indianapolis; Cardinals from St. Louis to Phoenix; Raiders back to Oakland; Rams from Anaheim to St. Louis; Browns to Baltimore, becoming the Ravens; and the Oilers to Nashville, becoming the Titans). See table 10.3 for a list of additional team relocations.

In 2001 many small-market MLB teams could not compete with large-market teams that received higher revenues from amenities such as club seats and luxury boxes and were thus able to pay higher player salaries. Because some of the smallest-revenue teams could not afford salaries demanded by quality players, MLB voted in favor of contracting from 30 to 28 teams following the 2002 season. MLB never specified exactly which teams were facing the prospect of **contraction**, but the Florida Marlins, Tampa Bay Devil Rays, and Minnesota Twins all feared that they would be targeted.

In response, the attorney general of Florida issued civil investigative demands to MLB, Commissioner Bud Selig, and the Devil Rays and Marlins under his statutory authority to investigate possible violations of the antitrust laws. Relying on the long line of earlier cases on the antitrust exemption, the court denied the attorney general's claims because the decision to force particular teams to cease operations (i.e., the decision to contract them) and the structure of the league itself were essential features of the business of baseball and therefore were exempt.

No teams were ever contracted, because MLB and the players union reached an

Table 10.3   Professional Sports Team Relocations Since 1950

Year	Franchise	New location and name
MAJOR LEAGUE BASEBALL		
1953	Boston Braves	Milwaukee Braves
1954	St. Louis Browns	Baltimore Orioles
1955	Philadelphia Athletics	Kansas City Athletics
1958	Brooklyn Dodgers	Los Angeles Dodgers
1958	New York Giants	San Francisco Giants
1961	Washington Senators	Minnesota Twins
1966	Los Angeles Angels	California (Anaheim) Angels
1966	Milwaukee Braves	Atlanta Braves
1968	Kansas City Athletics	Oakland Athletics
1970	Seattle Pilots	Milwaukee Brewers
1972	Washington Senators II	Texas Rangers
2005	Montreal Expos	Washington Nationals
NATIONAL FOOTBALL LEAGUE		
1961	Los Angeles Chargers (AFL)	San Diego Chargers
1963	Dallas Texans (AFL)	Kansas City Chiefs
1983	Oakland Raiders	Los Angeles Raiders
1984	Baltimore Colts	Indianapolis Colts
1988	St. Louis Cardinals	Phoenix Cardinals
1995	Los Angeles Raiders	Oakland Raiders
1995	Los Angeles Rams	St. Louis Rams
1997	Cleveland Browns	Baltimore Ravens
1997	Houston Oilers	Tennessee Titans
NATIONAL BASKETBALL ASSOCIATION		
1951	Tri Cities Hawks	Milwaukee Hawks
1955	Milwaukee Hawks	St. Louis Hawks
1957	Fort Wayne Pistons	Detroit Pistons
1957	Rochester Royals	Cincinnati Royals
1960	Minneapolis Lakers	Los Angeles Lakers
1962	Philadelphia Warriors	San Francisco Warriors
1963	Chicago Bullets	Baltimore Bullets
1963	Syracuse Nationals	Philadelphia 76ers
1968	St. Louis Hawks	Atlanta Hawks
1971	San Diego Rockets	Houston Rockets
1971	San Francisco Warriors	Oakland Warriors
1972	Cincinnati Royals	Kansas City Kings
1973	Baltimore Bullets	Washington Bullets
1973	Dallas Chaparrals	San Antonio Spurs
1978	Buffalo Braves	San Diego Clippers
1979	New Orleans Jazz	Utah Jazz

Year	Franchise	New location and name
NATIONAL BASKETBALL ASSOCIATION		
1984	San Diego Clippers	Los Angeles Clippers
2001	Vancouver Grizzlies	Memphis Grizzlies
2002	Charlotte Hornets	New Orleans Hornets
2008	Seattle Sonics	Oklahoma City Thunder
2012	New Jersey Nets	Brooklyn Nets
NATIONAL HOCKEY LEAGUE		
1976	California Golden Seals (Oakland)	Cleveland Barons
1976	Kansas City Scouts	Colorado Rockies (Denver)
1978	Cleveland Barons	Minnesota North Stars
1980	Atlanta Flames	Calgary Flames
1982	Colorado Rockies	New Jersey Devils
1993	Minnesota North Stars	Dallas Stars
1995	Quebec Nordiques	Colorado Avalanche (Denver)
1996	Winnipeg Jets	Phoenix Coyotes
1997	Hartford Whalers	Carolina Hurricanes
2012	Atlanta Thrashers	Winnipeg Jets

agreement putting off any discussion of contraction until the expiration of the agreement in 2006. Contraction was not discussed in the most recent collective bargaining negotiations. It remains to be seen whether MLB will again seek to contract teams that it deems not financially viable.

League Versus League

Other litigation has focused on competition between professional sports leagues themselves. A new league usually faces many challenges when it attempts to compete with an established league for players, facilities, or television revenues. Because of these challenges, the new league may end up suing the established league, claiming that its conduct violates the antitrust laws. The first litigation in this area was the *Federal Baseball* decision that led to MLB's exemption from antitrust laws, as already discussed. Since that time, new leagues have repeatedly sued established leagues under section 2 of the Sherman Act, claiming that the established leagues maintain illegal monopolies over their particular sports and that they use anticompetitive methods to maintain those monopolies. Remember, to sustain a claim under section 2, a plaintiff league must show that the established league has monopoly power in a relevant market and that the established league has engaged in anticompetitive conduct that maintained this monopoly power.

Historically, most professional team sports in the United States have maintained only one viable league. Although many competitors have surfaced over the years, none have successfully challenged the dominance of the NBA, NFL, NHL, or MLB. Several factors may explain this circumstance, including sports fans' preference for one champion at the highest level of competition in each professional sport. In addition, upstart leagues often quickly fold because of financial mismanagement, inability to generate revenue, or inability to find suitable facilities in which to hold their events.

One of the most interesting cases in this area was brought by a competitor to the NFL. From 1983 to 1985, the United States Football League (USFL) played its games in the spring and summer and thus did not compete directly with the NFL. The USFL debuted with a dozen teams and national television contracts with ABC and ESPN. Eventually, the USFL decided to move its season to the fall in direct competition with NFL games, but it was unable to secure any national television deals to carry the games. In 1984, right before it decided to fold, the USFL sued the NFL, seeking $1.7 billion in damages and claiming that the NFL monopolized professional football and used predatory tactics to limit the ability of the USFL to grow (*USFL v. NFL*, 1988). At the time, the NFL had television deals with all the major television networks, including CBS, ABC, and NBC. In addition, it rotated the Super Bowl among those networks. The USFL claimed that this arrangement gave the NFL leverage to ensure that none of those networks would carry USFL games.

Although the jury agreed that the NFL willfully maintained monopoly power in the market for professional football in the United States, its award of $1 to the USFL, even when tripled under the Clayton Act, was no consolation. One of the major reasons that the award was miniscule was that the jury believed that many of the problems the new league faced were the result of its own management decisions, such as deciding to discontinue its spring schedule even though national television contracts were available for those games. As a result, after three seasons and losses of approximately

$200 million, the USFL folded in 1985. In 1990 the USFL was awarded $5.5 million in attorney fees and more than $62,000 in court costs, but by that time the league had long since ceased operations.

Single-Entity Structure

Since the 1970s some professional sports leagues have attempted to avoid the problems discussed here by claiming that they are single entities. A single entity cannot violate section 1 of the Sherman Act because there is no combination or agreement between two parties, the first element needed for a violation of section 1.

The NFL has used the **single-entity defense** more than any other league. If a league attempts to defend itself against an antitrust claim by using this defense, it must demonstrate that instead of being an organization made up of separate business entities (the teams), it is one business entity itself and the teams merely buy into that entity in some way or another. For instance, in the late 1980s the owner of the New England Patriots attempted to sell a portion of the franchise to the public to raise money to pay off debts. He asked the NFL to waive its policy against public ownership so that he could proceed with the sale. The matter was never called for a vote among the owners of all the other teams, because he thought that a vote would have been futile. In 1988 he sold the team for $83.7 million. In 1991 he sued the NFL, claiming that the policy against public ownership forced him to sell the team at a fire sale price to pay off his debts (*Sullivan v. NFL*, 1994). A jury found that the NFL violated section 1 of the Sherman Act and awarded Sullivan $38 million. This amount was reduced to $17 million. Then, because the Clayton Act allows for damages in antitrust cases to be tripled, it was increased to $51 million. The

NFL appealed the decision, arguing that its member teams could not conspire with each other in violation of section 1 because they function as a single entity in relation to the public ownership policy. Although the appellate court reversed the verdict because of problems with the admission of evidence before the district court, it found that the single-entity defense did not apply. Specifically, NFL teams compete in many ways on and off the field for fan support, players, coaches, local broadcast revenues, and ticket sales, and therefore the teams were not acting as a single entity.

The circumstances leading to a more recent case began in 1963 when NFL teams formed National Football League Properties (NFLP) to develop and market their intellectual property. NFLP granted nonexclusive licenses to various venders, which allowed them to make and sell apparel with particular team or NFL logos. American Needle had one of these licenses, but in 2000 it lost its license when the NFLP gave Reebok International Ltd. a 1-year exclusive license for trademarked headwear with NFL team logos. American Needle sued, arguing that this agreement violated the Sherman Act. The NFL replied that it was not capable of conspiring under the act because it is a "single economic enterprise" and thus cannot be subject to antitrust scrutiny (*American Needle v. NFL*, 2010, p. 2207). Reversing the United States Court of Appeals for the Seventh Circuit and the district court, the Supreme Court found that NFL teams compete on and off the field for fans, ticket sales, staff, and players, and therefore that each team is an independently owned and managed separate business. As a result, when the teams license their individual trademarks to NFLP, this concerted action could be subject to antitrust scrutiny (p. 2213). The court remanded the case back to the Sev-

enth Circuit, which subsequently remanded it to the trial court. In February 2015 American Needle agreed to settle its claims against the NFL (Vehling, 2015). Although the settlement ended the parties' dispute, the Supreme Court's decision that the NFL's conduct could be subject to antitrust scrutiny remains unchanged.

In the 1990s several new professional team sports leagues also attempted to structure themselves as single entities, including the American Basketball League (ABL), the Women's National Basketball Association (WNBA), and Major League Soccer (MLS).

Soon after MLS was formed, MLS players contested the league's structure as a single entity. In MLS, the league office owned all player contracts, controlled all player salaries under a salary cap, and mandated transfer fees for player transactions among teams. To ensure that they could contest this conduct, the players did not create a players union because a union would have had to negotiate with management over terms and conditions of employment for all players. As a result, the league could not argue that its conduct was protected under the labor exemption previously discussed. The players then sued, claiming that the restrictive player restraints embodied in the salary cap and transfer system violated the antitrust laws (*Fraser v. Major League Soccer*, 2000).

MLS openly admitted that it had created this structure in an attempt to keep salaries and other costs down so that the league could develop a strong base of financial viability in its early years of operation. The league office specifically referred to the single-entity structure as a way to avoid antitrust scrutiny, create evenly matched teams, and capitalize on the ability to place local favorites in areas where they could help the team build a fan base. MLS also pointed to other factors showing that the league was a single entity; for example, all players were employees of the league and not a specific team, MLS could place marquee players on certain teams and had to approve all other player transactions, individual teams did not own their own logos, and profits and losses were shared in a way similar to that of a single corporation. The court agreed with MLS, finding that it was a single corporate entity, and therefore it could not violate section 1 of the Sherman Act.

This decision is important because it implies that new sports leagues that are set up in a way that is substantially similar to MLS will also be single entities protected from antitrust scrutiny. This structure allows new leagues to keep better control over their costs, especially over player salaries. Several new leagues, including the National Lacrosse League, the Women's Professional Soccer League, and the now defunct Continental Indoor Soccer League, have been formed following this model. As a result, although they may still be subject to review as illegal monopolies under section 2 of the Sherman Act, their single-entity status may protect them from review under other antitrust laws.

Of course, all this depends on whether the league stays true to its single-entity structure. Even in MLS things can change. In 2003 the players unionized, forming the Major League Soccer Players Union, and by 2004 they had signed a collective bargaining agreement with MLS that lasted until 2010. The league then entered a series of 5-year agreements, lasting from 2010 until 2014 and most recently from 2015 until 2019. As a result, although the league may be able to use the labor exemption to protect itself from antitrust scrutiny, it should no longer be able to use the single-entity defense to impose whatever terms and conditions of employment on the players that management prefers.

Application to Individual Performer Sports

The application of antitrust laws extends beyond the five major professional sports leagues discussed in the previous section. Professional boxing, tennis, golf, bowling, and automobile racing have all been found to be businesses engaged in interstate commerce. As explained earlier in this chapter, section 1 of the Sherman Act provides that such businesses engaged in interstate commerce can be sued for alleged violations of the antitrust laws.

Governing bodies of individual performer sports, such as the Professional Golf Association (PGA) Tour and the Professional Bowlers Association (PBA), bring together the best athletes at their particular sport and organize events for those athletes. If an athlete is excluded from membership in those organizations, he has no realistic alternative to make a living playing his sport. The focus of litigation in this area is on whether the necessary restraints on membership are legitimate business activities or suppress competition and violate the antitrust laws.

For example, a professional golfer who was denied entrance to PGA Tour events because of repeated poor performance sued the PGA, claiming that the tour's eligibility rule unreasonably restrained trade in violation of the Sherman Act. Finding that the purpose of the eligibility performance standards was to maintain a high quality of competition and that the rules were reasonably designed to accomplish this purpose, the court found that they were reasonable and did not violate the antitrust

Antitrust Law **241**

laws (*Deesen v. Professional Golfers' Assoc.*, 1966). In general, eligibility restrictions for individual sports leagues or associations have not been found to violate the antitrust laws because they promote the quality of the competition with the particular leagues, ensure uniformity of the rules, and assist in the orderly scheduling of tournaments and other events.

Application to College Sports

College athletics have seen their share of antitrust litigation. These cases predominantly involve the National Collegiate Athletic Association (NCAA). The NCAA is a membership organization made up of universities that agree to abide by its rules. But individual universities, players, coaches, and others often disagree with the application or effect of a particular rule and sue the NCAA, claiming that the rule itself violates the Sherman Act. One of goals of the NCAA is to preserve the amateur nature of intercollegiate athletics as a part of the educational process in college and to ensure that its member schools compete on a level playing field. To meet this goal, the NCAA has created extensive rules restricting the nature of participation in intercollegiate athletics. These rules include limits on recruiting, academic eligibility requirements, financial aid standards, agent regulations, amateurism rules, and a myriad of other topics. At the same time, revenues in university athletics have skyrocketed. As these revenues have increased, the NCAA often faces criticism that its commitment to amateurism is a sham and that its rules are therefore illegitimate.

Regardless of these arguments, schools see an incredible financial value in being part of the NCAA and succeeding within intercollegiate

© Zhukovsky/Dreamstime.com

In individual performer sports such as tennis, eligibility restrictions enforced by governing bodies may not violate the antitrust laws if the restrictions promote the quality of the competition, ensure uniformity of the rules, and assist in the orderly scheduling of tournaments and other events.

athletics. Many see no alternative to membership within the NCAA, so when NCAA rules negatively affect them, they sue, claiming that the rules violate the antitrust laws. Until the 1980s the NCAA was able to defend itself from antitrust claims because most courts found that intercollegiate athletics were not commerce as defined by the Sherman Act. In 1984 the Association for Intercollegiate Athletics for Women (AIAW) sued the NCAA, claiming that it unlawfully used its monopoly power in men's university sports to facilitate its entry into women's university sports and force the AIAW out of existence. The court disagreed, finding that schools simply chose to leave the AIAW and join the NCAA because the NCAA provided a superior product (*Association for Intercollegiate Athletics for Women v. National Collegiate Athletic Association*, 1984). It seemed that the NCAA would continue to avoid antitrust scrutiny, but that was not the case.

In the 1980s the NCAA's university football television plan set the price for televised Division I games and limited the number of televised games. The College Football Association (CFA) negotiated an independent television contract that allowed more appearances on television for its member schools. In response, the NCAA announced that it would begin to penalize schools that became members of the CFA. The University of Oklahoma and the University of Georgia sued, claiming that the NCAA's television plan violated the Sherman Act (*National Collegiate Athletic Association v. Board of Regents of the University of Oklahoma*, 1984). The Supreme Court agreed, holding that the NCAA's television plan violated the antitrust laws by unreasonably restraining trade and harming consumers by televising fewer football games. The case was the first successful antitrust challenge to the NCAA

and its rules. Litigation over NCAA rules only increased in the following years.

Another crucial decision involved NCAA Bylaw 11.02.3, which restricted the earnings of Division I assistant coaches to $16,000. The coaches sued, claiming that the rule was illegal price fixing in violation of the Sherman Act (*Law v. NCAA*, 1998). (See more about this case in the accompanying e-book, *Case Studies in Sport Law, Second Edition* [Pittman, Spengler, & Young, 2016].) The NCAA argued that the rule was necessary to help schools keep entry-level coaches, reduce costs to athletic departments, and maintain competitive equity among programs so that larger schools could not attract the most talented coaches by paying higher salaries. The U.S. Court of Appeals for the Tenth Circuit disagreed, finding that the rule artificially lowered coaches' salaries and therefore was illegal per se under the Sherman Act. A jury then returned a verdict in favor of the coaches for $22.3 million ($66.9 million if tripled under the Clayton Act). Instead of appealing the decision, the NCAA settled with the coaches by paying $54.5 million.

The NCAA may be subject to scrutiny under the antitrust laws when it acts in a commercial capacity, as it did in *Board of Regents* by restricting the output of television games and in *Law* by restricting coaching salaries. Rules that are less commercial in nature, however, typically have not been found to violate the antitrust laws. In these types of cases, the NCAA often argues that the particular rules, often dealing with academic eligibility, promote amateur intercollegiate athletic competition. Courts accept the preservation of amateurism as a justification for rules limiting competition among NCAA members for the services of athletes, which reduces the costs of producing university athletics.

Braxton Banks, a fullback at Notre Dame, had a year of university eligibility left when he declared his eligibility for the 1990 NFL draft. After he was not selected in the draft, he attempted to return to Notre Dame to pursue a graduate degree and still play football. The NCAA's no-draft and no-agent rules barred him from returning to play football at the university level because he had declared himself eligible and signed with an agent. Banks sued, claiming that the NCAA rules violated the antitrust laws (*Banks v. National Collegiate Athletic Association*, 1992). (See more about this case in the accompanying e-book, *Case Studies in Sport Law, Second Edition* [Pittman, Spengler, & Young, 2016].) Agreeing that the rules were necessary to maintain competition among amateur students pursuing their education, the court held that the rules did not violate the Sherman Act.

Most courts would agree that athletic participation is a valuable part of the educational process. Therefore, NCAA rules that promote amateurism for university student-athletes are typically upheld because they promote university sports as part of the educational process for the student. Still, since 2009 the NCAA has faced numerous lawsuits claiming that its eligibility rules violate federal antitrust laws. Although this litigation continues as new claims are brought seemingly every month, two important decisions could shape the future of collegiate athletics.

Initially, in a case brought by former football players claiming that NCAA rules capping the number of scholarships that a school could provide violated the Sherman Act, the United States Court of Appeals for the Seventh Circuit determined for the first time that the provision of scholarship funds for college athletes was a sufficient commercial transaction subject to antitrust review (*Agnew v. NCAA*, 2012). But the court dismissed the players' claims because they did not properly allege a cognizable market for review. Instead, in a similar case in Indiana, a district court adopted the Seventh Circuit's reasoning and denied the NCAA's motion to dismiss (*Rock v. NCAA*, 2013). Although still going through the court system, this and similar claims have opened up many NCAA rules to antitrust scrutiny.

Athletes have also challenged NCAA rules limiting the amount of aid that they can receive as part of their athletic scholarships. Although dozens of lawsuits with various claims against these rules have been filed, the most famous case involves former UCLA basketball start Ed O'Bannon. In August 2014 a California district court found that NCAA rules restricting athletes from receiving more compensation violated the Sherman Act (*O'Bannon v. NCAA*, 2014). Although it opened the door for some sort of limited additional compensation for student-athletes, the decision has been widely panned by antitrust and other scholars and is currently on appeal. Perhaps more important, at the same time that this litigation has been going through the court system, many collegiate conferences, starting with the newly minted Power 5 (Atlantic Coast Conference, Big Ten, Big 12, PAC 12, and SEC) voted in 2015 to provide full cost of attendance scholarships for their athletes. As other conferences follow suit, the issues that brought forth the bulk of the litigation against the NCAA may become moot.

LEARNING AIDS

Summary

The antitrust laws are intended to promote competition and efficiency in the market and to protect consumers from the monopoly power exhibited by some businesses. In sport these laws have been used by players and players associations to eliminate league rules related to free agency, player drafts, and salary caps that players believe limit their ability to receive high salaries and play for the team they choose. But leagues and teams have been able to defend these restraints on players because much of what the leagues and teams do is shielded from the antitrust laws by various exemptions. In the end, in professional sports, teams and players negotiate over the terms of employment and come to a collective bargaining agreement that includes free agency rules and player salary caps.

Although much of the discussion about antitrust law has focused on professional team sports, individual performer and college sports can also be subject to review under these laws. Whenever one party undertakes some sort of activity to restrict competition and efficiency in the marketplace, it may be subject to review under the antitrust laws.

Sport administrators need to understand the antitrust laws to keep their leagues, associations, teams, events, or other organizations within the law and to protect their organizations if another individual or group tries to change an agreement because of its potential negative effects on competition.

Discussion Questions

1. What is the purpose and function of sport antitrust laws?
2. Provide an example of antitrust applied in the sport context.
3. What is the value of free agency to a player?
4. Why do some professional sports leagues impose salary caps on their players?
5. Why is Major League Baseball the only professional sports league that has an exemption from the antitrust laws?
6. What is the difference between an antitrust exemption and a labor exemption and how does that affect the way a professional sports league operates?
7. Under what circumstances is the NCAA most likely not subject to the antitrust laws? Provide a hypothetical example.

Legal Challenge to an Established Professional Sports League

A group of Texas businessmen decided to start a new sports league to compete with the NBA. The league, called the Professional University Players Basketball Association (PUPBA), enlisted players from 4-year universities who either currently played in the National Basketball Development League (NBDL) or on professional teams in the United States or Europe or were talented, undrafted players who wanted to play in a new league at the next level. Teams would be formed that consisted only of players who had formerly played for a specific university. The idea was a hit and drew wide-based fan support from those with ties to the universities represented by the various teams. Sixteen teams were formed, and play began in 2016. The concept was so appealing that some players left their NBA and European teams to play for the new league. The league began play in the summer so as not to compete with the NBA and university basketball. The league debuted with national television contracts with CBS and ESPN. Eventually, the league decided to extend its season to include both the spring and early summer in direct competition with both NBA regular-season games and the NBA finals. Given the NBA's strength and position in the market, however, PUPBA lost its existing television contracts and was unable to secure any new national television deals to carry the spring games. At the time, the NBA had television deals with all the major television networks, including ESPN, TNT, CBS, ABC, and NBC. In addition, it rotated the NBA playoffs among those networks. PUPBA claimed that this arrangement gave the NBA leverage to ensure that none of the networks would carry PUPBA games. The new league experienced extreme financial hardships, and right before it decided to fold, PUPBA sued the NBA, seeking $2 billion in damages and claiming that the NBA monopolized professional basketball and used predatory tactics to limit the ability of the PUBPA to grow.

Labor Law

Alicia Jessop, Esq.

Chapter Objectives

After reading this chapter, you will know the following:

- How labor law developed in the United States

- What rights employees have in the United States under labor law

- What tools employers and employees can use to obtain their goals and gain concessions in collective bargaining negotiations

- What actions labor law prevents employers and labor organizations from engaging in

- What strategies professional athletes can adopt in the future related to labor law and antitrust law to further their interests

Since the dawn of the Industrial Revolution, managers and workers have worked to strike a balance in their workplace relationship that allows both parties to achieve their goals. The sport industry comprises a variety of types of employers and employees. From team owners who employ professional athletes to the referees who officiate games, examples of employer–employee relationships are abundant in the sport industry. Just like managers and workers during the Industrial Revolution, employees and employers in the sport industry today constantly seek ways to achieve their goals in the workplace relationship. Labor law is the type of law that governs those relationships. It does so by specifying what both employees and employers are allowed to do in these relationships and tells what kinds of actions both sides are prevented from engaging in under the law.

This chapter provides a history and framework of federal labor law in the United States. It also details the specific rights that employees in the United States have under labor law and examines the way in which those rights have been used and continue to be used in the sport landscape. Furthermore, this chapter looks at the types of actions that federal labor law prevents employers and labor organizations from engaging in. The chapter also discusses legal strategies, called *economic weapons*, which employers and employees can use in workplace-related negotiations.

Development of Labor Law in the United States

In the wake of the Industrial Revolution, American laborers in the early 1800s sought to join labor organizations, commonly referred to as *labor unions* or, more simply, *unions*. A **union** is an organized group of employees that uses their collective strength to protect the rights and interests of the group's members. Workers during this period often faced unfair labor conditions and sought to unionize to obtain greater rights and better working conditions from their employers. For years, workers ranging from shoemakers to railroad workers unsuccessfully sought to unionize as courts repeatedly struck down their union organization efforts (*Commonwealth v. Pullis*, 1806).

In 1935 American workers finally obtained the rights they were seeking when the United States Congress passed the National Labor Relations Act (NLRA). This piece of federal legislation, which still serves as the main body of labor law in the United States, provides several important rights to American workers. Additionally, the NLRA specifies what types of actions workers and employers are prohibited from engaging in. The passage of the NLRA meant that for the first time in American history, a federal law was in place to govern the relationship, rights, and responsibilities between workers and employees.

An independent federal agency, the National Labor Relations Board (NLRB), is responsible for overseeing and enforcing the NLRA. The NLRB was created by the executive branch of the federal government. Its head office is located in Washington, D.C., and it has 32 regional offices spread across the United States. The NLRB's responsibilities include conducting unionization elections, investigating charges of unfair labor practices, facilitating settlements of unfair labor practice cases, deciding cases, and enforcing orders. Thus, issues and disputes arising under the NLRA do not go immediately to the court system, but rather to the NLRB.

One notable aspect of the NLRA to consider as you work through this chapter is that it applies only to private employers and their workers. Public employers, such as government entities and public universities, do not fall under the scope of the NLRA. Thus, employees working in the public sector who seek labor law rights must look toward applicable state law.

As noted earlier, American employees in the private sector received several workplace rights through the passage of the NLRA. These rights are located in section 7 of the NLRA. The following lists the rights that 29 U.S.C. §157 (NLRA, section 7) provides to American employees:

- The right to form, join, or assist labor organizations
- The right to bargain collectively with an employer
- The right to engage in concerted activities

Notably, section 7 also grants American employees the right to refrain from using the rights it provides, unless membership in a labor union is a condition of their employment. Regardless, since the enactment of the NLRA, professional athletes throughout the United States have relied on the rights granted under section 7 to protect and promote their workplace interests.

The first right that employees in the United States are given under the NLRA is the right to form, join, or assist labor organizations. For decades, players in the four major leagues in the United States—MLB, NBA, NFL, and NHL—have used this right provided under section 7 to obtain union representation. As noted, a union is an organized group of employees that uses their collective strength to protect the rights and interests of the group's members. One way that a union accomplishes this is by representing members in collective bargaining negotiations with their employer on workplace issues that affect them, such as wages, hours, and conditions of employment.

Unionization of American Professional Sports Teams

Throughout the last two centuries, professional athletes have taken advantage of the right provided under section 7 of the NLRA to unionize. To unionize under the NLRA, the first step for a group of employees is to file a petition with the nearest NLRB office. This petition must show that at least 30% of employees support the decision to unionize. After the petition is filed, the NLRB engages in an investigation to ensure that it has jurisdiction, that the union is qualified, and that nothing would bar an election. After the filing of the petition, the employer is required to post Notices of Petition for Election in places easily visible to the employees. In the meantime, the NLRB negotiates a unionization election agreement between the employer and employees. Thereafter, unless legal challenges to the process or petition surface, an election is held. A union is certified if a majority of votes cast support it. American professional athletes have followed this process when seeking union representation.

NBA players were the first professional athletes in America to unionize. In 1954, frustrated with the players' lack of bargaining power to negotiate higher salaries, Boston Celtics point guard Bob Cousy decided that something had to be done to motivate the NBA to pay its players more. At the time, Cousy was the best player in the NBA. Due to his prominence, he was able to motivate the NBA and its team owners to meet the players' labor demands. Throughout the 1954 season Cousy wrote to leaders of other teams, encouraging them to work together to make demands collectively on the NBA's owners for higher salaries. Cousy's actions ultimately led to the 1954 founding of the union that represents NBA players today, the National Basketball Players Association (NBPA).

Subsequent to NBA players' formal unionization, players in the other three American major professional sports leagues (MLB, NFL, and NHL) began unionization efforts. The next to do so were NFL players. In 1956 the National Football Players Association (NFLPA) was organized after Creighton Miller, who was the Cleveland Browns general manager and also an attorney, was asked by players to help them unionize.

In 1966 MLB players became the next group of professional athletes in the United States to unionize formally. The Major League Baseball Players Association (MLBPA) was organized as an attempt by players to end baseball's reserve clause. Under MLB's reserve clause system, a player was bound to one team for the entirety of his career, unless the team traded or released him. Given this circumstance, MLB players' bargaining rights and earning possibilities were severely limited. Through

unionization and other legal mechanisms, MLB players have seen a drastic weakening of the reserve clause.

The final major professional sports league in the United States to unionize formally was the NHL. In 1967 the National Hockey League Players Association (NHLPA) was organized. Ten years before the organization of the NHLPA, a handful of players attempted to form a union after access to pension fund financials was withheld from players by NHL team owners. NHL team owners responded to that unionization effort by trading or moving the players involved down to the minor leagues. When the NHLPA was ultimately organized, it assisted players in negotiating better terms of employment with the NHL and the players' respective teams. A key point to understand about unions is that after a group of employees forms one, it becomes the group's exclusive representative for purposes of collective bargaining. Therefore, if a group of employees is unionized, an employer may not collectively bargain with employees individually or outside of the union's presence. This requirement is critical in ensuring that the union chosen by a group of employees to represent them maintains the greatest amount of bargaining power possible with an employer.

Another critical point to understand about the NLRA's section 7 right to unionize is that only employees in the United States can unionize. For purposes of the NLRA, not every worker is considered an employee. For instance, independent contractors, day laborers, and seasonal workers are not viewed as employees under the NLRA. Thus, they cannot unionize.

One test that courts apply to determine whether a worker is an employee is the right-to-control test (see the University Football Players' Right to Unionize sidebar). The right-to-control test considers the degree of control that an employer has over a worker under 11 factors (*Restatement (Second) of Agency*, § 220, 1958; *FedEx Home Delivery and International Brotherhood of Teamsters*, 2014):

- The extent of control that, by agreement, the employer may exercise over details of the work

- Whether the worker is engaged in a distinct occupation or business

- Whether the work is typically done under the direction of an employer or without supervision

- The skill required in the particular occupation

IN THE COURTROOM

University Football Players' Right to Unionize

Northwestern University and College Athletes Players Association (CAPA) (2014)

In January 2014 a group of Northwestern football players filed a petition with the NLRB to unionize. Through unionization, the group wanted to achieve better medical care, obtain guaranteed scholarships, and create less strict transfer rules. Northwestern University objected, arguing that the players were not employees and thus could not unionize under the NLRA. To determine whether Northwestern football players were employees, the NLRB applied the common law right-to-control test and its factors to the players.

In applying the common law right-to-control test, the NLRB regional office found that Northwestern football players on scholarship were employees. The regional office considered the scholarship compensation that players received to play football; the significant control that the athletics department exerted over players in terms of training camp schedules, school-year schedules and responsibilities, and rules of conduct; and the shifting of players' academic and career plans because of their playing football. Using itineraries and regulations provided by Northwestern to the players, the regional office found that the players engaged in 40 to 60 hours of football-related activities weekly. The regional office weighed the level of control exercised by Northwestern over the football players under these factors and against the backdrop of the revenue generated by the football program. Ultimately, this led the regional office to hold that Northwestern University's scholarship football players were employees who could vote to unionize. Notably, because non-scholarship players (i.e., walk-ons) do not receive compensation for playing, they were held not to be employees and thus unable to vote to unionize.

Northwestern University appealed the regional board's decision to the NLRB office in Washington D.C. In August 2015, the NLRB declined to assert jurisdiction in the case. In doing so, the NLRB did not rule on whether Northwestern football players on scholarship are employees under the NLRA. Rather, the NLRB argued that labor stability would not be promoted by its ruling on the issue, as the NLRA cannot be imposed upon state-run universities and their football teams. Nonetheless, the NLRB's decision to not assert jurisdiction meant that Northwestern football players on scholarship were unable to unionize for the time being.

It's important to note that the NLRB's decision to decline asserting jurisdiction in the Northwestern football players' case does not preclude other college athletes from attempting to unionize. However, those seeking to do so must work to overcome the issue of not damaging labor stability, which the NLRB raised in the Northwestern case.

- Whether the employer or worker supplies tools and the location where the work takes place
- The length of time that the worker is employed
- Whether the worker is paid for time or by job
- Whether the work is part of the regular business of the employer
- Whether the parties believe they are creating a master–servant relationship
- Whether the employer is in the type of business for which the work is being completed
- Whether the worker has significant entrepreneurial opportunity for gain or loss

None of these factors alone is determinative in finding a worker to be an employee. Rather, each of the factors must be assessed and weighed. Other relevant factors, depending on the circumstances, may also be considered. Finally, the factual circumstances of each case determine the weight to give each factor (*Roadway Package Systems, Inc.*, 1998). Thus, whether workers are considered employees who can unionize under section 7 of the NLRA is made on a case-by-case basis.

Right to Bargain Collectively

Another important right given to employees under the NLRA is the right to bargain col-

Team members must meet several criteria before being allowed to unionize. Kain Colter, former Northwestern University football quarterback, and Ramogi Huma, the founder and president of the National College Players Association, met with lawmakers while trying to earn college athletes the right to unionize.

© AP Photo/Lauren Victoria Burke

lectively with their employers. **Collective bargaining** is a negotiation process through which employers and employee union representatives have mutual obligations to meet at reasonable times and confer in good faith with respect to the three mandatory terms of collective bargaining: wages, hours, and conditions of employment.

The outcomes of collective bargaining negotiations are recorded in a **collective bargaining agreement (CBA)**. This contract documents the outcomes of collective bargaining negotiations and in turn outlines the rights and responsibilities related to the employment relationship that flows between employees and employers. The terms of a collective bargaining agreement are binding on all parties to the agreement.

Because collective bargaining agreements are contracts, they exist for fixed periods. After that period expires, the employer and union representatives must negotiate a new collective bargaining agreement. When the collective bargaining agreement expires, employers and employees have several options for how to proceed. The first option is for the sides to maintain the status quo and continue operating under the terms of the old collective bargaining agreement until a new collective bargaining agreement is negotiated. Generally, this option is used when there is labor peace between the two sides—when there are not any contentious disagreements about how wages, hours, or conditions of employment should be set.

In professional sports, contention in collective bargaining is common. Team owners and players often have different opinions about how much players should be paid, how many games should be played in a season, and what conditions a player must uphold to remain employed by the league. Thus, the NLRA sets forth tools called **economic weapons** that either side can use in collective bargaining to gain concessions from the other side in negotiations.

Lockouts

The economic weapon given to employers is the **lockout**. During a lockout, employers stop work and deny employment to employees. As such, employees are literally held out of employment. They may not access the employer's buildings, engage in work, or even collect a paycheck.

An employer is prohibited from locking out its employees when a collective bargaining agreement is in place. Thus, employers may lock out employees only after a collective bargaining agreement expires. Employers often do so to obtain concessions from employees in collective bargaining negotiations. The logic behind an employer's imposition of a lockout is that if employees are unable to receive a paycheck for a long enough period of time, they will become more inclined to make concessions at the collective bargaining table to end the lockout and return to work.

In response to being locked out, employees have the option to file an antitrust lawsuit under the Sherman Antitrust Act. When filing the antitrust lawsuit, employees assert that the action of their employer in locking them out is anticompetitive. The benefit to employees of filing an antitrust lawsuit is that if a court rules in their favor, the employer will be forced to lift the lockout. If the lockout is lifted, the employees will be able to return to work and collect a paycheck while a new collective bargaining agreement is negotiated. Another benefit to employees is that if they win, the Sherman Antitrust Act requires courts to award them **treble damages**. Under treble damages, the injured party (here, the employees) is awarded three times the amount of damages they incurred. Winning an antitrust lawsuit against an employer can be a lucrative opportunity for employees.

An important caveat about the ability of employees to sue their employer for violating the Sherman Antitrust Act by locking them out is that the employees cannot be unionized. Antitrust law exists separate from labor law and its remedies. Therefore, if unionized employees want to bring an antitrust lawsuit against their employer, the first thing they must do is decertify their union through the process of **decertification**.

Decertification is the vote of union members either to discontinue a union's representation of them or to be represented by another union. To decertify a union, at least 30% of union members must sign a card or petition requesting that the NLRB conduct an election. The union will be decertified if less than a majority of votes cast support union representation. After the union is decertified, employees, through the help of legal counsel, can file an antitrust lawsuit in an effort to end an employer's lockout.

At the successful conclusion of the employees' antitrust lawsuit, a court would order the lockout to be lifted. However, the parties would still need to negotiate a new collective bargaining agreement. Thus, the employees may wish to be represented again by a union to assist them with this process. Therefore, they would hold another election for union representation. Should employees vote in favor of being represented again by a union, the union would be reorganized. The union would then again begin collective bargaining with the employer to reach terms of a new collective bargaining agreement.

When an employer locks out employees, the employees are not required to file an antitrust lawsuit. Rather, doing so is an option they can engage in to reduce the length of the lockout and subsequently earn paychecks while the new collective bargaining agreement is negotiated. If employees do not file an antitrust lawsuit, their union representatives will continue collective bargaining with the employer during the lock-

out. However, they will not be paid when collective bargaining is ongoing during a lockout. Without a successful antitrust lawsuit, employees will only be able to work after a new collective bargaining agreement is negotiated, which will subsequently result in the employer lifting the lockout.

Strikes

The economic weapon that employees are given is the right to **strike**. A strike occurs when employees collectively refuse to work in an effort to obtain concessions from their employer on terms being negotiated through collective bargaining. Collective bargaining agreements exist for fixed terms and generally contain no-strike clauses that prevent unions from striking during the term of the agreement. Therefore, employees may only strike legally after a collective bargaining agreement has expired.

The logic behind a strike is that if the workforce collectively refuses to work, the employer will not be able to produce its goods or services. If the employer is unable to produce its goods and services, it will be unable to generate income. If the employer is unable to generate income for a long enough period of time, it may be forced to make collective bargaining concessions. Thus, a strike is seen as a way for employees to obtain an upper hand in collective bargaining.

Collective Bargaining in American Professional Sports

The four major sports leagues in the United States—MLB, NBA, NFL, and NHL—have entered into collective bargaining agreements with their respective league's athletes and representing unions. Each league's collective bargaining agreement covers the three mandatory terms of collective bargaining (wages, hours, and conditions of employment) and addresses other issues related to the respective league. For instance, the NBA and NBPA's collective bargaining agreement specifies the length hotel beds must be when players travel to away games. The NFL and NFLPA's collective bargaining agreement allows the payment of moving expenses for veterans or rookies who are traded.

Although each league's collective bargaining agreement contains clauses outside the three mandatory terms of collective bargaining, clauses related to those terms make up the bulk of the agreements. Each league's collective bargaining agreement contains several clauses related to the mandatory collective bargaining term of wages. For instance, each league specifies a minimum compensation amount that a player must receive under his playing contract. Often, as is the case with the NFL, the minimum salary that a player receives is based on the number of years the player has played in the league, and it increases over time. Three of the four major professional sports leagues in America—the NBA, NFL, and NHL—also specify an upper limit on the salary amount that players can be paid by teams. This upper limit is called a **salary cap**. Notably, MLB does not have a salary cap.

Generally, a league's salary cap is calculated by determining the amount of revenue a league generates and then multiplying that number by the percentage of revenue it agrees to share with its players. The greater the percentage is, the more money teams can spend on their rosters and, in turn, the more money players can earn through their playing contracts. Each league's collective bargaining agreement specifies what types of revenue—for instance, ticket sales, broadcasting, and sponsorship—are shared with players. Similarly, each league's collective bargaining agreement withholds certain types of revenue from being shared with players. The types of revenue that fall

within the calculation of a salary cap and the percentage of revenue to be shared with players are often the most contentious points of collective bargaining negotiations. This is because owners want to maintain the greatest percentage of revenue for themselves, and players want to earn the highest salaries possible.

The next mandatory term of collective bargaining is hours. Although many American employees collectively bargain for 40-hour workweeks, the focus for athletes when it comes to collective bargaining hours is different. Professional athletes and their unions focus on the number of games that will be played in a season and when and how often—in the season and off-season—players must report to team activities. Generally, leagues and team owners work to negotiate longer seasons, because playing more games means that teams have a greater number of opportunities to generate revenue. Furthermore, leagues want greater off-season workout requirements than players do, and they want players to report to training camp earlier. In contrast, given the toll paid by the body when playing a professional sport and the need for recovery time, union representatives work to negotiate shorter seasons and fewer training hours for the players they represent.

The third mandatory term of collective bargaining, conditions of employment, focuses on what each side must do to obtain and maintain the employment relationship. For instance, terms related to workplace safety may be negotiated as conditions of employment that employers must uphold. Furthermore, standards for employees to become or remain eligible for employment may be negotiated as conditions of employment.

One of the common conditions of employment that employees are subject to in the 21st century workplace is drug testing. To either obtain or maintain a job, employees

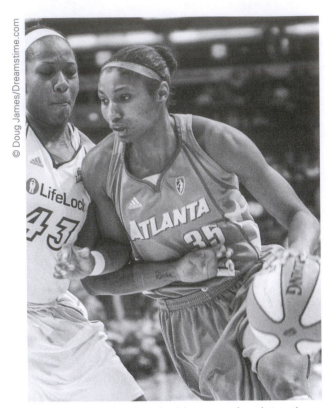

Unions for professional athletes work to keep the amount of time players are required to work out, practice, and play their sports reasonable.

are frequently required to submit to and successfully pass a drug test. Professional athletes are no different. All four major professional sports leagues have drug policies in place, although the substances banned and penalties for testing positive under said policies vary widely. Because drug-testing policies amount to conditions of employment, the terms of every policy must be negotiated between leagues and players associations through collective bargaining.

One substance that has posed problems in recent collective bargaining negotiations between leagues and players associations is human growth hormone (HGH). In 2011 the NFL and NFLPA negotiated a new collective bargaining agreement. One issue that the parties could not reach an agreement on, and therefore saved to negotiate later, was

an HGH testing policy. The sides needed over 3 years to agree on an HGH testing policy. One of the main sticking points in negotiating an HGH testing policy was determining how to structure an appeals system for players who tested positive under the policy. Players did not want to cede too much oversight power to the NFL commissioner in HGH testing, so they opposed a system in which he would oversee the appeals process.

The NFL and NFLPA weren't the only parties that faced difficulty in negotiating terms of an HGH testing policy. Like the NFL, the NBA and NBPA entered into a new collective bargaining agreement in 2011. Just like the NFL and NFLPA, the NBA and NBPA took over 3 years to negotiate an HGH testing policy for NBA players. One issue that the NBA and NBPA faced in reaching their agreement on HGH testing was determining adequate safeguards for testing. Furthermore, some in the NBA questioned the validity and strength of research demonstrating the negative effects of HGH.

The NHL reached a new collective bargaining agreement with the NHLPA in 2013, but an HGH testing policy was not present in the collective bargaining agreement. Although the NHL and NHLPA have reportedly met on the issue numerous times, both sides said that implementation of an HGH testing policy would not occur until the 2014–15 NHL season, at the earliest. The holdup in adopting a plan includes finding time to educate players on the issue and fully developing and implementing a testing plan. As of September 2015, the NHL and NHLPA had not agreed on an HGH testing policy.

The first major professional sports league in America to adopt an HGH testing policy was MLB. In 2013 MLB and the MLBPA reached an agreement allowing for random, in-season blood testing for HGH. First-time violators of MLB's drug-testing policy, which includes HGH, are subject to an 80-game unpaid suspension. Second-time violators receive a 162-game unpaid suspension. A player who tests positive for a substance banned under the agreement for a third time is banned from MLB.

The roadblocks that leagues and unions have faced in negotiating HGH testing policies signal the important considerations that each side must face when collectively bargaining conditions of employment. Employers must focus on maintaining the safety of their workforce, as well as the integrity of their brand. For employees and unions, conditions of employment must be negotiated in a way that protects an employee's job and provides specific safeguards and appeals processes should the employee violate a condition of employment.

Right to Engage in Concerted Activities

The final right that section 7 of the NLRA gives employees is the right to engage in concerted activities. A **concerted activity** is an activity two or more employees engage in to aid or protect the terms and conditions of their employment. Because section 7 specifies that employees may engage in concerted activity "for the purpose of collective bargaining or other mutual aid or protection," concerted activities may be carried out by unions or nonunionized employees. Examples of concerted activities include the following: two or more employees approaching their employer to discuss increasing their wages, two or more employees approaching management about workplace safety concerns, and two or more employees addressing their employer about receiving additional benefits. Although concerted activity generally requires the involvement of two or more employees to be protected under the NLRA, the NLRB

notes that the actions of one employee may be protected as a concerted activity under the NLRA if the employee involved other employees before acting on behalf of other employees.

One type of concerted activity that arises in the professional sports setting is a strike. As discussed earlier, a strike is a collective refusal by employees to work in an effort to obtain concessions from their employer in collective bargaining. Of the four major sports leagues in the United States, NBA players are the only group never to have gone on strike. Throughout their histories, MLB, NFL, and NHL players have all used strikes in efforts to gain concessions in collective bargaining negotiations with their respective leagues.

In particular, players in these leagues have engaged in strikes to obtain higher salary caps, improve pension plans and health benefits, create grievance systems, and develop free agency. Going forward, unionized professional athletes will likely continue to use strikes as an economic weapon to gain concessions in collective bargaining. What remains to be seen, however, are the issues that players will be willing to strike for to obtain concessions at the collective bargaining table.

Prohibited Conduct Under the NLRA: Unfair Labor Practices

While section 7 of the NLRA provides employees in the United States with certain rights, section 8 of the NLRA (29 U.S.C. § 158) prohibits private employers and labor organizations from engaging in certain types of activities called *unfair labor practices*.

If an unfair labor practice is alleged to have occurred, the person or group alleging the violation may file a claim, called an **unfair labor practice charge**, with the NLRB. Thereafter, the NLRB will conduct an investigation to determine whether any action should be taken on the charge. While the charge is being investigated, the NLRB may seek the order of an **injunction** from the district court. An injunction is a court order requiring someone to perform or refrain from performing a certain activity. Thus, in seeking an injunction, the NLRB works to stop behavior prohibited or to initiate action required under the NLRA.

After the NLRB has investigated the unfair labor practice charge, if it decides that formal action should be taken, it will file a complaint against the party alleged to be in violation of the NLRA. That party may then file an answer. Thereafter, a trial will be held. The trial will result in either an order to cease and desist engaging in the unfair labor practice or a dismissal of the complaint. Furthermore, the parties can reach a settlement ahead of the trial and choose how to remedy the unfair labor practice charge on their own. Table 11.1 highlights the most relevant examples of section 8 unfair labor practices for sport managers.

Section 8 of the NLRA makes it illegal for employers to interfere with, restrain, or coerce employees in the exercise of their section 7 rights. Remember that section 7 of the NLRA gives employees of private companies three important rights: the right to form, join, or assist labor organizations; the right to bargain collectively; and the right to engage in concerted activities. Thus, any action of an employer that interferes with these rights amounts to an unfair labor practice under section 8 of the NLRA.

What types of actions would interfere with, restrain, or coerce employees' section 7 rights? One example is threatening employees with unfavorable treatment if they participate in or support a labor organization. For instance, suppose that a team owner opposes the league's players association. In an effort to lessen the power of the players association, the team owner calls in the team's star player and tells him that he will be cut from the team if he actively supports the players association. Because the player has the right to assist labor organizations under section 7 of the NLRA, this action amounts to restraint and coercion of the player's NLRA section 7

Table 11.1   Section 8 Unfair Labor Practices

Unfair labor practice	Applicable to employer	Applicable to labor organization
Interfering with, restraining or coercing employees in the exercise of their section 7 rights	Yes	Yes
Dominating or interfering with the formation or administration of a labor organization	Yes	
Discriminating against employees in hiring, tenure, or conditions of employment to discourage labor organization membership	Yes	
Discharging or discriminating against an employee who files an unfair labor practice charge or testifies before the NLRB	Yes	
Refusing to collectively bargain	Yes	Yes

rights. Subsequently, it would violate section 8 of the NLRA.

Labor organizations are also prohibited from interfering with employees' exercise of their section 7 rights. Imagine a scenario in which at the expiration of their collective bargaining agreement, NFL players choose to strike to gain concessions in collective bargaining. After the strike begins, the NFL doesn't quickly grant concessions. As a result, several weeks of the regular NFL season end up being canceled. The striking players have not received paychecks during the strike, and the reality of canceled games has caused some of them to become worried that they could lose a season's worth of pay. A small group of players decides to stop striking and go back to play, but most players remain on strike. It would be a violation of section 8 of the NLRA for the union to threaten bodily injury or the loss of employment to the players who stop striking.

Section 8 also prohibits employers from dominating or interfering with the formation or administration of a labor organization. An employer dominates in the formation of a labor organization if it engages in the process to the point that the union is viewed as the employer's creation.

What exactly does that level of domination look like? Imagine a scenario in which an athletics director at a private university holds a meeting with her staff to discuss issues related to college athletes and their compensation. During the meeting, one department employee suggests that the college athletes unionize. The athletics director says that doing so may be beneficial for the athletes, because it will allow them to bargain collectively and possibly negotiate salaries. The athletics director, however, secretly has grave concerns over how collective bargaining could sway the current balance of power between the ath-

letics department and college athletes in terms of wages, hours, and conditions of employment.

Over time, the athletics director's staff continues to urge the unionization of the school's college athletes as a potential solution to criticism of not paying college athletes salaries beyond scholarships. The athletics director decides to take action herself and personally calls a labor organization to come on campus and begin the petition process with the NLRB. She does so with the hope that she will be able to guide the actions of the union if it is formed. This action would amount to an unfair labor practice, because the athletics director is dominating the formation of the labor organization.

Employers are also prohibited from discriminating against employees in terms of hiring, tenure, and conditions of employment as a method to discourage union membership. A team cannot refuse to sign, release, or impose additional work-related burdens on a player solely because of his affiliation or support with a union. See the Release of a Player Because of Union Activities sidebar.

Section 8 of the National Labor Relations Act also prohibits employers from discriminating against employees who file charges with or testify before the NLRB. In the preceding case, imagine a scenario in which after McCullum filed the charge against the Seahawks, he was never offered another contract to play in the NFL. If evidence showed that McCullum was being held out of opportunities to play with other teams because of filing a charge with the NLRB, that action would violate section 8 of the NLRA. Similarly, if the Seahawks released McCullum upon his filing of a charge with the NLRB, that action would likewise amount to discrimination in violation of section 8 of the NLRA.

IN THE COURTROOM

Release of a Player Because of Union Activities

Nordstrom, et al., d/b/a Seattle Seahawks and NFLPA (1989)

Sam McCullum was a wide receiver who joined the Seattle Seahawks in 1976. In 1981 he was elected the team's union representative by his fellow teammates. In 1982, while serving as the Seahawks' union representative, McCullum remarked during a press conference that he believed team doctors released injured players back into the game too soon. Those remarks allegedly drew a negative reaction from the Seahawks' general manager and coach. Furthermore, McCullum helped organize a solidarity handshake between Seahawks players and their opponents during the team's first preseason game. The solidarity handshake was supported by the NFLPA. This action also allegedly drew the opposition of the Seahawks' head coach.

After these events, McCullum was released by the Seahawks. He was offered a contract by the Minnesota Vikings, which he rejected because of the amount of money offered under the contract. In response to McCullum's release by the Seahawks, the NFLPA filed an unfair labor practice charge against the Seahawks on McCullum's behalf. The unfair labor practice charge alleged that the Seahawks discriminated against McCullum by releasing him from the team because of his labor organization membership. Ultimately, the charge was upheld by the NRLB, and the Seahawks were found to have committed an unfair labor practice violation.

Sport managers should be aware of one final action that amounts to a violation of section 8 of the NLRA—a refusal to bargain collectively. Both employers and labor organizations can commit violations of section 8 in this regard. The question, however, is what amounts to a refusal to bargain collectively in violation of section 8?

To comply with the terms of section 8 as it relates to collective bargaining, employers and labor organizations must meet at reasonable times to bargain in good faith about the mandatory terms of collective bargaining: wages, hours, and conditions of employment. During these meetings, the sides must provide each other with information that is relevant to the mandatory terms of collective bargaining upon the request of the other side. Requests about information can be made only at the collective bargaining table. Thus, refusing to provide information sought by the media or outlets outside the collective bargaining table is not a violation of section 8.

Sometimes, even when both an employer and a labor organization enter into collective bargaining negotiations in good faith and provide all relevant information, they are unable to reach an agreement. Does the inability of the parties to reach an agreement or negotiate a new collective bargaining agreement amount to an unfair labor practice?

The inability to negotiate a new collective bargaining agreement does not violate the good faith standard set forth under section

8 of the NLRA. Similarly, section 8 of the NLRA doesn't require either side to make concessions at the collective bargaining table. Rather, all that is required is for the parties to come together with any relevant information that has been requested by the other side at the collective bargaining table and make a good faith effort to bargain on the mandatory terms of collective bargaining.

Labor law, however, provides employers with a unique right if collective bargaining agreements are not fruitful in reaching a new labor agreement. If an employer determines that an impasse has been reached in collective bargaining, it may declare an impasse and unilaterally implement the terms of the last offer it made to the union. Although this option can result in the end of a work stoppage and labor dispute, it presents grave risks to an employer. Namely, if the union disagrees that an impasse has been reached, it can file an unfair labor practice charge with the NLRB, asserting that the employer failed to bargain in good faith. If the NLRB determines that an impasse was not reached, it or a federal court will order the parties back to the bargaining table. The terms unilaterally imposed by the employer will not be enforced.

Sport managers need to be aware of a range of issues when it comes to labor law. Athlete employees have significant rights under the law, and team employers must not overstep certain safeguards. Thus, an understanding of the rights provided under section 7 of the NLRA and the actions prohibited under section 8 of the NLRA is critical for any sport manager.

Labor law continues to play an integral role in the relationships between professional teams and athletes. As the 21st century unfolds, it remains to be seen what role, if any, labor law will play in the relationship between universities and college athletes. Furthermore, with the advancement of technology and continued concerns over doping in sports, labor law will likely continue to play a significant role in shaping boundaries for professional athletes in those areas. Overall, as it has since the 20th century, labor law will continue to be a guiding force in the relationship between athletes and teams as the 21st century continues.

LEARNING AIDS

Summary

Since the early 20th century, labor law has played an important role in protecting the rights and interests of professional athletes in the United States. Furthermore, it has also played an important role in shaping the history of professional sports leagues in the United States by delineating the leagues' responsibilities to players and setting forth guidelines that define the relationship between employer and employee.

As the 21st century unfolds, labor law will continue to shape the relationships between professional athletes, teams, and leagues. In this century, labor law has the potential to affect the relationship between intercollegiate athletes and their universities. Furthermore, it remains to be seen whether players will continue to rely on labor law to gain concessions in labor negotiations or begin to rely more heavily on antitrust law to obtain the terms they desire.

Discussion Questions

1. Do you believe that all college athletes are employees under the common law right-to-control test? Why or why not?

2. Should college athletes be able to unionize? What are the pros and cons of the unionization of college athletes?

3. One term that unions and leagues are required to bargain collectively is wages. For sports leagues, wages generally relate to how a salary cap is calculated. Should team owners always be required to open their financial books to players in negotiating a salary cap? Why or why not?

4. Why do professional athletes want to limit the length of a sport's season? What motivates team owners to negotiate for the greatest number of games possible in a season? What is the best way for players and owners to reach an agreement on this issue?

5. What issues did players and leagues face in agreeing to HGH testing policies? How could these issues be addressed?

6. To uphold section 8 of the NLRA, all that is required of employers and labor organizations is to meet and bargain collectively in good faith on the mandatory terms of collective bargaining. Neither side is required to make concessions, nor do they have to reach an agreement. Is this standard strong enough to promote strong labor relations in the United States? Why or why not?

7. How effective are lockouts and strikes when it comes to employers and employees gaining concessions in collective bargaining? Use examples from recent collective bargaining negotiations between sports leagues and their players in making your argument.

8. Should athletes use antitrust law instead of labor law in attempting to end lockouts imposed by leagues? Why or why not?

Opening the Financial Books in Collective Bargaining

The World Basketball League (WBL) is a professional basketball league that has teams across the United States. Its players are represented by a labor organization, the World Basketball League Players Association (WBLPA). Currently, the WBL and WBLPA are negotiating a new collective bargaining agreement. One of the issues the sides are having difficulty in reaching an agreement on is the salary cap. WBL owners have offered players a salary cap that results in their earning 10% less in league revenue than they did under the most recent collective bargaining agreement.

As time goes on and the likelihood of a lost season increases, collective bargaining negotiations have become more heated. The pressure being felt on both sides is demonstrated by the comments that WBL team owners have made recently.

Allison Baloof and her husband co-own the Palo Alto Queens, a team in the WBL. Along with holding this role, Allison stars in the cable television reality show *Real Richies of SoCal*. On a recent episode, Allison is shown riding in a limousine with her costars to a gala. As she swigs champagne, Allison brings up the WBL collective bargaining negotiations. She then says, "We are going broke! The Queens are losing money every day! My family is struggling to pay the bills. We cannot pay the players any more under a salary cap. If we cannot lower the percentage they receive, we'll fold."

The commissioner of the WBL, David Soft, is an avid viewer of *Real Richies of SoCal*. He watches the show to help him wind down after a long day of running the WBL. After hearing Allison's comments, he thinks, "She's right." That night, Soft gives a speech to a group of university students. When asked about the ongoing collective bargaining negotiations, Soft says, "Some of our teams are losing money. We cannot keep up this pace of increasing players' salaries."

Billy Gatherer is the executive director of the WBLPA. After a long day of collective bargaining, Gatherer walks in the front door and finds his wife watching *Real Richies of SoCal*. He hears Allison's comments and says, "This is garbage. Change the station." But he also thinks, "Allison and the other owners have never brought up this point in collective bargaining." His wife then changes to the local news, which is airing Soft's speech. Gatherer hears Soft's comments about WBL teams losing money.

After hearing Soft and Allison's comments, the next day during collective bargaining negotiations, Gatherer and the WBLPA request that the WBL and its owners open their financial books to players and the WBLPA. The WBL denies this request. Thereafter, the WBLPA files an unfair labor practice charge with the NLRB, alleging a violation by the WBL to bargain collectively in good faith.

Glossary

acceptance—The act of agreeing to an offer by words or conduct. Acceptance must be communicated to the person making the offer.

actual authority—Authority under which the agent reasonably believes that her actions are within the scope of authority given to her by the principal.

actual harm—Clear and convincing proof of physical or emotional injury to a person.

administrative agencies—Governmental agencies that have the authority to create laws, rules, and regulations to carry out the responsibilities of government.

affirmative action—Actions taken by employers to seek out, hire, and promote qualified individuals in protected groups.

Age Discrimination in Employment Act (ADEA)—A federal law that prohibits discrimination in employment matters because of age.

agency agreement—The oral or written agreement that formalizes the relationship between an agent and a principal.

agency law—The law that applies to and explains the relationship between principal and agent. Agency law specifically defines the rights and responsibilities of both principals and agents, the authority of the agent as he works for the principal, and the creation of the agency relationship itself.

agency relationship—The relationship between the principal and the agent.

ambush marketing—Practice of creating an advertising or promotional campaign that confuses consumers and misrepresents that a company is an official sponsor of an event.

Americans with Disabilities Act of 1990 (ADA)—A federal law that prohibits discrimination in employment matters because of disability.

answer—The response of a defendant to a complaint (accusation of wrongdoing).

antitrust exemption—A finding by a court or provision in a statute that exempts a party from review under the antitrust laws.

apparent authority—A situation in which the principal allows a situation to exist that may mislead others about the agent's actual authority. In these situations, a third party may be able to rely on the agent's actions to hold the principal accountable.

appropriation—The use, without permission and for one's own benefit, of the name, likeness, or other identifying characteristics of another person.

arbitrary or fanciful marks—Trademarks that are inherently distinctive because they describe the source of a good and not the good itself.

arbitration—Process in which a neutral third party (the arbitrator or panel of arbitrators) renders a decision after a hearing at which both parties are given a chance to be heard and to present evidence.

assault—An intentional tort involving the believable threat of a harmful or offensive touching of another.

assumption of risk—A defense to negligence recognized by some jurisdictions when three elements are met: (1) the risk entered into is inherent to the activity, (2) the plaintiff voluntarily consented to participate in the activity, and (3) the plaintiff had knowledge, understanding, or appreciation of the risks involved in the activity.

avoidance—The response to an evaluation of risks in which action is taken to eliminate the risk (e.g., by eliminating a program, facility, or service).

battery—An intentional tort involving the harmful or offensive touching of another.

bilateral contract—Contract that contains two promises: the offer and the acceptance.

bona fide occupational qualification (BFOQ)—A defense to claims of discrimination asserting that a particular trait of a job applicant or employee is necessary for a particular job even though excluding others without this trait is discriminatory.

breach of duty—A failure to act in a reasonable manner for the safety of others; a failure to meet the standard of care.

breach of warranty—The failure to uphold an express or implied promise to abide by certain terms and conditions relevant to the sale or lease of goods.

business necessity—A defense to claims of unintentional discrimination asserting that a legitimate hiring practice is a business necessity even though it has a discriminatory effect.

case law—Published legal decisions decided in a court of law by a judge or jury.

causation—The connection between an act (or failure to act) and harm.

cause in fact—But for the act (or failure to act), the injury would not have occurred.

cause of action—Circumstances that give rise to a lawsuit; often used interchangeably with the term *lawsuit*.

civil law—A category of law in which monetary damages are often claimed because of an act or failure to act by another that results in harm to persons or property.

collective bargaining—Negotiation process through which employers and employee union representatives have mutual obligations to meet at reasonable times and confer in good faith with respect to the three mandatory terms of collective bargaining: wages, hours, and conditions of employment.

collective bargaining agreement (CBA)—A written agreement between employers and employees that documents the outcomes of collective bargaining negotiations and provides the exact terms and conditions of the employment relationship between the parties. The terms of a collective bargaining agreement are binding on all parties to the agreement.

collective mark—Trademark used by the members of a cooperative, association, or other collective organization to indicate membership in that organization.

commerce—Trade, traffic, commerce, transportation, transmission, or communication between states, between a state and any place outside thereof, within the District of Columbia or a possession of the United States, or between points in the same state but through a point outside thereof.

commercial speech—An expression related to economic interests of the speaker or the audience. Commercial speech is protected by the First Amendment but is regulated by the government to protect consumers from false or misleading advertisements.

comparative negligence—A defense to negligence whereby some degree of fault and subsequent monetary damages are shifted away from the defendant. In a pure comparative negligence jurisdiction, the defendant is liable only for the proportion of fault attributed to himself.

compensatory damages—Damages (money) awarded by a court to compensate a defendant for the actual value of injuries or damages that she experiences.

complaint—A formal accusation of wrongdoing brought by a plaintiff against a defendant in a legal case.

concerted activity—Activity in which two or more employees engage in conduct to aid or protect the terms and conditions of their employment.

consequential damages—Monetary relief for economic losses that were caused indirectly by the original breach of contract.

consideration—The exchange of value or benefit that each party agrees to give up as a result of the contractual agreement.

Consolidated Omnibus Budget Reconciliation Act (COBRA)—A federal law that requires organizations to allow employees to retain their rights to insurance coverage under their employer's health plan for a certain length of time after they have left the organization.

constitutional law—The law relevant to the Constitution of the United States and to state constitutions.

Consumer Product Safety Commission (CPSC)—A federal regulatory agency that provides safety guidelines and recommendations for consumer products.

contact sport exception—Argument that contact sports such as football should not be taken into account in regard to a school's compliance with Title IX. Courts have consistently held that the statute includes no such exception.

contraction—Measures that would be taken to decrease the size of a professional sports league or organization.

contractual remedies—Ways in which contract law can be applied to resolve a wrong done to a plaintiff.

conversion—Taking and depriving another of his right to the exclusive possession of personal property.

copyright—A right granted by statute to the author or creator of a literary or artistic production that provides the author with the exclusive right to reproduce, publish, or sell the production.

copyright infringement—Unauthorized use of copyrighted material in a way that violates one of the owners' exclusive rights in the copyright.

criminal law—The body of law that identifies what behavior is criminal and stipulates penalties for violations.

crisis—An emergency or significant critical event that must be planned for proactively and can often be dealt with by the affected organization.

crisis management plan—A comprehensive, proactive plan designed to lessen the negative effect on an organization in the event of a crisis.

cybersquatting—Illegal action by which someone registers a domain name that is confusingly similar to a registered or unregistered trademark or dilutes a famous mark. The cybersquatter must intend to profit from this use in bad faith toward the true trademark owner.

damages—Money that is sought for a wrong committed by another in tort or contract.

de facto discrimination—Discrimination that occurs when a law or policy does not appear to have a discriminatory purpose but has a discriminatory effect.

de jure discrimination—Discrimination that occurs when a law or policy has a discriminatory purpose.

decertification—Vote of union members either to discontinue a union's representation of them or to be represented by another union. To decertify a union, at least 30% of union members must sign a card or petition requesting that the NLRB conduct an election. The union will be decertified if less than a majority of votes cast support union representation.

defamation—A false and defamatory statement made in the presence of a third party; may be either spoken (slander) or written (libel).

deliberate indifference—Behavior whereby someone in authority knows that sexual harassment has taken place but does not respond to remedy the problem.

deposition—A type of discovery in which a witness provides verbal information in preparation for trial.

descriptive mark—Trademark that describes a characteristic or quality of a good or service.

design defect—A product that is designed in a faulty manner that ultimately results in injury to consumers.

dilution—The loss of capacity of a famous mark to identify and distinguish goods or services, even in the absence of competition between the parties involved or no likelihood of confusion, mistake, or deception.

discovery—The part of the legal process that involves gathering information verified by oath in preparation for trial.

disparagement of property—Untrue statements about personal property that result in financial hardship to a business; types consist of slander of quality and slander of title.

disparate-impact discrimination—A type of discrimination that is unintentional in which the percentage of workers in a particular business does not mirror the percentage of those in protected classes in the local labor market.

disparate-treatment discrimination—An intentional form of discrimination in which a qualified job applicant in a protected class is denied employment.

diversity jurisdiction—The jurisdiction of a federal court to hear a case brought by people and organizations from different states.

doctrine of supremacy—A doctrine based on the supremacy clause in the U.S. Constitution stating that the U.S. and state constitutions and federal legislation are superior to common law and state legislation.

due process—A guarantee that a person cannot be deprived of life, liberty, or property without a fair process or hearing.

duty of loyalty—Duty under which the agent must act solely and completely for the benefit of the principal.

duty of obedience—The agent's duty to follow all reasonable instructions given by the principal.

economic weapons—Tools provided by the NLRA for employers and unions to use during collective bargaining to gain concessions from the other side in negotiations.

effective accommodation—Under the third part of the three-part test provided in the policy interpretation, a program must measure whether it effectively accommodates the interests and abilities of the particular gender to provide equal athletic opportunities for both sexes.

emergency action plan—A comprehensive, proactive plan that addresses potential medical emergencies occurring in a sport setting.

employment at will—A legal doctrine that holds that the employment relationship can end at any time and for any reason. Important exceptions to this doctrine are public policy, implied contracts, and the application of federal laws such as those governing discrimination.

Equal Employment Opportunity Commission (EEOC)—A governmental agency that monitors compliance laws relevant to employment discrimination.

equal opportunity—A standard set out in the regulations that enforce Title IX. It refers to the responsibility of a program to provide equivalent athletic opportunities for both sexes.

equal protection—A guarantee that laws will be applied in an equal and nondiscriminatory manner.

equal work—The concept that individuals of either sex must be paid similar wages for jobs that are substantially equal, although the skill, effort, and responsibility of the jobs need not be identical. The jobs must be substantially equal except for the fact that one employee is paid higher wages.

establishment clause—A sentence in the First Amendment of the United States Constitution that prohibits the government from establishing a state-sponsored religion, promoting religion, or favoring religion over nonreligion.

exemptions—Findings by a court or provisions of statutes that exempt a party from review under a particular regulation or statute. Exemptions allow the party to avoid liability because of its actions that otherwise could be found to have violated the regulation or statute.

expert witness—A person who, through skill, training, background, education, or experience, renders opinions on matters relevant to legal cases.

express authority—Any written or oral communication that grants the agent authority to perform an act.

express warranty—An express agreement (spoken or in writing) that the product will be of a certain quality and type, as well as other agreed-upon provisions.

Fair Labor Standards Act (FLSA)—A federal law that governs child labor practices.

fair use—Use of copyright for purposes such as criticism, comment, news reporting, teaching, scholarship, or research.

false imprisonment—The intentional, wrongful, and unreasonable confinement of another.

false light—The publishing of false ideas or information attributed to a person.

Family and Medical Leave Act (FMLA)—A federal law that requires organizations to provide employees with up to 12 weeks of leave to attend to family health issues.

fiduciary duty—Any duty to act for the benefit of someone else while subordinating one's own personal interests.

forensic expert—An expert who, through skill, training, background, education, or experience, renders opinions on matters relevant to legal cases.

foreseeability—The ability to foresee or anticipate whether a certain event will happen.

free agency—The period when a professional athlete is not under contract to any particular team and is therefore able to negotiate with any team.

free exercise clause—A phrase in the First Amendment to the United States Constitution that prohibits the government from restricting a person's right to exercise her religious beliefs.

free speech clause—A clause in the First Amendment to the United States Constitution that protects freedom of speech for all persons.

general supervision—The type of supervision typically employed with more mature or more skilled sport participants and activities involving less risk.

generic mark—Marks so common that they cannot receive federal trademark protection.

Glossary

gross negligence—A high level of negligence (subjectively determined), in which a defendant has demonstrated a high degree of carelessness.

group boycotts—Situation in which a league or a group of teams collectively agree not to bargain with a particular group of players, such as by setting draft rules that exclude certain players from being drafted.

hazard—Something that holds the potential to cause harm.

Health Insurance Portability and Accountability Act (HIPAA)—A federal law that provides rules for employers who provide health plans for their employees.

hostile and abusive work environment—An environment in which someone is so affected by sexual conduct and finds it so offensive or intimidating that it negatively affects his or her job performance. The working environment becomes filled with intimidation, ridicule, and insult.

hostile environment sexual harassment—Harassment by an employee, student, or third party that is sufficiently severe, persistent, or pervasive to limit a student's ability to participate in or benefit from an educational program, including an athletic program.

impasse—A situation that occurs when the parties negotiating an agreement have reached a point where they can make no further progress because they cannot agree on further changes to the agreement.

implied authority—The agent's authority and ability, not expressly provided in the agreement, to perform incidental acts that are reasonably necessary to accomplish the agent's express responsibilities as provided in the agency agreement (either oral or written).

implied warranty of fitness—An implied promise by the seller that the product is appropriate for the particular purpose for which it was sold.

implied warranty of merchantability—An implied promise by the seller that the product is reasonably appropriate for the general purpose for which it was sold.

industry standard—Standard practice within an industry or profession.

inherent risks—Risks that are a necessary part of an activity (e.g., trees on ski slopes; legal tackles in football).

injunction—Court order that requires someone to perform or refrain from performing a certain activity.

intentional infliction of emotional distress—Extreme and outrageous conduct that results in severe emotional distress to another.

intentional tort—An act that is both wrongful and knowingly committed.

interrogatories—A type of discovery in which written information is gathered in preparation for trial.

interstate commerce—Commerce that takes place between two or more states.

intrusion—The invasion of a person's home or personal belongings without permission.

invasion of the right to privacy—Interference with a private citizen's right to privacy in her personal life.

judge-made law—Legal decisions made in a court of law by a judge.

labor exemption—An exemption that provides that when employers and employees have bargained in good faith, one party cannot be subject to antitrust claims brought by the other party.

libel—The written form of defamation.

license—A right granted by an owner, known as the licensor, to a third party, the licensee, that permits the licensee to associate his goods, services, or business with the logos, names, and mascots of the licensor. Granting a license creates a contractual relationship between the licensor and the licensee.

liquidated damages—Specific amounts of damages that the parties agreed to within the contract itself that must be paid by the party that breaches the contract.

lockout—An economic weapon held by employers wherein they stop work or deny employment during a labor dispute. During a lockout, employees are literally held out of employment—they may not access the employer's buildings, engage in work, or even collect a paycheck.

loss of consortium—Loss of the services or involvement of a family member brought about by the wrongful actions of another.

mandatory subject of collective bargaining—Terms of employment such as wages or hours of work that must be agreed to in negotiations between employers and employees.

manufacturing defect—A defect that occurs during, or is associated with, the manufacture of a product.

mediation—A private, informal process in which a neutral third party (the mediator) helps the parties in a dispute reach an agreement; sometimes called *facilitation*.

monopoly—An organization that possesses exclusive control over the means of selling and producing a product.

monopoly power—The ability of an entity to exhibit characteristics of a monopoly by controlling the means of selling or producing a product.

moot case—A case in which actual controversy no longer exists and deciding the case would be pointless or of no practical significance.

necessity—A defense to trespass in which an innocent person enters the land of another to avoid imminent and serious injury to the body or property of oneself or another person.

negligence—An unintentional tort that results in personal injury.

negligent per se—Situation in which a plaintiff needs to prove only causation and injury to prevail on a negligence claim.

Occupational Safety and Health Act—A federal law that provides for the safety and health of employees in the work environment.

offer—A conditional promise to do or refrain from doing something in the future.

Parole Evidence Rule—Rule under which litigants cannot assert facts that existed before the contract was formed if those facts are inconsistent with or contradict the existing written contract.

partially disclosed principal—A situation in which an agent reveals that she has a principal but does not reveal the principal's identity

patent—A document provided by the federal government that gives the owner of an invention the right to exclude others from reproducing the patented invention for 20 years.

patent infringement—Action whereby someone other than the patent holder makes and, without permission, uses, sells, offers to sell, or imports patented material.

per se rule—Conduct that is inherently anticompetitive, such as price fixing and group boycotts, and therefore automatically violates the Sherman Antitrust Act.

personal property—Movable property such as sports equipment.

pleadings—Formal statements in legal documents prepared by attorneys that provide details about a case and may include an answer, a complaint, or both.

policy interpretation—An interpretation provided by the Department of Education in 1979 setting forth ways in a which a school can assess whether it complies with Title IX and the regulations implementing Title IX.

position statement—A professional association's stance on a matter of public importance. Position statements often provide recommendations on safety matters.

price fixing—Agreement among members of a group (such as a professional sports league) to set prices at a certain level to avoid competition among group members over prices.

primary sources—Sources of law derived from original sources such as published court decisions or statutes.

product liability—Liability attached to the manufacture or distribution of a product.

proximate cause—Requirement that the act (or failure to act) and the injury be strongly or directly linked.

public disclosure of private facts—Making factual information public about a person's private life that an ordinary person would find objectionable.

punitive damages—Damages (money) designed to punish a defendant for a wrongful act that results in pain and suffering by a plaintiff.

quid pro quo sexual harassment—Harassment involving "something for something." Such harassment includes requesting sexual favors in exchange for job-related benefits, or a coach telling a player that she or he must submit to the coach's advances to make the team. In the case of harassment by a coach, a school may be liable for damages.

ratification—The principal's affirmation of an agent's actions, even though the agent lacked authority to act on behalf of the principal at the time of those actions.

real property—Fixed property such as sport stadiums, fields, courts, or unmovable goals.

reasonable accommodation—Finding work responsibilities and environments that allow employees with disabilities to be successful in performing their job functions.

remand—The act of sending an appealed legal case back to the trial court to determine an issue of fact.

reserve clause—A clause that used to be contained within every professional baseball player's contract stating that if the player did not automatically sign a new contract with the team for the next season, all the provisions of his present contract would be automatically renewed.

respondeat superior—A legal doctrine that holds people and organizations high in the chain of command (principals) liable for the negligent acts of those lower in the chain of command (agents).

Restatement of Torts—A comprehensive document that provides a uniform set of rules relevant to the law of torts.

retention—Taking no action in response to an evaluation of risks. The situation is kept as is.

right of publicity—The right of any person to control the commercial use of her identity.

risk—The likelihood or probability of harm.

risk management—The process of reducing or eliminating the risk of harm to participants and loss to an organization through injury and subsequent lawsuits.

Rozelle rule—An NFL rule that required a team signing a veteran free agent to provide compensation to the team that was losing the player.

rule of reason—Rule used by courts in antitrust cases that applies when the conduct is not inherently anti-competitive; under this rule, a court focuses on whether the challenged conduct restrains trade unreasonably.

rules and regulations—Policies or principles that are publicly agreed on and that govern an activity or organization.

safe harbor—Criteria set out in a statute that if met allows the entity to avoid liability. The first part of the three-part test, dealing with a comparison of enrolled students to participating student-athletes, is often known as a safe harbor because a school that can meet this first part does not have to meet the other parts of the test and will not be found to have violated Title IX.

salary cap—An agreed-upon limit of the amount that a team and league will spend on player salaries for any particular year. Salary caps can limit what teams spend on individual player salaries, their entire roster's worth of salaries, or both. The amount is agreed to in negotiations between players and teams and is included in the league's collective bargaining agreement.

scope of employment—The realm of activities engaged in by an agent when acting on behalf of a principal.

secondary meaning—Meaning assigned to a trademark when it has received widespread use and public recognition so that it indicates the source of the good or service instead of the good or service itself.

secondary sources—Sources of law derived from sources secondary to an original source such as articles that interpret or analyze case law decisions or statutes.

service mark—Mark used in the sale of advertising or services to identify and distinguish the services of one entity from the services of others.

sexual harassment—Unwelcome conduct that is sexual in nature. In the employment context, such harassment creates a hostile or abusive work environment and may result in a lawsuit. In the high school or university setting, this conduct is a form of sexual discrimination prohibited under Title IX.

single-entity defense—A defense to an antitrust claim; a party using this defense must demonstrate that instead of being an organization made up of separate business entities, it is a single business entity and therefore cannot be a combination or conspiracy in restraint of trade as required to violate the antitrust laws.

slander—The spoken form of defamation.

slander of quality—Untrue statements about the quality of personal property that result in financial hardship to a business.

slander of title—Untrue statements about the ownership (title) of personal property that result in financial hardship to a business.

specific performance—An injunction issued by the court ordering the breaching party to carry out its contractual duties.

specific supervision—The type of supervision typically employed with less mature (younger) or less skilled sport participants and with activities involving greater risk; also known as arms-length or close supervision.

standard of care—The duty, or responsibility, of persons to act in a reasonable manner to provide for the safety of others.

standard representation agreements—Documents that many professional player unions require agents to enter into with any players they represent. Agents who do not use the standard representation agreement cannot represent players in the particular league.

stare decisis—A legal principle that requires courts to respect prior decisions, generally stand by them, and not disturb the law unless necessary.

state action—Any action of the federal or state governments or their subdivisions, such as city or county governments or agencies.

Statute of Frauds—Principle stating that three types of contracts must be in written form: (1) contracts concerning the sale, mortgage, or lease of an interest in land; (2) contracts that cannot be performed within 1 year of their making; and (3) contracts for the sale of goods that have a value in excess of $500.

statutory law—Laws (legislation or codes) created by legislators at the state and federal levels.

strict liability—Legal concept in which liability results regardless of fault; often used in product liability cases.

strike—A type of protest that occurs when employees collectively refuse to work in an effort to obtain a concession or concessions from their employer on terms being negotiated through collective bargaining.

suggestive marks—Trademarks that require some creativity to understand the product that they describe.

summary judgment—A written document (motion) produced by attorneys and brought before the court claiming that a case should be decided based on the applicable law, given that no facts remain in dispute.

summons—Official notification to a defendant that she must respond to a complaint.

theory—A legal concept or model on which the outcome of a case may hinge.

three-part test—Three-part analysis set out in the Title IX policy interpretation that measures whether the interests and abilities of both sexes are being equally accommodated by the provision of equal athletic opportunities as provided in the regulations.

Title VII of the Civil Rights Act—A federal law that prohibits discrimination in employment matters because of race, color, national origin, gender, or religion.

tort—A civil wrong or injury that often results in monetary damages.

trademark—Any word, name, symbol, or device that an organization uses to identify and distinguish its services from the services of another organization and to indicate the source of the service.

trademark infringement—When a non–trademark owner engages in some unauthorized use of a trademark that is likely to cause consumers to be confused or deceived about who really owns the trademark.

transfer—The response to an evaluation of risks in which methods are devised to place the risk of liability on another (e.g., through contractual agreements).

treatment—The response to an evaluation of risks in which some action is taken to reduce the risk.

treble damages—An award to the party of three times the amount of damages incurred.

trespass to personal property—The initial nonpermitted taking of another person's personal property.

undisclosed principal—A situation in which a principal uses an agent for negotiations with a third party, but the third party has no knowledge of the identity of the principal

unfair labor practice charge—A type of claim brought to the NLRB when a violation of section 8 of the NLRA is alleged to have occurred.

Uniform Athlete Agents Act—A standard act created by the National Conference of Commissioners on Uniform State Laws, the main purpose of which is to provide for uniformity in registration and certification of athlete agents among the states. The act becomes an enforceable law if a particular state enacts it within its state statutes.

Uniform Commercial Code (UCC)—A lengthy document, adopted in 49 U.S. states, that provides a uniform set of rules relevant to the sale of goods (contracts).

unilateral contract—A contract in which the offeree accepts by performance rather than by promise.

union—An organized group of employees that uses their collective strength to protect the rights and interests of the group's members. One way that unions accomplish this is by members' engagement in collective bargaining—through the representation of union leaders—with their employer on matters affecting them, such as wages, hours, and conditions of employment.

voidable contract—A contract that is invalid and allows one party to walk away from it without breaching the contract

voluntary consent—An agreement (express or implied) to participate in an activity in a manner, time, and place of one's own choosing.

waiver—A contract between a sport organization and a participant; the participant signs it before participating in a sporting event. By signing the waiver, the participant agrees to absolve the sport organization from liability for any injuries that the participant suffers because of participation.

References

Chapter 1

Carper, D.L., & McKinsey, J.A. (2012). *Understanding the law* (6th ed.). Mason, OH: South-Western.

Carper, D.L., McKinsey, J.A., & West, B.W. (2008). *Understanding the law* (5th ed.). Mason, OH: South-Western.

DeFunis v. Odegaard, 416 U.S. 312 (1974).

Pittman, A.T., Spengler, J.O., & Young, S.J. (2016). *Case studies in sport law* (2nd ed.). Champaign, IL: Human Kinetics.

Chapter 2

57A American Jurisprudence, § 227 (2005).

57A American Jurisprudence 2nd, § 427 (2003).

57A American Jurisprudence 2nd, § 429 (2005).

Avila v. Citrus Community College District, 111 Cal. App. 4th 811, 4 Cal.Rptr.3d 264 (2003).

Costa v. Boston Red Sox Baseball, 809 N.E.2d 1090 (2004).

Day v. Ouachita Parish School Board et al., 823 So.2d 1039 (La. App. 2 Cir. 2002).

Fidelity Leasing Corp. v. Dun & Bradstreet, Inc., 494 F. Supp. 786 (E.D. Pa. 1980).

Green v. Konawa Independent School District, 105 P.3d 840 (Okla. Civ. App. 2005).

Hackbart v. Cincinnati Bengals, Inc., 601 F.2d 516 (10th Cir. 1979).

Kavanagh v. Trustees of Boston University, 795 N.E.2d 1170 (Mass. 2003).

Keeton, W.P. (1984). *Prosser and Keeton on the law of torts*. St. Paul, MN: West.

Kiely, T.F., & Ottily, B.L. (2006). *Understanding product liability law* (3rd ed.). Newark, NJ: Lexis Nexis.

Leakas v. Columbia Country Club, 831 F. Supp. 1231 (Md. 1993).

Lowe v. California League of Professional Baseball, 65 Cal.Rptr.2d 105 (Cal. App. 4 Dist. 1997).

Mania v. Kaminski, 412 N.E.2d 651 (Ill. App. 1 1980).

Nabozny v. Barnhill, 334 N.E.2d 258 (Ill. App. 1975).

Neary v. Northern Pacific Railway, 110 P. 226 (Mont. 1910).

Owen, D.G., Madden, M.S., & Davis, M.J. (2000). *Madden & Owen on product liability* (3rd ed.). Minneapolis, MN: West.

Pittman, A.T., Spengler, J.O., & Young, S.J. (2016). *Case studies in sport law* (2nd ed.). Champaign, IL: Human Kinetics.

Regions Bank & Trust v. Stone County Skilled Nursing Facility, Inc., 49 S.W.3d 107 (Ark. 2001).

Restatement (Second) of Torts, § 282 (1965).

Restatement (Second) of Torts, § 432 (1965).

Restatement (Second) of Torts, § 500 (1965).

Restatement (Second) of Torts, § 907, Comment a (1965).

§ 324 (2005).

Sanchez v. Hillerich & Bradsby Co., 128 Cal. Rptr. 2d. 529 (1992).

Stringer v. Minnesota Vikings Football Club, LLC, 705 N.W.2d 746 (Minn. 2005).

Uniform Commercial Code, § 2-313.

van der Smissen, B. (2003). Elements of negligence. In D.J. Cotten & J.T. Wolohan (Eds.), *Law for recreation and sport managers* (3rd ed., pp. 56–65). Dubuque, IA: Kendall/Hunt.

Whitley v. Com., 538 S.E.2d 296 (Va. 2000).

Wong, G.M. (2002). *Essentials of sports law* (3rd ed.). Westport, CT: Greenwood.

Chapter 3

Access Now et al. v. South Florida Stadium Corp. et al., 161 F. Supp. 2d 1357 (S.D. Fla. 2001).

Americans with Disabilities Act of 1990 (ADA), 42 U.S.C. § 12101(b)(1) (2008).

Appenzeller, H., & Seidler, T.L. (1998). Emergency action plan: Expecting the unexpected. In H. Appenzeller (Ed.). *Risk management in sport: Issues and strategies* (pp. 297–309). Durham, NC: Carolina Academic Press.

Byrd v. State, 905 S.W.2d 195 (Tenn. App. 1995).

Connaughton, D.P., Spengler, J.O., & Bennett, G.B. (2001). Crisis planning and management for physical activity programs. *Journal of Health, Physical Education, Recreation and Dance, 72*(7), 27–29.

Definitions, 28 C.F.R. § 36.104 (2008).

Dougherty, N.J., Goldberger, A.S., & Carpenter, L.J. (2002). *Sport, physical activity and the law*. Champaign, IL: Sagamore Publishing.

Holle, R.L., & Lopez, R.E. (1999, October). Updated recommendations for lightning safety—1998. *Bulletin of the American Meteorological Society, 80*(10), 2035–2041.

Kleinknecht v. Gettysburg College, 989 F.2d 1360 (3rd Cir. 1993).

Locilento v. John A. Coleman Catholic High School, 134 A.D.2d 39, 42, 523 N.Y.S.2d 198, 200 (3d Dept. 1987).

National Collegiate Athletic Association. (2001). NCAA guideline 1d: Lightning safety. *2001–2002 NCAA sports medicine handbook*, 12–14.

Nondiscrimination on the Basis of Disability by Public Accommodations and in Commercial Facilities, 28 C.F.R. Subpart A (2006).

Peterson, J.A., & Hronek, B.B. (2001). *Risk management for park, recreation, and leisure services.* Champaign, IL: Sagamore Publishing.

Pittman, A.T., Spengler, J.O., & Young, S.J. (2016). *Case studies in sport law* (2nd ed.). Champaign, IL: Human Kinetics.

Rehabilitation Act of 1973, Pub. L. No. 93-112 (1973).

Spengler, J.O., Connaughton, D.P., & Pittman, A. (2006). *Risk management in sport and recreation.* Champaign, IL: Human Kinetics.

Title III, 42 U.S.C. § 12182(a) (2008).

Verni v. Aramark et al., 903 A. 2d 475 (N.J. App. 2006).

Walsh, K.M., Bennett, B., Cooper, M.A., Holle, R.L., Rakov, V.A., Roederell, W.P., Ryan, M. (2013). National Athletic Trainers' Association position statement: Lightning safety for athletics and recreation. *Journal of Athletic Training, 48*(2), 258–270.

Chapter 4

Black v. NFL Players Association, 87 F. Supp. 2d 1 (D.DC 2000).

Davis, T. (2007). United States. In R.C.R. Siekmann, R. Parish, R. Branco Martins, & J.W. Soek (Eds.), *Players' agents worldwide: Legal aspects* (pp. 655–691). The Hague, The Netherlands: T.M.C. Asser Instituut.

Drew Rosenhaus net worth. (n.d.). www.therichest.com/celebnetworth/athletes/agent/drew-rosenhaus-net-worth

Feinsand, M., & Madden, B. (2007, November 15). Alex works to stay a Yankee. Deal expected to be reached within 48 hours. *Daily News* (New York), p. 54.

Greenberg, M.J., & Gray, J.T. (1998). *Sports law practice* (2nd ed.). Charlottesville, VA: Lexis Law.

Gregory, W.A. (2001). *The law of agency and partnership* (3rd ed.). St. Paul, MN: West.

Hilliard & Taylor v. Black, 125 F. Supp. 2d 1071 (N.D. Fla. 2000).

Katz, A. (2008, May 13). Mayo denies ex-confidant's claims of gifts, including TV, cash. *ESPN.com.* http://sports.espn.go.com/ncb/news/story?id=3390695

Miller-Ayala Athlete Agent Act, Cal. Bus. & Prof. Code, §§ 18895 et. seq. (2015).

National Collegiate Athletic Association. (2014, July). *2014–2015 NCAA Division I manual.* Indianapolis, IN: NCAA.

National Conference of Commissioners on Uniform State Laws (NCCUSL). (2000). Uniform Athlete Agents Act. www.law.upenn.edu/bll/archives/ulc/uaaa/aaa1130.htm

NCAA Division I Committee on Infractions. (2003, September 10). *California State University, Fresno Public Infractions Report.*

NFL Players Association. (2012, June). *NFLPA regulations governing contract advisors.*

Pittman, A.T., Spengler, J.O., & Young, S.J. (2016). *Case studies in sport law* (2nd ed.). Champaign, IL: Human Kinetics.

Pryor, B. (2013, October 9). Sports agent Terry Watson indicted related to UNC athlete-agent case. *Dailytarheel.com.* www.dailytarheel.com/article/2013/10/second-indictment-in-related-to-unc-athlete-agent-case

Pugmire, L. (2008, May 13). Tito Maddox sees himself in O.J. Mayo saga. *Los Angeles Times.* www.latimes.com/sports/la-sp-maddox13-2008may13,0,3380367,print.story

Restatement (Third) of Agency, § 1.01 (2006).

Restatement (Third) of Agency, §§ 8.03–8.05 (2006).

Robinson, C., & Cole, J. (2006, September 15). Cash and carry. *Yahoo Sports.* http://sports.yahoo.com/ncaaf/news?slug=ys-bushprobe

Sharp, L.A., Moorman, A.M., & Claussen, C.L. (2007). *Sports law: A managerial approach.* Scottsdale, AZ: Holcomb Hathaway.

Sports Agent Responsibility and Trust Act, 15 U.S.C. §§ 7801–7807 (2015).

Steinberg, Moorad & Dunn, Inc. v. Dunn, Case No. CV 01-07009 RSWL, 2002 U.S. Dist. LEXIS 26752 (C.D. Cal. 2002).

Uniform Athlete Agents Act, Wis. Stat. §§ 440.99 et seq. (2013).

Uniform Commercial Code (2012).

Uniform Law Commissioners. (n.d.). *Legislative fact sheet—Athlete agents act.* www.uniformlaws.org/LegislativeFactSheet.aspx?title=Athlete%20Agents%20Act

United States v. Walters & Bloom, 913 F.2d 388 (7th Cir. 1990).

Wikipedia. (n.d.). Scott Boras. http://en.wikipedia.org/wiki/Scott_Boras

Wolohan, J. (2007). United States. In R.C.R. Siekmann, R. Parish, R. Branco Martins, & J.W. Soek (Eds.), *Players' agents worldwide: Legal aspects* (pp. 637–653). The Hague, The Netherlands: T.M.C. Asser Instituut.

Chapter 5

Amended and Restated Lease Agreement by and Between Southeast Wisconsin Professional Baseball Park District, and Milwaukee Brewers Baseball Club, Limited Partnership. (2004, January 1).

Amended and Restated Non-Relocation Agreement by and Among Southeast Wisconsin Professional Baseball Park District, State of Wisconsin and Milwaukee Brewers Baseball Club, Limited Partnership. (2004, January 1).

Berkowitz, S., Upton, J., Schnaars, C., Dougherty, S., Klein, S., Gauthier, S., Marske, M., Weeden, A., & Baumer, B. (n.d.) NCAA salaries. *USA Today*. http://sports.usatoday.com/ncaa/salaries

Farber, D.C. (Ed.). (2014). *Entertainment industry contracts*. LexisAdvance, https://advance.lexis.com

Imig, P. (2013, March 12). Lambeau Field will be bigger, louder in 2013. *Foxsports Wisconsin*. www.foxsports.com/wisconsin/story/lambeau-field-will-be-bigger-louder-in-2013-031213

Indiana University. (2007, April 20). *Employment agreement between the Trustees of Indiana University and Kelvin Sampson.*

Lease Agreement by and Among Green Bay-Brown County Professional Football Stadium District, City of Green Bay, and Green Bay Packers, Inc. (2001, January 1).

Levert v. University of Illinois, 857 So.2d 611 (La. App. 2003).

McMillen, J.D. (2007). Game, event, and sponsorship contracts. In D.J. Cotten & J.T. Wolohan (Eds.), *Law for recreation and sport managers* (4th ed., pp. 334–341). Dubuque, IA: Kendall/Hunt.

Miller, W.S., & Anderson, P.M. (2001). *Major league leases: An overview of major league facility leases and how they are negotiated.* Mequon, WI: Front Office.

National Basketball Association. (2011, December). *Collective bargaining agreement.*

National Collegiate Athletic Association. (2008, February 8). *Notice of allegations to the President of Indiana University, Bloomington.* http://assets.espn.go.com/media/pdf/080213/ncb_noticeofallegations.pdf

National Collegiate Athletic Association. (2015, August 1). *2015–2016 NCAA Division I manual.* Indianapolis, IN: NCAA.

National Football Players Association. (2011, August 4). *Collective bargaining agreement.*

National Letter of Intent. (n.d.). Financial aid requirement. www.ncaa.org/wps/wcm/connect/nli/nli/nli+provisions/financial+aid

O'Brien v. The Ohio State University, 2006 Ohio 4737 (Ct. Claims 2006), *aff'd*, 2007 Ohio 4833 (Ct. App. 2007).

Pittman, A.T., Spengler, J.O., & Young, S.J. (2016). *Case studies in sport law* (2nd ed.). Champaign, IL: Human Kinetics.

Reevy, M. (2014, December 20). 8 NFL coaches earning over $6 million. *Sports CheatSheet*. www.cheatsheet.com/sports/the-8-nfl-coaches-earning-over-six-million.html/?a=viewall

Restatement (Second) of Contracts, § 2 (1990).

Restatement (Second) of Contracts, § 24 (1990).

Restatement (Second) of Contracts, § 350 (1990).

Separation Agreement Between the Trustees of Indiana University and Kelvin Sampson. (2008, February 22).

Taylor v. Wake Forest University, 191 S.E.2d 379 (N.C. App. 1972).

The world's highest paid athletes: 2014 ranking. (n.d.). *Forbes*. www.forbes.com/athletes/list/#tab:overall

USADA v. Landis, Case No: 30 190 00847 06 (September 20, 2007).

Chapter 6

Americans with Disabilities Act of 1990, 42 U.S.C.A., § 511.

Americans with Disabilities Act of 1990 (ADA), 42 U.S.C. §§ 12101 et seq. (2008).

Anderson v. Little League Baseball Inc., 794 F. Supp. 342 (Az. Dist.Ct. 1992).

Civil Rights Act of 1964, 78 Stat. 253; 42 U.S.C. § 2000e.

Coleman v. Western Michigan University, 336 N.W.2d 224 (Mich. App. 1983).

Martin v. PGA Tour, Inc., 984 F. Supp. 1320 (D. Ore. 1998), *aff'd*, 204 F.3d 994 (9th Cir. 2000), *aff'd, PGA Tour, Inc. v. Martin*, 532 U.S. 661 (2001).

Moore v. University of Notre Dame, 22 F. Supp. 2d 896 (N.D. Ind. 1998).

Occupational Health and Safety Act, 29 U.S.C. chapter 15.

OSH Act of 1970, Pub. L. No. 91-596 (1970).

Pittman, A.T., Spengler, J.O., & Young, S.J. (2016). *Case studies in sport law* (2nd ed.). Champaign, IL: Human Kinetics.

Prohibition of Discrimination by Public Accommodations, 42 U.S.C. § 12182(a) (2008).

Rehabilitation Act of 1973, 219 U.S.C. § 794.

Spengler, J.O., Connaughton, D.P., & Pittman, A. (2006). *Risk management in sport and recreation*. Champaign, IL: Human Kinetics.

Chapter 7

Adler v. Duval County School Board, 250 F.3d 1330 (11th Cir. 2001), *cert. denied*, 534 U.S. 1065 (2001).

Arlosoroff v. NCAA, 746 F.2d 1019 (4th Cir. 1984).

Bethel School District v. Fraser, 478 U.S. 675 (1986).

Board of Regents v. Roth, 408 U.S. 564 (1972).

Borden v. School District of Township of East Brunswick, 523 F.3d 153 (3rd Cir., 2008).

Brentwood Academy v. Tennessee Secondary School Athletic Association, 531 U.S. 288 (2001).

Chilingirian v. Boris, 882 F.2d 200 (6th Cir. 1989).

Codd v. Velger, 429 U.S. 624 (1977).

Cohen, C., & Sterba, J.P. (2003). *Affirmative action and racial preference*. Oxford, UK: Oxford University Press.

Cureton v. NCAA, 198 F.3d 107 (3rd Cir., 1999).

Dambrot v. Central Michigan University, 55 F.3d 1177 (6th Cir., 1995).

Esbeck, C. H. (1990). The Lemon test: Should it be retained, reformulated or rejected? *Notre Dame Journal of Law, Ethics and Public Policy, 4*, 513–548.

Gillum v. City of Kerrville, 3 F.3d 117 (5th Cir. 1993).

Goss v. Lopez, 419 U.S. 565 (1975).

Green v. City of Hamilton Hous. Auth., 937 F.2d 1561 (11th Cir. 1991).

Grutter v. Bollinger, 539 U.S. 306 (2003).

Jennings v. Wentzville R-IV School Dist., 397 F.3d 1118 (8th Cir. 2005).

Lee v. Weisman, 505 U.S. 577 (1992).

Lemon v. Kurtzman, 403 U.S. 602 (1971).

Lockhart, W.B., Kamisar, Y., Choper, J.H., & Shiffrin, S.H. (1991). *Constitutional rights and liberties* (7th ed.). St. Paul, MN: West.

Louisiana High School Athletic Ass'n v. St. Augustine High School, 396 F.2d 224 (1968).

Ludtke v. Kuhn, 461 F. Supp. 86 (S.D.N.Y. 1978).

Ludwig v. Board of Trustees of Ferris State University, 123 F.3d 404 (6th Cir. 1997).

Lynch v. Donnelly, 465 U.S. 668 (1984).

Mann, R.A., & Roberts, B.S. (2010). *Essentials of business law and the legal environment* (10th ed.). Mason, OH: West.

Marshall, W. P. (1986). We know it when we see it: The Supreme Court and establishment. *Southern California Law Review, 59*, 495–550.

Menora v. Illinois High School Association, 683 F.2d 1030 (7th Cir. 1982).

Miller, R.L., Cross, F.B., & Jentz, G.A. (2011). *Essentials of the legal environment* (3rd ed.). Mason, OH: West.

National Collegiate Athletic Association v. Tarkanian, 488 U.S. 179 (1988).

Pittman, A.T., Spengler, J.O., & Young, S.J. (2016). *Case studies in sport law* (2nd ed.). Champaign, IL: Human Kinetics.

Price v. Univ. of Alabama, 318 F. Supp. 2d 1084 (N.D. Ala. 2004).

Santa Fe Independent School District v. Doe, 530 U.S. 290 (2000).

Siegert v. Gilley, 500 U.S. 226 (1991).

Stanley v. The Big Eight Conference, 463 F. Supp. 920 (W.D.Mo. 1978).

Tinker v. Des Moines Independent Community School District, 393 U.S. 503 (1969).

Wallace v. Jaffree, 472 U.S. 38 (1985).

Wong, G.M. (2010). *Essentials of sports law* (4th ed.). Santa Barbara, CA: Praeger.

Chapter 8

Athletics, 34 C.F.R. 106.41 (2015).

Biediger v. Quinnipiac University, 728 F. Supp. 2d 62 (D. Conn., 2010), *aff'd*, 691 F.3d 85 (2nd Cir. 2012).

Boucher v. Syracuse University, 1998 WL 167296 (D.C. NY 1998), *motion granted*, 50 Fed. Appx. 643 (4th Cir. 2002).

Cannon v. Univ. of Chicago, 441 U.S. 677 (1979).

Carpenter, L.J., & Acosta, R.V. (2014). *Women in intercollegiate sport: A longitudinal, national study: Thirty-five year update: 1977–2014.* http://acosta carpenter.org/AcostaCarpenter2012.pdf

Civil Rights Restoration Act, 20 USCS § 1687 (2015).

Cohen v. Brown University, 809 F. Supp. 978 (D. RI 1992), *aff'd*, 991 F.2d 888 (1st Cir. 1993).

Cohen v. Brown University, 101 F.3d 155 (1st Cir. 1996).

Daniels v. School Board of Brevard County, 985 F. Supp. 1458 (M.Dist. Fla. 1997).

Davis v. Monroe County Board of Education, 526 U.S. 629 (1999).

Equal Pay Act, 29 U.S.C. § 206(d) (2015).

Equity in Athletics, Inc. v. Department of Education, 639 F.3d 91 (4th Cir. 2011).

Equity in Athletics Disclosure Act, Pub. L. No. 105-244 (1998).

Financial Assistance, 34 C.F.R. 106.37(c) (2015).

Franklin v. Gwinnett County Public Schools, 503 U.S. 60 (1992).

Gebser v. Lago Vista Independent School District, 524 U.S. 274 (1998).

Grove City College et al. v. Bell, 465 U.S. 555 (1984).

Jackson v. Birmingham Board of Education, 544 U.S. 167 (2005).

Kelley v. Board of Trustees, 35 F.3d 265 (7th Cir. 1994).

Landow v. School Board of Brevard County, 132 F. Supp. 2d 958 (M.Dist. Fla. 2000).

Lapchick, R. (2014, May 7). *The 2014 racial and gender report card: Major League Baseball.* Orlando, FL: Institute for Diversity and Ethics in Sport.

Lapchick, R. (2014, June 24). *The 2012 racial and gender report card: National Basketball Association.* Orlando, FL: Institute for Diversity and Ethics in Sport.

Mason v. Minnesota State High School League, 2004 U.S. Dist. Lexis 13865 (D. Minn. 2004).

McCormick v. School District of Mamoroneck, 370 F.3d 275 (2nd Cir. 2004).

Mercer v. Duke Univ., 190 F.3d 643 (4th Cir. 1999).

Mercer v. Duke Univ., 181 F. Supp. 2d 525 (M.D.N.C.2001), *vacated in part and remanded per curiam*, 50 Fed. Appx. 643 (4th Cir. 2002).

Miami Univ. Wrestling Club v. Miami Univ., 302 F.3d 608 (6th Cir. 2002).

Murphy v. University of Cincinnati, 72 Fed. Appx. 288 (6th Cir. 2003).

National Center for Education Statistics. (2013, May). *The condition of education 2013*. U.S. Department of Education, NCES 2013-037.

National Collegiate Athletic Association. (2012a). *1981– 1982 – 2011–12 NCAA sports sponsorship report and participation rates report*. Indianapolis, IN: NCAA.

National Collegiate Athletic Association. (2012b, July 16). *Emerging sports for women*. www.ncaa. org/wps/wcm/connect/public/NCAA/Resources/ Emerging+Sports+for+Women

NCAA v. Smith, 525 U.S. 459 (1999).

National Federation of State High School Associations (NFHS). (2012). *2011–12 High school athletics participation survey*.www.nfhs.org/ParticipationStatics/ PDF/2011-12%20Participation%20Survey.pdf

National Federation of State High School Associations (NFHS). (2014). *2013–14 High school athletics participation survey*. www.nfhs.org/ParticipationStatics/ PDF/2013-14_Participation_Survey_PDF.pdf

National Wrestling Coaches Assoc. v. Department of Educ., 361 U.S. App. D.C. 257 (D.C. 2004).

Office for Civil Rights. (1996). *Clarification of intercollegiate athletics policy guidance: The three-part test*. Washington, DC: U.S. Department of Education.

Office for Civil Rights. (1997). *Sexual harassment guidance: Harassment of students by school employees, other students or third parties*. Washington, DC: U.S. Department of Education.

Office for Civil Rights. (2000, April 11). *Letter from Dr. Mary Frances O'Shea, national coordinator for Title IX athletics, to David V. Stead, executive director, Minnesota State High School League*. Washington, DC: U.S. Department of Education.

Office for Civil Rights. (2000, May 24). *Letter from Dr. Mary Frances O'Shea, national coordinator for Title IX athletics, to David V. Stead, executive director, Minnesota State High School League*. Washington, DC: U.S. Department of Education.

Office for Civil Rights. (2001). *Revised sexual harassment guidance: Harassment of students by school employees, other students, or third parties*. Washington, DC: U.S. Department of Education.

Office for Civil Rights. (2003) *Further clarification of intercollegiate athletics policy guidance regarding Title IX compliance*. Washington, DC: U.S. Department of Education.

Office for Civil Rights. (2008, September 17). *Dear colleague letter: Athletic activities counted for Title IX compliance*. Washington, DC: U.S. Department of Education.

Office for Civil Rights. (2010a, October 26). *Dear colleague letter: Harassment and bullying*. Washington, DC: U.S. Department of Education.

Office for Civil Rights. (2010b). *Intercollegiate athletics policy: Three-part test*. Washington, DC: U.S. Department of Education.

Office for Civil Rights. (2011, April 4). *Dear colleague letter: Sexual violence*. Washington, DC: U.S. Department of Education.

Office for Civil Rights. (2013, May 9). *Dear colleague letter*. DOJ Case No. DJ 169-44-9, OCR Case No. 10126001. Washington, DC: U.S. Department of Education.

Pittman, A.T., Spengler, J.O., & Young, S.J. (2016). *Case studies in sport law* (2nd ed.). Champaign, IL: Human Kinetics.

A Policy Interpretation: Title IX and Intercollegiate Athletics, 44 Fed. Reg. 239 (1979).

Rios, E. (2015, April 8). The feds are investigating 106 colleges for mishandling sexual assault. Is yours one of them? *Mother Jones*. www.motherjones.com/politics/ 2015/04/department-of-education-investigation-colleges-sexual-assault

Roberts v. Colorado State Board of Agriculture, 998 F.2d 824 (10th Cir. 1993).

Secretary of Education's Commission on Opportunity in Athletics. (2001). *Open to all: Title IX at thirty*. Washington, DC: Department of Education.

Simpson v. University of Colorado, 372 F. Supp. 2d 1229 (D. Co. 2005), *reversed & remanded*, 500 F.3d 1170 (10th Cir. 2007).

Stanley v. University of Southern California, 178 F.3d 1069 (9th Cir. 1999).

Title IX of the Education Amendments of 1972, 20 U.S.C. §§ 1681–88 et seq. (2015).

Title VII, 42 U.S.C. § 2000e-2 (2015).

U.S. Equal Employment Opportunity Commission. (1997, October 29). *Enforcement guidance on sex discrimination in the compensation of sports coaches at educational institutions* (EEOC Notice No. 915.002). Washington, DC: EEOC.

U.S. General Accounting Office. (2001, March 8). *Intercollegiate athletics: Four-year colleges' experiences adding and discontinuing teams* (GAO-01-297). Washington, DC: GAO.

U.S. Government Accountability Office. (2007, July). *Intercollegiate athletics: Recent trends in teams and participants in national collegiate athletic association sports* (GAO-07-535). Washington, DC: GAP Report to Congressional Addressees.

White House Council on Women and Girls. (2014, January). *Rape and sexual assault on campus: A renewed call to action*. www.whitehouse.gov/sites/default/files/ docs/sexual_assault_report_1-21-14.pdf

Chapter 9

Anti-Cybersquatting Consumer Protection Act, 15 U.S.C. § 1125(d) (2008).

Baltimore Orioles, Inc. v. Major League Baseball Players Assoc., 805 F.2d 663 (7th Cir. 1986), *cert. denied*, 480 U.S. 941 (1987).

Boston Athletic Association v. Sullivan, 867 F.2d 22 (1st Cir. 1989).

C.B.C. Distribution & Marketing, Inc., v. MLB Advanced Media, 443 F. Supp. 2d 1077 (E.D. Mo. 2006), *aff'd*, 505 F.3d 818 (8th Cir. 2007).

Cardtoons, L.C. v. Major League Baseball Players Assoc., 95 F.3d 959 (10th Cir. 1996).

C.B.C. Distribution & Marketing, Inc. v. MLB Advanced Media, 443 F. Supp. 2d 1077 (E.D. Mo. 2006), *aff'd by*, 505 F.3d 818 (8th Cir. 2007).

Collegiate Licensing Company. (2015). Clients. www.clc.com/Clients.aspx

Copyright Act, 17 U.S.C. §§ 101–810 et seq. (2015).

Dallas Cowboys Cheerleaders, Inc. v. Pussycat Cinema, Ltd., 604 F.2d 200 (2nd Cir. 1979).

Dauster, R. (2014, June 9). NCAA settles for $20 million in Keller v. NCAA lawsuit. *NBC Sports.* http://collegebasketballtalk.nbcsports.com/2014/06/09/ncaa-settles-for-20-million-in-keller-v-ncaa-lawsuit

Dream Team Collectibles, Inc. v. NBA Properties, Inc., 958 F. Supp. 1401 (E.D. Mo. 1997).

Fantasy Sports Properties, Inc. v. Sportsline.com, Inc., 287 F.3d 1108 (Fed. Cir. 2002).

Federal Trademark Dilution Act, 15 U.S.C. § 1125(c) (2015).

Goddard, E. (2014, March 5). Exclusive: Red Bull wins Sochi 2014 "Ambush Marketing" gold, says report. *Inside the Games.* www.insidethegames.biz/articles/1018733/exclusive-red-bull-wins-sochi-2014-ambush-marketing-gold-says-report

Haelan Laboratories, Inc. v. Topps Chewing Gum, Inc., 202 F.2d 866 (2nd Cir. 1953), *cert. denied*, 346 U.S. 816 (1953).

Hall, E. (2012, July 25). Paddy Power resists having Olympic ambush ads taken down in U.K. *Ad Age Global.* http://adage.com/article/global-news/paddy-power-resists-olympic-ads-u-k/236302

Harjo et al. v. Pro-Football, Inc., 50 U.S.P.Q.(2d) (BNA) 1705 (1999), *rev'd, summary judgment granted in part, summary judgment denied in part*, 284 F. Supp. 2d 96 (D.C. Cir. 2003).

Keller v. Elec. Arts Inc. (In re NCAA Student-Athlete Name & Likeness Licensing Litigation), 724 F.3d 1268 (9th Cir. 2013).

Lanham Act, 15 U.S.C. §§ 1 et. seq. (2015).

March Madness Athletic Assoc., LLC v. Netfire Inc., 120 Fed. Appx. 540 (5th Cir. 2005).

Martin v. PGA Tour, Inc., 984 F. Supp. 1320 (D. Ore. 1998), *aff'd*, 204 F.3d 994 (9th Cir. 2000), *aff'd, PGA Tour, Inc. v. Martin*, 532 U.S. 661 (2001).

Morris Comm. Corp. v. PGA Tour, 117 F. Supp. 2d 1322 (M. Dist. Fla. 2000).

Morris Comm. Corp. v. PGA Tour, 235 F.Supp. 2d 1269 (M. Dist. Fla. 2002).

Muhammad Ali v. Playgirl, Inc., 447 F. Supp. 723 (S.D.N.Y. 1978).

National Collegiate Athletic Association. (n.d.). *NCAA trademarks.* www.ncaa.org/championships/marketing/ncaa-trademarks

National Hockey League and Lemieux Group LP v. Domain for Sale, Case No. D2001-1185 (WIPO Arbitration and Mediation Center, December 6, 2001).

NBA v. Motorola, 105 F.3d 841 (2nd Cir. 1997).

NFL. (2013, October 15). *NFL.com terms and conditions.* www.nfl.com/help/terms

National Football League v. McBee & Bruno's Inc., 792 F.2d 726 (8th Cir. 1986).

Patent Act, 35 U.S.C. §§ 1 et seq. (2015).

Pittman, A.T., Spengler, J.O., & Young, S.J. (2016). *Case studies in sport law* (2nd ed.). Champaign, IL: Human Kinetics.

Pittsburgh Athletic Co. v. KQV Broadcasting Co., 24 F. Supp. 490 (W.D. Pa. 1938).

San Francisco Arts & Athletics, Inc. v. United States Olympic Committee, 483 U.S. 522 (1987).

Smith, N. (2012, June 12). North Dakotans vote to let UND retire Fighting Sioux nickname. *Bismarck Tribune.*

State of North Dakota v. NCAA, Memorandum Decision and Order, Civil No. 06-C-1333 (November 11, 2006).

Ted Stevens Olympic and Amateur Sports Act, 36 U.S.C. §§ 220501 et seq. (2015).

WCVB-TV v. Boston Athletic Association, 926 F.2d 42 (1st Cir. 1991).

Chapter 10

Agnew v. NCAA, 683 F.3d 328 (2nd Cir. 2012).

American Needle v. NFL, 130 S.C. 2201 (2010).

Arbitration of Messersmith, Grievance No. 75-27, Dec. No. 29 (1975).

Association for Intercollegiate Athletics for Women v. National Collegiate Athletic Association, 735 F.2d 577 (D.C. Cir. 1984).

Banks v. National Collegiate Athletic Association, 977 F.2d 1081 (7th Cir. 1992).

Brown v. Pro Football, Inc., 518 U.S. 231 (1996).

Chicago Professional Sports Limited Partnership v. National Basketball Association, 95 F.3d 593 (7th Cir. 1996).

City of San Jose v. Office of the Commissioner of Baseball, 776 F.3d 686 (9th Cir. 2015).

Clarett v. NFL, 306 F. Supp. 2d 379 (S.D.N.Y. 2004), *reversed & remanded*, 369 F.3d 124 (2d Cir. 2004).

Clayton Antitrust Act, 15 U.S.C. § 15 (2015).

Curt Flood Act, 15 U.S.C. § 26(b) (2015).

Deesen v. Professional Golfers' Assoc., 358 F.2d 165 (9th Cir. 1966), *cert. denied*, 385 U.S. 846 (1966).

Denver Rockets v. All-Pro Mgt., Inc., 325 F. Supp. 1049 (C.D. Cal. 1971).

Federal Baseball Club v. National League, 259 U.S. 200 (1922).

Flood v. Kuhn, 407 U.S. 258 (1972).

Fraser v. Major League Soccer, 97 F. Supp. 2d 130 (D. Mass. 2000), *aff'd*, 284 F.3d 47 (1st Cir. 2002).

Law v. NCAA, 5 F. Supp. 2d 921 (D. Kan. 1998).

Los Angeles Memorial Coliseum Commission v. National Football League, 726 F.2d 1381 (9th Cir. 1984).

Mackey v. NFL, 543 F.2d 606 (8th Cir. 1976).

National Collegiate Athletic Association v. Board of Regents of the University of Oklahoma, 468 U.S. 85 (1984).

O'Bannon v. NCAA, 7 F. Supp. 3d 955 (N.D. Cal. 2014).

Piazza v. Major League Baseball, 831 F. Supp. 420 (E.D. Pa. 1993).

Pittman, A.T., Spengler, J.O., & Young, S.J. (2016). *Case studies in sport law* (2nd ed.). Champaign, IL: Human Kinetics.

Powell v. NFL, 930 F.2d 1293 (9th Cir. 1989).

Rock v. NCAA, 2013 U.S. Dist. LEXIS 116133 (S.D. Ind. 2013).

Sherman Antitrust Act, 15 U.S.C. §§ 1 et seq. (2015).

Smith v. Pro Football, Inc., 593 F.2d 1173 (D.C. Cir. 1978).

Sports Broadcasting Act, 15 U.S.C. §§ 1291 et seq. (2015).

Sullivan v. NFL, 34 F.3d 1091 (1st Cir. 1994), *cert. denied*, 513 U.S. 1190 (1995).

Toolson v. New York Yankees, 346 U.S. 356 (1953).

USFL v. NFL, 842 F.2d 1335 (2d Cir. 1988).

Vehling, A. (2015, February 17). NFL, American Needle to settle antitrust suit. *Law360*.

Wood v. NBA, 809 F.2d 954 (2d. Cir. 1987).

Chapter 11

Commonwealth v. Pullis (Philadelphia Mayor's Court, 1806).

FedEx Home Delivery and International Brotherhood of Teamsters, 361 N.L.R.B. No. 55 (2014).

National Labor Relations Act (NLRA), 29 U.S.C. §§ 151 et seq. (2014).

Northwestern University and College Athletes Players Association (CAPA), Case 13-RC-121359 (NLRB Region 13, 2014).

Nordstrom, et al., d/b/a Seattle Seahawks and NFLPA, Case 2-CA-19101 (NLRB, 1989).

Pittman, A.T., Spengler, J.O., & Young, S.J. (2016). *Case studies in sport law* (2nd ed.). Champaign, IL: Human Kinetics.

Restatement (Second) of Agency, § 220 (1958).

Roadway Package Systems, Inc. (Roadway III), 326 N.L.R.B. 842 (1998).

Index

About the Authors

John O. Spengler, JD, PhD, is a professor and director of the University of Florida's Sport Policy and Research Collaborative. Spengler received his bachelor's degree from Wake Forest University, his law degree from the University of Toledo, and his PhD from Indiana University. His research focuses on legal and policy issues relevant to sport and recreation, obesity prevention and physical activity, and structural environmental factors (social and physical) that influence health. Spengler's research has been funded by the Robert Wood Johnson Foundation to study policies relevant to improving opportunities for physical activity. He is a volunteer with the American Heart Association, where his research has informed AHA policy and advocacy efforts at the state and national level to improve community health through physical activity.

Spengler's work has been published in numerous journals, books, and commissioned research papers and presented through webinars, panels, and professional presentations. He serves on the advisory board of the Aspen Institute's Project Play and Physical Literacy Working Group and has served as president of the Sport and Recreation Law Association, associate editor of the *Journal of Legal Aspects of Sport*, and a board member for SHAPE America. Honors include selection as a University of Florida Research Foundation professor in recognition of research and scholarly achievements and two-time UF College of Health and Human Performance Teacher of the Year. He also received the Fame for Fitness Award from the Florida Sports Hall of Fame in recognition of his work on childhood obesity prevention, the University of Toledo School of Law Order of the Coif Jurisprudence Award, and SHAPE America's Distinguished Scholar award. He is a research fellow for both the SHAPE America Research Consortium and the Sport and Recreation Law Association.

Spengler resides in Gainesville, Florida. He enjoys sports and outdoor activities.

Courtesy of Paul Anderson

Paul M. Anderson, JD, is the associate director of the National Sports Law Institute of Marquette University Law School in Milwaukee, Wisconsin. He is also associate director and professor in the Sport Law program at Marquette University Law School, the most comprehensive and advanced sport law program in the world. He has taught, written, and consulted on all areas of sport law for the past two decades.

As part of his role in the National Sports Law Institute, Anderson researches all areas of sport law and coordinates multiple publications for the sport industry, including annual surveys devoted to developments in the field. He has written numerous books, book chapters, articles, and other publications related to various areas of sport law. In his law practice, Anderson has represented many clients in the sport industry.

Anderson is co-faculty advisor to the *Marquette Sports Law Review*, a former editor of the *Journal of Legal Aspects of Sport*, and managing editor of the *Journal of Sport and Social Issues*. He is a reviewer for the *Journal of Legal Aspects of Sport, Communication and Sport,* and *International Sports Law Journal*. He is past chair of the Sports and Entertainment Law section of the State Bar of Wisconsin. Anderson is a member of the Sport and Recreation Law Association, the Sports Lawyers Association, American Bar Association's Forum on the Entertainment & Sports Industries, and the International Association of Sports Law.

In 2008, Anderson received the Faculty Advisor of the Year Award from the Marquette Moot Court Association. He also received the President's Award from the Sport and Recreation Law Association in 2005 and was awarded the Sports Law Alumnus of the Year Award from the Sports Law Alumni Association of Marquette University Law School in 2003. In 2002 he received a Leadership Award from the Society for the Study of the Legal Aspects of Sport and Physical Activity.

In his free time, Anderson enjoys reading science fiction, writing, and watching and participating in various sports. He and his wife and daughters reside in Milwaukee.

Daniel P. Connaughton, EdD, is a professor in the sport management program and an associate dean in the College of Health and Human Performance at the University of Florida. His teaching and research are focused on the study of law and risk management in sport and physical activity programs.

A frequent conference presenter and author of many publications, Connaughton has received several teaching and research awards. The American Heart Association has funded his research investigating implementation constraints and risk management practices related to automated external defibrillators in sport and recreation programs. Since 2008 he has served as the principal investigator of the Bicycle Safety and Risk Management Project, which is funded by the Florida Department of Transportation Safety Office. Connaughton is a research fellow with the Sport and Recreation Law Association and Research Consortium of SHAPE America.

With an educational background in exercise and sport sciences, Connaughton also holds advanced degrees in recreation administration (University of Florida), physical education (Bridgewater State College), and sport management (Florida State University). Connaughton has held management positions in campus and public recreation departments, aquatic facilities, and health and fitness programs. He holds several professional certifications and frequently serves as a consultant and expert witness in sport and physical activity–related lawsuits.

In his free time, Connaughton enjoys cycling, running, and traveling. He resides in Gainesville.

Courtesy of Thomas Baker

Thomas A. Baker III, JD, PhD, is a commercial litigator turned associate professor in the sport management and policy program at the University of Georgia. He conducts research in sport management that focuses on the application of the law to sport. Within that focus he specializes in how commercial laws influence sport marketing, such as legal issues concerning brand management and the use of social media in sport marketing. Additionally, he conducts risk management research focused on preventing sexual abuse in sport, and terrorism management at sports facilities. He is also editor in chief of the *Journal of Legal Aspects of Sport.* Dr. Baker received his PhD in sport management from the University of Florida, where he was a Dr. Charles W. LaPradd PhD fellow and earned the Clifford A. Boyd Graduate Scholarship Award and the Norma M. Leavitt Scholarship. He earned his JD from Loyola University New Orleans School of Law, where he graduated in the top 10 percent of his class (cum laude) earning the distinction of William L. Crowe Sr. Scholar.

About the Contributor

Courtesy of Alicia Jessop

Alicia Jessop is an assistant professor at the University of Miami, where she teaches courses on legal aspects of sport, sports governance, and globalization of sport. Alicia holds a BS in economics from the Colorado School of Mines and a JD (cum laude) from Chapman University, where she was an editor of *Chapman Law Review*. Alicia is the founder of the widely read sport law website Ruling Sports.com and a former sport business contributor to *Forbes*. She currently covers sports for *The Huffington Post* and CNBC.